Humanitarian Politics

By the Same Author:
United Nations Peacemaking: The Conciliation Commission for Palestine

Humanitarian Politics

The International Committee of the Red Cross

David P. Forsythe

The Johns Hopkins University Press
Baltimore and London

Written under the auspices of the Center of International Studies, Princeton University

Manufactured in the United States of America

The Johns Hopkins University Press, Baltimore, Maryland 21218
The Johns Hopkins Press Ltd., London

Library of Congress Catalog Card Number 77–4781
ISBN 0-8018-1983-0

Library of Congress Cataloging in Publication data will be found on the last printed page of this book.

For
Lindsey,
my daughter

Contents

Figures

Tables

Preface

This book constitutes a study of the process by which the International Committee of the Red Cross (ICRC) tries to protect and assist persons around the world. It deals primarily with the period 1945–75. It is directed to a very elusive, and perhaps mythical, reader—the general but sophisticated observer of world affairs.

Because the basic activity of the ICRC is not widely and analytically understood, I have tried to present systematic description and analysis of the functions, roles, and structure of the ICRC in the context of world politics. I have tried to keep legal technicalities to a minimum. The reader interested in the status of the ICRC under international law is directed to my article, "Who Guards the Guardians: Third Parties and the Law of Armed Conflict," *American Journal of International Law* 70, no. 1 (January 1976):41–61. I have also tried to hold to a minimum the jargon from political science. The reader interested in an application of some of the perspectives found in the literature of political science is directed to my article, "The Red Cross as Transnational Actor: Conserving and Changing the Nation-State System," *International Organization* (Autumn 1977). Finally, I have not tried to write an exhaustive history of the ICRC, either for the modern period or certainly for earlier times.

In one sense, this book is one individual's view toward the ICRC. That having been said, a word is in order about my qualifications to write such an interpretation. As an independent academic, I initially gained some understanding of ICRC affairs while carrying out research under a grant from the National Endowment for the Humanities. Subsequently I became a consultant to the Henry Dunant Institute, the Red Cross research center in Geneva, in order to work on a study of political prisoners. In this capacity I gained further insights into ICRC matters. Then I became a consultant to the Joint Committee for the Reappraisal of the Red Cross. In that position, and charged with studying Red Cross protection, I obtained further understanding about the ICRC. I worked not only in Geneva but also had the opportunity to accompany several ICRC missions in the field. Some of my conclusions from working as a consultant have been published in my *Present Role of the Red Cross in Protection,* Background Paper No. 1 (Geneva: Red Cross, 1975). Some of my conclusions also found their way into another Red Cross publication authored by the Study Director of that Reappraisal Committee, Donald D. Tansley, *Final Report: An Agenda for Red Cross* (Geneva: Red Cross, 1975).

I should add, however, that this present book is authorized neither by the ad hoc Reappraisal Committee, nor by the ICRC. While the book could not have been written without some cooperation from these two Red Cross agencies, all statements of fact and interpretation are the sole responsibility of the author.

My interpretations are based primarily on public documents and on interviews with Red Cross, governmental, and academic officials during 1971–76. Many records held by the ICRC and/or governments are regarded by these institutions as confidential. Perhaps in time the ICRC or a government will release its own version of some of the general subjects and specific situations covered in the following pages, making direct reference to ICRC documents; thus my own study must be regarded as tentative. But it is likely that a fully authoritative account will be a long time in appearing, given the sensitivity of many matters discussed below, the desire of governments to avoid controversy, and the penchant of the ICRC for caution in the face of governmental sensitivity. Ergo this book. I believe it offers a useful introduction to the work of the ICRC, even if it cannot be offered as a definitive analysis. To the best of my knowledge, after much research and cross-checking of interview information, nothing in the book is false. But there may be, and probably is, additional information on a subject, unknown to me. What is presented below, however, should be a clear, net increase in general understanding of who the ICRC is and what it does.

If journalism is the first draft of history, as someone (no doubt a journalist) once said, perhaps this book can be considered the second draft on the subjects covered. Without doubt the most fully authoritative draft is yet to come.

The use of specific names and places is controlled by a desire not to complicate further the already complicated life of the ICRC. Where a situation is terminated, or a government no longer in power, I have employed specifics. Where there is high probability that the use of specifics would jeopardize an ongoing or future ICRC action, I have been intentionally vague.

While the book is a personal one, it is in reality a product of many people.

The late Pierre Boissier, then director of the Henry Dunant Institute, a member of the ICRC, and the official historian of the early period of the ICRC, gave me much valuable information from his rich store of knowledge. Jean Pictet, vice president of the ICRC, warmly received me in Geneva and continued to give of his time after that, even when we disagreed on matters. It should be said that he never sought to infringe on my academic freedom, even when he thought my analysis wrong or the ICRC wronged. Jacques Moreillon, ICRC director of principles and law, greatly facilitated my work with his analytic mind, his willingness to have me participate in several operations in the field, and in countless other ways at which I can only guess. Other officials of the ICRC were willing to talk candidly with me: Eric Martin, president; Roger Gallopin, president of the Executive Council; Pierre Basset, Gallopin's chef de cabinet. My thinking was greatly affected by rather consistent interaction with the ICRC's middle level of management over a three-year period.

In addition to these and other interactions with ICRC officials, I benefited from several long sessions with Jacques Freymond, former acting president of the ICRC and now director of the Graduate Institute for International Studies in Geneva, and with his most helpful assistant Thiery Hentsch. Donald Tansley, study director for the Red Cross Reappraisal Committee, was a most accommodating "boss" during 1973–75.

Among the many governmental officials contributing in some way to my understanding of humanitarian law and diplomacy were Frank Sieverts (United States), David Miller (Canada), Hans Blix (Sweden), and several professors who also held governmental posts such as Georges Abi-Saab (Egypt), G. I. A. D. Draper (United Kingdom), and I. P. Blishchenko (USSR).

Especially encouraging in my long studies were Leon Gordenker of Princeton and R. R. Baxter of Harvard. The former gave me valuable comments on the manuscript as did a reader, unknown to me, for the Johns Hopkins University Press. Nicholas Onuf of the American University gave me comments on Chapter 5.

The later stages of manuscript preparation were accelerated by grants from the University Consortium for World Order Studies and by Princeton University; these grants made possible my spending a valuable year as a visiting fellow at Princeton's Center of International Studies. Cy Black, the Center's director, was most accommodating. The University of Nebraska granted several leaves of absence from my teaching duties. A travel and maintenance grant from the Ford Foundation was of great help during 1976 and 1977.

A final word is in order about my personal views toward the ICRC (these are further explicated in a Postscript). As these views necessarily affect what follows, it is best to be explicit about my general orientation. I consider myself a sympathetic critic of the ICRC. I am sympathetic toward what the ICRC tries to do for the individual around the world. But at times I am critical of how the ICRC goes about its protection and assistance efforts.

The ICRC is an old and, in many quarters, a venerated institution. Some believe that to criticize it publicly is to damage its image and hence its humanitarian work. I believe the contrary. *Not* to engage in discussion and constructive criticism is to damage its work. One of the problems for the ICRC is that so few outsiders have really known the organization and its work that it has been wellnigh impossible to stimulate ICRC officials with different perspectives based on a knowledge of the recent past.

One ICRC official told me, having read this manuscript: the ICRC is an old thing, old things get worn smooth, sometimes it is good to use a wire brush on them, and this book is the wire brush.

I am content with that evaluation.

Humanitarian Politics

Introduction:
The Meaning of
Humanitarian Politics

Since the International Committee of the Red Cross (ICRC) has traditionally claimed to be a nonpolitical organization, it is well to explain why a book about the ICRC is entitled *Humanitarian Politics*.

The words "politics" and "political" in the English language (and in other languages as well) are used to cover a multitude of sins, both literally and figuratively. While those words have many meanings, three are relevant here: "realpolitik," "partisan politics," and "politics," broadly defined.

"Realpolitik" refers to the competition among actors in world politics for power, prestige, and—in general—who gets most of the pie.

"Partisan politics" is factional politics—competition among groups within a nation for what there is to get. The groups can be political parties, factions within parties, interest groups, or any other type of political actor. What is sought may be votes, financial gain, a new law, or a million other things.

The ICRC has traditionally tried to stay apart from these two types of politics. At a minimum, the ICRC has tried to avoid any intentional action based on either realpolitik or partisan politics. That is to say, it tries to avoid action motivated by a desire to help one actor win some sort of victory in world politics over another actor, or to help one faction triumph over a rival within a nation. Sometimes in its attempts to help an individual, the ICRC may take action on humanitarian motivation that inherently works to the advantage of a state or faction. For example, if the ICRC is concerned about the fate of political prisoners in nation

1

X and makes an overture to that state for permission to visit places of detention, that humanitarian démarche inherently works to the advantage of those critical of detaining state. Conversely, once the state accepts ICRC visits, that acceptance tends to become an advantage to the state. Therefore the ICRC can be said to be involved in ''politics'' because of this undesired but sometimes necessary impact on realpolitik and partisan politics—and because, by essence, the ICRC tries to protect and assist the victims of politics.

Beyond this, however, there is a third type of politics that the ICRC engages in. Indeed, the ICRC must engage in this third type of politics, must be a political animal, if it is to do the job it has set for itself. In one broad sense of the word, ''politics'' refers to the competition and struggle to make and implement public policy. If the ICRC wishes to promote human rights in armed conflicts, if it wishes to improve the international protection of political prisoners, if it wishes to bring material assistance to those in need, it frequently must engage in struggle to get these values implemented in the public life—the public policy—of nations.

It is in this sense that the ICRC is most fully and consistently engaged in humanitarian politics: the struggle to implement humanitarian values as official policy in the nations of the world.

To talk of what the ICRC does in this way is not to rule out the possibility that in some cases humanitarian values may be implemented without competition, struggle, and conflict. It is at least possible in theory, and there may be actual examples, where some authority undertook a humanitarian policy because of purely humanitarian motivation—a pure concern for the well-being of the individuals in question. In the world as we know it, however, it is generally the case that actors in the political process do not exist for purely humanitarian reasons. If they undertake a policy that has a humanitarian aspect, they do so as a result of a costs-benefits analysis in which they compare the costs and benefits of the humanitarian aspect with such things as security needs and economic considerations.

For example, when the ICRC desired to help promote the humanitarian objective of securing the prompt return of Pakistani prisoners of war held by India after the war for Bangladesh, ICRC overtures ran into Indian interests of a nonhumanitarian nature. India, like other states, found that prisoners of war were a good bargaining weapon. And India was interested in such things as promoting Pakistani recognition of Bangladesh and in supporting a Bangladesh effort to bring to trial certain Pakistanis as war criminals. Therefore India, in pursuing policies which to it seemed just, did not want to release its prisoners of war for those purely humanitarian reasons that found legal expression in the Third Geneva Convention of 1949.

In this situation the ICRC had to struggle to implement humanitarian values. The ICRC tried to persuade India to change its policy and to separate the return of the Pakistani prisoners of war from the other goals that interested India. This ICRC effort necessarily resulted in a certain amount of conflict with established

Indian policy. But if humanitarian values on the issue of Pakistani prisoners of war were to become part of public policy in south Asia, the ICRC had to engage in struggle. The ICRC had to decide which overtures to make, on what grounds, and how hard and far to push them—both in the context of general Indian policy on prisoner of war matters, and in the context of Pakistani and Bangladesh policy as well.

Thus humanitarian politics—in the sense of struggling to implement public policy of a humanitarian nature—is practiced by the ICRC. The ICRC has to do this in many situations if it is to remain true to its humanitarian values. Not to struggle would be to abandon those values, to have no impact on many situations. Not to struggle would mean allowing one's self to be manipulated by others. That is why Jacques Freymond, a former acting president of the ICRC, has written:

> Above all, we should recognize that all humanitarian action cannot be isolated from its political context and that it therefore has a political content. This means that all humanitarian organizations must define a long term humanitarian policy based on a serious analysis of several factors. ... This humanitarian policy in turn implies a humanitarian strategy distinct from tactical moves imposed by the variety of crises. Neglect of this work of reflection leads to contradiction, confusion, and, what is worse, the degradation of humanitarian action to the level of an instrument of political interests.[1]

While Freymond's own use of the word ''political'' is not always consistent, the thrust of his argument is clear. Humanitarian organizations need a policy, that is, a specific set of ends and means, based on strategy, that is, a general conception of goals and roles, in order to make a humanitarian impact on parties operating on the basis of realpolitik and partisan politics.

The key for humanitarian organizations is to engage in cooperation *and conflict* with actors in the political process, in a context of realpolitik and partisan politics imposed by those actors, but to maintain consistent action motivated by humanitarian values.

A humanitarian agency needs to be aware of its impact on other parties' nonhumanitarian goals and policies, for a humanitarian agency may be charged with ''political'' bias. As James E. Bond has written, ''Unfortunately, one man's humanitarianism may be another's political maneuvering; and even the ICRC has been accused of favoritism.''[2]

Now observers may disagree on the extent to which the ICRC takes these things into account. Does the ICRC have a humanitarian strategy? Is it aware of its political context? Does it recognize the need to struggle? Is it easily manipulated by states and various nonstate parties?

But whether one is talking about what the ICRC actually does or what it should be doing, one is talking about humanitarian politics—the struggle to implement humanitarian values as part of public policy.

1 The ICRC and the Red Cross Movement

The International Committee of the Red Cross (ICRC) is hardly known, and the International Red Cross is poorly known.

First of all, the International Red Cross, which is not so much an organization as a transnational movement, is a complicated thing. It is badly known because it is complex. Secondly, the world's press has not helped matters by confusing the transnational movement with one agency in that movement; both the movement in general and the ICRC are referred to as the International Red Cross. Thirdly, the ICRC, which handles much of the diplomacy for the International Red Cross, frequently employs a policy of silence. When the ICRC visits prisoners of war or political prisoners, it sends a private report to the authorities concerned. While this may be necessary, given governmental attitudes, it does not lead to an understanding of what the ICRC is and does. And fourthly, the ICRC itself has not explained its activities clearly, apparently believing there is some safety in obscurity. If one does not analytically explain activities, one does not have to draw the line between what can be divulged and what should remain a diplomatic secret.

In 1962 an ICRC official remarked that the ICRC is unknown ten kilometers from its headquarters next to the Palais des Nations in Geneva. But he was wrong. The ICRC is unknown two kilometers from its headquarters. Even the

Genevois Swiss do not have a clear understanding of the agency that founded the Red Cross movement. In the early 1970's when the ICRC was being criticized even in the Genevois press, the Swiss public reduced its financial contributions to the Swiss Red Cross!

The International Red Cross, to those who have any view on the matter at all, is frequently and vaguely viewed as associated with disaster relief. To the extent that the ICRC is known as a separate entity, it is vaguely associated with prisoners of war.

THE ICRC AND THE RED CROSS MOVEMENT

The International Red Cross is a transnational movement with two heads and many arms. To carry the metaphor further, we can say that the heads do not control the arms, and that the heads are not always looking in the same direction.

The ICRC is the founding head of the movement. To the all-Swiss ICRC were added national Red Cross Societies between the 1860's and the present. These are the independent arms, in the past not responsible to the ICRC, once recognized by that head. The second head, the League of Red Cross Societies, was added after World War I. As a federation of the national societies with a multinational secretariat, it is independent of the ICRC. The two heads and all the arms formally get together once every four years, in principle, at the International Conference of the Red Cross. As if there were not enough difficulty in coordinating the heads and the arms, this Conference is also attended by the states that have adhered to the Geneva Conventions on the laws of war.

It is possible, however, to make some analytical sense out of this loosely knit movement. Figure 1.1 represents at least a theory of organization, even if it does not fully explain the Red Cross movement.

The chart in figure 1.1 identifies the units in the movement. The connecting lines indicate patterns of interaction, rather than formal authority. All of the lines represent "two-way streets." There is a lack of clear patterns of authority within the movement that could be represented by a "one-way street." There are three sets of "statutes" in the movement: one each for the ICRC, the League, and the "International Red Cross." The last statutes pertain somewhat ambiguously to the interactions of the ICRC, League, and Conference. Sometimes the statutes are inconsistent. For example, the statutes of the ICRC say both that only the ICRC can change its statutes and also that the ICRC will accept the directives of the International Conference. Now suppose the Conference, taking "decisions" under the IRC statutes, directs the all-Swiss ICRC to change its statutes so as to add members from the major groupings found in world politics! Some ICRC officials argue that this scenario could not arise. Other observers are not so sure the Conference might not attempt to interpret IRC statutes exceedingly broadly,

Figure 1.1. The International Red Cross and the Nation-State

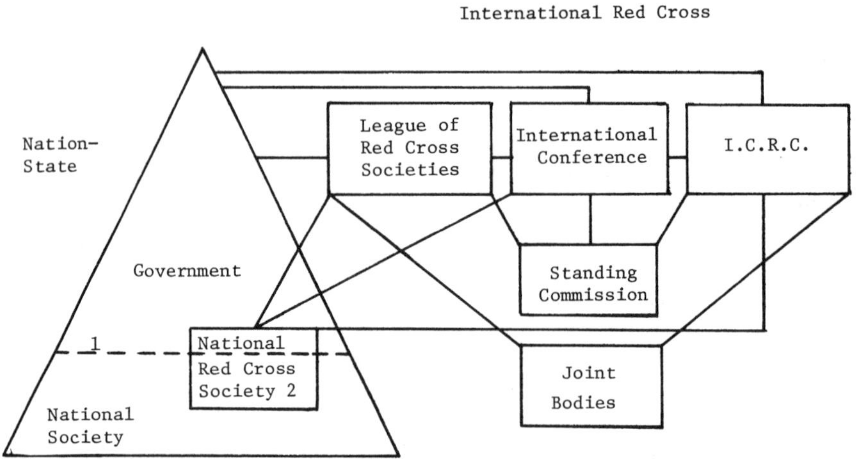

¹The location of this line will vary, depending on whether the government is limited or totalitarian.
²The Red Cross Society may be more or less within the governmental sector, varying with each case.

thus reducing the scope of ICRC statutes. Certainly the wording of the three sets does not guarantee that conflicting interpretations will not arise. The units of the movement are formally joined in a tenuous way.

There is some order in the movement, however. It is produced by tradition and by cooperation among the Red Cross agencies. A closer look at each agency will make this clear.

THE ICRC

The ICRC, the original Red Cross agency, grew out of an effort by a group of Swiss citizens to help the wounded in the war of Italian succession in the late 1850's.¹ Over the years, the basic function of the ICRC came to be that of helping individuals through protection and assistance. Protection came to mean the presence of a third party to see that an "enemy" was treated humanely by his captor. Assistance came to mean the providing of material goods or medical services—and sometimes social services like legal or family help.

The basic approach of the ICRC in its attempts to protect and assist people was pragmatic action: it would do what was possible, then later make an effort to formalize agreement in general so that what had been possible in the past was guaranteed in the future. Ad hoc diplomacy was followed usually by efforts at legal development to insure legally guaranteed action in the future. Specific concern led to efforts to systematize help.

Thus the original concern for wounded soldiers at the battle of Solférino in 1859 by Henry Dunant led not only to immediate medical assistance to the wounded but to the 1864 Geneva Convention. Concern for prisoners of war in the Franco-Prussian War of 1870 and then in World War I led first to pragmatic protection and assistance, then to the 1929 Geneva Convention on prisoners of war. Increasing concern for civilians in modern war, which was dramatized by the urban bombings and occupations of World War II, led to both pragmatic help and the Fourth Geneva Convention of 1949. Likewise, concern for individuals in civil wars led both to humanitarian involvement in these wars (as in Spain in the 1930's and the Congo and Nigeria post-1945) and to pushing for new law on the subject (reflected in Common Article 3 of the Four Geneva Conventions of 1949 and efforts to expand that legal regulation in the mid-1970's). Finally, efforts to help victims of weapons of mass destruction were followed periodically by efforts legally to limit or prohibit the use of such weapons.

This historical resumé not only demonstrates the approach of the ICRC to its work, but also it shows that the original focus of the ICRC—and therefore of the Red Cross movement—was on the individual in armed conflict. This was where the need seemed greatest. It was paradoxical that the greatest active concern for the individual, at least on the part of many citizens, should arise in time of war. Let there be peace, and the fate of an Austrian citizen was of little concern to outsiders. Let there be war between Austria and Italy, and that same Austrian citizen—now a soldier—was the subject of greater international concern. (It should be added that at the time the Red Cross movement started, philosophers like Hegel and Marx were concerned for individuals regardless of national boundaries *and* regardless of peace or war. But the historical fact remains that for many in the West, it was the state of war that legitimized and stimulated interest in other citizens.)

This early Red Cross focus on armed conflict was maintained by the ICRC for about a century, so that it was written of the ICRC that it existed to try to humanize war.[2] At the start of the second century of ICRC existence, there was some change in focus evident. While the amount of blood spilled was still one indication of whether the ICRC would become interested in the plight of indi- . viduals in a given situation, the ICRC was showing a broader focus in its protection and assistance efforts. The ICRC was displaying more and more interest in persons that might be affected by violence in the future, or who were affected by small-scale violence. It could be said that the ICRC was tending toward a concern for the individual affected by political conflict, whether armed conflict or not. This was true especially when no other agency appeared to be protecting or assisting the individual in need. In Red Cross jargon, it was the presence of a "man-made disaster" that defined the focus of ICRC protection and assistance efforts. Other "disasters" and other subjects were left to other institutions.

It is against this background that the "special role" of the ICRC within the Red Cross movement can be understood, as specified in Article 4 of the Statutes of the ICRC. The present version of the "special role" was formally restated in May 1974: The special role of the ICRC shall be:

a) to maintain the fundamental and permanent principles of the Red Cross, namely; impartiality, action independent of any racial, political, religious or economic considerations, the universality of the Red Cross and the equality of the National Red Cross Societies;

b) to recognize any newly established or reconstituted National Red Cross Society which fulfills the conditions for recognition in force, and to notify other National Societies of such recognition;

c) to undertake the tasks incumbent on it under the Geneva Conventions, to work for the faithful application of these Conventions and take cognizance of any complaints regarding alleged breaches of the humanitarian Conventions;

d) to take action in its capacity as a neutral institution, especially in case of war, civil war or internal strife; to endeavour to ensure at all times that the military and civilian victims of such conflicts and of their direct results receive protection and assistance, and to serve, in humanitarian matters, as an intermediary between the parties;

e) to contribute, in view of such conflicts, to the preparation and development of medical personnel and medical equipment, in co-operation with the Red Cross organizations, the medical services of the armed forces, and other competent authorities;

f) to work for the continual improvement of humanitarian international law and for the better understanding and diffusion of the Geneva Conventions and to prepare for their possible extension;

g) to accept the mandates entrusted to it by the International Conferences of the Red Cross.

The ICRC may also take any humanitarian initiative which comes within its role as a specifically neutral and independent institution and consider any question requiring examination by such an institution.

To carry out this special role, the ICRC has progressed from the ideas and action of one man, Henry Dunant, through a committee of five, to an agency of over two hundred permanent employees—which mushroomed to an agency employing some 4,000 people during Word War II. This agency is a private corporation under Swiss law, but it is generally regarded as a nongovernmental international organization (NGO).[3] This is because of the scope of its activity and because the ICRC is recognized in international law.

The details of ICRC organization are considered at a later point (Chapter 8). It is important to note briefly, however, that recent changes in ICRC organization may affect some of the conventional wisdom about the agency.[4] Until 1973, the ICRC was dominated by a governing council called the Comité. One observer, by no means uninformed about international affairs, referred to this council as "dominated by a group of very conservative Swiss businessmen who are more strongly anti-Communist than most Americans."[5] The Comité also had the image of being greatly conservative in the general sense. One member of the ICRC staff demonstrated in scholarly fashion that the Comité was more cautious about protecting political prisoners than staff members in the field were.[6]

These and other views toward the ICRC during the time of dominance by the Comité must be reexamined because of major changes in the agency's organization. Is the ICRC ethnocentric? Is it deferential to states? Does it seek to avoid controversy at the price of protecting human rights? Is it impartial and effective? Is it composed of skeptical humanitarians, wary of governmental actions and promises whether of the "left" or "right"? Answers to these and other questions, traditionally raised in regard to the ICRC, should be—if not answered—at least debated with more facts in the light of the rest of this book.

One further introductory word about the ICRC seems appropriate. The ICRC obviously has close relations with the Swiss government. This is true legally and financially. But the ICRC is probably more independent of the Swiss government than most national Red Cross Societies are of their respective governments.[7]

The ICRC and the Swiss government work closely in the development of humanitarian law for armed conflicts; the ICRC hosts preparatory meetings to, and presents working documents to, the diplomatic conferences called and chaired by the Swiss government, which is the official depository for the Geneva Conventions on humanitarian law. More strikingly, the Swiss government provides about seventy-five percent of the regular budget ("permanent" and "temporary" sectors) of the ICRC. Moreover, the Swiss people take up an annual collection for the ICRC's emergency actions. (While this public collection is not directly part of ICRC-Swiss government relations, it is indirectly part of the same picture.)

These legal and financial interactions, however, do not necessarily lead to the conclusion that the ICRC bends to the will of the Swiss government. First of all, the government has given the ICRC a declaration guaranteeing the inviolability of ICRC buildings and grounds, as if they were diplomatic property. More importantly, there does not appear to be any record of governmental dictatorial interference in the affairs of the ICRC. Rather, the pattern of interaction is one of mutual exchange of information based on mutual desires. Where ICRC communications are not adequate and where open communication is not advisable, the ICRC will use the communication network of the Swiss government—or other governments—when necessary. From time to time Swiss governmental officials will help ICRC officials in times of diplomatic difficulties, as in the Nigerian Civil War when August Lindt, formerly Swiss ambassador to the Soviet Union, then an official of the ICRC, was detained by Nigerian authorities but eventually released after representations by the Swiss Embassy in Lagos. At other times, however, both the government and the ICRC keep a certain distance between their respective operations for varying reasons. The fact that some ICRC representatives carry a Swiss diplomatic passport in addition to a Red Cross laissez-passer is a reflection of governmental support for the ICRC but not evidence of governmental interference or control.

If it were not for the rest of the Red Cross movement, one could perhaps view the ICRC as an independent bureau of humanitarian affairs for Switzerland, supported by both the public and the government. And it has been said by some Swiss that, since the government has only an economic foreign policy, it is good to have the ICRC for humanitarian affairs. Most ICRC personnel strongly reject this perspective, arguing that there have been many important differences between the ICRC and the Swiss government.

In any event, the rest of the Red Cross movement does exist, further enhancing the independence of the ICRC from both the Swiss government and the Swiss people, even as the presence of that movement ties the ICRC into a set of complex relations.

THE ICRC AND NATIONAL RED CROSS SOCIETIES

The statutes of the ICRC and the tradition of the Red Cross movement indicate that it is the ICRC that shall recognize new national Red Cross Societies. As the British scholar G. I. A. D. Draper has pointed out, "It is this role which has of recent years placed the ICRC in a position of considerable difficulty."[8] There are rules governing the recognition procedure, but like the recognition of states in international law, the rules are capable of flexible interpretation (see Appendix A).

Complicating the process of recognition is the fact that admission to the League is a separate question from recognition by the ICRC. It is possible that a group could be admitted to the League of Red Cross Societies without having been recognized as an official Red Cross Society by the ICRC. This has, so far, not occurred. But there have been times when the possibility of League admission apparently was used as a weapon to push the ICRC toward formal recognition. The possibility of a conflicting result between the process of recognition by the ICRC and the process of admission by the League has been avoided either because the ICRC agreed to recognition in deference to League wishes, or the League agreed to nonadmission in deference to ICRC wishes. At the time of writing, there is some possibility that the Magen David Adom Society of Israel, unrecognized by the ICRC because it does not use one of the three symbols approved by the Red Cross Conference and by the Geneva Conventions, will seek admission to the League despite that nonrecognition.

The question of recognition and admission is of course important for the internal workings of the Red Cross movement, affecting who attends and votes at Conference meetings. But there is a broader significance to these matters which explains why the ICRC has had some difficulty in recognition matters.

Recognition of a national Red Cross Society is frequently part of the game of realpolitik and partisan politics. Therefore the ICRC is sometimes confronted with a choice that, irrespective of the ICRC's humanitarian orientation, has an impact on the struggle among states and groups. A challenging faction will seek ICRC recognition for its "Red Cross Society" as part of its quest for general acceptability as a legitimate state or government. And a "Red Cross Society" meets considerable difficulty in trying to operate internationally without ICRC Recognition.

The Kurdish element within Iraq presented the ICRC with a petition in 1974, requesting recognition of the Kurdish National Red Cross Society.[9] This was obviously part of the attempt by the Kurdish people to create a new state, since the Red Cross rules of recognition specify that there can be only one national Red Cross Society within a state. Given the existence of the Iraqi Red Crescent, the ICRC could not recognize a Kurdish Red Cross without recognizing, de facto, a Kurdish state. The ICRC was able to duck the question rather easily, since there were—and are—few if any states that officially recognize a Kurdish state in what is now part of Iraq. But the very fact that the ICRC did not respond affirmatively to the Kurdish petition was a decision favorable to Iraq, however well argued the ICRC decision was on the basis of a literal interpretation of the Red Cross rules of recognition.

A similar situation has presented itself with regard to the group that calls itself the "Palestinian Red Crescent." It too has sought recognition from the ICRC, and the ICRC has so far failed to give that formal recognition. In this case, since the group exists in fact as well as on paper, the ICRC has followed its long-standing practice of cooperating with the Palestinian Red Crescent on a pragmatic basis in medical and diplomatic matters. For example, during one of the violent conflicts within Lebanon in the 1970's, the ICRC, the Palestinian Red Crescent, and the Lebanese Red Cross cooperated in arranging a truce and in evacuating the wounded from a Palestinian refugee area where there had been fighting between Palestinian and Lebanese forces. Likewise in the Jordanian Civil War of 1970, the ICRC interacted with the Palestinian Red Crescent as if it were a Red Cross Society, nonrecognition notwithstanding. As with the case of the Kurdish petition, the Palestinian petition was easily rejected on formal grounds, since the Palestinian movement had declared neither a government in exile nor the existence of a state. Moreover, a National Society must be able to extend its work to national territory in its entirety—which of course is not possible for a national society created in exile. Be that as it may, an ICRC decision to recognize would necessarily affect the struggle between the Palestinians on the one hand and the Jordanians and Israelis, both of whom would be immediately affected by the creation of a Palestinian state, on the other. While the rules of recognition provide some shield for the ICRC from the full pressures of realpolitik, it is only a partial shield.

That the rules of recognition for Red Cross Societies as applied by the ICRC constitute only partial isolation from realpolitik is demonstrated by recognition tangles in East Asia in the early 1950's with regard both to China and the Koreas. Contrary to the Kurdish and Palestinian examples, in East Asia the question was not directly one of recognition of a brand new society—and state—but the problem of successor societies and governments within a state. The formal rule in question was not whether a state existed that was entitled to have a national society, but whether a state had become a party to the Geneva Conventions— which is also a necessary precondition for recognition of the society. The Red Cross Society must be able to carry out its duties under the Geneva Conventions in order to merit recognition.

With regard to China, the ICRC considered the Red Cross Society of the People's Republic of China to be the sole Chinese Red Cross after the triumph of Mao Tse-tung in the Chinese Civil War.[10] This was contested by the faction led by Chiang Kai-shek and entrenched on Taiwan, especially since Chiang's government had signed the 1949 Geneva Conventions, whereas Mao's government had not. (It was only in 1956 that the government of the People's Republic of China adhered to the Conventions.) Nevertheless, the ICRC persisted in its policy of recognizing only the Red Cross Society on the mainland. From 1950 on, the ICRC argued that Mao's government, as the successor to Chiang's government, succeeded to the legal obligations accepted by the latter, despite the fact that the Communist government did not explicitly accept the obligations under the Geneva Conventions at the time of ICRC recognition. To the ICRC, there was only one state of China, represented by Mao's government. Moreover, the "Taiwanese Red Cross" was not seen as having sufficient activity to merit recognition, and in any event was claiming—unpersuasively—to be the sole Chinese national society. Also humanitarian action by the ICRC argued in favor of good relations with Mao's government. Despite lack of cooperation with the ICRC by the Chinese Communists during the Korean War, the ICRC continued its course of action.

This ICRC policy had the result of introducing two Chinese governments into Red Cross Conferences, as the ICRC notified the government on Taiwan of the Conferences because it was a signatory to the Conventions, even though the ICRC did not recognize a Taiwanese Red Cross Society. Between 1952 and the early 1970's, this situation led to much wrangling at those conferences, based on realpolitik.

The ICRC's policy toward the Chinese National Red Cross Society also contributed to hypothetical complexity on the question of ICRC access to political prisoners in Taiwan. The ICRC, through 1975, had not requested such access. Were the ICRC to do so, it is conceivable that the government might request recognition for its National Society as part of the price for access. The ICRC clearly would like to deal with recognition questions solely on principle. But it is doubtful if governments view matters in the same light.

The ICRC's recognition policy toward the Chinese National Society could be defended on its merits, and increasingly that policy was supported by international consensus. But it could complicate the protection of political prisoners on Taiwan. And the policy had not resulted in any great degree of cooperation from Mao's government.[11] Such were the difficulties for the ICRC in recognizing national societies.

A similar tangle occurred in Korea. Neither North nor South Korea was—or is—a member state of the United Nations; neither had formally adhered to the Geneva Conventions at the time of the war in 1950–53; and as the war progressed the ICRC recognized neither of the groups claiming to be the "Korean Red Cross" for the unitary state of Korea (both societies claimed to be *the* Korean society). There was a group functioning in the South, anxious for recognition and cooperation. There was a group in the North, at least on paper. The Red Cross Conference had accepted the principle that no recognition should occur during armed conflict. This principle provided the ICRC with grounds for delaying decision.

As the status quo ante settled upon Korea after 1953, the ICRC said that it wanted to resolve the recognition tangle, and did in fact recognize the national society in the South after that society limited its jurisdictional claims to south of the seventeenth parallel. This recognition occurred despite the fact that the government in Seoul had not formally adhered to the 1949 Geneva Conventions in behalf of the Republic of Korea (and did not do so until 1966, despite promises to the ICRC to act earlier). The ICRC said that the Republic of Korea succeeded to the legal obligations of the previous Korean empire under an earlier Geneva Convention, thus permitting recognition.

The ICRC used the same fragile argument in order to recognize the national society in the North shortly thereafter. The government of the People's Republic of Korea had likewise not adhered to the 1949 Conventions, and its very legitimacy as a government representing a state was questioned and indeed challenged by many in the 1950's—as was true to only a slightly lesser degree for Seoul as well.

ICRC officials, in reviewing these events, see themselves as having acted pragmatically, *tant bien que mal,* in a difficult situation without adequate guidelines—but without disregard for principles. Others outside the ICRC, some in other Red Cross agencies, see the ICRC as having acted, at least partly, under Western—and specifically American—pressure. It seems to have been the case that the American Red Cross was lobbying—in the period immediately after the 1953 Korean armistice—for the admission of the national society from the South into the League. Such lobbying, if strong enough, would have generated pressure on the ICRC to recognize at least the southern national society. Otherwise, that society might become a member of the League without ICRC recognition, thus bringing into the open the contradictions or fragmentation of the Red Cross movement.

Since recognition did in fact precede admission, it is difficult to pass definitive judgment on how much principle, and how much practical recognition of

Western influence, played in those decisions, especially since individual perspective now varies.

There were numerous other recognition problems for the ICRC, most of them touching upon some aspects of realpolitik. In Rhodesia, Ian Smith's 1965 declaration of an independent state was not recognized by the British government (or anybody else). The British Red Cross continued to exercise jurisdiction over its Rhodesian section, authority which was *not* resisted by that latter Red Cross group. But the very fact that the Rhodesian section had *not* sought independent recognition led to problems for the ICRC.

At a point after 1965, the British Red Cross requested copies of ICRC prison reports from Rhodesia. The British government did not. The British Red Cross believed that it was entitled to receive the reports since that had been previous practice. ICRC prison reports pertaining to a number of British territories abroad had been transmitted to the British Red Cross, so that that society—and its sections abroad—could provide assistance to detainees and their families, as suggested by the ICRC.

The ICRC, however, declined to respond affirmatively to this British Red Cross request. The ICRC believed that, given the conflict between the British and Rhodesian governments, the ICRC might antagonize the latter by sending reports to the British Red Cross. That, in turn, might cause the ICRC to be barred from prison visits. Thus the ICRC replied that it could only send reports to those authorities in factual control of detainees not protected by the Geneva Conventions, and that such a policy did not imply any jurisdictional recognition of the detaining authority.

The British Red Cross viewed this position as a breaking-off of the normal—e.g., the previous—relationship between the British Red Cross and the ICRC. The ICRC viewed disagreement with the British Red Cross as preferable to possible friction with the Smith government that might prevent future ICRC visits. Therefore, continuing recognition of British Red Cross's jurisdiction in Rhodesia was the framework within which choices had to be made by the ICRC.

The question of the recognition of Magen David Adom in Israel presented still other problems. The ICRC, as part of its attempt to relate to non-Western groups, had deferred to the recognition of two other symbols in addition to the red cross on a white background—the reverse of the Swiss flag—as symbols for national societies. First the red crescent was accepted in response to the desires of a number of Muslim societies who found the symbol of the cross unacceptable. Then the Red Lion and Sun was accepted for the national society of Iran. At that point the ICRC, and others, had second thoughts about accepting other symbols that would negate the value of having a symbol (or a few symbols) associated with humanitarianism. Thus the line was drawn at three symbols. (The Red Cross Conference has the final, formal say about symbols for the movement; a diplomatic conference has the final, formal say about symbols insofar as international law is concerned. The two processes do not have to arrive at the same judgment, although at present they have.)

But for the group in Israel that desired to be affiliated with the international Red Cross movement, the cross was as unacceptable as it had been to the Muslims. The Red Cross and diplomatic conferences, however, were heavily influenced by African and Asian delegations hostile to the state of Israel, and it appeared very difficult to achieve any change toward official acceptance of the red star of David as one of the substitutes for the red cross. Hence the ICRC neither recognized Magen David Adom nor submitted a resolution of change to the conference.

Certain ICRC officials stressed that the nonrecognition of Magen David Adom was strictly a matter of proper symbols. Other officials appeared to believe that as long as the practical job of protection and assistance was being achieved—in general—in the Middle East, the question of recognition could await an improvement in Arab-Israeli relations. The leaders of Magen David Adom, however, believed that they were being unfairly discriminated against within a humanitarian movement and that the prestige and legitimacy of Israel was also damaged. A number of observers believed that the only way out of the impasse was to return to the idea of one symbol which the Israelis—and others—could adopt, either a single, new symbol or a red cross on a white background *joined by* whatever national symbol the local society desired. As with other problems of recognition, the core of the dispute was the legitimacy of the government and state in question as an issue in realpolitik. In this case, the ICRC deferred to majority sentiment, especially since the practical work of the ICRC was progressing in the Middle East, and since the ICRC was opposed in principle to any further substitution for the original symbol.

Once a society has been recognized as a national Red Cross Society, the ICRC has exercised virtually no control, and very little influence, over the group. The two entities have interacted on the basis of mutual desires, a situation that can lead to cooperation, conflict, or mutual detachment.

Nothing in the statutes of any of the Red Cross agencies says anything about withdrawal or recognition. Withdrawal of recognition could be inferred from the right to recognize, but withdrawal of recognition has not been practiced by the ICRC in its 110-year history. There has been, therefore, no official attempt by anyone to insure that national societies act in keeping with the values of the Red Cross movement as adopted by the International Conference. Those values are: humanitarianism, impartiality, neutrality, independence, voluntarism, unity, and universality.

It is no secret that certain national Red Cross Societies have violated one or more of these principles. First of all, it is very difficult for any national society to be really independent from the government. As writers have noted, the independence of national societies is increasingly menaced.[12] This is part of the historical trend of increasing governmental impact on all phases of life within a nation. Where a powerful government aspires to totalitarian control, there is very little independence for a Red Cross Society. But even in nontotalitarian states, it is difficult for a society to be truly independent from government, since the latter charters the society and appoints several of its top officials. Moreover, the Red Cross tends to be an establishment group. That is to say, it tends to recruit into the group the same type of person that goes into government. Thus there is a similarity in governmental and Red Cross outlooks within many nations that is not so much produced by government as it simply arises because of the similarity of people in both organizations. The tendency in the West for many retired military and civilian government workers to join the Red Cross Society accentuates the trend. It is also true that many Red Cross Societies perform quasigovernmental functions. It is the American Red Cross that holds the blood reserve of the nation; that is something the government can hardly be unconcerned about. Thus the independence of the national society is circumscribed by federal legislation. In Norway, the Red Cross Society is the main channel of humanitarian foreign assistance from the government, and neither the government nor the society can afford to ignore the other. While this sort of situation does not erase the independence of the national society, it limits it considerably. And although variations in funding are great among the more than 120 societies, in general, national societies are funded by governments and public collections.

While the degree of independence of the society from the government varies, the societies that *could* take action in opposition to the government are not so numerous. The societies that would *want* to take such action are fewer still. Thus *if* the ICRC is looking for a national group to oppose governmental policy on the torture of political prisoners, or to pressure the government to give better treatment to captured enemy personnel, or to lobby the government to change its position at a diplomatic conference, or to pressure the government to permit relief supplies to reach civilians in a secessionist area of the nation, many times the national Red Cross Society is not a reliable partner for the ICRC. It is more an arm of the government than a humanitarian agency independent of the government and tied to a humanitarian international movement.

When the lack of independence is combined with a lack of impartiality, the utility of the national society for humanitarian endeavors is reduced to the point of extinction. Impartiality for the Red Cross movement means humanitarian action without regard to distinctions based on race, religion, partisan politics, ethnic differences, sex, or any other discriminating factor. It is unfortunate but true that the writing down of the principle of impartiality by the national society, and the joining of that group by citizens of a nation, does not mean the principle will have meaning for members. When the dominant view within the government characterizes the national society as well, and when that dominant view is hostile toward a particular group within the nation, the society becomes an arm of the government for a policy of discrimination.

In Burundi in the early 1970's the ICRC withdrew from the country in the context of intertribal violence because the ICRC did not obtain what, to it, were satisfactory guarantees that material relief offered would be provided on an impartial basis. The Burundi Red Cross was as dominated by the Tutsi as was the government, and in that situation the ICRC did not want to be associated with a national society that might have been as anti-Hutu as the government. The League entered into the dispute after the ICRC withdrew and helped in the distribution of material relief, on governmental terms. The ICRC remained unhappy about the situation but was unable to alter it.

In Bangladesh in 1971–72, it was common knowledge that the Bangladesh Red Cross was led by officials greatly influenced by the Awami League, the political movement of most Bengali during the struggle for independence from Pakistan. It was also common knowledge that most Bengali, particularly the politicized Bengali, had little love for that minority group called Bihari who had cooperated with the Punjabi in West Pakistan in the suppression of the Bengali independence movement. When the state of Bangladesh was created through war in 1971, following a bloody attempt at maintaining control over the East by the West, the dominant Awami League in the new state coordinated social, economic, and physical attacks against the Biharis, who were left defenseless by the withdrawal of the Pakistani army. For a time the Biharis benefited to some extent from an uneasy order maintained by the Indian army. But when that army withdrew, the situation for the Biharis became acute.

The ICRC sought to protect and assist this threatened group during the violent winter of 1971–72. That course of action eventually brought the ICRC into conflict with the Bangladesh Red Cross, which sought to assert its control over relief operations as an exercise of nationalism. Under the traditions of the Red Cross, the national society was entitled to control assistance when the armed conflict was ended. Yet the ICRC was not convinced that in the spring of 1972 the Bangladesh Red Cross could be fully trusted to distribute relief on an impartial basis so soon after the antagonisms of war. Finally it was decided that the national society would have ultimate authority over assistance and would distribute that assistance to Bihari enclaves; the ICRC would supervise the relief operation through spot checks to insure that Red Cross principles were upheld. Assistance was finally provided on that basis. (The United Nations was able to help in this process, in part because the head of the UN mission was also a member of the ICRC.)

Because some violations of Red Cross principles have become of general concern at International Conferences, there has been a slight movement toward acknowledgement of the right of the ICRC to retract recognition as a weapon to enforce maintenance of Red Cross principles. The ICRC on its own had threatened to withdraw recognition from the national society in Haiti in the 1950's because of discrimination based on partisan politics within that Red Cross Society. Negotiations between that society and the ICRC led to fundamental changes, allowing the question of withdrawal of recognition to be shelved. Also, there was some informal discussion both within the ICRC and at the International Conferences in the 1960's about the status of the South African Red Cross and racial discrimination there. At the International Conference in 1973, a vaguely worded resolution was passed that appeared to authorize the ICRC to withdraw recognition in certain cases.[13]

Like recognition, however, withdrawal of recognition is likely to be a difficult step for the ICRC. It will be difficult to keep the process free from partisan politics and realpolitik. And the government in question is not likely to view international criticism of its national Red Cross Society benignly, especially since the government itself may be legally liable for the policies of the national Red Cross Society under international law. If the government has committed the state to one of the international legal conventions, for instance, prohibiting racial discrimination or protecting the status of women, then ICRC action toward the national society for engaging in discrimination may be prima facie evidence of illegal behavior on the part of the state, in that the state has permitted that behavior to exist.

Whatever the future of withdrawal of recognition, and some ICRC officials believe it has great potential, it can be safely said that—to date—beyond the point of recognition the Red Cross movement has been ''nationalized'' to a great extent. The national Red Cross Societies, once recognized, have been free in fact to adopt the dominant values of the nation. Whether these national values are consistent with Red Cross values all too frequently becomes an academic question to the members of that national society. ''Red Crossers'' think more in terms of action per se than in terms of philosophical consistency according to vague standards.[14]

While problems of implementing Red Cross values have been exceedingly serious in places like Burundi and Bangladesh, it is a universal problem to get members of national societies to treat ''enemies'' humanely. It is difficult enough to get citizens of a nation to treat an enemy soldier from another nation in keeping with Red Cross values. It is even more difficult to get intranational ''enemies'' to treat each other humanely. It is not just the Spanish Civil War that demonstrates the intensity of hostility among conflicting groups of the same nation, although it is worth noting that neither the Spanish Red Cross nor any European Red Cross national society played a significant role in that internecine slaughter.[15] In Uruguay, it is difficult to find many citizens concerned about the welfare of the Tupamaros, the Marxist urban guerrillas. Within party and government circles in the Soviet Union, it is difficult to find much interest in the conditions of political prisoners detained for slandering the state. The dominant national values are reflected in the national Red Cross Society, for usually that society is one composite of the nation. Thus the ''nationalization'' of the Red Cross movement means that the ICRC, once recognition is finished, may have few allies—even within the Red Cross movement—in its humanitarian activity in keeping with Red Cross principles. And the threat or actuality of withdrawal of recognition is as likely to produce retrenchment behind the national values as conversion to the values of the Red Cross.

All of this is not to say that the ICRC has a monopoly on humanitarian values and that national Red Cross Societies have no humanitarian role to play. While the ICRC has learned from painful experience over some 110 years that some national societies are not always independent and not impartially humanitarian, there are other examples to the contrary. While the ICRC had twelve of its delegates killed in World War II out of the 180 serving, the Honduras Red Cross had some of its members wounded trying to give first aid during the 1969 war with El Salvador.

The existence of the International Red Cross as a transnational movement opens up possibilities for humanitarian action, but the existence of Red Cross agencies in more than 120 states guarantees nothing. In some cases the ICRC, based in a small and neutral state and therefore free from imperial entanglements, may find support for its work of humanitarian assistance and protection from a national Red Cross Society. In other cases, the ICRC has to bypass the national society and deal directly with the authorities.

This ICRC independence tends to occur when the ICRC engages in ad hoc diplomacy rather than action under the Geneva Conventions, for by definition ad hoc diplomacy is not spelled out in international law and is thus something relatively new, unstructured, and poorly understood. While national societies do not like the idea of the ICRC doing things independently—viz., without consultation and coordination with them—they also dislike being asked to approach the government in behalf of Tupamaros, or Russian political prisoners, or American Indians at Wounded Knee. This sort of overture is, first of all, frequently regarded by the national society as ICRC meddling in internal affairs of the nation; and, secondly, it is the type of thing that gets the national society in trouble with the government and with the majority of the population as well. It is easier for national societies to cope with floods, to collect blood, and to give doughnuts to the army than it is to lobby the government in behalf of individuals who, from the national view, have violated national law—or perhaps just violated majority sensitivities. Hence while the national societies want to be informed, when they find out what is going on they frequently prefer not to be involved. And in some cases the national society is opposed to what the ICRC wishes to do.

In sum, the arms of the Red Cross movement have been responsible to the ICRC head only through the point of recognition. Beyond that point, each of the Red Cross agencies tends to go its own way, adopting programs based on the needs of a given society and the predilections of its leaders, with passing attention to common symbols and slogans. It has been difficult to isolate ICRC recognition of national Red Cross Societies from issues in realpolitik, not because the ICRC wanted it that way but because states and movements viewed these "humanitarian" questions in light of their significance for state power, prestige, and legitimacy. The subject of withdrawal of recognition is likely to be characterized by the same problems.

It is unlikely that the ICRC could acquire the power within the Red Cross movement to direct a unified movement. The national societies are not convinced that this would be a good change, and in any event governments would not allow it—especially totalitarian ones. The International Red Cross is therefore likely to continue to be a very fragmented movement, characterized by both selective cooperation and mutual exclusion between the ICRC and the national societies.

The presence of the League of Red Cross Societies has not changed this situation.

THE ICRC AND THE LEAGUE

The League of Red Cross Societies was a direct result of World War I. During that war, national societies had increased greatly their membership and activity. After the war, there were a number of people who believed that the international linkages established among Red Cross Societies during the war should not be dismantled. Even if the war of 1914–18 were the war to end all wars, there was a belief that the national societies could be turned into agencies to cope with natural disasters. Thus the League was created.

The League was also a result of lack of leadership by the ICRC, for that latter agency was unresponsive to these demands for a new Red Cross focus on peacetime activities based on the national societies' newly found energy. This lack of leadership in the Red Cross movement was especially noticeable since several national societies, notably the American one, had attracted dynamic leaders because of wartime exigencies. Thus the ICRC preoccupation with its traditional, wartime tasks led to a bypassing of that agency by those members of national societies committed to pushing ahead with new, peacetime Red Cross plans.

Moreover, the years after the Great War were times of great expectations, as well as sweeping assumptions about the arrival of the era of democracy. Not only was the ICRC's leadership rather elevated in age and not prone to bold, new undertakings, the ICRC was undemocratic: its recruitment was by cooptation— viz., election to membership by those already members. Therefore age, lack of dynamism, and lack of democracy on the part of the ICRC all contributed to the creation of a new institution in the Red Cross movement—the League.

The League was created for two basic functions: to deal with natural disasters, and to promote the development of the national societies so that the Red Cross movement could be better prepared for disasters, whether natural or "man-made."

This distinction between the functions of the ICRC on the one hand and the League on the other seemed reasonable enough in the abstract. But the division of labor was, in fact, based upon a premise that either never existed or increasingly broke down: that peace could be distinguished from war. In peace the Red Cross head for assistance was to be the League, as coordinator of the national societies, while in peace the ICRC was to be the head of Red Cross efforts to develop humanitarian law. In war, the ICRC was to become the head of both assistance and protection, with support from the League and the national societies. But what if the dividing line between peace and war became blurred? Who led Red Cross assistance efforts in internal strife, and civil wars, and undeclared wars? And who was responsible for protection outside the situation of formal war? And when the violence tapered down, or simply dragged on in the same pattern, who within the Red Cross movement decided that it was time for the ICRC's wartime leadership to cease and time for the League and national societies to assert themselves under the assumption that the situation was as normal and peaceful as could be expected? And what if a natural disaster occurred within a war setting?

As if these problems in dividing peace from war, and man-made from natural disasters, were not enough to make organization and coordination difficult within the Red Cross movement, that movement was also characterized by institutional jealousy that exacerbated the analytical problems. Having lost clear leadership of the movement after World War I, the ICRC retreated into its version of isolationism. The agency became defensive, fearful, and resentful of the efforts of the League and national societies to assert themselves. These attitudes confirmed the League's beliefs that the ICRC was passé, out of touch with current needs and possibilities. As led by first the Americans and then the Scandinavians, the League was assertive to the point of being undiplomatic toward its partner in humanitarian work.

This institutional jealousy between the ICRC and League was compounded by the jealousy of some national societies toward them both. It was ironical that the split between the two heads in Geneva was accompanied by criticism of both heads by national societies who were interested in promoting their own autonomy at the expense of "Geneva"—whether ICRC or League. This three-cornered jealousy proved especially debilitating to the League, which as a federation of national societies was pushed in the direction of assertiveness toward the ICRC by some societies and in the direction of passivity toward everybody by others. While the international secretariat of the League had the ability to be assertive at times through the personalities and diplomatic skills of its leaders, it lacked the authority to command the national societies and so lacked the authority and power to insure a followthrough on what it had initiated. The League was thus similar to a United Nations agency like the United Nations Relief and Works Agency for Palestine Refugees (UNRWA): it had the power to initiate but was easily stalemated by the countervailing power of national societies, not to mention governments.[16]

To demonstrate the overall situation with brutal succinctness, while the ICRC and League were competing over who was to deliver wheat and rice in Bangladesh, the Russian Red Cross dispatched a medical team there, to be led and coordinated by no one in Geneva. Or, while the ICRC and the Nigerian Red Cross were discussing who was to coordinate material and medical relief on the Nigerian side of the civil war, the French Red Cross was unilaterally flying material and medical relief to Biafra on French military planes also carrying French arms for the Biafran army.

These sorts of problems in organizing the movement have led to a long-standing effort to clarify roles, particularly between the ICRC and League. These two heads, not totally unlike warring states, signed an agreement in 1951 that reaffirmed the leadership role of the ICRC in all protection matters and in assistance for man-made disasters.[17] If the 1951 agreement reaffirmed past principle, it did little to clarify problems in applying the principle to real world situations. The '51 agreement has been followed by a 1969 protocol (see Appendix B). And that protocol has been followed by a series of meetings to define what the protocol means. And all of this has recently been accompanied by committee action under the International Conference to re-evaluate the statutes of the League, to see what organizing principle can be introduced through that approach.

If one takes the post-1945 situation, it is difficult to find a clear pattern in ICRC-League relationships. In Bangladesh in 1971–72, the national society and League felt that the ICRC was controlling assistance too long; the ICRC felt the other two were insensitive to protection tasks linked to assistance. In the Algerian War, especially during the latter stages, the League pursued its program of refugee relief in Tunisia and Morocco without keeping the ICRC fully informed, with the result that the ICRC asked the Secretary General of the League to appear before the full Committee to give an explanation. There seemed to be a considerable spirit of competition, if not mistrust, beneath the surface of these events. Yet there is probably a trend toward improved relations, Bangladesh notwithstanding; and despite the fact that in the Indochina War, the government of South Vietnam invited various Red Cross Societies to become involved in the South without full coordination with either the League or ICRC.

The ICRC and League seem to be cooperating more on an ad hoc basis, due in part to changes in personnel on the ICRC side. More importantly, there is a growing feeling within the ICRC that it is important to accommodate the contributions of other Red Cross agencies in assistance. They want to participate, and their participation is needed for at least the collection of goods. And some in the ICRC believe that the ICRC may not have any particularly superior abilities regarding the management of large-scale assistance. In both Indochina, from 1973, and in the Jordanian Civil War of 1970, there was an integrated Red Cross assistance effort directed by a joint ICRC-League committee, headed by an official on loan from a national society—in Indochina by a Swede and in Jordan a Finn. These integrated efforts handled material and medical assistance coordination, while the ICRC handled protection tasks. It seems to be the case that both operations went about as well as expected, and the core bureaucracy has been left in existence for future use. This is an encouraging sign for prospects of coordination.

If there is an emerging pattern in ICRC-League relations, it seems to be one of fluctuating coordination, slightly systematized, with some awareness that mutual detachment and exclusion is detrimental to the status and effectiveness of the movement as a whole. Just as the ICRC has learned from the bitter experience in Nigeria and Bangladesh that managing a large-scale material relief program is different from small-scale assistance to prisoners of war, so the League has apparently begun to appreciate that responding to floods and earthquakes is different from negotiating with hijackers and kidnappers.

Yet the movement is far from being unified. League officials were fond of comparing the International Red Cross to an orchestra, in which many instruments were played; ICRC officials were fond of saying that even an orchestra needed a conductor. It seems doubtful that the International Conference can do anything to improve the situation.

THE ICRC AND THE INTERNATIONAL CONFERENCE

One longtime observer of, and participant in, Red Cross affairs referred to the International Conference in Teheran in 1973 as that "enormous vanity fair." This seems to sum up the observations of many regarding the importance of the Conference.

This characterization may be slightly unfair—but only slightly. The seemingly endless debates of the Conference, while they have no legally binding effect, can result in resolutions that can have some practical merit on occasion.[18] The ICRC has been known to introduce draft resolutions endorsing this or that objective, so that after Conference approval the ICRC can make overtures to various governments, claiming that it has a mandate to do so from the Conference. The ICRC has used the Conference to request information from governments about what they were doing to implement the Geneva Conventions. The ICRC has also used regional Red Cross conferences in Latin America to endorse the idea of Red Cross interest in political prisoners. Given its broad representation—delegates from the ICRC, the League, the national Red Cross Societies, and all states signatory to the Geneva Conventions are present—the International Conference every four years is, in particular, an apt time and place for the ICRC to try to have some ideas and action endorsed as a legitimate Red Cross concern; this has some practical pay-off—difficult to measure—in ICRC diplomacy after the Conference.

But there are many problems inherent in the Conference. State delegations can vote for resolutions without officially committing their states to a policy of support for what has been voted. Many state and national Red Cross delegations, presumably distinct entities, have engaged in the most blatant forms of debate based on realpolitik, which is supposedly excluded from the Conference. Like most international conferences attended by more than 125 entities from around the world, it is terribly difficult to organize, focus, and streamline. The result is much talk and little change in behavior after the talk, a process not unknown in other collective meetings such as the UN General Assembly.

There is a suborgan of the Conference of some potential importance. This is the Standing Commission, composed of nine individuals: five elected by the Conference, two by the League, and two by the ICRC. In addition to making decisions with regard to the Conference, the Commission is charged with settling "any difference of opinion which may arise as to the interpretation and application of the present Statutes [of the International Red Cross—viz., the movement] as well as any questions which may be submitted to it by the International Committee or the League."[19] These same statutes later say, however, "The independence and initiative of the various bodies of the International Red Cross in their respective spheres shall, however, continue to be strictly safeguarded."[20]

As we have noted before, the various statutes of the Red Cross movement are not clear and consistent about who can do what, either within one set of rules or among the three sets. The Standing Commission does, however, possess some potential to become a "super-agency" for the movement—one executive organ that could institutionally embody "the International Red Cross" and be elected by the constituent members of the movement while being responsible ultimately only to the International Conference. Whatever this potential, and precisely because of it, the exercise of influence by the Commission is consistently resisted by the ICRC, which fears for its image of impartiality and independence from realpolitik. An increase in influence for the Commission is likewise resisted by many national societies, which continue to favor local autonomy within the movement, whether it be autonomy from the ICRC, League, or Standing Commission. The members of the League secretariat have mixed feelings about deferring to the Commission, but have seemed less opposed than the other constituent parts.

The International Conference of the Red Cross and its Standing Commission at the moment have largely symbolic meaning for the movement. There is some symbolic importance from a conference every four years and from a Commission that represents that meeting in the intervals, in the sense of helping to pull the movement together and reminding the parts that the whole does exist. Whatever the limitations on the practical effects of the Conference and the Commission, the movement would be less unified without them. It remains true, however, that the Conference consistently reflects the disunity of the movement. Conference debates are frequently acrimonious, and resulting resolutions are not enforced. The Commission is weaker in terms of practical influence than the other centers of power in the movement—especially the ICRC and the national societies.

THE RED CROSS IN REVIEW

The International Red Cross is a transnational movement with great potential for humanitarian action accompanied by great problems of organization and coordination. The movement comprises a network of humanitarian agencies potentially available for global action. Its presence opens the door to certain possibilities, but the movement in its present condition guarantees nothing by way of probable results.

The movement can function as an integrated whole, as it did in the Hungarian crisis of 1956 until the Hungarian government terminated Red Cross action.[21] In that situation of domestic instability followed by Soviet military intervention, the ICRC was the sole international agency to gain access to the scene of violence. The ICRC cooperated with the Hungarian Red Cross, as well as various competing political factions, to bring in material and medical assistance to individuals in need. The collection of assistance was coordinated by the League, with the particular cooperation of the Austrian Red Cross, which served as the base agency for the assistance operation. The ICRC then ran convoys from Austria into Hungary, negotiating truces in order to assure the safe passage of the convoys and the distribution of the assistance in Budapest. The Red Cross movement functioned quickly and efficiently, engaging in humanitarian action without controversy as long as the Hungarian situation was unstable. With the reimposition of control by the Kadar government, the leadership of the Hungarian Red Cross was changed and the ICRC was no longer permitted to enter the nation.

On the other hand, in places like South Vietnam prior to 1973 and Bangladesh, the Red Cross movement was represented by various parts of the movement; there was slight coordination in the Red Cross presence. In both South Vietnam and Bangladesh, the ICRC functioned independently to protect prisoners of war, civilian detainees, and political prisoners. The League was involved in certain assistance roles. In addition a number of national societies "did their own thing" with the permission of the local government and Red Cross Society. The attempt of the ICRC and League to coordinate assistance throughout Indochina from 1973 on was largely successful, but this joint program did not alter the separate status of protection functions directed by the ICRC or some separate programs in South Vietnam run by national societies.

And in some situations where Red Cross activity might be expected, the movement does not function at all because of countervailing power. Legal arguments aside, there was general expectation that American combatants held in North Vietnam were to be visited by the ICRC during the Indochina War. Neither the ICRC, nor League officials, nor national Red Cross Societies like the American and Polish ones which served as intermediaries, were able to secure a Red Cross presence in the places of detention. While this absence was not due to any lack of motivation and desire on the part of various Red Cross officials, it still bears noting that the movement was not able to function in accordance with general expectations. The barrier to Red Cross operations in cases like this was not so much lack of coordination within the movement as the weakness of Red Cross values as a universal code of behavior when faced with local—in this case, national—behavior based on different values.

In the context of a universal Red Cross movement characterized by great potential for action yet fluctuating action in fact, and characterized by aspirations toward unity but factual disunity, the ICRC has become quite clearly the protection agency of the movement, utilizing other parts of the movement or bypassing them according to its understanding of the needs of a given situation. The function of assistance is less clearly the prerogative of any one agency, in peace or in war, particularly because of the sheer size of the job entailed in large-scale relief operations. In situations like Nigeria or Bangladesh, the sheer scope of needed assistance tends to favor a movement-wide operation rather than an "ICRC job" or a "League role." And neither the ICRC nor League can perform adequately in the assistance field without the competence of national Red Cross Societies—the grassroots collection and distribution agencies.

The lack of institutional change in the Red Cross movement since the present parts were more or less formally put together in 1928, plus the ICRC's historical role since the 1860's, has given it great independence which it jealously guards. Symbolic both of the present condition of the transnational movement and of the independent attitudes of the ICRC was the question of a new Red Cross headquarters in Geneva. The International Labor Organization was moving out of its building next to Lake Geneva, and the premises were offered to the League, the ICRC and the Henry Dunant Institute for an integrated headquarters of the International Red Cross. The League was in favor of putting itself and the ICRC under the same roof, for symbolic as well as for administrative reasons. But the ICRC was opposed, believing the ILO building was too costly and ostentatious, and also that the ICRC should be housed apart from the League to guarantee its independence from a federation that was subjected to national pressures and thereby to protect not only its neutral image but also its diplomatic secrets. The ICRC was able to make its view prevail.

The above example conveys clearly the independence and influence of the ICRC within the Red Cross movement. Because of this independence and influence, what the ICRC does and says has great importance for what is done and said in the name of the International Red Cross. And it is equally important for the movement what the ICRC does *not* do, and why.

Therefore we now turn to the basic functions of the ICRC, its rationale for these functions, in the form of Red Cross philosophy, and alternatives to ICRC action in world affairs.

2 The ICRC in Global Context: Functions, Philosophy, Alternatives

From the 1860's to World War I, what the ICRC did and what was done in the name of the International Red Cross were almost one and the same. There was no League, and while national societies might "do their own thing," the international dimension of Red Cross activity was dominated by the ICRC.

The ICRC during this period provided humanitarian protection and assistance in armed conflicts. Progressively into this century, the ICRC extended this protection and assistance to individuals in need short of armed conflict—that is, to individuals in some sort of conflict situation that was not violent enough to be called war. But in general the ICRC has always oriented its basic activity to conflicts—emphasizing the protection of individuals from some type of adversary, and assisting them with medical and material aid as a concomitant or secondary activity.

From about the 1920's, the other components of the Red Cross movement increasingly turned to nonconflict work, such as assistance in natural disasters and various community service programs (e.g., collection of blood, first aid training). But these other functions adopted by the rest of the movement did not alter the basic functions of the ICRC—humanitarian protection and assistance in conflict situations.

Eventually the ICRC, and other Red Cross agencies, developed a philosophy as an official rationale for Red Cross actions. That this was a secondary effort, compared with pragmatic action as the primary effort, is seen in the fact that there was no official statement on "Red Cross philosophy" until 1921—some sixty years after the start of the movement. Prior to 1921 and the first, formal ICRC statement on "Red Cross principles," the movement as a whole had contented itself with "unofficial" statements explaining philosophy of action. These ranged from Henry Dunant's *A Memory of Solférino* to various statements by Red Cross officials. During these first sixty years, the ideas behind Red Cross action were largely explained through the action, especially as demonstrated by the ICRC.

With the creation of the League and the expansion of Red Cross activity to nonconflict situations in the 1920's, the ICRC felt the need to articulate more clearly and formally the motivating ideas of Red Cross action. This trend toward development of a Red Cross philosophy took on greater impetus after World War II because of: (1) the expanded activity during that war, and (2) the increased number of national societies from new states participating in the movement. In the late 1940's there occurred something of an orgy of rule-making within the movement, with the ICRC adopting ten rules for the recognition of national societies and the League adopting seventeen basic rules for admission to that federation. The 1952 Red Cross Conference followed by formally adopting for the first time some basic principles for the movement.

Finally in the 1960's an official set of seven basic principles was adopted by the Conference; this supposedly explained what the components of the movement had been doing in the preceding 100 years.

ICRC action of humanitarian protection and assistance, and to a lesser extent the formulation of Red Cross principles, permit one to place the ICRC in global context in the last quarter of the twentieth century. What the ICRC does, and to some extent the official rationale for this action, allows one to compare the ICRC with other actors in world affairs—especially other nongovernmental organizations (NGOs) active on humanitarian issues. What the ICRC does and says can be compared not only with other NGOs, but also with intergovernmental international organizations and with states.

FUNCTIONS OF THE ICRC

The Protection Function

Protection has been the main contribution of the ICRC to the Red Cross movement. That ICRC protection has been of special significance in the broader world of international relations. The ICRC has exercised almost a monopoly of direct protection roles in the name of the Red Cross. And while there have been, and are, other efforts in international relations at protecting the individual, the position of the ICRC in protection matters is both widely accepted and exceptional in many ways.

An analytical view of ICRC protection indicates three basic roles; each role has a direct and an indirect dimension. They are (1) ad hoc diplomacy; (2) development of law; (3) application of law.

1. The ICRC engages in attempts to protect individuals on the basis of ad hoc diplomacy. (This is more fully treated in Chapters 3 and 4.) The ICRC seeks to become involved in a situation on the basis of ad hoc agreement among the parties involved, even though the ICRC has no legal right to enter a country. In Red Cross jargon, this type of involvement is called the right of initiative—the right of the ICRC to try to initiate protection attempts on the basis of humanitarian concern. Sometimes the ICRC will wait to be asked to exercise an initiative, on other occasions it will initiate protection action completely on its own. When the American official, Dr. Claude Fly, of the Agency for International Development (AID) was kidnapped in Uruguay in the early 1970's, the ICRC became officially involved upon request of a member of the family. In a number of hijacking situations in the Middle East, the ICRC has become involved either initially on its own or at the request of a Palestinian group or a state. In these situations of kidnappings and hijackings, and with regard to political prisoners, the ICRC has attempted to protect individuals from harm not because the ICRC was guaranteed a legal right to execute protection but because the parties involved agreed to an ICRC direct presence and participation in diplomacy.

This direct protection through ad hoc diplomacy has an indirect dimension. When the ICRC explains its actions or when it interacts with other units in the Red Cross movement, it is building an image and reputation that affects its ad hoc diplomacy. When the ICRC interacts with other NGOs like Amnesty International and the International Commission of Jurists to obtain information on political prisoners, it is indirectly engaged in protecting individuals. Thus there is a preparatory stage to ad hoc diplomacy that can be referred to as the indirect aspect of ad hoc protection attempts.

2. The second basic protection role is that of developing law for the protection of individuals. (This role is covered in Chapter 5.) The direct dimension is exemplified by the activities of the ICRC in the preparatory conferences and the diplomatic conferences that draft the law and formally approve the draft law prior to state signature and ratification. The ICRC interacts with the Swiss government as well as with the United Nations and the Red Cross Conference to help initiate legislation. Then the ICRC plays a direct role in the preparatory and diplomatic meetings: writing draft articles, hosting meetings of legal experts, writing revised draft articles, and commenting at the diplomatic conference as a legal expert and unofficial cohost of the conference. (The Swiss government is the official host

for diplomatic conferences related to humanitarian law in armed conflict, even though the ICRC itself is the official host for the preparatory meetings of legal experts. Such are the legal games that states play—e.g., only states can be full participants in the diplomatic conferences that formally approve the draft law and open it to state adherence.)

This direct role for the ICRC in helping to develop humanitarian law has evolved historically; there is nothing that guarantees an ICRC role in the legislative process except precedent and the ICRC's current utility. Indeed, in the late 1960's and early 1970's, there was competition between the ICRC and certain UN agencies over who was to do what in supplementing the 1949 Geneva Conventions. The pull of tradition, as well as the explicit preferences of a number of states, was sufficient to produce once again a direct legislative role for the ICRC. This legislative role is limited to the development of humanitarian law in armed conflict, primarily because the ICRC itself has not sought to expand its legislative scope of interest to human rights in general.

There is an indirect dimension to this role. Other ICRC actions have educative effects that impinge on its legislative role. Past ICRC ad hoc diplomacy with regard to prisoners of war and civilians in a war zone indirectly contributed to direct legislative efforts in behalf of these persons. ICRC publications and seminars likewise contributed indirectly to direct protection efforts, at a later time. Whatever the ICRC's legislative scope of interest, either upon request or at its own choice, its past record in ad hoc diplomacy will be a major, if indirect, ingredient in new attempts at legislation. It will be against the background of ICRC ad hoc visits to political prisoners, among other efforts, that any attempted new international legislation for those individuals will occur.

3. The third protection role for the ICRC is that of helping to apply the law once legislated. (This is treated in Chapters 6 and 7.) The direct aspect of this role is by far the easiest of the three roles to identify, for that role is by and large spelled out in treaty law. It involves executing specific tasks, general tasks, and substituting for the Protecting Power. (A Protecting Power is a neutral state appointed by a belligerent in international armed conflict to help implement humanitarian law.) While many of the rights and duties of both the detaining authority and the detainee are spelled out in the law, as well as the rights and duties of the ICRC (and other Red Cross agencies), there are some aspects of legal protection which historically have been left to the practice of the ICRC— such as the disposition of prison reports after a visit to prisoners of war or civilian detainees. It is ICRC practice and not the statutory law that has determined that the reports will be private rather than public and will go only to the state of origin and the detaining state. Whatever the ambiguity of certain aspects of this role, the overall role of helping to apply the law is an ICRC task—rather well recognized, at least by specialists in the international law of armed conflict.

The indirect aspect of this role consists of the dissemination and inculcation of the humanitarian law of armed conflict. Whereas the parties directly concerned in the armed conflict, along with the ICRC, have a direct role in ongoing legal protection, all states that are parties to the Geneva Conventions, as well as all Red Cross agencies, can play an indirect role through preparation for humanitarian protection. Instruction in the law prior to direct protection may be as important, or more so, than direct protection. The serious teaching of the law, both to the military establishment and to the educated public, is a sine qua non to the systematic application of the law during armed conflict. It is for this reason that James E. Bond has written:

> To a great extent there is no law of war except what the soldier does in the field. He does not read the Geneva Conventions before he acts. He may recall his training. He may consult field regulations or field manuals. The soldier thus inevitably makes law on the battlefield. If he has received sound instruction in his responsibilities and if he has been issued directives that embody sound principles, he will usually make good law. The quality of the directives is all-important because every army runs on directives.[1]

This need for indirect legal protection through training in the law can be contrasted with the limits of actual training and dissemination, leading to acute problems in armed conflicts like the Indochina War. According to an American veteran,

> We were told repeatedly from basic training through advanced infantry training through OCS [Officer Candidate School], when you got to the Nam, you threw the book [The Geneva Conventions] away.... I went through infantry OCS and was trained to be an officer and nobody ever showed it to me.... I was never taught ... how to handle a prisoner if I captured one.... I never received any instruction about how to take prisoners of war.... You are given a Geneva Convention card sometimes that has the rules on it, treat women with respect and so forth, but like I told you, and they told us when you get to the Nam, you just throw the book away.[2]

During the Indochina War, the United States government was sending numerous reports to Geneva demonstrating the existence of various regulations requiring military decision-makers to take account of the laws of armed conflict, as requested by the Red Cross Conference. But without doubt there was a gap between what was issued as a rule at the Pentagon, and what was done in the field. No Red Cross agency seems to have concerned itself with this gap.

Indeed, much of the difficulty in applying the humanitarian law of armed conflict in the past lies not so much in the lack of effort by the ICRC in direct protection as in the lack of acceptance of the general idea of international protection for one's enemies. This situation stems from inadequacies in *in*direct protection—that is, in the inculcation of the legal principles in the military in particular and in the nation in general. Direct protection attempts have occurred in a sea of ignorance and lack of concern. The fact that certain ICRC activity may be considered "indirect" protection through the teaching of legal principles does not make it less important than actual ICRC supervision of the law in an ongoing conflict.

The Assistance Function

In addition to protection, the ICRC engages in assistance. When assistance is tied to protection, as it frequently is, ICRC assistance may be said to have all the characteristics of protection analyzed above. When the ICRC provides material goods and medical help to detainees, there is a meshing of the protection and assistance functions. Where assistance is separate from protection, as is also frequently the case, the ICRC has less of a monopoly over Red Cross action in the assistance field—and a less unusual position in the larger world of international affairs. Even in armed conflicts, where the ICRC is supposed to be the uncontested head of Red Cross assistance efforts, the national Red Cross Societies and the League are—by necessity—playing an increasingly significant part. By tradition within the Red Cross movement, the ICRC plays no part in assistance in natural disasters. Beyond the Red Cross movement, there are many agencies concerned with assistance, especially in natural disasters, but also in the context of "man-made disaster." With regard to needs for assistance stemming from situations of the latter type, there are agencies of a permanent sort—like the UN High Commission for Refugees, and ad hoc organizations—like Joint Church Aid in the Nigerian War. Because of assistance by other Red Cross agencies and by organizations outside the Red Cross movement, ICRC assistance roles are more complex than protective roles—and thus more difficult to identify and analyze in satisfactory fashion.

The ICRC, in the context of conflict, may engage in assistance efforts by providing (1) material goods, (2) medical goods and services, or (3) sociolegal services. These assistance roles may either be large-scale or small-scale.

Material goods may be money, food, clothing, or housing. Medical goods and services are self-explanatory. Sociolegal services may take a variety of specific forms. The most common examples of social services provided by the ICRC would be legal and family counseling, and provision of reading and recreational matter, plus religious services. In the territories occupied by Israel after the 1967 and 1973 wars, for example, the ICRC advised Arab civilians, upon their request, about state requirements for the reunification of families and for internation travel for the purpose of education. Particularly with regard to the movement of persons between Israel-controlled areas and the Arab states, the ICRC became a "humanitarian travel agency," assisting in arranging family holidays and movement of students. This seemed to have little to do with protection of these people from any party. Likewise after World War II, the ICRC assisted German nationals in France and non-Germans in Germany with legal services. Since workers deported to Germany were in particular need immediately after the collapse of the Third Reich, the ICRC became a de facto consulate for these persons, providing them with the necessary legal materials—principally the Red Cross travel document—so that other states could attach their visas to it. Likewise, much of the activity of the Red Cross Central Tracing Agency, an administrative arm of the ICRC, centers on providing social and legal services to individuals—like the location of individuals for family and insurance reasons.

ICRC assistance through these roles can be large-scale or small-scale. The significance of using this distinction is that the size of the assistance effort has a great deal to do with whether the ICRC can—and should—handle that operation as an ICRC program, or whether assistance should be a Red Cross or even UN operation. The dividing line between small- and large-scale is not objectively definable. But administratively it is easy to distinguish millions of Bengalis streaming into India out of what is now Bangladesh from several thousand Bihari in need of assistance within that new state. It is also fairly easy to distinguish a large-scale assistance operation involving the feeding, clothing, housing, and medical care of thousands in an armed conflict, as in Nigeria, from the provision of blankets and medical care to hundreds of political prisoners in Rhodesia.

In addition to types of assistance and its overall dimension, one can identify assistance roles such as: assessment of needs, collection and distribution of goods, and overall planning and management. (See further Chapter 7, section on the Nigerian War.)

PHILOSOPHY OF THE ICRC

Content

Through protection and assistance the ICRC tries to apply the philosophy of the Red Cross movement to conflict situations. Historically, one can say that ICRC protection and assistance in conflicts had a profound influence on the development of the official Red Cross principles. The ICRC was the oldest and most experienced Red Cross agency. Moreover, the ICRC took upon itself to be the "guardian" of Red Cross principles, a position officially agreed to by the rest of the movement.

What the ICRC has had to say about Red Cross philosophy has not always been clear. For a long time the ICRC said nothing—officially. In 1921 the ICRC formally adopted four principles: charity, universality, independence, and impartiality. Subsequently, these four differed from those adopted by the League in the late 1940's, and from those adopted by the Conference in 1952. In 1956 the ICRC's Jean Pictet attempted to bring some order out of this chaos by arguing in behalf of seven basic principles (humanity, equality, due proportion, impartiality, neutrality, independence, and universality). Finally in 1965 the Red Cross

Conference adopted an altered seven: humanity, impartiality, neutrality, independence, voluntary service, unity, and universality.

The core idea, for the ICRC as well as for the Red Cross movement, has been expressed either as charity or humanity. Charity was the original idea, reflected in the motto of the ICRC: *Inter Arma Caritas*. Over time charity gave way to humanity, or to the word ''humanitarianism.'' Charity seemed to convey a lack of systematic action, and a lack of action directed to the causes in contrast to the consequences of human suffering.[3] Moreover, some were inclined to read an upper-class bias into ''charity,'' as if it denoted an aristocratic duty toward the lower classes.

However expressed, it was clear that the central idea for the Red Cross was help to fellowmen in need. It was a product of Western Christianity. ICRC spokesmen in particular were fond of using the parable of the good Samaritan to demonstrate the essential nature of Red Cross action and thought.[4] There is reason, therefore, for humanity to be listed as the first of the 1965 official principles.

Beyond the broad agreement that a concern for humanity denotes the most fundamental Red Cross principle, there has been much semantic confusion, of two types. First, there has been a good deal of hair-splitting about meaning. There has been an effort to consider ''impartiality'' and ''neutrality'' as referring to qualitatively different things.[5] And independence has not always been separated from impartiality and neutrality. Neutrality alone has proven just as elusive an idea to Red Cross thinkers as to others who have wrestled with the term. Does it mean impartiality formally recognized? Does it mean abstinence from a conflict if a Red Cross role is not agreed upon by all conflicting parties? Does it mean having a balanced impact on a situation? Does it mean action consistent with Red Cross values, whatever that action's impact on the parties and whatever their views?[6]

A second semantic problem has been, not the unpersuasive effort to distinguish among words, but rather the use of some concepts as principles and the nonuse of others. Why should ''voluntary service'' be listed as a principle, but Pictet's 1956 ''due proportion'' be downplayed (''due proportion'' refers to the idea of giving help in due proportion to the need, as the only permissible discrimination in the work of the Red Cross). Or why should ''unity'' and ''universality'' be listed as basic principles when one already has the term ''humanity''; are not unity and universality already present in the idea of humanity, insofar as Red Cross philosophy is concerned? Why, furthermore, should the official seven be used, but not the idea of discretion, or cooperation with public authorities, or action as a temporary ''fireman'' until the public authorities can take over the activity? These ideas, too, have long characterized the history of the Red Cross.[7]

In sum, neither the 1965 seven principles, nor the unofficial commentary preceding them, has met with full and widespread appreciation. This may be, in part, because of differences among ''Continental philosophy,'' ''Anglo-Saxon pragmatism,'' and other values. But to numerous observers, writing on Red Cross principles appears unclear and inconsistent.[8] It is not at all clear that the principles have practical meaning, for most members of the Red Cross movement appear to pay only lip service to them while concentrating on their real interest—pragmatic action.[9]

There is, however, real meaning to Red Cross philosophy, if it is understood to mean the essence of Red Cross thinking as derived from past and present action. As indicated above, there is a *Grundnorm* in Red Cross thinking: humanitarianism, or help to the individual in need. At a second level, there is the idea that this help should be nondiscriminatory, except on the basis of a hierarchy of need (due proportion; or ''to each according to his need''). Therefore all men are equal; there is to be no discrimination whether for nationality, race, class, party membership, religion, or sex. This means, in other words, that the motivation of the members of the movement, and of course of the ICRC, should be impartiality. And this impartiality requires an independent base for its exercise. Red Cross help to individuals is thus to be impartial and not subjected to any pressures that would result in discrimination.

At a third level, there is the idea that Red Cross help to individuals of a nondiscriminatory nature should occur with the cooperation of public authorities and be primarily of a temporary nature. Now this third level of operational guidelines is not found in the official principles or commentary in any form, but has constituted an important element of Red Cross thinking in the world of applied action. From the very beginning of the Red Cross movement, Red Cross agencies and programs have existed to work with, and supplement, public authorities. The ICRC in particular has sought to operate on the basis of consent given by public authorities, either as written into international law or as given on an ad hoc basis.[10] Moreover, the ICRC in particular has seen itself as basically an emergency actor, especially in war or other times of crisis. If it has tended to become something of a rather permanent actor in certain areas, such as detention inspections, it is because no other actor seems able to perform this task as effectively; and the ICRC maintains the official view that it is prepared to give up such tasks when another actor is able effectively to do the job.

Current Red Cross philosophy, therefore, can be initially understood in these terms: (1) a core idea (help to fellowmen in need); (2) a derivative tenet (nondiscriminatory help); and (3) a basic operational guideline (help on the basis of the consent of public authorities, usually temporarily).

It is on the basis of this thinking that the ICRC has carried out protection and assistance in conflict situations.

Strengths

The Red Cross core idea and its derivative tenet have had wide appeal. This is especially true in the Western world, where the Judeo-Christian ethic has long emphasized individuality and the intrinsic or metaphysical equality and dignity of all persons. In theory at least, the state exists to protect and promote the welfare of the individual. In general terms, there is no fundamental conflict between Red Cross nondiscrimination and values widespread in the West.

In the non-Western world, Red Cross nondiscrimination meets some difficulties of a general nature. While it can be noted that the 1965 version of Red Cross principles was adopted unanimously, nevertheless there seems to be in the non-Western world greater acceptance of the idea that it is permissible to think in terms of a superior nation, class, ethnic group or political party. Moreover, overlaying this discriminatory group thinking one also finds in some places a formal ideology creating discriminatory hierarchies among men on some basis such as social origin or class. While some of these barriers to nondiscriminatory action exist in the West as well—official or unofficial racism is one example—it remains true that discriminatory group thinking is more official, acceptable, and prevalent in the non-Western world.

Nevertheless, there remains rather wide acceptance for Red Cross humanitarianism that is nondiscriminatory and directed toward the individual. The Red Cross basic tenet is similar to "to each according to his need," which is a widely accepted principle in the Marxist and third worlds. This is especially true with regard to Red Cross assistance. But beyond, either a "communist," "socialist," or "capitalist" might agree that "enemies of the regime" should, if detained, be treated according to certain humanitarian standards. And the "group versus individual" dichotomy is in some ways a false issue, for the individual is found in a group at the same time that he is an individual. All groups of individuals may have certain minimum needs met without violating the rights of other groups. A "reactionary" when detained can be protected from physical and psychological torture without violating the rights of the "preferred class."

It is a historical fact that Red Cross protection and assistance in conflict situations has not been widely accepted in the socialist world since 1949. But this is not necessarily due to the content of Red Cross philosophy (see also pp. 47–49.)

The third level of essential Red Cross thinking is widely supported by public authorities of all kinds in all places, thus providing an important support for many Red Cross activities. Since Red Cross activity is not viewed as a threat or challenge to these authorities, and since they can view Red Cross activity as an advantage to them, these authorities frequently cooperate with permission, goods, cash, and in other ways.

Weaknesses

First, the Grundnorm of Red Cross thinking, help to people in need and suffering, does not limit or focus the activities of the movement. This, the main weakness of this norm, is a trade-off with the positive element of wide acceptance. But what is not said is what kind of need, what type of suffering is to be the focal point of Red Cross activity.

Historically this was not a problem as long as the ICRC had a single focus— help to war wounded. It was still not seen to be a problem when that focus was expanded to other war victims. It *was* perceived as a problem after World War I when Red Cross activity was accelerated in nonwar situations. This was precisely the period in which the first attention was paid to the subject of formal principles—1920–21. It was also perceived to be a problem after World War II when the heterogeneity of the Red Cross context and the strength of group thinking—especially in Eastern Europe—made a strong impact on Red Cross leaders. This was the period of what can be called an orgy of rule-making— 1946–48.

There has, up to the present, never been a resolution of this weakness. Red Cross activity is so broad and diverse as to defy categorization. There probably is no longer any agreement on the three categories of suffering Max Huber said should be of concern to the Red Cross: suffering from violence, suffering from natural catastrophes, suffering from basic deficiencies in a society. And if there were agreement, these three categories are still so broad that the problem of lack of focus remains unresolved.

For the ICRC, this means that national societies are engaged in all sorts of activities unrelated to conflicts, and indeed the League encourages them in a variety of nonconflict programs. The attention given to the ICRC and conflict situations is therefore reduced.

Secondly, the basic tenet of nondiscriminatory help is frequently found to be weak in competition with other value systems and other ways of thinking. The current, major opposition to it comes from those whose priority is group welfare rather than individual welfare. This, the basic, modern tension between Red Cross and other values, is avoided at the level of the Grundnorm, but becomes manifest at the level of the basic tenet.

The strongest group thinking currently is nationalism, in the Western, so-cialist, and third worlds alike. The modern age is an age of nationalism. Thus the Red Cross basic tenet of nondiscriminatory humanitarianism is frequently evaluated in the light of nationalistic values—and frequently dominated by those values. Red Cross agencies and programs are generally accepted when they are compatible with nationalism and the interests of the nation-state which is the voice of nationalism. Red Cross agencies and programs are rejected when in-compatible with nationalism as defined by a government. This basic weakness of the Red Cross tenet, inferior appeal compared to nationalism, is compounded when nationalism is insecure, for what emerges is chauvinistic nationalism which further rejects Red Cross values. And this basic weakness is also compounded when a formal ideology of class supremacy is superimposed upon nationalism. A national superiority complex, especially one that is the result of insecurity, and a class superiority complex must logically reduce the support given to a movement based on individual equality without regard for nationality or class or any other factor save extent of need (due proportion).

The result is that Red Cross nondiscriminatory help is accepted *to the extent* that it is instrumental to the dominant values of nationalism, whether that nationalism is expressed as simple national sovereignty, or national sovereignty overlaid with some form of imperialism, or national sovereignty clothed in some version of Socialism.

Red Cross socioeconomic programs are accepted insofar as they promote national unity and national viability. ICRC protection activities are rejected when they are seen as promoting national disunity and contravening national jurisdiction. Thus if a nation has 100 starving children and 100 political prisoners, it will be more inclined to accept Red Cross help in feeding, clothing, housing, and medically caring for the children, for this effort enhances the domestic image of state effectiveness in providing for the people. That hypothetical state will be less inclined to accept Red Cross help in establishing humane detention standards, as the effort is frequently perceived as conveying status to, and concern for, those who have disrupted national unity as defined by the government.

Thus the modern dominant value for many is group solidarity, group welfare, and group control. The Red Cross is accepted frequently only as a supplement to those ends. And even where accepted, the Red Cross is limited by the predominance of group values. The national society is not fully independent of most governments. The League is not allowed to command the national societies, nor is the ICRC (with the exception of recognition), and ICRC overtures and programs are sometimes rejected.

While there are some individuals who rally to the Red Cross tenet of nondiscriminatory humanitarianism as a *dominant* value, there are many more who accept the Red Cross only as something *instrumental* to some form of nationalism. The Red Cross movement has been "nationalized" to a great extent. And this emphasis on nationality is also accompanied by other forms of group discrimination, such as that based on race, social class, political party, or other criteria.

Thirdly, the Red Cross idea of acting on the basis of consent by public authorities, usually temporarily, while supported explicitly by public authorities and implicitly by a number of individuals, meets considerable opposition.

This idea has been a firm principle of operation in Red Cross history, but it is poorly explained and poorly understood. ICRC officials have not clearly and effectively explained that they are seeking the greatest humanitarian good for the greatest number. They have not made the point that ICRC in-country action requires future acceptability and systematic action over time—and thus recurring consent from powerful actors in world affairs. They have not made the point that more revolutionary actors exist in both the protection and assistance fields; thus that the Red Cross, often viewed as the "establishment humanitarian agency," occupies a particular place on the spectrum of humanitarian actors—a place supplemented by other types of actors. Red Cross leaders have not in general made an analytical examination and exposé of their own past successes compared to the achievements of these other organizations (did the revolutionary church groups achieve more by way of humanitarian assistance in the Nigerian War than the Red Cross, and could they act again; did the Council of Europe achieve more protection for political prisoners in Greece than the ICRC?). Thus the Red Cross has not done an effective job of explaining *why* it acts within the bounds of general expectations. Nor has it explained its contribution to raising general expectations on humanitarian matters over time.

Even if well explained, the operational principle of acting within the bounds of some type of consent (explicit or tacit), and usually temporarily, remains of weak appeal to a number of persons. Those who seek total and rapid change on the basis of their particular values or who seek to challenge or overthrow a particular establishment, do not see the need of doing what is expected and deferring to the wishes of public authorities. Thus a number of Scandinavian churches did not see the need to take the wishes of the Nigerian government into account in trying to feed starving people in Biafra. Thus Amnesty International does not see the need to defer to state wishes regarding publicity concerning torture of political prisoners in various regimes. Moreover, even certain Red Cross agencies have not always perceived the obligation to act within the bounds of consent in a given situation or with regard to a given subject.

OTHER ACTORS

ICRC protection and assistance, and the philosophy behind the action, must be analyzed in the context of other organizations. The ICRC seeks to achieve a "temporary" rather than "total" implementation of humanitarian values, and does so through cooperative behavior, for two reasons. First, there are other groups seeking total change through public and controversial behavior. Secondly, the ICRC has found that intermediate goals pursued by discretionary means leads to some improvement, in the sense of increased attention to humanitarian issues.

An Overview

Without doubt, there has been a worldwide increase in interest in human rights in the twentieth century. However much the individual may be victimized in any given concrete situation, there has been a clear increase in numbers of international agencies active in support of human rights. However weak is the authority and influence of these agencies, they are attempting to do more now than ever before. While the historical trend is not of sufficient strength to *guarantee* international defense of individual rights, that trend clearly exists.

From the sporadic attempts at defending human rights prior to World War I via the humanitarian intervention of states, through League of Nations' concern with protecting minorities, to the UN era of increasing debate on issues of and lip service to principles of human rights, one can chart the growth of an idea: that states are not free to treat even their own nationals without regard to certain minimum principles of human rights.[11] While the limitations of implementation are all too easily apparent, it is still true that a fundamental change in attitude is under way. What was once regarded as the absolute domain of state prerogative has increasingly become a matter of community concern.[12] The relationship between an individual and his government is increasingly a relationship that is expected to be governed by community standards. That this new attitude is not completely accepted, and that behavior is not always consistent with the new attitude, should not obscure recognition of its growing appeal.

At a minimum, there has been a proliferation of agencies attempting to do something about the condition of the individual on a global scale. These agencies may, at present, be in the stage of promoting the idea of human rights rather than implementing human rights.[13] But it is in the context of this proliferation of agencies and increased attempts at humanitarian action that the ICRC operates.

On a global scale, there are the agencies of the United Nations system, and there are NGOs that interact with that system. As far as the UN system is concerned, the entire system is more and more oriented to what can be called socioeconomic programs rather than security questions. While the latter issues are not absent, the weaknesses of the organization in matters of collective security and peacekeeping are well known. While the UN is involved in security matters in the Middle East and Cyprus, among others, the general assumption is that consistently somewhere between seventy-five and ninety percent of UN expenditures and manpower goes into socioeconomic concerns.

As part of this orientation, the Human Rights Division of the UN Secretariat has been quite active in making studies and interacting with states on various issues associated with human rights. The General Assembly itself has created suborgans to inquire into human rights questions. Admittedly, the Assembly organs have been instructed to inquire into the practices of states like Israel and South Africa, where the votes of the Afro-Asians can be mobilized for UN inquiries and debates vis-à-vis those states. What the Afro-Asians have wanted for Israel and South Africa they have been unwilling to accept for themselves—international supervision of governmental policy with regard to treatment of individuals under their control. The same trend is evident in UN agencies reporting to the UN Economic and Social Counsil (ECOSOC). Especially in the UN Human Rights Commission, there has been an absence of consistent concern for the condition of individuals regardless of nationality and race. Abortive debates on the policies of Chile, Greece and Haiti have been the exception; the general rule has been to avoid explicit mention of any state, consistent with an early orientation by the Human Rights Commission along these lines. The only state persistently drawing explicit attention from the Commission has been South Africa.

Despite this critical examination of the UN record on human rights, one can note more positive aspects. Both the Human Rights Commission and ECOSOC have approved the idea of a UN High Commissioner for Human Rights.[14] The creation of this office is now dependent upon Assembly action. If created, such a UN official might be able, like the UN High Commissioner for Refugees, or the Secretary General of the organization himself, to build an image of responsible neutralism in the area of realpolitik that could be translated into productive work in support of human rights. Even if the office of Commissioner for Human Rights is never established, and there is considerable doubt that it will be, the debate over its creation represents a new stage in governmental concern over international human rights. Moreover, the UN Human Rights Commission has a subcommission that has accepted the principle of individual petition. Thus there has been some slight shift away from the monopoly that states have exercised over UN procedures in relation to human rights. In addition to ECOSOC itself, there are the specialized agencies such as the International Labor Organization (ILO), the World Health Organization (WHO), and the Food and Agriculture Organization (FAO). It is FAO that has coordinated humanitarian assistance in much of Africa. It was WHO that put up the money for Red Cross hospitals in the Congolese Civil War. And it is the ILO that has sought to protect laborers through international supervision of labor conventions.

Outside the formal UN system, there is a global network of NGOs concerned with human rights. One of the most active of these and one which interacts consistently with the ICRC is Amnesty International, the London-based NGO concerned especially with political prisoners. Amnesty, which pays particular attention to person deprived of their liberty because of political belief or nonviolent political action, relies especially on publication as a means of combating governmental policies with which it disagrees. Amnesty also engages in observation of what it calls "political trials," tries to get material assistance to political prisoners—especially through the action of the national sections of its organization, and from time to time makes prison visits.

Another NGO active in this field and with a record of long interaction with the ICRC is the Geneva-based International Commission of Jurists. The ICJ engages in legal work in behalf of human rights. It publishes a journal in which it analyzes the legal aspects of various situations of concern to it, and it provides legal advice to governmental and international organization personnel in matters of human rights.

Whereas the ICJ has been Western in origin and membership, the International Association of Democratic Lawyers is an NGO interested in human rights issues but from a decidedly Marxist perspective. Although the association is not headquartered in Eastern Europe, it has focused its attention exclusively on alleged violations of human rights in Western or pro-Western states.

And there are a number of other NGOs active in this field. There is the International Institute of Human Rights in Strasbourg, the International League for the Rights of Man based in New York, and numerous others. The World Council of Churches has recently been active, not only in the Nigerian Civil War but also with regard to humanitarian aid to the liberation movements of Africa.

Thus on a global scale the UN system is supplanted and in some ways surpassed by an NGO network concerned with human rights. If the UN agencies have been slow to push for fundamental change on a universal basis, the NGOs have not. If the state-dominated UN organs have been slow to name names, the NGOs have not.

In addition to agencies with a global scope, there is much action in defense of the individual at the regional level. This is most striking in Western Europe. In addition to the Council of Europe with its Commission and Court of Human Rights under the European Convention on Human Rights, the Common Market has recently shown an interest in providing surplus commodities to the ICRC for humanitarian assistance. Outside of Western Europe, the Organization of American States has been moving toward acceptance of a regional convention on human rights for the Americas, which would supplement the already existing Inter-American Commission on Human Rights. Also the Organization of African Unity has held meetings on the subject of human rights in Africa, but on that continent there is no functioning regional machinery expressly devoted to human rights. Likewise, there is no regional machinery for human rights in Eastern Europe, the Arab world, or Asia. Be that as it may, the regional institutions in Western Europe and the Americas, which exist to promote and implement human rights without regard for nationality, are among the most effective and the most authoritative of all the international agencies concerned with human rights.[15] It is because of developments in these two geographical areas that some observers have become optimistic about the prospects for regional humanitarian action.

On both a global and regional scale, there has been increased attention to the quality of life, understood not only in the sense of improved protection of the environment but also in the sense of improved protection of the individual in legal and civil terms. Increasingly, humanitarian values compete with realpolitik. If realpolitik continues to be dominant, nonetheless it can be argued that those supporting increased attention to humanitarian values are closing the gap between the dominant policies based on a competition for state power and prestige and the secondary values associated with bettering the life of the individual. It is for this reason that Jacques Freymond, the former acting president of the ICRC, was fond of quoting Albert Sorel: "if history is not morality in action, neither is it action without morality."[16]

International Organizations and Movements

It is in the context of these humanitarian institutions—global and regional, UN and otherwise—that the ICRC operates. It seeks to maintain its independence from them all, especially from the UN, in an attempt to guard its neutral image.[17] In 1951 the General Assembly requested the ICRC to cooperate in naming a commission to work on the settlement of prisoner of war problems stemming from World War II. The ICRC refused to become involved, arguing that the General Assembly had not acted unanimously and thus the ICRC could not act as an impartial institution. In point of fact, the ICRC feared that its image would be that of an extension of the United-States–dominated General Assembly. On the other hand, when, in the Korean War, Western states in the Security Council requested the ICRC to investigate charges of the use of germ warfare by troops defending the regime in the South, the ICRC agreed to create a neutral commission of inquiry under its aegis, pending agreement. This move sparked controversy, especially since those raising the charges, the Chinese and North Koreans, refused to agree to inspection. A Soviet veto in the Security Council formally blocked the inspection. Nevertheless, and despite this episode, as a general rule the ICRC does seek to maintain independence from other international agencies in an effort to avoid becoming the agent for one coalition or another in realpolitik. For that reason the ICRC has refused to give specific testimony on what it has found in the prisons it has visited—a refusal applied alike to the UN Commission on Human Rights and the Council of Europe.

The ICRC also refuses to cooperate with other agencies because of the unwritten principle of discretion.[18] In the case of the Council of Europe's investigation of Greek detention policies in the late 1960's, the petitioning Scandinavian states appeared to have no motivation other than humanitarian. But the ICRC still refused to cooperate with the Council's investigation in any meaningful way. For the ICRC, it was not only a matter of defending the principles of independence and neutrality but also that of discretion. Even if the ICRC had knowledge of a violation of the European Convention on Human Rights, the ICRC did not feel obligated to testify to that effect, for it had a bilateral agreement with Greece that its findings would go only to the government. The ICRC believed it had to be faithful to that agreement in order to maintain the confidence of governments, thus ensuring access to individuals in future situations around the world, whatever the unhappiness of the Scandinavian governments in the Greek case.

Where one of these principles is not at stake, the ICRC has no hesitancy about cooperation. The ICRC works closely with the UN High Commissioner for Refugees in places like Uganda and Chile. In Bangladesh, the ICRC worked very closely with representatives of the Secretary General in efforts to protect the Bihari minority. After a period of some competition in the late 1960's, the ICRC and the UN Human Rights Division of the Secretariat arrived at mutually acceptable relations. The ICRC constantly interacts with other NGOs like Amnesty and the ICJ, although this interaction is not without its competitions.

However much these organizations may cooperate for a specific task, there is one fundamental difference between the ICRC and most of these other institutions. The ICRC is more content with intermediate results than the others. While

Amnesty International, for example, challenges the reasons that a man is detained as a political prisoner, the ICRC never questions the fact that the man is detained—unless for a humanitarian reason such as health, age or family considerations. While Amnesty raises the question of the reason *for* detention, the ICRC raises the question of the conditions *of* detention. Whereas the Security Council may vote that North Korea was the aggressor in the Korean War, and whereas the General Assembly may vote to dispatch troops to oppose that North Korean policy, the ICRC contents itself with attempts to obtain access to persons detained by North Korea and by the Chinese on North Korean territory. Therefore the ICRC does not seek a total solution to a problem.

Of course what is an intermediate and what is a total solution may be in the eye of the observer. In a hijacking, the ICRC does seek the total release of the passengers, and does condemn the taking of hostages as a statement of principle. In this sense ICRC action is oriented toward a total solution of a particular problem. In the case of the 1970 Palestinian hijacking of planes to Jordan, the ICRC refused to accept a Palestinian offer to release all passengers except Jewish ones. On the other hand, the ICRC does not take action against hijackers, either diplomatically or legally. When, in 1972, Israeli armed forces captured Palestinian hijackers using the flag of the Red Cross for cover, the ICRC protested strongly to the government. In this sense, the ICRC role in hijackings is intermediate rather than total; it seeks the protection of the hostages but it takes no action to eliminate the hijacking itself, aside from a reiteration of principle. The ICRC has not, for example, lobbied in support of anti-hijacking treaties.

Even where the ICRC is serving as some type of legal agent under the Geneva Conventions, and therefore has some responsibility to see that the law is observed, the ICRC tries to be legal adviser to the state rather than policeman. Hence when India persisted in violating the Geneva Conventions with regard to the return of Pakistani prisoners of war after the end of the war for Bangladesh, the ICRC, while noting the wording of the Third Convention, concentrated on improving the conditions of detention for the illegally held Pakistani rather than engage in constant argument with the Indian authorities about total right and wrong.

It is this intermediate objective in the humanitarian work of the ICRC that provides so much of the criticism of what it does. It is also one of the things that makes ICRC protection and assistance unique, for if it provokes criticism from NGOs and some governments, it is the very factor that makes it so acceptable among governments in general. Like UN peacekeeping, ICRC roles are useful precisely because they do not pretend to be total solutions. Total solutions require either total agreement, always difficult to get in world affairs, or violence. What is useful is what can be done on the basis of consensus diplomacy—which is also diplomacy based on incomplete agreement.[19]

Therefore the ICRC interacts with a number of NGOs and with intergovernmental organizations like the UN which have shown increased attention to the cause of human rights. But it is still the state that commands the most power and authority in the world.

States

The ICRC is, to a great extent, "the establishment" humanitarian agency. It has achieved a certain quasi-authoritative status in a world dominated but not completely controlled by nation-states. Its measure of general acceptability among states—not attained by other humanitarian NGOs—is the product of over a century of ICRC humanitarian action. The ICRC has discovered by trial and error what governments will permit and what they will not, and in pursuing what can be done on the basis of governmental consent it has built its reputation for responsible action—with responsibility defined by governments.

Despite all of the Red Cross jargon about avoidance of politics, the ICRC has been a very political animal, in the sense of recognizing the importance and content of policies pursued by governments. Historically the ICRC has been very pragmatic about what it can and cannot do in the face of government emphasis on realpolitik, and in the face of government leaders' interest in partisan politics. It is for this reason that the ICRC's Jean Pictet has written, "Humanitarianism mixes a little irrationality—the ideal, impossible to define, toward which one tends—with a lot of realism."[20]

Of course there is controversy about what is possible in a given situation. Particularly under the impetus of concern for what seems like the worst possible abuse of human rights, there may be strong argument for dispensing with the niceties of governmental consent. In a number of situations the ICRC has engaged in internal debate, and has been pressured from the outside, regarding what is possible and constructive action in defense of individuals.

The classic example of this type of controversy was the ICRC's position vis-à-vis the Third Reich of Adolph Hitler during World War II. ICRC representatives were in Germany visiting prisoners of war, and the institution had some knowledge of the situation in the concentration camps for the Jews. The ICRC made repeated efforts to obtain governmental permission to visit the concentration camps. It did obtain access to a few of the camps under a number of restrictions by the Third Reich in both 1935 and 1938. Complete permission was not forthcoming, and the ICRC believed it could not continue visiting the camps without full access to the camps and without private discussions with the detainees. The ICRC resumed its petitions to Hitler's subordinates, seeking the sort of access that it had regarding prisoners of war. This permission was not forthcoming until the very end of the war, when Germany was on the brink of total defeat. Throughout this long and frustrating sequence, the ICRC never published accounts of what it knew of the camps or in any other way contravened the wishes of the German government (except in the sense that repeated petitions and critical private reports no doubt were against the wishes of the government). The

ICRC took a broad view of its humanitarian pursuits, particularly its responsibilities toward Allied prisoners of war held by the Germans. Since the Third Reich had explicitly threatened to bar the ICRC from these prisoners of war if it took provocative action with regard to the Jewish detainees, the ICRC elected to pursue what was possible, to try for new possibilities, but not to contravene the desires of the government and thereby run the risk that the humanitarian action then possible—i.e., with prisoners of war—would be terminated.[21]

A similar situation—but a different ICRC response—arose in the Nigerian Civil War, where elements of Western opinion believed the Ibos in the eastern region to be threatened by genocide—either directly by conscious policy of the government in Lagos or indirectly from the governmental blockade. The ICRC was pressured by these Western elements to pursue policies of assistance without regard to the wishes of Lagos. The ICRC, in a context where legality and impartiality did not exist in "black" and "white," finally took action resulting in its chief representative in Nigeria being declared *persona non grata,* and the ICRC's role of coordinating assistance on the governmental side being terminated (see Chapter 7). With hindsight one can say that the genocide in the Nigerian War was much less real than the genocide in the Third Reich (although there is no doubting the reality of starvation in Biafra). But the pressures on the ICRC to take firm action were as real in the Nigerian War as in World War II. Equally real were the debates within the ICRC about what was, pragmatically, possible.

Therefore, while there may be controversy about what is justified pragmatism in a given case, and while the ICRC itself may alter its behavior in different situations, ICRC action in pursuit of individual welfare within the bounds of governmental consent has led, in historical perspective, to great acceptability among governments. The ICRC was the only humanitarian agency to operate on both sides in Nigeria. This status as a responsible humanitarian agency in the eyes of governments has carried over to liberation movements and various other nonstate, nongovernmental parties. The ICRC has been an acceptable intermediary for the Palestinian groups in the Middle East, most of the black liberation movements in Africa, some of the revolutionary groups in Latin America, and a few of the various antigovernment factions in Asia.

Such a position may guarantee criticism of the ICRC by elements totally opposed to a party with whom the ICRC cooperates in some way. In the 1960's and 1970's, the ICRC was criticized for being present in South Africa, Rhodesia and the Portuguese territories in Africa. It was argued by those totally opposed to the white regimes that the presence of the ICRC gave a certain legitimacy to those regimes. But the ICRC continued its visits to detainees in those states, believing that it had a humanitarian obligation to try and protect those individuals caught up in the struggles in southern Africa. While the ICRC roles were generally acceptable to black and white elites (despite some conflicts from time to time), that acceptability was accompanied by strong cirticism from extremist elements on both sides of the racial struggle.

ICRC acceptability to states (and nonstate parties, too), accompanied as it is by criticism and controversy, is of varying degrees in the last quarter of the twentieth century. The ICRC is most acceptable to Western states, increasingly is building rapport with the third-world states, and least acceptable to Marxist states.

The Red Cross movement is a Western movement by origin and leadership, and as already noted its philosophical underpinnings stem from Western Christianity. The ICRC as the original Red Cross agency has always been staffed by Swiss, and however much the state of Switzerland may be neutral with regard to military alliances; Switzerland is Western culturally and in terms of economic structures. National Red Cross Societies formed first in the West, and the League as the federation of these societies was led first by the Americans and then by the Scandinavians. The entire orientation of the Red Cross movement—its focus on the individual—arises from Western philosophical views of man and society.

It is not surprising then that the financial base of the ICRC should be Western governments: first the Swiss government, then the American, then the other Western governments. (Relatively high levels of financial support by the American government to the ICRC have, however, been of very recent origin.) And it is not surprising that some Western states pushed for new international law that would make the ICRC an automatic substitute for the Protecting Power under the Geneva Conventions—a supervisor of the law who would not need to secure state permission in order to act in each case. It is the Americans who turned to the ICRC in places like Tibet in the late 1950's to administer AID assistance. It is the British who permitted the ICRC to visit administrative detainees arrested because of events in Northern Ireland. It is the French who agreed to ICRC involvement in the Algerian War, who permitted prison visits not only in North Africa but also in metropolitan France, and who in the process set in motion events that helped to discredit the French Army and a government.

This is not to say that the ICRC has had a carte blanche to do what it pleased toward the Western states. If the British accepted the ICRC in the conflict over Northern Ireland, it was also the British that for a long time kept the ICRC out of the violent conflict in Kenya for fear that an ICRC presence would lend legal status to the independence movement there. If the Americans found the ICRC useful in Tibet, not to mention Korea, Vietnam, and Nigeria, etc., it was the Americans that declined to exert diplomatic pressure in support of the ICRC vis-à-vis the military junta in Chile in 1973. If the French progressively accepted a large involvement by the ICRC in the Algerian War, it was also the French that at first rejected ICRC offers of involvement and only later accepted them under the pressure of domestic criticism and escalation of the war itself.

Western acceptance of the ICRC in general does not imply that these states neglect claims to domestic jurisdiction and always accept the ICRC under any circumstances. The historical record shows simply that for reasons of domestic and international politics, as well as some humanitarian motivation, Western states have, in relative terms, been supportive of the ICRC.

The ICRC has also become widely acceptable in the third world, and it is in the third world that most ICRC action is now occurring—i.e., Nigeria, Bangladesh, Indonesia, Indochina, the Indian subcontinent, the Middle East, and so forth. The ICRC has achieved this level of involvement despite being largely unknown, even by political elites. Indeed, sometimes the ICRC capitalizes on its obscurity, as in Malaysia and the Philippines where it obtained access to detainees by riding the locally prestigious coattails of the national Red Cross Society. Since the national society was acceptable to the government, so was the ICRC. In that situation, the ICRC did not bother to explain the difference. The ICRC has also achieved a high level of involvement despite being an all-white organization. And the ICRC has been involved in a number of protection and assistance efforts in the third world despite the fact that it did not have extensive experience in Third World affairs at the start of this pattern of involvement. But the lack of nonwhite faces and the lack of Third World experience has created difficulties for the ICRC, especially in Nigeria but more generally as well.

Despite these problems, the ICRC appears to be building rapport with African, Arab, Asian and Latin American elites. It is doing so by demonstrating to these elites the services it can render to the state. These services include all of the traditional tasks of the ICRC, like protecting prisoners of war. Then there are services of special significance to the developing state. These services include the providing of much needed material and medical assistance. The ICRC also provides a certain amount of administrative expertise in penal matters, pointing out to the developing state what is going on in the rest of the world *and* allowing the central government to have a source of information as to what is really going on in the provinces. The ICRC is probably also acceptable to Third World states because of the ICRC's general status. After all, if the ICRC is accepted by the established states, and if a new state gets established by playing the game of politics by the established rules, then one of the rules is to accept the ICRC. There are three major symbols of national independence: extension of diplomatic recognition by the major states, membership in the United Nations, and becoming a party to the 1949 Geneva Conventions. The last symbol implies acceptance of the ICRC for at least some humanitarian tasks.

ICRC acceptance in the socialist world is problematical. There is the problem of reconciling Red Cross doctrine and Marxism as an ideology. There is the lack of socialist financial contribution to the ICRC (see Chapter 8) and lack of acceptance of ICRC visits to detainees, especially political prisoners (see Chapters 3 and 6). The bourgeois and historically conservative nature of the ICRC Assembly has created at least an ICRC image problem in the socialist world—and perhaps a substantive problem as well.

Despite these problems, which are considerable, the ICRC has had some mutually satisfactory relations with Marxist states. In the Cuban missile crisis of 1962, the ICRC was acceptable to the Soviet Union in the highly unusual role of supervising the Soviet ships incoming to Cuba, to ascertain the absence of missile parts. Although the ICRC did agree to act outside its normal roles in the ''interests of peace,'' and in response to Soviet-American requests and the blessings of UN Secretary-General U Thant, it did not have to carry out this task in fact, since the USSR ceased all shipping to Cuba for a time. Nevertheless, in this most major of crises in the modern period of international relations, the ICRC was acceptable to the Soviet Union. North Vietnam, despite its opposition to ICRC visits to American flyers during the Indochina War, accepted a supervising role for the ICRC in the transfer of individuals from Thailand to North Vietnam. North Korea, despite its refusal to allow ICRC representatives to enter its territory during the Korean War, accepted a supervising and active screening role for the ICRC in the transfer of individuals from Japan to North Korea. China, despite past antagonisms, cooperated with the ICRC in the repatriation of South Vietnamese and Americans captured on the Paracel Islands.

The conclusion suggests itself that the lesser acceptability of the ICRC in the socialist world, relatively speaking, is not a philosophical or image problem so much as it is a divergence of policy between what the ICRC and the socialist states want to do. While this policy difference may have philosophical and ideological overtones, the main problem has been the relative lack of interest in humanitarian concerns by these states on certain issues. When a socialist state wishes to pursue a policy that can be said to be humanitarian or have strong humanitarian content, it will use a Red Cross channel at times. In addition to the example cited above concerning the ICRC, there are other examples pertaining to other Red Cross agencies. When in 1956 China finally decided to release Japanese prisoners of war captured in World War II, it did so through the two national Red Cross Societies. When North Korea wanted to discuss certain matters with South Korea, it agreed to utilize the two national Red Cross Societies. When Poland agreed to serve as a go-between with regard to American flyers in North Vietnam, the diplomatic explorations took place through the Polish Red Cross.

ICRC problems in the socialist world stem from a divergence in policies on certain issues, not because the ICRC is always unacceptable for ideological, social, and economic reasons.

HOW THE ICRC OPERATES

The actual administrative process of the ICRC is discussed in Chapter 8 and need not detain us here. But the ICRC's style of action—the pattern of its specific actions—stems from its functions and philosophy as well as its administrative process. Before going on to specific functions and case studies, then, I think it useful to provide some overview of how the ICRC acts, so that the reader does not have to construct that general view inductively.

It is by no means clear that a *complete* pattern of action can be identified. For example, the use of legal or moral overtures by the ICRC may vary with each situation or even with the delegate involved. Likewise, how the ICRC tries to act may depend on such things as the malleable security of a regime.

Nevertheless, at the risk of possible redundancy, not only with what has been presented thus far but also with what will be said about ICRC administration, some generalizations can be made about the ICRC's structure or style of action.[22]

The Red Cross manifests certain operational principles. These principles can be distinguished from both channels of access and influence, and from tactics. The operational principles are three. First, the ICRC claims to be impartial. It is part of the growing number of actors in world affairs that would like to avoid national authority and realpolitik. Just as multinational corporations would like to treat all markets the same, the ICRC would like to treat all suffering the same. Thus it is said by Red Cross spokesmen that "blood always and everywhere has the same color."

Second, the ICRC has traditionally and on balance taken a cooperative approach to governments, not one of confrontation. Where armed conflict is concerned, the agency has tried to be a "friendly legal adviser" rather than policeman. In other situations the ICRC has presented itself as an adjunct to public authority, not a competitor. Thus the Red Cross fits the mold of those actors in world affairs that have tried to come to terms with nation-states and "have attempted to deal with states in a conciliatory manner."

Third, the ICRC in conflicts has been a discreet actor. While claiming a right to express a view—for example, as to when the law applies or when there is need for new law—the institution has not made public the details of its activities, so that it will be acceptable to states in future conflicts. The ICRC has treated even flagrant violations of the law of armed conflict or widely recognized humanitarian principles without publication of details. Some statements and reports of a general nature are made.

Beyond principles, the ICRC as the center of Red Cross activity in conflicts can utilize many channels to protect and assist individuals because of its loosely knit structure and ties to the establishment.

In some situations, the ICRC would seem not to need a variety of channels for action, for the law of international armed conflict guarantees it automatic access to prisoners of war and civilian detainees. While this legal basis has some importance, legal issues have been sufficiently complex to cause the ICRC to seek access to individuals primarily by voluntary grant of national authorities rather than by claims to automatic right.

In its search for voluntarily granted access to individuals who may need third-party protection or assistance, the ICRC can act through national societies, as it has done in places like Greece, Cyprus, Malaysia, and Algeria, obtaining introductions to key governmental officials, information, or logistical support. The ICRC can also utilize the secretariat of the League for these purposes. At times—and this has been the pattern of action in the past—the ICRC judges it useful to bypass all elements in the movement and deal directly with governments or other detaining authorities such as terrorists or private armies. The same channels are available for attempts to exert influence once access is gained.

The ICRC has also obtained more access to individuals held as "enemies" in political conflict than any other third party. Since World War II it has obtained access to more than 400,000 detainees in more than seventy countries. The ICRC has also obtained access to large numbers of nondetained individuals. For example, in the Nigerian Civil War, the ICRC at the peak of its operations provided assistance to some 2.5 million persons.

In trying to gain access and generate influence, the ICRC has sometimes not only played upon the fragmented nature of the movement but upon the fragmented nature of governments as well. For example, in preindependence Cyprus in the 1950's, the ICRC obtained its first access to detainees by permission of local authorities; London was not consulted. These early visits to places of detention were repeated systematically, still under local authority. Finally, formal endorsement of what was transpiring was sought—and obtained—from London. Similarly, in Brazil the ICRC obtained permission to visit certain prisons from provincial officials. More recently, the ICRC in cooperation with the Brazilian Red Cross secured access from central authorities to visit almost 4,000 detainees in three provinces.

On occasion, therefore, the ICRC plays a sophisticated game of bureaucratic politics. Indeed, one of the raisons d'être of the ICRC and Red Cross protection relates to bureaucratic politics. The ICRC can present itself to central authorities as an independent agent of those authorities to obtain information about what is transpiring at the lower levels and to observe whether central directives are being implemented. Many central authorities welcome this role. The ICRC believes that detainees, along with central authorities, benefit, since one of the problems in securing humane treatment is the autonomy of middle- or lower-ranking officials. The ICRC thus acts like an ombudsman: seeking a nonlegal resolution of problems stemming from national administration, without challenging either law or general policy, and reporting back to established authority for the final resolution of a problem.

The predominant tactical approach of the ICRC is that of friendly persuasion based on moral grounds. At times the ICRC appeals to the self-interest of states, as well as to legal argument. In the field operations of the ICRC, legal considerations have been frequently downplayed in order to avoid questions of jurisdiction. Thus the ICRC visited detainees in Northern Ireland under British jurisdiction, without reference to the law of armed conflict. The ICRC was primarily interested in moral, as distinct from legal, standards.

Beyond principles, channels, and tactics, a word can be said about two general resources of the ICRC that are rather highly valued by states and other actors: (1) efficacy and (2) integrity. Both resources exist empirically and also ascriptively. Either empirically or ascriptively, each resource is difficult to define or measure precisely.

1. Empirically, we do not know very much about the efficacy of the ICRC

related to conflicts. If we observe functional roles and start with the development of law, we know that in the mid-1970's the ICRC was once again used as a drafting secretariat for supplementing the 1949 Geneva Conventions, in preference to any other body. Reactions to ICRC performance both as drafting secretariat and as lobbyist for the law, however, have been mixed.

As for the ICRC and the application of law, we have little sure knowledge about efficacy. While we know what the ICRC tries to achieve and how it acts, there is no detached observer present to record whether some other agency might have acted more efficaciously, because of the nature of war plus ICRC discretion. We know a few specifics. From such bits and pieces of evidence we can construct some idea of the efficacy of the Red Cross in helping to apply the law of armed conflict. But there is much law, and the activity of the Red Cross is varied; consequently, an overall, empirical picture is elusive. If it is granted that the ICRC is relatively effective in supervising detention conditions (which seems probably true), what about the implementation of the rest of the law, such as judicial protection, or material-medical assistance to nondetained civilians?

The elusiveness of empirical evidence is equally pronounced with regard to ICRC ad hoc diplomacy. Little as we know about Red Cross efficacy in war, it is more than we know—for sure—about Red Cross effectiveness vis-à-vis political prisoners and other individuals not covered by the law of armed conflict.

2. Empirically speaking, there has never been evidence that the ICRC acted on any motivation other than that of a humanitarian agency. It has been accused of not being diligent in overseeing the use of the Red Cross travel documents by officials of the Vatican at the close of World War II, a deficiency claimed to have aided flight from justice by certain Nazi officials. And of course the ICRC has been criticized for failing to understand various parties and situations—from North Vietnam to Nigeria. But there has never been any evidence that the ICRC acted on the basis of realpolitik or partisan politics. Absence of such evidence can, indeed, be said to constitute empirical evidence on the other side of the coin.

Beyond empirical evidence, the ICRC and the rest of the Red Cross seem to be viewed as efficacious and responsible by an important segment of transnational opinion, including certain political elites and certain elements of the attentive public. The favorable image of the Red Cross in conflict situations does not seem to be in doubt for this important segment of opinion, although the effectiveness ascribed to the Red Cross varies according to specific role performed. The ICRC reputation for efficacy and integrity appears to be very high for applied protection and assistance to detainees, somewhat lower for assistance to civilians en masse, and probably lowest for its recent efforts in behalf of the ·development of law. Despite the difficulty of establishing ascriptive traits with any precision (since the needed attitudinal studies have not been done), it seems clear for a sector of transnational opinion that the general reputation of the Red Cross for efficacy and integrity is favorable.

That is not to say that criticism does not exist. Some specific criticism is included in the framework of a generally positive attitude. Others offer more general criticism, believing that the Red Cross does not go far enough in support of human rights and is not politically astute. There is some feeling, so far unmeasured, that the Red Cross "whitewashes" humanitarian problems in deference to the wishes of states.

To this criticism the Red Cross argues that it wants to take in-country action in a given situation so that it will also be able to act in future situations. The ICRC, unlike the Joint Church Agency in the Nigerian war, but like the High Commissioner for Refugees, seeks the greatest good for the greatest number over a long time span. The Red Cross can also be distinguished from human rights groups like Amnesty International that do not primarily emphasize in-country action and therefore do not worry greatly over acceptability for direct protection and assistance in future conflicts. When the Red Cross has differences of opinion with other human rights groups, frequently it is because of the different time span used to evaluate the merits of in-country action.

The Red Cross position, while certainly not eliminating all criticism, has considerable support. There is a widespread belief that the Red Cross, largely via the ICRC, can protect and assist individuals, can establish communication among individuals and states, and can make a contribution to the resolution of differences.

Moreover, in the context of this generally favorable view toward the Red Cross, actors frequently want the presence of the Red Cross in a conflict, whether or not its effectiveness is proven. An ICRC presence in Chile since the 1973 coup has been desired by both the Chilean junta and the American government, at a minumum because of the impression thereby created that the junta is doing something in support of human rights. In situations like Chile post-1973, a political process ensues between the ICRC, seeking to do as much as possible for detained individuals and their families, and the government, elements of which seek to do as little as possible for those individuals, while seeking not to provoke an ICRC statement of criticism, or an ICRC suspension or withdrawal of its presence, or some other manipulation of Red Cross resources viewed negatively by the government.

In evaluating Red Cross resources and their use, an important point is that, whatever deficiences exist, empirically speaking, there is no other actor in world affairs that has done—or will be likely to do—what the Red Cross has done with regard to conflicts. The United Nations Secretariat has argued that it has no clear role in implementing the laws of war, the UNHCR is limited by statute from doing what the ICRC does, Amnesty International and other human rights groups are not able to make systematic visits to political prisoners, the movement in the UN for a High Commissioner of Human Rights has slowed and perhaps stopped, and so forth. Thus insofar as international and internal wars continue, and as detention occurs for political reasons in the context of internal or foreign criticism, many actors are likely to continue to express a desire for a Red Cross presence in conflicts—either to create a certain image, or to help individuals, or both.

Red Cross resources are therefore relatively highly valued in conflicts. Certainly no state, and probably no other organization, can provide exactly what the ICRC and the rest of the Red Cross provide, especially in terms of an image of integrity and an accepted way of acting.

Finally, an introductory word can be said about the general impact of the ICRC. It is clear that when there is a confrontation between the Red Cross and states, the latter win. Thus when Nigeria shot down an ICRC plane flying into Biafra in 1969, declared the ICRC regional delegate persona non grata, and terminated ICRC coordinating activities for assistance on the Federal side of the civil war, the ICRC complied with Federal policies (although it continued to play a reduced role in Biafra). Thus when Greece in 1970 decided not to renew the written accord with the ICRC, under which the ICRC was given access to all places of detention—including civilian police installations—within Greece where political or administrative detainees were held, the ICRC complied (although it was the ICRC that finally decided to terminate its presence in Greece).

Direct confrontations between the ICRC and states, however, are not common. The Red Cross is generally cooperative, with the ICRC avoiding total confrontation with states on the basis (1) that some humanitarian good can be achieved even if a government is remiss on certain points, and (2) that some bad is prevented by a Red Cross presence even if some of it continues. There is also the widespread attitude of governments that (1) even if they win a confrontation there is a political price to be paid for victory, and (2) the Red Cross is generally useful to states' interests and thus should not be ''beaten'' too much, if at all.

The latter two points merit elaboration. First, when states reject ICRC proposals, programs, or personnel, there is a cost attached. For example, there was some confrontation between North Vietnam and the ICRC over detained American combatants. The ICRC thought the Third Geneva Convention should apply and that Red Cross visits and flows of information should occur; Hanoi disagreed. Hanoi had the power to pursue its policy on this matter. But that policy of rejecting the ICRC point of view had the effect of damaging Hanoi's reputation in diplomatic circles, and—more concretely—of providing the American government with an issue on which the Executive Branch could mobilize support in a critical Congress and a fragmented and disenchanted public.

Similarly, when the ICRC in 1965 presented its view to Washington to the effect that the Geneva Conventions should apply in Vietnam, a rejection of the ICRC position would have cost the American government dearly. Washington was claiming that Hanoi was engaged in international aggression against a legitimate regime in the South. To deny that the law of international armed conflict applied would have left the government open to intensified criticism at home and abroad. Despite the significant reservations of elements in the White House about activating this law, the United States generally accepted the ICRC position. When, subsequently, the United States did not accept the ICRC view that the Fourth Geneva Convention pertaining to civilians applied to detainees in

Saigon's civilian prisons, this decision to disagree with the ICRC—no matter how well-founded legally—brought the American Executive considerable criticism, as the subject of "political prisoners" in the South became a salient issue in debates about American policies in Indochina. (The American position on the issue was not helped by the ICRC decision to withdraw from visits to "civilian defendants" in 1972, on the basis of lack of cooperation from Saigon.)

The actual price paid for disagreement with the ICRC varies from situation to situation. In the above two examples, the price paid by Hanoi and Washington on the issues mentioned was relatively high. On the other hand in Ethiopia in 1975, when—in the context of an obvious internal war producing tens of thousands of casualties—the ICRC sought access to the war area around the city of Asmara, and the government replied that "there was no emergency," the price paid by the government was relatively low because few actors or observers at that time cared about Red Cross access, or about Ethiopia for that matter. Likewise, Iraq does not appear to have paid a high price for denial of Red Cross access to its rebellious Kurdish regions during the mid-1970's, again because few parties were interested in the humanitarian aspects of the situation.

On the second point previously mentioned, many governments are hesitant to seek a confrontation with the ICRC because they value its resources and the ends to which they can be put—the protection and assistance offered to nationals under foreign control, the supervision of lower administrative units, and so on.

Therefore, while states are obviously more powerful than the ICRC, they find themselves dependent on the Red Cross for certain services and circumscribed by certain Red Cross actions. States can break through this circumscription, but sometimes the costs are high, with damage to services that may be desired in the future.

REVIEW

The ICRC is a unique institution. The product of historical evolution, in Darwinian fashion the ICRC has survived by adjusting to its changing environment. An early "mutation" in the world of nation-states, the ICRC as an NGO has evolved to a point where its "Good Housekeeping Seal of Approval" is desired by authorities as a symbol of their humanitarian behavior. Its presence in diplomacy is also desired for more concrete reasons: to secure the release of a hostage or to check on the condition of nationals detained abroad, inter alia.

ICRC evolution is summarized by Max Huber:

> The Committee is not a public body, nor is it an institution of international law. It is a mere association of at most twenty-five private citizens of Swiss nationality. It is not a richly endowed foundation; it has no assurance of financial support from any quarter whatsoever. It has neither the political nor the economic strength of a Great Power to lean upon, but only that of the little country as its seat and origin.

And yet it has no mean function in the world. The national societies, the governments, public opinion, look at it for things that are asked of no other private organization in all the wide realm of international relations.[23]

Much is expected of the ICRC because it has proven its usefulness in the past. From the 1860's to the last quarter of the twentieth century, the ICRC has acted to help individuals through protection and assistance roles. In so doing, the ICRC has helped governments to promote the well-being of their own nationals and foreigners. The ICRC has also executed tasks which governments were not able to do because of national hostilities and antagonisms. There is no doubt but that the ICRC has acted to promote the welfare of the individual for some 110 years. That action has taken varying foci: the wounded in battle, prisoners of war, civilians in a war zone; individuals in an internal war or in domestic strife; political prisoners; hostages.

But most of this action occurred in the Western world when the authority of the nation-state was less challenged. The central question for the ICRC, and an important question for those who support humanitarian values, is whether the ICRC as a Western creation of the nineteenth century can utilize its past record of action and concomitant status in further humanitarian action. Can the ICRC translate its past experiences, occurring in a world of nation-states, to a world of transnational relations in which liberation movements and international organizations compete with the state for power and authority? Can the ICRC, against the background of a white and bourgeois history, develop rapport with nonwhite and nonbourgeois parties? Can the ICRC, with its traditional focus on conventional and interstate warfare, adjust to situations in which violence is also guerrilla and terroristic and is executed by individuals and groups?

This inquiry is an attempt to examine these questions, if not to answer them. We do so by first looking at the functional roles of the ICRC: ad hoc protection; protection through development of law; applied protection under law; and assistance. We then look at the administration of the ICRC. Finally, we try to pinpoint the crucial areas of choice for the ICRC as it charts its future.

3 Ad Hoc Diplomacy: Part One–Political Prisoners

ICRC attempts to protect individuals through ad hoc diplomacy have been a primary concern of the organization for the last one hundred years. Even action which is now authorized in treaty law was once ad hoc. The classic example is ICRC protection for prisoners of war, which was ad hoc protection in the Franco-Prussian War of 1870 and in World War I; it only became legal protection after 1929. Much of ICRC history has therefore centered upon ad hoc diplomacy. This is still the case.

While a great deal of what the ICRC does in the field of protection is thus without an explicit basis in international law, there is a relation between ad hoc diplomacy and law. Customary law is a very murky thing, but it is possible to argue that on the basis of long practice, the ICRC has a legal right to *ask* state permission for access to individuals. This right to ask without being charged with interference in domestic affairs has been explicitly approved by Common Article 3 of the 1949 Geneva Conventions with regard to noninternational armed conflicts. It is possible that this legal right to ask, affirmed for the ICRC in civil wars, is also in existence for situations of domestic instability (what the French-speaking circles call internal disturbances and tensions) on the basis of customary law.[1] We shall not know if the ICRC has this legal right based on customary law in *all* situations of conflict until some court says so. In the meantime, one can simply note that the ICRC has asked to see so many individuals in so many states that its attempt to protect individuals is becoming part of the diplomatic landscape. That being so, perhaps it does not matter whether ICRC ad hoc diplomacy is initially based on diplomatic practice or customary law. In any event, frequently ICRC action after a request is made is strictly ad hoc and not governed by either statutory or customary law. (The exception to this statement is armed conflict, where parties have legal rights and duties under the Geneva Conventions; this is taken up in a subsequent chapter on legal protection.)

In contemporary perspective, ICRC ad hoc diplomacy is becoming more, not less, important. ICRC protection activities related to political prisoners, hijackings, kidnappings, and a whole host of other situations such as the Cuban missile crisis of 1962 are on the increase. Such actions are taking a greater and greater percentage of ICRC time and money, and are increasingly demanded by states and other parties. It is reasonable to assume that if the ICRC role in past events were better known, there would be even more demands for ICRC ad hoc diplomacy in the future.

This increase in protection tasks undertaken on an ad hoc basis stems from two sources. There is a certain lack of desire to address issues in legal fashion—a preference to treat matters in an alegal way. One example of this is the fighting of undeclared wars, where the resulting detainees are not clearly and officially recognized as prisoners of war. A second reason accounting for increased ICRC ad hoc diplomacy is not the lack of desire but the lack of ability to handle matters in an authoritative, legal way. In a hijacking, there may be enough states that do not go along with the majority hard-line on these things, and the hijackers themselves may have enough coercive power, to thwart the majority sentiment for enforcing an anti-hijack law. In this situation, the lack of ability of states to enforce a law—despite majority sentiment in favor—results in alegal action: get the passengers and crew off, if possible save the aircraft, but do not worry too much about enforcing a law against the hijackers in the light of the first two objectives.

Precisely because such action as visiting individuals in a situation of domestic instability or negotiating with hijackers is not governed by explicit law, it is controversial. If law is a formalized consensus, then action not based on such an explicit consensus runs a high risk of being criticized. ICRC ad hoc protection is useful when international law is not, or cannot be, implemented. But that utility runs a high risk of controversy. It is not surprising then that many observers, both within the Red Cross movement and outside, are critical of ICRC diplomacy related to political prisoners and hostages, among other issues. It is highly probable that when the ICRC originally expanded its concern from the wounded in war to those taken prisoner, there were those who argued that the ICRC had no business taking action without legal basis. The same argument was probably raised when the ICRC started showing concern for civilians in addition to the more active participants in international armed conflict, and to noninternational armed conflicts as well. Because a subject is new and lacks legal regulation, ICRC ad hoc action tends to be more controversial; but then this has probably always been the case.

ICRC attempts to protect individuals, despite lack of legal authorization in international law to do so, center primarily on: (1) political prisoners and (2) those taken hostage in hijackings and political kidnappings, but may extend into other unpredictable situations. As an example of this last category there was the Cuban missile crisis, where the ICRC was asked to supervise arriving Soviet ships to Cuba; there, the ICRC may have had the opportunity to make its greatest contribution to world order. In situations where hostages are taken, the ICRC may be asked to take action related to dozens if not hundreds of lives. But it is the question of political prisoners that, day in and day out, occupies most of the ICRC's attention. And it is this question of political prisoners that will greatly influence the immediate future of the organization—and maybe the long-range future. Yet in 1974, *Saturday Review/World,* in an article on political prisoners, printed the following: "Many may assume that the Red Cross or the United Nations looks after the problem. The Red Cross, in most instances, is involved only with prisoners of war."[2]

POLITICAL PRISONERS

The ICRC has been concerned with political prisoners almost from its very beginning.[3] Starting with sporadic concern for political prisoners in the nineteenth century, then with limited efforts at involvement in more drawn-out situations such as the Russian Civil War, and leading up to protracted efforts to protect Jews in Hitler's Germany, the ICRC has shown increasing interest in the subject. In addition to ICRC diplomatic history, once can also find a progressive interest in the question in the Red Cross Conferences, which at the initiative of the ICRC debated the question and approved ICRC action.

Political prisoners became a *major* subject for the ICRC, however, only after World War II. Up until the late 1950's, conventional thinking within the ICRC was that action should be limited to situations of armed conflict—either international or noninternational. This attitude began to change under the impact of personnel changes at Geneva in the 1950's. The result was increased ICRC attention, between about 1958 and 1968, to the plight of detainees in situations short of civil war. For example, the ICRC attempted—without success—to see members of the Muslim Brotherhood detained in the 1950's in Egypt. The ICRC attempted—eventually with some success—to see Mau Maus detained in Kenya, even though the British refused to characterize the situation as a civil war, much less an international one. Visits were made in Guatemala in the wake of the 1954 coup, even though there was no protracted and large-scale violence. And visits were made in South Vietnam on a very limited basis after Dienbienphu and before the American military intervention. There are other examples of ICRC visits to detainees in "nonwar" situations in the 1950's and 1960's. It was frequently a colonial situation which attracted the attention of the ICRC.

The real spurt in ICRC interest in political prisoners occurred in the late 1960's. The new states of Africa and Asia were plagued by domestic instability, resulting in many detentions, either for incurring the displeasure of a government that had little regard for human rights, or for violently attacking the government. In some cases this domestic instability was accompanied by foreign intervention, as in Indochina, the Congo, and Cyprus.

Outside the third world, in the West, there was domestic instability, too, as in Northern Ireland and Quebec, plus a rash of real, threatened, or alleged violence by individuals and small groups. All of this resulted in detention for reasons related to partisan politics. Chronic political instability continued in Latin America, with resulting detention of widespread and harsh nature. And in the socialist states, while detention for opposing the dominant faction of the party-state had long characterized these totalitarian regimes, the creation of Amnesty International in 1961 did much to reawaken interest in the question of political prisoners in the 1960's. While Amnesty was a nonideological organization as prone to criticize such nonsocialist regimes as South Vietnam and Taiwan as the Soviet Union, the sheer size of the political prisoner population in the socialist states—plus Amnesty's commitment to public criticism as a policy weapon—did much to focus the eyes of the attentive public in the West on the question. The rise to fame of Alexander Solzhenitsyn in the late 1960's and early 1970's also contributed to this process, as his books on Soviet repressive policies likewise focused attention on political prisoners.

The result of these changing facts and perceptions was that the ICRC took the question of political prisoners more seriously, without forgetting about its more traditional concern for developing humanitarian law in armed conflicts and protecting persons under that law. From 1958 to 1970, the ICRC visited some 100,000 political prisoners in 65 different states. In the three years after 1970, another 170,000 political prisoners were visited by the ICRC around the world.[4] In 1973 alone, the ICRC was visiting in 35 different states. These figures did not cover visits to detainees in situations officially acknowledged as civil wars, as in Chile in 1973–74. And the statistics did not cover visits to protected persons under the full Geneva Conventions, as on the Indian subcontinent in 1971–74. The ICRC's increasing concern was reflected not only in the number of persons visited but also in its adoption of an official policy on the question, first in 1965, then again in 1968 and 1973.

In 1973–74, the ICRC recognized that the question of political prisoners was important enough to merit a complete review by the organization—a rather unusual step by an organization characterized in the past by pragmatism and decentralization rather than by centralized making of official policy. The ICRC brought together those officials of the organization with the most experience in political prisoner affairs for a series of meetings, during which it implicitly reaffirmed its commitment to continue to seek ad hoc protection for political prisoners. In an effort to define the scope of this protective action, the ICRC continued to view political prisoners as those detained in situations short of civil war and international war. Further, the ICRC used the concepts of internal trouble and tension—an internal trouble being closer to civil war, and an internal tension being closer to pure tranquility.

In trying to determine when an ICRC attempt at protection would be made in a situation of internal trouble, the ICRC noted four conditions that could trigger its involvement: serious violence, prolonged rather than occasional troubles, struggle among organized groups, some type of victims in need. In situations of internal tension, the ICRC listed six possible triggering conditions: serious events related to a civil war or internal trouble; existence of serious political, religious, racial, or social tension; suspension of judicial due process, or introduction of emergency laws, or nonobservance of national laws; administrative detention, or expulsion or deportation; excessive penalties; prima facie evidence of inhumane treatment.

These criteria, internal, subject to revision, nonbinding, and supposedly governing the scope of ICRC attempted protection of political prisoners, are—of course—broad in range, and vague. They do not define what a political prisoner who needs ICRC protection is. They constitute a check list of conditions to watch for. And given the state of the world in the 1970's, these conditions—especially pertaining to internal tensions—are almost omnipresent. Therefore, while the ICRC reaffirmed its interest in political prisoners on a very broad scale, it did not have much luck in precisely defining its scope of interest.

Indeed, one of the biggest problems for the ICRC, and others, in attempted protection of political prisoners is the unresolved question: what *is* a political prisoner?

Political Prisoners and Law

To answer the question one can logically look to law. If law contains the concept "political prisoner," then one has a legal answer to the question. And even though the ICRC has not been authorized by law to protect political prisoners from inequitable treatment, some law somewhere may use the concept, thus providing insight into the category of persons commonly called "political prisoners."

One can look to general international law, regional international law, and national law. In all three, the term "political prisoner" is not explicitly used, but can be inferred as a state resulting from either the committing of a crime against "national security" or persecution for political reasons. Whatever field of law one looks to, one can find references to political crime, security crime, and special detention because of security needs. One can find international regulation for situations of political persecution, on a limited basis, under refugee law. And one can find types of national law which are alleged to constitute persecution. But there is no clear definition of security crime. And there is no clear definition of political persecution. (See Appendix C.)

Now there is a logical convergence between security crime and persecution. What the government may regard as a long-term security need, someone else with a different time perspective may regard as unjustified action and hence persecution. The person may be evaluating the immediate situation, and the government looking to the future. The government of South Korea in the mid-1970's defended its 1972 constitution, and executive orders under that constitution, not as repression of human rights but as steps necessary to insure the security of the state in the light of agressive *intentions* on the part of North Korea. Because, as in the Korean case, there is challenge to the government's point of view about legitimate security needs, there have been attempts at international regulation of these matters, such as under the European Convention on Human Rights and the 1973 Paris Accords. Under the former, the Greek government's view of a legitimate security need was officially challenged; and under the latter, the Saigon government's view was the target of unofficial challenge. In both cases, the central issue was the line between legitimate governmental security need and persecution. Both national law and attempts at international regulation revolve around this point.

Therefore in law, the term "political prisoner" can have three meanings: to refer to those persecuted for reasons connected to partisan politics; to refer to those detained for security reasons; to refer to those either persecuted or detained for security reasons but without distinction between the two. The law is clearly not clear.

Given this fact, the ICRC has tended to act on an ad hoc basis, using the third definition—that a political prisoner is either a security prisoner or one persecuted for political reasons, and it does not matter to the ICRC which he is. In either case, the detainee is viewed as an adversary of the detaining authority. For the ICRC, that is the crucial variable. De facto enemy status, whether as persecuted, or as prosecuted for security crime, is the situation in which the ICRC believes the individual to be in need of some third-party protection. The only legal concept that provides the ICRC with a clear focus for action is administrative detention. Where there is detention of a special nature under administrative ruling that excludes other branches of government—especially courts—from a role the ICRC tries to act. Under administrative detention, the executive is often left with a free hand, unchecked by other national authorities. Where administrative detention is used as a "special" law, the ICRC has learned that it is almost always in a situation where the government alleges it is threatened by an enemy, from within the nation or from outside. Thus the individual detained under administrative order is almost always regarded as an enemy, and left without prospect of adequate national protection. As the legal director of the ICRC said in 1970: "whenever an interest is taken in the plight of political detainees, this category of detainee must first be defined. When detention is the result of an administrative decision, without any charge being preferred and without trial, there is no room for doubt."[5]

Political Prisoners and ICRC Practice

Against this background of confusion about the meaning of the term "political prisoner," the ICRC has great difficulty in achieving adequate protection for individuals detained in relation to political conflict. Despite the argument that the ICRC has a right to inquire into their welfare based on customary law, and even in those situations where administrative detention is practiced, thus providing a clear legal category of detainees, the ICRC encounters numerous problems.

Where there is prima facie evidence of "enemy status" for detainees coupled with lack of adequate protection from other sources, national or international, the ICRC tries to achieve what it can. Stimulated to action by press reports, published national laws, third-party claims, and eye-witness reports, the ICRC tries to use the technique of a prisoner-of-war visit: systematic observations on the site, with private interviews with the detainees, followed by a conversation with, and a written report to, the detaining authorities. Through this procedure the ICRC hopes to better the conditions for political prisoners.

Normally there is no publicity from an ICRC visit, unless the detaining authority itself chooses to publish a statement or the ICRC report. If it does the latter, by agreement with the ICRC it must publish the entire report. The British, Greek, and South African governments elected to publish ICRC prison reports in the 1960's and 1970's. The Greek government and the ICRC had discussions about a correct interpretation of the meaning of the ICRC reports. The ICRC also protested to the government of the Republic of South Vietnam regarding governmental statements as to what the ICRC had reported about the prison situation there. The ICRC does publish the bare outline of what it is doing through its regular publications, but it rarely publishes the substance of what its delegates have seen.[6] While a keen observer can piece together much of what is going on from these ICRC publications, the attentive public and most governmental officials are unaware of events, unless the detaining authority chooses to go public. Because a government can choose to publish a favorable report but remain silent about a critical one, some believe the ICRC should alter its policy on reports. One option is to demand that the government publish all ICRC reports if it wishes to publish one.

Even with the current ICRC publication policy, which is generally regarded as favorable to governments, the ICRC still has difficulties in its efforts. The first of a series of problems is that the lack of an agreed definition of who constitutes a political prisoner leads to governmental sensitivity in response to an ICRC inquiry. Since the ICRC has great room for discretion in deciding whether to seek involvement in a situation (that is to say, since it has varying criteria for involvement), a government may resent the implications of an ICRC request to see a category of detainees. From the point of view of the ICRC, it is difficult to determine fairly just what is, for example, excessive penalty in the context of an Asian society. The Indonesian government has a forced labor camp for political prisoners on the island of Buru. But is it possible that it is more humane for a political prisoner to be there, doing something in the open air, than to be in an unhygenic urban prison doing nothing? The ICRC, without guidelines from international law aside from the vague provisions of the UN Charter and the Universal Declaration of Human Rights, must make these evaluative judgments on its own, and its conclusions may antagonize a government that believes it has acted in accordance with local standards and security needs.

Because of varying standards of what is humane, or legal, or normal, the ICRC decision to seek involvement is frequently interpreted by the detaining authorities as an unwarranted interference by outsiders in the domestic affairs of the nation. Even if legal specialists in the foreign office have heard of customary international law, which is not always the case, then it is unlikely that those in the military and prison administrations have. Even in the unlikely event that these officials had heard of customary law and the ICRC's past practice, it is by no means sure that they would care or that it would make any difference to how they interpreted the overture of the ICRC. Moreover, possible emerging customary law may pertain to an ICRC right to ask for visits only with regard to internal troubles, not to detention outside a situation of violent conflict. Whatever the law and factual situation, government officials frequently resent having the ICRC imply that penalties are unusually severe, or that normal rights have been violated. This is especially true when the government does not recognize a separate category for the people about which the ICRC is concerned. In many states, the people of concern to the ICRC are regarded by the government as regular prisoners who have committed treason or subversion and who should therefore be punished according to national standards. Even in places where courts-martial have broad jurisdiction over civilians and where secret proceedings are the rule, as in Morocco and Iran among other places, these practices are regarded as normal and fair by the political elites in control. The ICRC's presence is unrequested and usually unwanted.

Moreover, the ICRC may be resisted because of the government's fear of conferring legal status upon an opponent. The ICRC is associated with the Geneva Conventions, which pertain, inter alia, to prisoners of war. Many governments are afraid that admitting the ICRC to prisoners will cause those prisoners to be viewed as prisoners of war instead of regular prisoners under national law, regardless of what the ICRC says or what the law itself says. Particularly if the detainees are part of a movement to destroy the existing government and/or state, the detaining authorities do not want to give the detainees the status of being part of a government in exile or in any other way a protected person under international law. In the struggle to affect images, the detaining authority tends to reject the offered services of the ICRC. This was true of the British in Kenya and initially of the French in Algeria. The ICRC was only admitted to the territory in question either when the conflict had subsided or when it had escalated to the point where the government found it impossible to deny that a civil war existed. Until either point was reached, the ICRC was rejected by the authorities in control as part of a governmental effort to characterize the opponents as insignificant common criminals. It is ironic that the ICRC's reputation for humanitarian action in armed conflict causes it to be persona non grata in some situations where the detaining authority does not wish to create or further the impression that an armed conflict exists.

Therefore the first problem for the ICRC is that of gaining access to persons in possible need of international protection. Given governmental claims to domestic jurisdiction accompanied by sensitivity toward foreign investigations and fear of conferring legal status upon opponents, it is an achievement in itself for the ICRC to be admitted to the prisons of twenty-five percent of the states of the world, in a given year, to see individuals detained in connection with political conflicts.[7]

When, and if, the hurdle of initial access is cleared, other problems remain. The second problem confronting the ICRC is how much access is enough, at any given point in time. In Cyprus in the mid-1950's, the ICRC slowly worked its way up to systematic visits, starting with one unofficial visit, then one official visit, all the while dealing with local officials rather than London. While this partial-access approach is usually without controversy if it leads to more complete access over time, the danger is that the ICRC will become locked into partial access through governmental action. Thus the government will be able to say the ICRC is present, when in fact the ICRC is only partially present.

In general, the ICRC will accept partial access to detainees because that is all the government will give. The ICRC has tended to act on the "one more blanket theory." As long as it can bring in one more blanket to someone in need (or family news, or medical supplies, etc.), it will do the humanitarian good it can. The ICRC has not practiced group ethics as a general policy. That is, it has not used its presence and threat of withdrawal as a bargaining tool to obtain more access. It has been a "pure" humanitarian actor in the sense of trying to do good for as many individuals as possible; it has hesitated to stop doing good for some because its presence may have helped the government to do evil to others. The ICRC has not had an all-or-nothing approach to political prisoners.

This approach is not only the result of being able to do good for some. It is an approach based on the hope of future extension of permission. In Rhodesia between 1959 and 1974, the governments permitted the ICRC to see only those administrative detainees under the emergency regulations; those charged and convicted under Rhodesian law were off limits. But in 1974 the ICRC asked for and received some permission to visit the regular sections of the Rhodesian prisons and thus to visit detainees convicted of sabotage and other "political crimes." The ICRC's long demonstration of its manner of operation under partial access finally led to broader permission.

That extension of access does not always come, however. In the Republic of South Africa, the situation is just the reverse of Rhodesia. The ICRC is permitted to visit the convicted prisoners associated with political crime—viz., the blacks on Robben Island—but not administrative detainees. As of the time of writing, no extension of access had been granted within the Republic, or for visits to prisons in Namibia (Southwest Africa).

The problem for the ICRC concerning partial access is that the government may manipulate the organization into continuing its policy of partial access, relying on the ICRC's desire to continue the good it is doing; this provides the government with a public relations shield for what it wishes to do elsewhere. In this regard it should be noted that ICRC access has always been partial, in the sense that it never supervises interrogation. There have been two exceptions to this pattern.

The ICRC does not supervise interrogation for a very simple reason: governments do not allow it. The ICRC, like other groups concerned with human rights, is well aware that the probability of mistreatment is greatest during interrogation, especially if the individual is interrogated by the same forces that took him prisoner. This probability of mistreatment increases for the political prisoner as compared to the regular prisoner, for the detaining authorities frequently believe the political prisoner possesses information affecting the security of the state. Thus the motivation to obtain that information, regardless of means used, increases, and with it the government's determination to exclude the ICRC during the interrogation process.

The ICRC has accepted this limitation in part because it has believed that it is better to visit detainees after interrogation than not at all. And in part the ICRC has accepted this limitation because it believes it can have an impact on interrogation even if ICRC representatives are not present at that time. If the higher authorities commit themselves to a policy of opposing mistreatment, and if the ICRC representatives interview the detainees after interrogation and make a report to these higher authorities, then its prison visits may have some deterrent effect on mistreatment during interrogation.

The validity of this belief is very difficult to ascertain. If ICRC visits after interrogation *do* deter mistreatment during interrogation, there is nothing to measure, nothing to count. One cannot ascertain the bad that is *not* done because of ICRC private interviews and reports to higher authorities. On exceptional occasions one can clearly determine the impact of ICRC visits in this regard. Now that the government in Lisbon has changed, it can be stated that on one of the ICRC visits to prisons in the Portuguese colony of Mozambique in the

1970's, the ICRC delegation encountered almost four dozen cases of allegations of severe mistreatment, almost three dozen of which were accompanied by physical marks that verified the allegations. The ICRC delegation immediately suspended the visit, and the Geneva headquarters discussed the matter with Lisbon. A governmental inquiry was made, with officials sent from Lisbon to Mozambique. Subsequent ICRC visits verified that mistreatment had ceased after that inquiry, and was not resumed for the rest of the time that Lisbon controlled Mozambique.

While this sort of dramatic impact from ICRC visits is the exception rather than the rule, it is still true that the ICRC can be an effective arm of the central government in bringing lower officials under control.

In only two situations—setting aside a brief experience in Bolivia, for a few months in 1971—has the ICRC apparently gained access to individuals held for interrogation. In Greece in 1969 and 1970, the ICRC had access to *all* places of detention where political prisoners were held. The written àgreement under which the ICRC operated was not renewed by the Greek government after the fall of 1970. In Chile after the coup against Allende in September 1973, the victorious military junta officially declared that a civil war existed, and then in 1974 declared that while the civil war had ended a stage of siege remained. In that context, the ICRC based its action on Common Article 3 of the Geneva Conventions pertaining to noninternational armed conflict. Hence, technically speaking, the ICRC was not dealing with political prisoners but with protected persons under international law. Just how they differed from political prisoners was not clear. The more important point for present purposes is that the ICRC in Chile gained right of access to certain detainees, including those held for interrogation. As in Greece, the ICRC ran into difficulty with the detaining authorities. For a time in 1974 ICRC visits were suspended. Also the ICRC chose to alter the composition of its entire delegation. At the time of writing it is not clear what the denouement of this situation will be.

In both instances where the ICRC was granted access to detainees held for interrogation, there ensued serious friction between the government and the ICRC. It would be erroneous, however, to attribute this friction solely to the fact of ICRC visits. In Greece, for example, there were factions in the government opposed to any presence of the ICRC, regardless of what it did or did not do. An evaluation of what these two cases mean for the future of ICRC supervision of interrogation leads to considerable ambiguity. The ICRC continues to believe it can have an impact on interrogation despite governmental restrictions.

Beyond the problem of initial access and partial access, the ICRC has faced a third problem: whether it should ever agree to conduct visits to political prisoners without private interviews. ICRC discussions with detainees, in the absence of representatives from the detaining party, are regarded by the ICRC as the sine qua non of its protection efforts, once access has been obtained. Without this private interview, visits are relatively insignificant, for there are few detainees who will speak candidly when the captor is present. Yet in the past the ICRC has agreed to visit political prisoners in the presence of a government official. It has done this on occasion when it had reason to believe the situation was so bad for the detainee that any visit was preferable to no visit. There are probably situations at the time of writing that would lead the ICRC to make this type of visit again. It is also the case that the ICRC will agree to an accompanied visit when a new state is unaware of how the ICRC operates. Thus it may agree to one round of visits to demonstrate its procedures to the government.

ICRC policy as of the mid-1970's is that it will not, in general, conduct a round of accompanied visits. Any deviation from this policy requires specific approval from Geneva. It is not clear what would cause Geneva to approve a round of accompanied visits, or to approve a second round of accompanied visits. There is no pattern of action as yet.

A fourth problem is whether the ICRC should ever raise a question with the detaining authority about the reasons for, as compared to the conditions of, detention. The ICRC has maintained the position for some time that it should not raise any question about the reasons for detention except on humanitarian grounds. It does not question the fact of detention, unless by reason of age, health, or family considerations. This ICRC policy is the price of admission that the organization pays to get into the prison. It is also a policy that allows the ICRC to claim to be nonpolitical.

Now the ICRC is sometimes aware of the laws under which the detainees are held. Indeed, the nature of those laws is part of the complex of factors that the ICRC evaluates in deciding when to seek involvement. And the reasons for detention, as reflected in those laws, affects what the ICRC says and does vis-à-vis the detaining authority. While there is some variation in ICRC practice from one geographical region to another, in at least some regions the ICRC delegates structure their overtures to the government according to the reasons *for* detention. For example, where a detainee is an administrative detainee, held without indictment or prospect of trial, the ICRC tends to urge that the conditions of detention should be as good as economics and security will allow. The ICRC has argued in several situations that for administrative detainees, the conditions should be nonpunitive, since the individuals have not been convicted of an offense. If the government finds itself in a situation where it lacks evidence of criminal violation, or perhaps does not want to pursue formal charges because of having to divulge the identity of an informer, that government finds itself urged to upgrade detention conditions or let the detainees go. Although the ICRC does not directly challenge the government's reason for detention, it points out to the government the consequences of its detention policies. Such an ICRC argument depends on the status of the detainees as administrative detainees (or perhaps in some cases on the length of time detained) and on the government's responsiveness to considerations of equity. In a number of situations such ICRC appeals find little response. But ICRC focus on the conditions *of* detention from a humanitarian perspective does not totally ignore the reasons for detention.

Nevertheless, this aspect of ICRC policy had led to criticism by those circles who believe protests should be launched against the very fact of detention. The ICRC is seen as getting in the way of the conflict over whether a certain type of detention should even exist. It has been argued that the ICRC's presence primarily works to the advantage of the detaining authority, in that what should not even exist is approved by the ICRC as humanitarian.

To this criticism the ICRC replies that since other groups are attacking the reasons for detention, it does not have to, but can concentrate on trying to improve the present situation while waiting for a change from other forces. The ICRC also believes that when other forces bring about a change in the situation, that change is not likely to be the panacea hoped for. The 1974 coup in Portugal replaced the old political prisoners with the political police themselves— decidedly a change, but not one that erased the problem of political prisoners in Portugal. Moreover, the ICRC argues that it is better to get in the prisons under humanitarian rules than to criticize the detaining authority from a distance; the latter may only create more difficulties for the detainees. In certain situations, the ICRC has asked the detainees themselves whether they prefer the ICRC to continue visits or to withdraw in order to increase international diplomatic pressure on an uncooperative regime. In these situations the detainees have preferred to maintain contact with the outside world through the ICRC than to have the ICRC withdraw in protest.

It is difficult to evaluate the validity of criticism, as well as of the ICRC's response, on this point. That the government receives a public relations value from an ICRC presence is unquestioned. But the detainees themselves tend to favor continued ICRC involvement. An exception was IRA detainees in Northern Ireland, who apparently were so antagonistic toward the British government that they did not want the ICRC to verify humane detention; they destroyed prison facilities and abused ICRC delegates.

It might be remembered that those outside the situation, criticizing the government for detention and the ICRC for trying to make bearable something that ought to be overthrown, are politicized elements. They are politicized in the sense of caring enough about the political conflict going on in Rhodesia, South Africa, or someplace else to pay attention and get involved themselves. They are willing to sacrifice the detainees to the political cause, to say the detainees should do without ICRC visits in order to dramatize the evils of the detaining regime. But among the detainees are frequently a number of nonpolitical individuals that have been swept up in the political conflict—relatives of suspected or detained persons, individuals coerced into the struggle against their will, persons who perhaps at an early age voluntarily opted to fight in the struggle but have now been separated from friends and relatives for years. Should the ICRC respond to their individual wants or ignore them because of the larger question of the legitimacy of detention? It is not an easy question. The ICRC as a humanitarian organization has in the past avoided the larger issue, relegating it to the realm of "politics."

In only one situation in the modern period has the ICRC unilaterally terminated its visits to political prisoners. In South Vietnam in 1972 the ICRC finally withdrew from visiting political prisoners because of the persistent lack of cooperation on the part of that government. This withdrawal was not so much because of the reasons for detention as it was of the refusal of the government to grant private interviews, to agree to systematic visits, and to stop hiding individuals from the ICRC.

A fifth problem is how often ICRC visits must occur, to be of benefit to the detainees. In some situations ICRC visits have been widely spaced, most often because of delays in obtaining governmental permission but in some cases because of lack of manpower and money on the part of the ICRC. In some cases the ICRC visits detainees each month or perhaps every two months. The normal minimum emerging from ICRC practice seems to be six months: the ICRC must see a detainee twice a year to keep effective check on where he is and how he is treated, as well as on whether the government takes the ICRC seriously and implements ICRC recommendations. In situations where there is a rapid turnover of the prison population, as in internal troubles and civil wars, more frequent visits are required.

A sixth problem concerns whether the ICRC should focus exclusively on the conditions of detention or whether the organization should show increased attention to the judicial process. If mistreatment occurs during interrogation because the courts place emphasis on confessions in order to obtain convictions and do not appear to be concerned about coerced confessions, should the ICRC devote more time to trial observation and/or make an attempt to secure adequate defense counsel for the accused? Answer to this query in part depends upon another question: of what value is an observer at a trial? Amnesty International and the International Commission of Jurists, which engage in extensive observation of political trials, have frequently been unable to measure their impact. A judicial decision favorable to the accused may be the result of many factors, including the mood of the judge on that particular day. It is impossible to say with any certainty what effect an ICRC delegate's presence in a courtroom would have in producing judicial due process and equity. The ICRC has engaged in trial observation and in limited legal assistance to persons under the law of armed conflict; this was true in the Algerian War and to a small extent in the Middle East since 1967. There is a continuing question whether the ICRC should attempt some form of judicial protection of political prisoners. Having shown concern for the detainee in prison, should the ICRC follow him into the courts?

A seventh problem completes this survey of difficulties confronting the ICRC as it tries to protect political prisoners. It also closes the circle, returning us to the original problem of trying to define a political prisoner. In a number of states, all prisoners are detained together. This makes it practically impossible, as well as ethically difficult, for the ICRC to visit one type of prisoner—the political prisoner—and to ignore the other—the regular prisoner. Moreover, in a number of states, all prisoners have poor detention conditions or are mistreated, not because they are regarded enemies of the government but because the government lacks the financial resources and administrative expertise to run a humane penal complex. Where the prisoners constitute a mélange, and/or where prison conditions are just plain poor, the ICRC tends to visit all prisoners, not just political prisoners. This poses the question whether the ICRC has the capability to do this on a serious basis.

Compounding the difficulty is that this role of global prison inspector is not only forced on the ICRC in certain cases by circumstances, but in certain situations is sought by the ICRC. Where a state does not have political prisoners at a given time, but has had them in the past or is likely to have them in the future because of chronic domestic instability, the ICRC has intentionally visited the regular prisoners in order to be on the scene, acting with the permission of the government, when the next batch of political prisoners arrives. This has been ICRC policy especially in Africa, and at times in Latin America, where chronic political instability is accompanied by poor prison conditions. While this may be a shrewd move toward guaranteeing future protection of political prisoners, the question remains as to the capacity of the ICRC to carry out this wide-ranging task.

Despite all of these problems, the ICRC continues to try to protect political prisoners through its ad hoc diplomacy. One reason is need. A second reason is lack of adequate protection from other sources.

Political Prisoners and World Politics

To understand why the ICRC has increased its interest in political prisoners, it is useful to keep in mind these two factors of need and alternatives. Only someone with vested interests in avoiding reality can deny that political prisoners—whatever they are called—constitute an increasing problem in world affairs, either from the humanitarian or from the realpolitik point of view.

This is not the place to attempt a factual survey of the global dimensions of the political prisoner problem. Numbers are elusive, depending as they do on an agreed definition, which is lacking. Moreover, there are simply no numbers available to the public in the West for political prisoners in certain places. No one knows how many political prisoners there are in the Soviet Union or China—not Amnesty International, the ICRC, or the CIA. One can read of figures like two or three million in the world, or perhaps five million. But like the statistics on how many people are dying of starvation, or how much money the oil companies are really making, no one knows. One can also read figures on how many states allow torture to go on.[8] But these figures, too, depend upon an elusive definition of what is torture, what is mistreatment, and what is only psychological pressure on a detainee that is to be regarded as normal and acceptable in an imperfect world.[9]

When all the numbers are in, however controversial they are, it is clear that there are more and more people in the world detained by reason of political events. As a former ICRC official has written: "Since 1945, and despite the solemn proclamation of the Declaration of Rights of Man, the number of political detainees locked up in the course of internal troubles—or more simply through a measure of precaution—by the challenged governments has not ceased to grow."[10] This trend has several specific causes.

Governments have increased both their ambitions of national control and their potential technology for controlling their citizens. While this attempt at control of political factions is pronounced in totalitarian regimes, it is also present in those regimes with a tradition of limited government. The Watergate affair in the United States, not to mention the use of the Internal Revenue Service against political opponents, can be viewed in the same context as totalitarian surveillance and control. The dimension of the problem is different, but the intent and technological basis is very similar. The extent of governmental attempts at influencing the nation are increasing, and thus the political elites tend to expand the political system—that is, tend to regard more and more things as the proper domain of partisan politics. Along with this trend is the government's belief that more and more things—individuals, groups, and events—have a negative effect on the government's position. Thus the government tries to control more—frequently through detention.

On the other hand, the research of T. R. Gurr has shown that the individual tends to see the political elites as more and more responsible for controlling his life, and when he becomes disenchanted and frustrated, the resulting action increasingly tends to be *political* action. This political action, stemming from negative feelings combined with a sense of frustration about peaceful politics, increasingly tends toward violence.[11]

Thus a vicious circle is created in which both governments and citizens see things in political terms—i.e., related to decisions by those engaging in conflict over public policy. The result is that action by both elite and mass is political action. And since the individual tends toward violence, the government tends toward exceptional detention and exceptional interrogation in an effort to preserve itself and the state. It is a formula producing increasing numbers of political prisoners.

A compounding problem is that both the legitimacy of the government, and the procedures for peaceful change within the nation, are fragile in so many places. In most of the world beyond the North Atlantic area, the legitimacy of the government is not shored-up by a long tradition of democratic elections. And the procedures for conflict-resolution and legislation are dominated by a particular faction, which promotes extremism in other factions. Where this lack of legitimacy and equitable legislation is accompanied by lack of governmental efficiency, as is true in much of the world, one can expect violent attempts at change accompanied by extreme measures on the part of the government.

These general trends can be demonstrated by specific examples. A classic case is the Republic of South Vietnam. The basic legitimacy of the government was challenged by a large percentage of the population of the South, not only by the Viet Cong but also by the neutrals. Governmental institutions were inequitable in the sense of not permitting representation and free interaction to the various interests. Efforts of the various governments representing the Republic at control were inefficient. The entire situation was compounded by lack of social cohesion in the South and foreign intervention both for and against the government.[12] The result was that as of the mid-1970's, not counting prisoners of war, there were between 40,000 and 200,000 political prisoners held by the Thieu regime—people detained by reason of the conflict between the government and its adversaries, but who were not official combatants.[13]

The case of South Korea is similar. The Park government desired to enlarge its control of those citizens disagreeing with the president on some issue. A number of elements in the South opposed this trend, charging that the 1972 constitution and subsequent executive orders were illegitimate. The regime argued that control was necessary and that full representation and discussion could not be permitted because of the alleged threat to the South from North Korea. Frustration with this view led to violence, clearly represented by the 1974 attack on President Park that killed his wife. This event in turn gave the government reason to engage further in detention of critics and opponents. The actual numbers of those detained for challenging the president's policies were controversial, but the situation in the mid-1970's was serious enough for an official of the U.S. State Department to state publicly and officially that "law and practice do not appear to guard adequately against arbitrary detention or to guarantee fair and public trial." This statement was published as part of an official Department of State report; the cover page stated more directly, "In January [1974] the Government of Korea promulgated three emergency measures which violate human rights."[14] When the United States government, the major defender of and contributor to the Republic of Korea, makes that kind of statement, there is no doubt as to the seriousness of the situation for the detainees there.

Lest one think that political prisoners are found only in Asia or only in regimes supported by American military assistance, it is well to recall the works of Solzhenitsyn with regard to political prisons in the Soviet Union and the use of mental hospitals to persecute and mistreat opponents of the ruling elite there. Also one can compile a list of other states that have engaged in exceptional detention or harsh treatment for reasons related to partisan politics. Almost every state in Latin America consistently holds political prisoners. A clear exception, and perhaps the only one, in the mid-1970's was Costa Rica. By contrast, in Bolivia, according to the *New York Times,* there has been general disregard for national laws by the government, and arbitrary detention and torture are reportedly widespread.[15] In Africa, almost every government, whether black or white, holds political prisoners. In Uganda alone, the reports of those who by 1974 had "disappeared" at the hands of the government range up to 90,000.[16] In Asia, virtually every regime holds political prisoners, with the possible exception of Japan. Indonesia freely admitted holding some 55,000 individuals allegedly connected to the 1965 attempted communist coup. By the mid-1970's some of these had been in detention for a decade without charge or trial. And lest one think that the subject of political prisoners pertains only to the socialist and third worlds, it should be recalled that the Canadian government of Pierre Trudeau arrested several hundred suspected advocates of an independent Quebec under a wartime emergency statute even though Canada was not at war; none of those detained were ever indicted. And a governmental commission of the British government concluded that administrative detainees in Northern Ireland had been mistreated as a result of official governmental policy there.[17]

It is clear, without trying to describe the situation in every state, and without having to, that political prisoners are a global problem. They are a problem by the standard of humanitarian values—e.g., unfair detention and harsh treatment and conditions. They are a problem by the standard of realpolitik values—e.g., they constitute a cause of struggle (as in South Vietnam, where the detention of certain individuals gave the Viet Cong reason to continue the fight), and they constitute an embarrassment to states trying to give aid to, or trade with, the detaining state (as in the case with the United States in giving aid to South Korea or in trading with the Soviet Union).

Given this global situation, the ICRC continues its efforts to protect political prisoners. It might be able—and willing—to retire to the sidelines if some other agency were able to provide international protection. This has not been the case.

Other NGOs are active on these political prisoner problems. It may be, and probably is, the case that some of these, like Amnesty, are very effective vis-à-vis certain regimes. It is quite possible that Amnesty's publications on Eastern European regimes have caused those regimes to mitigate some of the harshness toward dissidents. It is very difficult, if not impossible, to tell. It can be recalled that back in the early 1950's the Western states utilized the United Nations to debate forced labor in the Soviet Union. A subsequent ILO report in the mid-1950's indicated some reduction in the use of that practice. But it is impossible to tell whether it was UN debates or other factors—such as the death of Stalin—that accounted for the change in Soviet policy.[18] Likewise it is impossible to evaluate the precise impact of other NGOs active on human rights issues.

What can be said is that no other organization but the ICRC has access to prisons and other detention centers around the world. There are gaps in the ICRC's record of gaining access, most notable in the case of socialist regimes. But it is interesting that the ICRC is measured according to where it fails to enter; other NGOs are measured by where they do gain entry. It is noteworthy that the ICRC fails to enter certain states; this is a measure of the general expectation that it will get in. For Amnesty, it is noteworthy that in its history it has entered the prisons of only some half a dozen nations; this is a measure of the general expectation that it will *not* be allowed in. Now it should be kept in mind that Amnesty officially seeks to liberate chosen prisoners; thus a detaining government is not anxious to allow an Amnesty representative in the prison. Also, Amnesty places more emphasis on collecting information and in attending political trials than in visiting detention centers. But that choice of policy does not change the fact that it is the ICRC that gets in. No other NGO but the ICRC consistently gets to visit with the political prisoners face to face around the world. Thus the ICRC continues its efforts because, in part, it recognizes that it can do some things that other NGOs cannot.

United Nations bodies have never shown consistent interest in the political prisoner question. The High Commissioner for Refugees is limited, by statute, to working with those individuals who are *fugitives* from their state of origin or usual residence for reasons of political or other persecution; his office is barred by law from helping those still under their own government's control. The UN Human Rights Commission first denied to itself the right to make specific inquiries and reports, then departed from that orientation but without moving toward a consistent examination of political prisoner problems. Specific states became temporary targets of concern, but only South Africa remained a permanent concern. The Commission's subcommittee on protection of minorities moved to accept, in the early 1970's, the idea of individual petitons, rather than state complaints, as a stimulus for committee action. But it is improbable that this procedural decision by a committee made up of nongovernmental personnel can achieve much when the organs it reports to are legally composed of governmental representatives.

This is the fundamental problem in all UN action to promote and protect human rights. Any collective action in support of human rights strikes at the very core of governmental interest, since such action is concerned with what the target government and every government holds sacred—the relationship between the citizen and his government. Human rights questions are always "political questions" in the sense of touching upon vital interests—the security of the government. All states have recognized the danger to them of opening the Pandora's box of international inquiry into human rights on a specific basis. Even though the target regime is somebody else at a given point in time, the precedent and logic of that situation pertain to all other governments and can return to haunt them in the future. UN bodies have not been effective promoters or protectors of human rights precisely because the UN is an intergovernmental organization asked to deal with a question that inherently undermines governmental interests as governments perceive them. Because of that inherent contradiction between the Charter articles calling for human rights action, on the one hand, and on the other hand governmental perspectives, there is no reason to believe the UN will become an effective actor for human rights in the near future. Too many past reports compiled by individuals in the Secretariat have been buried by governmental bodies to give much optimism.[19] There have been too many resolutions of vague wording or weak supervisory machinery.[20]

While the historical trend is for international organizations like the UN to be the scene of increased debate on human rights, and while one cannot predict the end product of this trend, there is no UN body able to replace what the ICRC does with regard to political prisoners.

If one takes a regional rather than a global view of international organizations and human rights issues, the result is somewhat different. The European Convention on Human Rights does provide legal protection to political prisoners, as well as other types of individuals, as a check on national governments. Given a change in regimes in Portugal and Greece, and given a change in policy on the part of France and Switzerland, this Convention and its concomitant supervisory machinery will be legally binding in almost twenty states by 1980. What can be said about the ICRC and political prisoners in these Western European states, on the basis of the first two decades of experience, is that there has been a need for the ICRC to carry out its tasks while a legally definitive settlement of issues is pending. These legal judgments have been a long time in coming. In the one case so far where a government was determined to be violating the Convention to which it was a party—the Greek case—the judgment of violation was not followed by a change in governmental policy. This would seem to suggest that even where there is regional international protection of human rights, there may very well be a need for an intermediate role for the ICRC in relation to political prisoners. Outside Western Europe this set of questions does not arise, for, with the exception of the Inter-American Commission on Human Rights, no other regional organization exists that has played a significant role in protecting political prisoners.[21]

There is no one example that perfectly demonstrates the situation of political prisoners. The types of detainees and the types of laws controlling are much too varied. Thus there is no model of global need which can be used to explain ICRC concern. Nor is there one situation which demonstrates the interaction among the various organizations interested in protection of political prisoners. But certainly one of the most interesting case studies out of ICRC recent experience was the question of political prisoners in Greece, 1967–74.

The Greek Case

In April of 1967, a group of military officers seized control of the government of Greece. This military junta alleged that the nation faced a threat to its security from communists and communist sympathizers and proceeded to rule on the basis of that view. "Apparently over 6,500 were arrested.... The junta destroyed the visible Left... the independence of the judiciary was eliminated.... Civil liberties of all kinds were severely curtailed."[22]

This crackdown on civil liberties, with the political Left as a special target, gave rise to criticism especially within Western Europe, since the junta's actions violated regional expectations of the limits of permissible governmental action. The various governments of Greece had more or less adhered to the basic tenets of Western parliamentary democracy since World War II, and Greece was a party to the European Convention on Human Rights. Criticism of the junta centered on two points: (1) was there a real threat to the security of Greece, justifying the deprivation of normally accepted individual rights; (2) were detainees tortured or otherwise mistreated during detention?

The ICRC became involved in this controversy, especially from 1967 to 1970; its involvement reached a highpoint in 1969–70 when the ICRC signed a bilateral agreement with the government permitting ICRC access to places of detention. At the end of that one-year agreement the government did not choose renewal, and the ICRC was excluded from systematic visits for the duration of the junta's role—until summer 1974.

The Greek case, pertaining to political prisoners in Greece between 1967 and 1974, gives rise to certain questions: (1) what was the nature of ICRC involvement; (2) what did the ICRC achieve; (3) was the ICRC used by the government to block other inquiries and actions, especially by the Council of Europe?

Before the Accord. Between the coup in April 1967 and the autumn of that year, the ICRC obtained permission to visit some places of detention. The ICRC acted quickly after the takeover, and received important help from the Greek Red Cross in approaching the government and securing governmental cooperation. The ICRC had in Greece at this time one delegate, a person who did not always convey an impression of forcefulness. According to the wife of a detainee, who of course was emotionally involved in the situation, her meeting with the ICRC official was less than encouraging. "A wrinkled old man with a whispery voice was ushered into the living room, physically in danger of being blown out the window by a dog's loud bark, and my heart sank when I saw whom I would be dealing with."[23] The ICRC, during this early stage of involvement, sought to track down the whereabouts of detainees, observe the conditions of detention— especially on the two island camps of Yaros and Leros, and to report its observations and recommendations to the government. ICRC focus was on medical- nutritional needs and physical conditions of detention, especially for administrative deportees. In November, after detention visits in May, July, and October, the ICRC issued a statement in Geneva saying detention conditions had improved.[24]

From the fall of 1967 until the bilateral accord was signed in the fall of 1969, criticism of both the military junta and the ICRC grew. The European press began to pay increasing attention to the Greek situation in the fall of 1968, led by the British press and in particular *The Manchester Guardian*. Torture was a central issue.[25] The American press was slower to cover the situation, but *Look* did much to direct American public concern to Greece in the spring of 1969.[26] NGOs like Amnesty International and the International Commission of Jurists were also publishing criticisms of the Greek government, and both the UN Human Rights Commission and the International Labor Organization debated the question of Greek violations of human rights.

Much of the international criticism was directed at Greece's obligations under the European Convention on Human Rights. In September of 1967, when the controversy was starting to build, the Scandinavian governments sought legal action against Greece under the Convention.[27] These governments filed a petition with the European Human Rights Commission, challenging the legality of a number of Greek policies. In January of 1968, legal proceedings continued, and officials of the Council of Europe approached the ICRC in quest of reliable information on the Greek situation. The ICRC refused to divulge any knowledge on the subject. It cited as precedents its refusal to cooperate with the League of Nations inquiry into Italian attacks on medical personnel in Ethiopia in the 1930's,[28] and also its refusal to cooperate with the UN in inquiries into South African detention policies earlier in the 1960's. (Officials of the American government also approached the ICRC in search of information during 1968; the ICRC likewise officially refused information to that party, despite American suggestions that it could support the ICRC vis-à-vis Greece.)

In 1969, after over a year of proceedings, the Council of Europe progressively moved toward a critical judgment of the junta's policies. In January the European Consultative Assembly recommended to the Committee of Ministers that Greece be expelled from the Council of Europe. In May, the Committee warned Greece that expulsion was being considered. During the summer, new hearings were held by the organs of the Council. By October of 1969, the Commission on Human Rights had finished its deliberations and was preparing its report (the ICRC had attended one of the hearings upon request but had refused to divulge any substantive information.) The general assumption, in the fall of 1969, was that the Commission's report would be highly critical of the junta's policies pertaining to civil liberties and detention practices.

During this period from fall 1967 to fall 1969, the United States—while not a party to the European Convention and therefore not involved with the European regional institutions—was deeply involved in the situation because of its military interest in Greece. Greece was a member of NATO, and the United States was the largest supplier of military assistance to that state. In the U.S. view, Greece was important to the southern flank of NATO.

Just after the coup, the United States had implemented a selective embargo on military assistance to Greece, presumably because of the junta's illegal assumption of power. But in January of 1968 it recognized the government of the colonels as legitimate, and American military assistance was progressively resumed. By February of 1969, heavy military equipment such as jet aircraft was again being delivered to Athens. While the Executive Branch was beginning to deal with the junta as a normal military ally, elements in Congress remained critical of the detention policies of the regime. In the fall of 1969, these critical circles used the Senate hearings on the nomination of Henry Tasca as ambassador to Greece as a forum to debate the junta's policies. The Senate was not satisfied with administration policy and delayed confirmation.

Also at this time, in the fall of 1969, NATO officially voted to condemn the junta for its domestic policies, with the American executive opposed and Congressional elements working closely with the NATO majority.

Thus the American government was sharply divided on how to deal with the Greece of the colonels.

In this context of American division and European criticism, the ICRC continued to try to protect political prisoners in Greece from harsh conditions and treatment on an ad hoc basis. As criticism in Europe and in the American Congress increased, the ICRC stiffened its bargaining position with Greece. The ICRC focused more and more on the question of detention treatment in mainland prisons and police stations.

With regard to permission for visits, the ICRC engaged in conflict with the junta in late 1967 and again in 1968 over the extent of ICRC access and whether private interviews were to be held. At one time, an ICRC delegate refused to visit a locale in the presence of a government official. There was also some conflict over whether the ICRC was to be allowed to visit the Greek ship *Elli,* where torture was alleged to occur.

With regard to detention conditions, the ICRC played a large part in securing the closing of the detention camp on Yaros in December 1968. From the summer of 1967 the ICRC had been pressing the government to terminate use of that installation for political deportees on the grounds that conditions were unacceptable and inadmissable. The ICRC also made strong representations about the camp at Leros and about the conditions in certain prisons on the mainland.

With regard to treatment, from the summer of 1967 the ICRC conveyed claims about torture and mistreatment to the government. The ICRC thus initially acted as it does when acting under the Geneva Conventions, calling the government's attention to allegations of illegal and inhumane actions. As the ICRC proceeded to build up its own experiences inside Greece, it brought the attention of the junta to its own findings. The major problem for the ICRC, in attempting to verify charges of torture or mistreatment, was how to ascertain torture if no physical marks were left. The ICRC's "four-wall theory" was useless. That is to say, while the ICRC had at times used the policy of reporting to the government as a fact only that which the ICRC delegate could see within the four walls of a detention place, such an approach to establishing facts could not be usefully applied to a situation where, for example, beating might have occurred on the soles of the feet (this is called falanga, is very painful, leaves no permanent trace, and is alleged to have been widely practiced in Greece). In this 1967–69 period, the ICRC compiled prima facie evidence that torture existed: it reported that systematic patterns of allegations constituted prima facie evidence.[29] It compiled a report on the Bouboulinas Street Prison in Athens, where much torture was alleged to occur. That report tended to confirm torture allegations—that is, the ICRC's description of the prison confirmed allegations by detainees about what the interior of the prison was like, where the secret tortures supposedly occurred, etc.[30] The ICRC made other representations to the government.

With regard to publicity, the ICRC engaged in conflict with the junta on a number of issues. In 1967 it raised a question about misquotation of its delegates in government statements to the press. In 1968, the government printed a brochure, *The Truth About Greece,* which quoted from part of an ICRC report. The ICRC strongly protested this action, implied that the ICRC might have to issue its own publication regarding torture and mistreatment in Greece, and secured a governmental promise not to repeat such partial quotations. Again in the spring of 1969, the ICRC privately discussed with governmental officials the way in which the regime was using ICRC reports—in particular the junta's tendency to refer to such reports inaccurately, without quoting or publishing them, in an effort to dispel allegations of torture.

In the 1967–69 period, then, the ICRC, despite criticism that it was unresponsive to charges of torture and being manipulated by the colonels, was trying to protect political prisoners more and more extensively within Greece, at the price of increased conflict with the regime.[31] The ICRC could not defend itself against criticism without publishing the details of its work. It did not want to publish the details of its work for fear of being expelled from Greece.

The Accord. Despite increasing friction between the ICRC and the Greek government, the two parties signed an accord on 4 November 1969, under which the ICRC was guaranteed access to all places of detention in Greece in which were kept administrative deportees and those detained for political delicts. The ICRC had been attempting to obtain written permission from the government throughout the summer and early fall of 1969, in an effort to remove or reduce conflict between the regime and the ICRC. It has been widely suggested that the junta agreed to such an accord because of the growing criticism of the regime in foreign circles. In particular, it has been suggested that the junta signed the accord in an effort to forestall critical action by the Council of Europe.

Under the terms of the accord (see Appendix D), the ICRC was to have general access to detention places, including police stations where political prisoners were held, infirmaries, hospitals, and places of prisoner transfer, as well as camps and prisons. When the prisoner's family was unable to obtain information from the government, the ICRC was entitled to supply information as to: the place of detention; the nature of the alleged delict, if any; the conditions of detention; and the government's terms for family visits. The ICRC was authorized to provide material assistance to indigent families of those detained for more than two years, with the ICRC working in cooperation with the Greek Red Cross and the government's Department of Social Affairs. The ICRC was to consult with the government in the appointment of ICRC delegates. Action under the accord was to remain private. The government was not to engage in partial reporting of ICRC findings. The ICRC was not to pass judgment on the government's reasons for its policies. The accord was to last one year, tacitly renewable unless explicitly denounced by either party.

The ICRC moved quickly to implement the accord. By the end of November 1969, the ICRC had secured special funding permitting the expansion of the ICRC delegation in Greece, and on 24 November extensive ICRC visits throughout Greece began, including visits to places never before visited. By early 1970, certain factions within the Greek government were clearly opposed to the vigorous ICRC attempt to implement the accord. Conflicts occurred, and on several occasions an ICRC delegate was physically barred from entering a place of detention. Later in 1970, the Greek minister of justice was changed; he was the official in charge of prisons, and he had been a principal point of friction between the government and the ICRC.

As a summary statement on the year of the accord, it can be said that the ICRC's serious efforts to implement the letter and spirit of the agreement resulted in increased conflict with the government. It can also be said that during the twelve-month period when the ICRC had a carte blanche vis-à-vis the political prisoners in Greece, allegations of tortures virtually ceased. It is argued by some that this stemmed from the ICRC's effectively checking the actions of the various police, by others that it stemmed from the ICRC's exposing the false nature of detainee allegations.

Beyond ICRC-Greek relations, events were transpiring that were probably to have an effect on the renewal of the 1969 accord. Within the Council of Europe, the Human Rights Commission had made its report to the Committee of Ministers on 18 November 1969. This report, charging the junta with numerous violations of the Convention on Human Rights, leaked to the public on 29 November. On 12 December, the junta denounced the Convention, citing the leak as evidence of irresponsibility and bias. Subsequently in 1970, the Committee of Ministers decided to publish the Commission's report officially and voted to urge Greece to restore civil liberties and to "abolish immediately torture and other ill-treatment of prisoners and to release immediately persons detained under administrative order." But because Greece had indicated a clear policy of non-cooperation with the Council of Europe, the Committee of Ministers decided that "in the present case there is no basis for further action."[32]

Despite the Council of Europe's judgment that no state of emergency existed in Greece justifying the government's departure from the civil liberties protected under the European Convention on Human Rights, and despite the Council's conclusion that torture and mistreatment existed in Greece as an "administrative practice," the threat of sanctions on the junta from the Council was a dead letter by the summer of 1970. New petitions were submitted by the Scandinavian states during 1970; these had the effect of helping to keep the legal issues alive. And the members of the Common Market debated whether Greece should be denied certain privileges in trade. But the fact remained that by mid-1970 the regional institutions of Western Europe had gone as far as they were willing to go in challenging the policies of the junta. The government showed no willingness to change its policies under the pressure of adverse publicity, and the states of Western Europe showed no willingness as a group to apply economic sanctions.

Also during 1970 in the United States, the Executive Branch moved ahead with efforts to "normalize" relations with the junta. This effort finally predominated over Congressional opposition. Full military assistance was resumed in September of that year (and restoration of full foreign aid followed in December). The Executive Branch had never deviated from its support of the junta, once it became clear in late 1967 that the colonels had a firm grip on the nation. From that point the State Department became a defender of the regime, as spokesman for the White House and Pentagon. The State Department, despite the findings of the Council of Europe, implied strongly that no torture existed in Greece. In a State Department paper on Greece, the United States said, "no instances of torture were confirmed by the Red Cross."[33] Beyond this type of statement to the benefit of the colonels, it was generally argued that U.S. military assistance worked to the advantage of the junta and constituted de facto support for the regime's detention policies. Further, it was argued that the frequency with which U.S. Ambassador Tasca was seen in public with members of the junta helped to confer legitimacy on that government and to freeze the status quo.[34]

Be that as it may, by the early fall of 1970 the United States had resumed full military assistance, and the Council of Europe had stated it had no "basis for further action."

After the Accord. On 3 November 1970, one day before the 1969 accord would have been automatically renewed by the tacit consent of the parties, the Greek government denounced that agreement. The ICRC had consciously decided not to raise the question of renewal explicitly but to hope for tacit renewal. The junta's action took by surprise not only the ICRC but also the American government. The Greek regime coupled its statement of nonrenewal with private overtures to the ICRC to continue its delegation in Athens, although just what that delegation was to do was not clear. Negotiations followed from late 1970 to early 1971, as the ICRC explored with the Greek government just what type of international protection could be agreed upon. In February of 1971 the ICRC elected to end its presence in Greece, believing that continuation of that presence would work to the advantage of the colonels without corresponding advantage to the political prisoners.

In November of 1971, the ICRC made an unsuccessful démarche with the colonels with regard to the detainees. Then in 1973, at a time of student disturbances, the ICRC exercised its right of initiative and approached the colonels, requesting that information about the student detainees be conveyed to their families, since the families had no word from the authorities as to where and how the detainees were. The government's response was positive. Finally in 1974, as violence erupted in Cyprus, the ICRC offered its services to the parties under the

Geneva Conventions. Despite the long record of friction between the ICRC and Athens, the ICRC was as acceptable to the Greek government as to the Turkish. The ICRC, however, in the early stages of Cypriot violence, took care to obtain permission to enter Cyprus from the Cypriot government and then to obtain the consent of Athens for its humanitarian tasks under the law of armed conflict.

Aside from the brief—and successful—undertaking with regard to the Greek students in the summer of 1973, the ICRC did not resume action with regard to Greek political prisoners in the 1970–74 period. As part of the 1974 Cypriot crisis, the junta resigned, and the subsequent Greek government released those detained for political reasons.

Conclusion. In the Greek case, the ICRC probably pushed to the limit of what was possible vis-à-vis the military junta. ICRC diplomacy, although slow to perceive the seriousness of the situation within places of detention on the mainland, as well as on Greek ships off the coast, became progressively more dynamic and assertive after the summer of 1967 up to termination of its activity in early 1971. What was achieved in the Greek case was something entirely new in the history of international relations: the international supervision by legal agreement of a nation's army and police units throughout the country on a day-to-day basis. (In the Nigerian Civil War of 1967–70, the government in Lagos permitted an international observer team to observe the Federal army in its treatment of Ibos. The observer team did not observe the Federal police, and its observations were not as widespread nor as thorough as the ICRC's in Greece. The observer group was permitted to act on the basis of a vague grant of the government, not by written and precise permission.) At a minimum, some six thousand Greek detainees were helped by the ICRC's presence as an observer, and by its communications to family, provision of material and medical assistance, and reports to the detaining authorities—coupled with verbal discussions and at times arguments and protests.

This achievement was obtained in large part because of the international context of criticism of the Greek junta, along with that regime's weak legitimacy and weak support from Greek citizens. What terminated the ICRC's role in Greece was: (1) the organization's serious efforts to implement the 1969 accord, (2) an anti-ICRC faction within the government, and (3) the collapse of the probability of international pressure and sanctions during 1970. (Throughout the Greek case, the socialists were relatively unimportant. There was socialist criticism of the junta during the early stages of their rule, but the Soviets apparently perceived that the existence of the junta was disruptive to NATO's solidarity. Soviet criticism of the junta was progressively muted, and in the early 1970's the Soviet Union entered into new trade agreements with the colonels.)

In this context of international criticism, the ICRC made thorough visits to places of detention, and subsequently took up the major issues with the government, both verbally and in writing. It pursued subjects when governmental responses were unsatisfactory. It changed personnel to maximize opportunities for protection, although it can be argued that certain ICRC personnel became emotionally involved, in that they became antigovernment. It recalled its chief of delegation in one instance to dramatize its unhappiness with governmental policies. The ICRC was particularly good in maintaining rapport with different factions in the government; this aided in the accumulation of information. It took pains clearly to inform the political prisoners about its scope of action, so as to reduce false hopes among the detainees. The ICRC was also able to maintain its independence from various parties; while this was not a policy designed to enhance ICRC popularity in Western Europe, it was a policy on which the ICRC could build action in the future.

On the other hand, the ICRC was not assertive toward the colonels until others became interested in the situation and began to note its seriousness. Early press releases by the ICRC tended to be overly favorable to the government. (Certain individuals within the ICRC in the mid-1970's still tended to picture the Greek case as a massive public relations campaign by the Greek emigrés in Europe, similar to the public relations job done by the Biafran authorities during the Nigerian Civil War.) Some observers date allegations of mistreatment on the prison ship *Elli* from February 1968; the ICRC apparently did not take up the matter until July of that year. While it can be argued that the ICRC was used for public relations purposes by the regime, there is no evidence that political elites in Western Europe or in the United States were significantly influenced by the junta's statements and publications regarding ICRC findings.[35]

In sum, the ICRC appeared slow in recognizing the seriousness of the situation in Greece after 1967, but as the context changed the ICRC changed along with it, obtaining an unmatched basis for protection efforts, from which systematic protection proceeded on a broad-ranging scale. It is true that the ICRC did not deal with the substantive issues causing the detention and treatment; it is also true that the Council of Europe *did* make that attempt—unsuccessfully. With the benefit of hindsight, it is possible to suggest—but not prove—that had the United States been more concerned with civil liberties in Greece, the position of the ICRC might have been truly revolutionary instead of only provocative.

Political Prisoners: Summary

It cannot be emphasized too much that one case study cannot be an accurate microcosm of all situations concerning political prisoners with which the ICRC deals. Nevertheless, the Greek case does demonstrate certain things that are more generally characteristic of ICRC attempts at ad hoc protection of political prisoners.

Where there are people who may be badly treated by a government, or unfairly detained, and where other options regarding international protection do not appear to be working, the ICRC has determined a need to act. Such ICRC involvement will be controversial because of inflated accounts of mistreatment coupled with the government's deflated versions, and because of differing standards of equitable detention.

Controversy will also be insured because of a central tension between security needs and humanitarian values, or, to phrase the issue differently, between differing conceptions of which humanitarian policy has priority. Many parties place humanitarian values second to security needs—however broadly defined. This was the view of the Greek military junta. Some reject that dichotomy and argue that security policies constitute a priority form of humanitarian values. As Henry Kissinger has argued with regard to Soviet-American relations (in the face of Congressional criticism that he had forgotten about the plight of Russian Jews in search of Soviet trade), reduction of general tensions through trade—and reduction of armaments along with a credible deterrent against aggression—is also a humanitarian policy.[36] From either approach, there is a controversy over the extent to which one should pay attention to human rights or civil liberties in world politics.

If most states take the first approach, and if the Kissinger approach is gaining some currency, it is still the case that the reverse of the Kissinger approach is largely ignored. That is, if security policy is a form of humanitarian policy, then humanitarian policy is also a form of security policy. This has been well argued by Maurice Cranston:

> To claim the traditional rights of man is to claim, among other things, both security *and* liberty. Security is not something which is at odds with human rights, because it is itself a human right; it is nothing other than the right to life restated. The security of the individual is bound up with the security of the community; the private enjoyment of the right depends upon the common enjoyment of the right. The demand for liberty and security is not the demand for two things which can only with difficulty be balanced or reconciled; it is a demand for two things which naturally belong together. Part of the traditional Western faith in freedom is a belief that a free country is *safer* than an unfree country. History gives us good grounds for continuing to think that this belief is true.[37]

If in the Greek case the junta followed the first view, and if the United States followed the Kissinger view, then the fall of the junta in 1974 because of lack of internal support and latent opposition to its policies indicated the validity of the third view: a government is not likely to be secure if in its quest for security it violates widespread expectations that civil liberties will be protected.

In the last quarter of the twentieth century, the need for international protection for persons detained in relation to political conflict—either realpolitik or partisan politics—is likely to continue. This need will be compounded by the lack of adequate legal protection for political prisoners, primarily because of the impossibility of achieving a clear definition of "political prisoner" and because of lack of governmental interest in the entire subject. While the concept of administrative detention is clear in law, there are types of political prisoners that do not fit within that concept. The law is too flexible an instrument of social policy to permit an easy definition; too many political prisoners can be tucked under other laws having nothing to do with administrative detention or security crimes. And there is no global legal standard to distinguish legitimate prosecution from use of law to persecute.

Despite legal problems, where the ICRC can gain systematic access to individuals, the history of its actions demonstrates that the organization can improve the psychological, material, and medical conditions of the detainees.

But the debate remains, whether that improvement is worth the price of cooperating with the detaining authorities and ignoring the substantive issues that cause the detention in the first place. The ICRC is convinced of the usefulness of its approach, because of its concern for the welfare of the detainees. Others are not convinced.

4 Ad Hoc Diplomacy: Part Two

INTRODUCTION

ICRC ad hoc diplomacy since 1945 has comprised much more than attempted protection of political prisoners. The ICRC has been asked to do a variety of things by a variety of groups. It has been asked to inquire into the fate of Russian military personnel on a helicopter that mistakenly landed in China—an inquiry requested by the Russian Red Cross Alliance. It has served as an intermediary between China on one side and the United States and South Vietnam regarding the repatriation of persons seized by Chinese military forces when those forces took control of the Paracel Islands in the South China Sea. It has arranged the release of Portuguese businessmen seized by African liberation movements. Requests to the ICRC for some sort of ad hoc protection for an individual or groups of individuals are numerous—and increasing.

The ICRC has also projected itself into a variety of situations, exercising its right of initiative without waiting to be asked. This has been done in several international incidents regarding aircraft, and it has been done in other situations as well—such as in the civil war in Yemen.

ICRC ad hoc attempts at protection beyond the subject of political prisoners, either as a result of a request or as a result of ICRC initiative, may be broken down into two major categories: (1) hijackings, (2) kidnappings. The ICRC has also participated in a miscellany of other incidents.

Especially in the late 1960's and early 1970's, the ICRC became involved in a dozen hijackings, plus four other aircraft incidents. During this short period at least, hijackings constituted a major focus in ICRC ad hoc diplomacy. One may very well raise questions as to whether this focus will be more than temporary (for reasons that will be explained). But from the perspective of the mid-1970's, hijacking has been an important subject for the ICRC.

Political kidnappings have also led to ICRC diplomatic involvements, although on a smaller scale than hijackings.

There is also a miscellaneous category of ICRC diplomatic involvements without precise legal basis, involvements covering such things as supervising agreements upon request, exercising protection *sans demande,* providing technical services, and participating in diplomacy directed toward a reduction of tension in world affairs. A number of these diplomatic involvements not only did not relate to the Geneva Conventions but also did not relate to the statutes of the ICRC.

Thus the scope of ICRC ad hoc protection was immensely broad. While none of these activities matched ICRC concern with political prisoners, each carried its own significance both for the ICRC and for the individuals involved, and frequently for states and nonstate parties engaged in international politics as well.

HIJACKINGS

Hijackings became a serious international problem in the late 1960's and early 1970's. From 1930 until 1967, the number of aircraft hijacked across an international boundary had ranged between zero and ten per annum (see figure 4.1).[1] Most of these incidents had been primarily nonpolitical in nature, resulting from individual attempts to leave one country for another. While some significance in international politics flowed from such events, the "political" significance was secondary to the personal motivations. The pattern of hijackings was "East to West" and from Cuba to the United States. Everything considered, these incidents prior to 1967 caused little general difficulty in world affairs.

Starting in 1967, however, both the number and political significance of hijackings changed. Hijackings in 1969 were ten times more numerous than two years previously, and the political character of the event was much more pronounced. In fact, the reverse of the previous situation existed: hijackings became primarily political events, with some humanitarian overtones. (Political hijackings to dramatize some political cause were accompanied by psychopathic hijackings and extortionary hijackings.)

The institutions of international law and organization were generally ineffective in dealing with this situation. The Security Council of the United Nations

Figure 4.1. Aircraft Hijackings, 1930–75

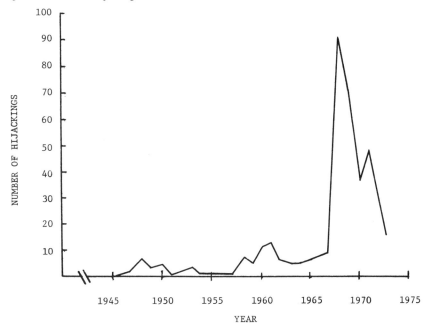

Source: Compiled from U.S. Congress, House, Committee on Foreign Relations, *Aircraft Hijackings,* 91st Cong., 2nd Sess., 1970; and *New York Times,* 1970–73.

passed several resolutions recommending that states take action necessary to eliminate disruption of normal air traffic. While these resolutions were useful as a record of who was opposed to hijacking and who was not, no change in the situation followed the passage of these measures, which were not legally binding. Efforts to conclude new conventions in international law, while successful, did not lead to a change in the situation. There remained some states that refused to commit themselves to extradition of hijackers or to their sure punishment in the state of capture. Thus the conventions did not guarantee legal enforcement against hijackers. Political asylum still existed for hijackers in some states.[2]

The ICRC became entangled in a number of these hijackings, as table 4.1 shows. The ICRC became involved both by request and by its own initiative. The scene of involvement was frequently the Middle East, in part because Palestinian groups—especially the Popular Front for the Liberation of Palestine (PELP)—used hijacking as a tactic and in part because the the ICRC was rather well known to most Middle Eastern parties through its protection and assistance roles in armed conflict. On three occasions, the involvement of the ICRC led to important diplomatic complications.

In general, it can be said that the achievements of the ICRC in these hijackings were three. The release of the hostages was achieved on a number of

Table 4.1. Aircraft Hijackings Involving ICRC, 1968–73

Year	Airline involved	Place of landing	Origin of ICRC involvement
1968	El Al	Algeria	Israeli request
1969	TWA	Syria	ICRC initiative
	Portuguese Commercial	Congo	ICRC initiative, then Portuguese request
	South Korean private	North Korea	South Korean request
1970	Olympic	Egypt	ICRC initiative*
	TWA, BOAC, SwissAir	Jordan	Palestinian request, then 3 governments' request*
	JAL	North Korea	Japanese Red Cross involvement; ICRC informed
1971	Portuguese private	Congo	Congolese request, then Portuguese Red Cross
1972	Lufthansa	Aden	Requests from USA, West Germany, Japanese Red Cross re passengers
	Sabena	Israel	"Palestinian Red Crescent" request*
	Turkish private	Bulgaria	United Nations request
1973	MEA	Israel	Lebanese request

Other Aircraft Incidents Involving ICRC, 1968–73

Year	Airline involved	Place of landing	Origin of ICRC involvement
1970	BOAC	Israel	Emergency landing in Israel; government arrests 2 Algerians; Algeria requests ICRC role
1973	Libyan Airlines	Sinai	Shot down by Israel; ICRC initiative; then Libyan request
	USSR military helicopter	China	Mistaken landing; Russian Red Cross request
	Iranian military helicopter	Iraq	Iranian Red Lion and Sun request

*Major diplomatic complexities ensued.

occasions. The presence of the ICRC provided negotiating time to the parties involved; once the ICRC representative was *sur place* there was protection for the passengers and crew in the sense that the probability of violence was reduced (but not eliminated, as we shall see) while negotiations through the ICRC took place. And finally, some assistance was rendered during the negotiations by the

ICRC via the provision of food or medical assistance. ICRC material and medical assistance, however, was not always needed.

These achievements were accompanied by a number of problems for the ICRC. First, since some parties desired not to negotiate with the hijackers, the room for diplomatic maneuver by the ICRC was sometimes reduced to the point of extinction. If no bargains were to be struck then it was up to the hijackers either to release the hostages or not, and there was no room for the ICRC to facilitate an agreement.

Secondly, both sides in the hijacking tended—as a general rule—to try to manipulate the ICRC for their own purposes. Thus the ICRC, with its concern for the individuals involved, had to be wary of lending the symbol of the Red Cross to some political cause. The classic example of this was the Sabena affair in the spring of 1972.

A Sabena airliner was hijacked to Tel Aviv by "Black September"—a radical Palestinian group. Palestinian elements requested ICRC involvement, and the government of Israel did not object. The ICRC thus began to serve as an intermediary.

At one point an ICRC representative sought a statement from the Israelis that force would not be used during the ICRC involvement. Israel offered a statement of some ambiguity. According to the ICRC, that statement was: "We are very very careful not to use force in this case. It is most dangerous to take this plane by force, it might cause a disaster inside. We are very conscious about it and shall use force only if we think this is the only way to save the passengers. This is not a military situation."[3]

Subsequently, in the process of transmitting information from the hijackers in the plane to the authorities some distance away, an ICRC representative asked to communicate certain information to Geneva, as had been done during earlier stages of the situation. This request was refused by Israeli authorities. The delegate returned to the aircraft, followed shortly thereafter by some fifteen members of an "El Al maintenance crew" who were supposedly to make certain repairs on the aircraft. The ICRC official called this fact to the attention of the hijackers, who, after ordering that the men be searched by a crew member, allowed the "maintenance men" to approach the plane. These men were in fact armed security forces, and they proceeded to subdue the hijackers by force, with some injury to passengers.

An ICRC presence was, therefore, involved in an Israeli use of force after those authorities had led the ICRC to believe force would not be used. Moreover, according to ICRC statements to the press, a bargain allowing the passengers to deplane peacefully was imminent at the time force was used.

The ICRC, believing that its image of impartiality had been damaged, lodged a protest with Israel and made known what had happened.

A third problem for the ICRC has been the attempt of hijackers to get the ICRC to guarantee the terms of an agreement. Hijackers have sometimes sought an ICRC endorsement for a negotiated agreement in the wake of hijacking. This the ICRC has been reluctant to provide on the grounds that it has no way of insuring the implementation of the agreement, and therefore the ICRC would only be putting its good name out on a limb. In fact, an ICRC delegate did make certain decisions on his own in 1970 (see below), and Geneva did carry through with its part of the bargain once the delegate *sur place* had made a commitment in the name of the ICRC. But after 1970, the ICRC explicitly rejected that course of action.

Fourthly, the ICRC has found that its involvement in hijackings has led to difficult choices. Should the ICRC lend its approval to a proposal by one party? Should the ICRC make its own proposals? These complex and difficult choices were pronounced in the Jordanian affairs (covered in detail below) when the ICRC was called upon either to support or to reject a release proposal that would have left certain hostages in the hands of the hijackers while freeing others.

Because of these problems, the ICRC slowly developed a policy with regard to its involvements in hijackings. Prior to 1970, the ICRC had proceeded on the basis of pragmatism, attempting to do what it could for the hostages without much attention to questions of "policy." Events in the period 1970–72, however, caused the ICRC to establish a formal policy in 1970 and to revise it in 1972. That revised policy, continuing to the time of writing, is, in essence, the following: (1) as a matter of principle, the ICRC condemns violations of principles of law and humanity, notably those affecting innocent lives; (2) in general, the ICRC will not participate in negotiations, but will only provide material and psychological help to the victims; (3) as an exceptional matter, the ICRC may become further involved, if one party requests it to do so and other parties agree; in that case, the ICRC will demand the abstention of force and other acts prejudicial to the victims, and will demand full liberty for its representatives; (4) the ICRC will ask for help for the victims, including the placing in security of special cases such as wounded, sick, children, etc.; (5) the ICRC will accept no responsibility for execution of agreements, decisions, or acts entered into by the principal parties.

This policy is best understood against the background of events in Greece and Jordan (and Israel).

The Athens Affair

On 22 July 1970, a group of Palestinians seized an Olympic airliner on the ground at the Athens airport. An ICRC delegate, by chance passing through Athens, offered his services to the parties concerned, without instructions from Geneva. The hijackers demanded safe passage out of Greece for themselves and for seven Palestinians detained in Greek jails. These seven had either tried to hijack an El Al plane in Greece in 1968, or had attacked the El Al airline office in Greece. They were serving sentences handed down by Greek courts. The ICRC delegate served as intermediary between the hijackers and Greek authorities and helped secure an agreement permitting the safe passage of the hijackers out of

Greece. As part of this agreement, the seven detained Palestinians were to be released within thirty days. The ICRC delegate was deeply involved in fashioning the agreement, and he then escorted the hijackers out of Greece as planned.[4] The plane carrying the delegate and hijackers was originally destined for Beirut, but while airborne the decision was made to go to Cairo. The ICRC delegate had some influence in the making of this decision.[5]

While all of this was transpiring, and unknown to the ICRC delegate, officials of the International Air Transport Association (IATA) were strongly opposed to any bargaining with the hijackers. IATA was lobbying both the ICRC in Geneva and the Greek government to stand firm. Upon learning of the hijackers' intentions of going to Beirut, IATA officials had taken steps to secure the arrest of the hijackers upon landing there. There IATA officials, already unhappy over the ICRC's involvement at Athens, became incensed when the plane was diverted to Cairo. Moreover, the Egyptian government was not happy at being embroiled in the situation, for it had voted against asylum for hijackers at the 1970 meeting of the International Civil Aviation Organization (ICAO). The arrival of the plane in Cairo forced the Egyptians to choose between supporting the Palestinian cause and supporting orderly air communication. They reluctantly permitted the plane to land, then allowed the hijackers to depart for another Arab country without prosecution.[6]

Other governments, too, were critical of the ICRC in arranging and supporting the Athens agreement, and in unintentionally thwarting the planned arrest in Beirut. Interestingly, however, Senator Jacob Javits of the United States, a strong supporter of Israel, praised the role of the ICRC, while Israel was quite critical of the ICRC.[7]

The actions by the ICRC delegate placed ICRC headquarters in a very difficult position. While the headquarters saw clearly the problems created by its man *sur place*, the ICRC also recognized that its own image as a responsible organization was at stake. Its delegate had guaranteed the agreement in the name of the ICRC, and if the ICRC reneged on the agreement it would damage its reputation—and ipso facto its future opportunity for humanitarian work—with the Palestinians and perhaps with other revolutionary groups. While this was of little concern to states, the ICRC recognized that nonstate groups were both detainees and detaining parties. Thus the ICRC needed the confidence of these groups (the ICRC must have the confidence of detainees to obtain accurate information about conditions of detention).

Even after the hijackers had left both Greece and Egypt, the ICRC was lobbied by IATA not to go through with the release of the detained seven. At a minimum, IATA asked the ICRC to seek some sort of punishment, even if token, in the state of asylum where the ICRC was to escort the seven upon their release. But the ICRC refused either to reject the second stage of the Athens agreement or to alter it by seeking prosecution after release.[8] Supporters of the Palestinian cause were of course satisfied with the role of the ICRC. The Greek government was satisfied to be rid of a dangerous and difficult situation. But others were critical of both the ICRC and the Greek government for giving in to "blackmail" diplomacy.

Before the ICRC had fully evaluated its role in the Athens affair, and before the organization got around to sending out a restrictive policy statement to its delegates around the world regarding hijackings, the ICRC became involved in the even more complex Jordanian affair. The tendency present at ICRC head-quarters to avoid all hijackings in the aftermath of the Athens affair was abruptly overturned by this new hijacking and request for ICRC involvement.

The Jordanian Affair

On 7 September 1970, Palestinians belonging to the Popular Front for the Liberation of Palestine (PFLP) hijacked four planes. One, an El Al, was flown to London after the hijackers were overcome in a shoot-out on board; one of the hijackers (Leila Khalid) was detained there, the other having been killed. A second plane, belonging to Pan Am, was blown up on the ground at Cairo after the passengers and crew were removed. Two others, belonging to TWA and SwissAir, were flown to a makeshift landing strip in Jordan. Three days later a fifth plane, owned by BOAC, was hijacked and flown to where the other two were sitting in the Jordanian desert.

Initially more than 600 persons were made hostage by the events of 7 September. The ICRC was contacted almost immediately by the Palestinians and the Egyptians to arrange the repatriation of some 125 women and children. At about the same time, the ICRC was contacted by Western governments that had citizens or planes involved; these governments sought the ICRC's help in securing the release of the rest of the hostages.[9]

The PFLP demanded the release of seven Palestinians detained in Western Europe (Ms. Khalid in the United Kingdom, three in West Germany, and three in Switzerland). Subsequently it escalated its demands to include the release of a number of Palestinians detained in Israel.[10]

In order to respond to these demands, the involved Western governments formed a bargaining group committed to a group policy; this was called the Berne group because Berne, Switzerland was the locale of policy coordination. The Berne group asked the ICRC to represent it as one party in the negotiations. Israel did not want to join this group. It stayed in close contact with the Berne group, but it issued a statement in which it refused to bargain with the hijackers. Israel was also critical of the ICRC for its past role in the Athens affair.[11] The ICRC agreed to serve as intermediary between the PFLP and the Berne group, but it insisted on having a free hand in the negotiations. That is, the ICRC refused to become the representative of any party and insisted on being an independent party in the negotiations. This was agreed to by both sides.[12]

The ICRC proceeded to make contact with all parties, dispatched a delegate to Jordan to talk directly with the PFLP (the same delegate that had handled the Athens affair), and began to provide food and medical assistance to the hostages, sweltering in the cramped quarters of the three planes in Jordan. Living conditions were initially very bad for the hostages, and the ICRC secured vast improvements with the cooperation of the PFLP. The ICRC operated efficiently out of its Beirut office and warehouse, and later out of Amman. The Jordanian government, embarrassed by the PFLP's flaunting of its authority, also cooperated with the ICRC.[13]

The diplomatic bargaining quickly centered on the following point: would it be acceptable to all if the PFLP were to release all hostages except those Israeli citizens of military significance, in return for the release of the seven Palestinians detained in Europe—the ''European seven.'' A second stage of bargaining would then entail the question: would the Israelis release some of their Palestinian detainees in return for the release of the remaining Israeli hostages held by the PFLP?[14]

This two-stage proposal, involving first a partial release of hostages, split the Berne group. The Western European states were favorably inclined; the United States—and Israel—were opposed. A complicating factor was that some persons regarded by the PFLP as Israelis had dual citizenship and were carrying both Israeli and American passports. Thus some of those who would remain as hostages were viewed as Americans by the United States government.

At this stage in the negotiations, the ICRC made known its opposition to the PFLP proposal. An ICRC vice president, who had taken over the negotiations and who was instrumental in fashioning the ICRC's position, felt very strongly that the ICRC could not endorse a plan whereby some hostages would receive preferential treatment—release—over others. The view that the ICRC had to act impartially prevailed as official ICRC policy. The ICRC's stand was congruent with the United States and Israeli position. As such, the stand helped, rightly or wrongly, to block agreement on the PFLP proposal.[15]

Whereas the ICRC's stand was based on an interpretation of impartial humanitarianism, there was a further consideration blocking acceptance of the PFLP's proposed stage one. There was uncertainty as to what was involved in the proposed stage two. The Israelis wanted to know exactly how many Palestinian detainees they would have to release, and which ones. But the PFLP did not want to give the Israelis names and numbers early in the negotiations, for by so doing the PFLP would tell the Israelis which detainees were most important to the PFLP. Moreover, the Israelis were reluctant to agree to any open-ended scheme whose numbers were not precise. The uncertainty regarding stage two caused the Israelis to object to stage one. If the Israelis objected to stage one, it was difficult for the Americans to accept it either. And if the Americans rejected stage one, it was difficult for the Western European states to accept it—even though they wanted to.[16]

On 12 September the PFLP blew up the remaining three planes and released all but 58 hostages, who were split up into small groups and dispersed within Jordan into secret PFLP sanctuaries. The ICRC suspended negotiations in protest. Later the ICRC issued a statement saying it would no longer participate in negotiations but would only try to check on the conditions of detention for the hostages. On 15 September the government of Israel detained some 450 new Palestinians from the occupied territories, in an obvious effort to obtain a bargaining weapon. On 15 September, the Berne group, finding few options open to it, asked the ICRC to resume negotiations regarding the remaining hostages. The ICRC reversed its stand and agreed to do so, dispatching another negotiating team.[17]

On the morning of 17 September, however, the Jordanian army moved against Palestinian guerrilla organizations throughout the country, thus bringing a latent civil war into the open. The army, loyal to King Hussein, moved not only against the PFLP but also against the larger Palestine Liberation Organization (PLO) in an effort to restore control of the country fully to the king. Such a confrontation between the king and Palestinian armed elements had been the precise objective of the PFLP in the hijacking, for the PFLP sought to force other, more moderate Palestinian elements like the PLO to join it in a direct rejection of Hussein's authority. The PFLP thought the combined Palestinian groups were stronger than the Army.[18]

The outbreak of the Jordanian Civil War prevented the ICRC negotiating team from reaching Amman. Reaching Beirut, the chief negotiator had difficulty making contact with anyone in a position of authority from the PFLP. At this time, fears about the safety of the hostages increased, for the Jordanian authorities did not know where the hostages were and thus could not limit military operations in order to guarantee their safety. Neither the ICRC nor Western or Israeli intelligence knew their whereabouts either.[19]

On 26 September, the Jordanian army found fifteen of the hostages during a military operation and turned them over to the ICRC, which subsequently repatriated them. As the war went against the Palestinians in succeeding days, the PFLP released another thirty-two hostages, with the Egyptian Embassy in Amman serving as intermediary. At the end of September, the final few hostages were released, again through the Egyptian Embassy, with some supporting role for the ICRC.[20]

As all the hostages were in good condition, and since the hostages and others asked Western governments for a reciprocal act in return for the good treatment, the "European seven" were finally released by the three detaining states. And Israel, while denying participation in any deal, subsequently released two Algerians it had seized from an airliner that had made a transit stop in Israel, and ten Libyans, for "humanitarian reasons."[21]

Hijackings and the ICRC

If the Athens affair demonstrated the difficulties for the ICRC in projecting itself into a hijacking, the Jordanian affair indicated that being requested to act by the parties concerned was no guarantee of freedom from difficulty.[22]

In the Jordanian affair, the ICRC made an ethical judgment against the PFLP proposal for a stage-one partial release. This antagonized the PFLP, even as it was officially—if temporarily—accepted by the Berne group. It was a judgment tacitly supported by Israel for different reasons. But this ICRC evaluation meant that all the passengers and crew became the hostages of the Israeli-American minority of passengers. The difficulty of choice for the ICRC was obvious. First one evaluation and then another became the official policy of the organization.

The ICRC was unable to make any impact on the bargaining positions pertaining to stage two. The problem lay in the logic of the situation. As long as the PFLP would not make specific demands on Israel, Israel would not agree to the two-stage proposal. The ICRC finally reached the judgment that the best it could do was to lend its weight to a partial release in stage one and then hope for the best in stage two. There was no prospect of hostage release otherwise; the PFLP had at least promised to give the ICRC a list of the names of the detainees it wanted; and Israel had quietly agreed to the principle of an exchange.

After 1970, states improved their security measures for departing aircraft, and some parties had reservations about the utility of hijacking in bringing favorable attention.[23] For whatever combination of reasons, the number of hijackings declined noticeably by mid-1970, and, ICRC involvement in hijackings also declined.

It remains to be seen whether the cautious policy statement of the ICRC with regard to hijackings will be put to the test in future situations, and, if it is, whether the ICRC will be able to stick to its objective of playing a noncontroversial role as simple provider of "good offices." In particular, it remains to be seen if the ICRC can avoid participating in the negotiations in favor of simply transmitting messages. For after all, in almost all hijackings, the opposing parties can talk to each other directly by radio; the actual need for third-party transmission of messages is slight to nonexistent.

Whatever the outcome on this point, the Athens affair caused the ICRC to view more closely its personnel situation in the field and to re-evaluate slightly its long-standing belief that the man in the field must be given a great deal of freedom of action. The Athens affair demonstrates all too painfully for the ICRC the need to have capable delegates in the field ready to respond competently to hijackings—or any other emergency that arises and results in ICRC involvement.[24]

KIDNAPPINGS

The subject of political kidnappings demonstrates yet another area where the ICRC may be called upon to try and protect individuals in some way. The ICRC has not been involved in many political kidnappings during the period under review. Even so, the ICRC has encountered some of the same difficulties in this métier as found in hijackings. (The ICRC had peripheral involvement in the Maalot affair in Israel in 1974. Armed Palestinians, after seizing a school containing a number of students, listed the ICRC along with two states as acceptable intermediaries. The ICRC quickly prepared for involvement, but Israel chose the French government as interlocutor before storming the school with soldiers.) The ICRC had a central involvement in the 1970 kidnapping of an American official in Uruguay.

The Uruguay Affair

The kidnapping and killing of the American official Dan Mitrione in Uruguay in 1970 by the Tupamaros was front-page news and eventually the subject of a movie (*L'Etat de Siège* [*State of Siege*]). Related to that series of events was another, less publicized kidnapping—that of Dr. Claude Fly, an American under contract to the Agency for International Development (AID) of the U.S. government. In the wake of the Mitrione kidnapping the ICRC became involved in the effort to secure the release of Dr. Fly.

The basic situation in Uruguay in the late 1960's and early 1970's was one of economic problems combined with a trend toward authoritarianism. A vicious circle was created: strikes and protests over economic issues led to governmental repression, which in turn led to greater disruption—and violence—in an effort to resist governmental policy. The situation had its international dimensions, as Uruguay's government obtained support from the United States, while the threat grew of some foreign intervention on one side or another from groups in Brazil and Argentina. One of the active forces in Uruguay was the Tupamaros, a Marxist group with anarchistic tendencies and committed to "urban guerrilla warfare."[25]

On 1 August 1970, the Tupamaros kidnapped Mitrione and the Brazilian consul A. M. Dias Gomide. The Tupamaros alleged that Mitrione was engaged in teaching techniques of torture and mistreatment to the Uruguayan police in an effort to help the Uruguayan government obtain information on dissidents and suppress opposition. The expected American denial was accompanied by the facts that Mitrione was associated with the Federal Bureau of Investigation (FBI) and was assigned to a Uruguayan police station.[26]

On 7 August, Fly was kidnapped by the Tupamaros. It was alleged that he, too, was engaged in the teaching of torture techniques. It was specifically alleged that Fly was the superior of Mitrione and that both were agents of the Central Intelligence Agency (CIA).[27]

It is difficult to form sure judgments about events beyond this point, as an authoritative version of matters has yet to appear. From press reports it appears that the Uruguayan government was not anxious to make concessions in return for the release of hostages.

Mitrione was found dead on 10 August. The Tupamaros were widely criticized within Uruguay, even by those who supported them. This, too, tended to confirm the government's hard line, as the killing seemed clearly to alienate the public from the Tupamaros.

After several months without a change in the situation, Dr. Fly's family sought help from the ICRC, which then became involved, with the permission of the Uruguayan government and in liaison with the Uruguayan Red Cross. Whatever transpired after that point, no doubt part of the problem confronting the ICRC was that some of the most important leaders of the Tupamaros were detained. Thus the issue of ICRC access to detainees probably arose, despite evidence that detained Tupamaros were linked to the world outside their cells by an intricate system of clandestine communication.[28]

In any event, the ICRC was ultimately unsuccessful in obtaining the release of Dr. Fly. It appeared to be the case that, whatever the flexibility or inflexibility of the Tupamaros' leadership, the head of the government became increasingly inflexible on the question of bargaining over hostages; impending elections in late fall 1970 did not seem to increase the ICRC's room to maneuver. In March, 1971, Dr. Fly was released in ill health, after the ICRC had terminated both a first and second effort in his behalf. After Fly's release, there was speculation the Tupamaros may have feared that Fly might die during detention, thus creating image problems for the movement similar to the situation after Mitrione's death.[29]

There has not been, to date, criticism of the ICRC's role in this kidnapping.

Kidnappings and the ICRC

In the Uruguayan affair, insofar as one can conclude on the basis of scant public information, the fate of the hostages was inextricably tied up with the realpolitik and partisan politics of the situation. The ICRC was apparently unable to get the parties to recognize any humanitarian concerns that could be viewed apart from these political causes.

In kidnappings, unlike hijackings, "the individual is it." That is to say, in a kidnapping the individual is the only weapon available to the kidnappers. In a hijacking, the hijackers can bring attention to the cause by blowing up a plane. This difference reduces the field of diplomatic maneuver in kidnappings.

In the Uruguayan affair especially, the ICRC appeared ready to act to try and secure freedom for the hostages. When this quiet diplomacy failed to bring results, the ICRC retired to the sidelines without criticizing the intransigence of any party and without any public effort to defend what it had attempted. Its role was prudent, carefully aimed at probing the boundaries of the possible. The failure of the approach to bring results is explained by the commitment of the parties to their political goals at the expense of individual welfare.

MISCELLANEOUS PROTECTION TASKS

There are a number of protection tasks performed by the ICRC unrelated to political prisoners or hostages. These tasks are without integral connection (except in the sense that perceived successful performance tends to generate more requests on the organization), but it is possible to group some of them together under analytic headings.

Supervision of Agreements

The ICRC has long supervised agreements between two conflicting parties related to armed conflict but not specifically covered in the Geneva Conventions. Truces and surrenders have been observed by the ICRC at the request of the parties, the latter being vividly demonstrated in 1973 by the decision of Israeli authorities to request the presence of an ICRC official for the surrender of certain Israeli units surrounded in the Sinai. But recently the ICRC has been requested to supervise agreements far beyond the scope of the Geneva Conventions.

First, the ICRC has been called upon to supervise agreements that are essentially humanitarian in nature. It is noteworthy that in at least two of these recent humanitarian agreements, the ICRC dealt with regimes that had been highly antagonistic toward the ICRC on other issues. In the early 1960's, the ICRC supervised the movement of some Vietnamese from Thailand to North Vietnam. North Vietnam cooperated with the ICRC despite its failure to cooperate on detainees during the Vietnam War. This population transfer went without difficulty. Thailand was happy to see the aliens go, the civilians had themselves chosen North Vietnam, and that state was receiving additional manpower. The role of the ICRC was simply to assist in implementing what the parties had already agreed to. Since the parties did not have direct and official relations, an intermediary was desired.

Similarly, despite lack of extensive and harmonious dealings between the ICRC and North Korea, from 1959 to 1973 the ICRC supervised the movement of over 90,000 Koreans and their relatives from Japan to North Korea. In this case, the ICRC was involved in the sometimes controversial task of screening the individuals to assure that a voluntary choice had been made to go to North Korea. The question of screening by an international agency to establish individual freedom of choice—possibly in opposition to state policy—had been controversial in the past, with regard to the forced repatriation of North Korean prisoners of war detained by United Nations forces. That same subject was a controversial part of the debate about whether Palestinian refugees in the Middle East could participate in a legitimate vote on their future without being subjected to controlling state pressure. In this population transfer, the ICRC performed the requested tasks to the satisfaction of both Japan and North Korea. Subsequently the government of South Korea raised charges that some Japanese wives of Koreans had been forced to go to North Korea, and also that the ICRC had participated in a deal that had led to inhumane treatment in North Korea for those arriving.[30] A number of observers believed that South Korea was mainly interested in trying to disrupt the developing rapport between Japan and North Korea. If that was true, this case indicates that the ICRC may be criticized for reasons of realpolitik even when it operates in the humanitarian field within the bounds of governmental agreement. By and large, however, ICRC supervision of humanitarian agreements has gone without great difficulty or controversy.

There is also the rare case in which the ICRC is asked to supervise an agreement that is regarded as more political than humanitarian. The most striking example pertains to the Cuban missile crisis of 1962. In that the United States and the Soviet Union were engaged in a direct military confrontation, the situation was regarded as basically political and military, even though there were humanitarian concerns involved (such as whether the world would be blown up!).

As tense and delicate negotiations proceeded in 1962 regarding whether, and under what terms, the USSR would withdraw its missiles from Cuba and cease shipping new missile parts to that state, a high-ranking ICRC official informally offered his services to a United Nations official who was close to the negotiations then taking place at UN headquarters in New York.[31] When this information reached the Secretary General, he took up the matter with the Soviet and American negotiators. ICRC on-the-spot inspection in Cuba proved unacceptable. But the Soviet Union did agree to permit the ICRC to inspect ships incoming to Cuba, in order to ascertain that no missile parts were on board. It was finally agreed that the U.S. itself would verify the departure of missiles from Cuba by aerial surveillance.

When this deal was struck, the involvement of the ICRC was officially requested, although the ICRC had been informally involved in the fashioning of the agreement. The ICRC agreed so to serve because of the gravity of the situation and proceeded to create a pool of 180 special delegates for the task.

Actual ICRC supervision of part of the Soviet-American agreement of 1962 became unnecessary, for the USSR delayed all shipping to Cuba for a time after the confrontation. Nevertheless, the availability of the ICRC was useful in providing the Soviet Union with a way to alter its policy without on-board American inspection of Soviet ships, which would have been embarrassing, and possibly unacceptable, to the USSR. This availability and acceptability thus added an important element of flexibility to the negotiations. United Nations officials were looking for ideas that might divert the Soviet-American direct confrontation into a negotiated agreement, and the informal offer of help from the ICRC proved to be an important, if symbolic, element in that effort.

The way in which the ICRC assumed a task in the Cuban missile crisis was not without its problems. The Cuban government was not kept fully informed of developments involving the ICRC. The Cubans subsequently made known their unhappiness to the ICRC, both verbally and through actions. Whereas Fidel Castro before coming to power had cooperated with the ICRC in the medical care and exchange of detainees under his control, and whereas he had permitted visits to detainees as premier of Cuba, he refused to renew these visits. Cuban officials subsequently and privately linked this policy to what had transpired in the missile crisis. Thus the ICRC, while finding acceptance by the Americans and Russians in the crisis, created a residue of resentment that added to ICRC difficulties in trying to see political prisoners in Cuba. Apparently the ICRC was led to believe that the Cuban government had given its approval to American-Soviet arrangements; this was either not the case or was not subsequently viewed as the case by Castro.

There have not been many such "political" agreements entailing ICRC supervision, although—as the Korean-Japanese case indicated—a humanitarian agreement can have political implications. This mix of humanitarian and political motives was found in the UN request to the ICRC to participate in the naming of a UN commission on prisoners of war, and in the U.S. request to the ICRC to investigate charges of biological-chemical (B/C) warfare in the Korean War (see Chapter 2, above).

It would seem that the ICRC must be extremely wary of giving its consent to supervise projected agreements. The ICRC continues to defend its refusal to serve on the UN prisoner-of-war commission, in order to avoid being linked with a Western point of view. With regard to the Korean War, even if it be argued that the ICRC acted too hastily in agreeing to conduct an investigation into the use of B/C warfare, since that investigation could only be conducted with the permission of all parties concerned, it is unlikely that the ICRC would repeat its behavior in similar situations in the future. The ICRC prides itself on being acceptable to all for the promotion of fundamental—some would say minimum— human rights. It prefers agreement—some would say conservatism—to attempted action without agreement. The institution tends to second-guess itself when it gets involved in a situation without full and clear agreement among the parties about what is to be supervised, and how. This it does to protect its image of impartiality, for the sake of future utility.

Involvement Sans Demande

In the history of ICRC ad hoc diplomacy, most of the time the ICRC is asked by some party to exercise its right of initiative vis-à-vis another party. There have been several occasions, however, when the Red Cross symbol was employed in some protection task without a request from anyone. These involvements sans demande have arisen primarily through delegate action in the field rather than by official decision in Geneva.

The Athens hijacking and ICRC involvement through delegate decision *sur place* has already been noted. Another example of this type of ICRC involvement in a situation occurred in the Yemeni Civil War. The ICRC head of delegation in the area, the same one who decided to project himself into the Athens affair, was active in visiting detained combatants and in managing an ICRC medical station, among other things. Upon receiving reports that an air attack had created a number of civilian wounded in a certain area, he went there directly on his own initiative (not unlike countless other delegates in countless other violent situations). The Yemeni royalists and Saudi Arabia supported this initiative. What made the situation in Yemen different was what the delegate found in the wake of the air attack: clear indication of the use of poison gas. Compounding the situation was the subsequent fact that this ICRC report, sent first to Geneva and then to the parties involved in the conflict, wound up published in toto in the *New York Times*.

The ICRC believed it had to take firm action on the basis of the report's findings. The report by the delegate and three other ICRC officials, two of them doctors, stated in part:

> The head of the mission had one of the four communal graves opened. There were 15 corpses in it. An immediate autopsy . . . left no doubt that death was due to pulmonary edema. [effusion of serous fluid into the interstices of tissue cells]
>
> The four survivors who were in the contaminated area are all in pain from their eyes and almost blind. All have pains in the chest and none has any wound.
>
> The doctors cannot testify to an air raid with gas bombs of which they were not personally witness. On the other hand, they stress that all the evidence leads to the conclusion that edema was caused by the breathing of poison gas.[32]

In addition to the quiet overtures, the ICRC issued a public protest against the use of poison gas in Yemen, but without naming the user. While there were other allegations of gas bombing in Yemen after the bombing raid of 10 May 1967 investigated by the ICRC, there were no subsequent confirmations of use of gas warfare. Any change in Egyptian policy may have been due to the furor stirred up by publication of the ICRC report and the ICRC public protest. (At a minimum, publicity had an effect on Israel, which dispatched troops to the Egyptian front in the 1967 war equipped with gas masks.) There was no criticism of the ICRC for lodging a public protest, as most commentators believed the ICRC to be justified in taking unusual action because of the widespread opposition to gas warfare.

By contrast, the Geneva headquarters and not the delegate in the field took the unrequested initiative in 1971 to project the organization into the conflict between East and West Pakistan. As violence in the eastern sector increased, the ICRC dispatched two plane loads of medical assistance to Pakistan. The government was informed of the arrival of the planes and accompanying delegates just prior to their arrival. Permission from the government was not requested.

The government viewed the episode as a challenge to its policies in East Pakistan and denied entry to the ICRC officials. It did not wish to have ICRC officials, with or without medical assistance, in the country, for that would draw more international attention to the seriousness of the situation. The rejection of the ICRC delegates by the government was made easier by the fact that one delegate had been dispatched in such a hurry that his Swiss diplomatic passport had expired; thus he could be rejected on technical grounds. This poorly calculated move by ICRC headquarters, while it caused temporary problems between the government of Pakistan and the agency, did not prove to be a barrier to ICRC traditional roles under the Geneva Conventions once the violence escalated to the international war for Bangladesh later in 1971.

This 1971 episode, however, caused some observers of the ICRC to regard its diplomacy as both rigid and unstable: rigid in the sense of generally sticking to traditional activities through traditional means, even when change was demanded; but unstable in that it sometimes made a radical departure from past practice without diplomatic preparation and tact. This move also raised questions about the ICRC's political astuteness in understanding the views and policies of participants in a conflict. In that the decision to assert an abrupt initiative was made by the highest levels of decision-making in Geneva, questions were raised about the coordination between this level and the middle- and lower-rank specialists on Asia in the organization.

In the history of the ICRC its delegates have continuously asserted themselves in an effort to do things not specifically authorized by treaty law, like attempts to create neutral zones and truces (these are mentioned in the Geneva Conventions but are not required). When these attempts are linked to the treaty tasks of the ICRC under the Geneva Conventions, they are not so controversial and have become somewhat expected. Thus in the 1974 violence in Cyprus, the ICRC took the initiative to establish a neutral zone in the strongest building in Nicosia—the Hilton Hotel—in an effort to protect civilians. Similar action was pursued successfully in the 1970 Jordanian war. Some initiatives that occur without a specific request but are related to legal interpretations are at least regarded as normal, even if not agreed to. Thus it is increasingly accepted that the ICRC can assert its view as to when the Geneva Conventions come into force, as it did in 1965 regarding Vietnam. A party may disagree with the ICRC view, but it rarely challenges the right of the ICRC to assert that view.

But when involvements sans demande occur beyond the scope of the Geneva Conventions (or beyond a generally accepted definition of that scope), the probability is high that complexities will ensue for the ICRC. It is for this reason that the ICRC has been cautious in its use of the right of initiative without request. Many ICRC officials are now critical of ICRC policy vis-à-vis Pakistan in 1971; the agency has officially eschewed self-projection into hijackings and kidnappings; and it regards its self-projection into the subject of investigating the use of B/C warfare as an historical accident not likely to be repeated. Only on the question of political prisoners does the ICRC continue to assert a role for itself without request (although in many situations the ICRC is asked to become involved by NGOs such as the International Commission of Jurists or Amnesty, or by relatives, or by states).

Technical Services

In some situations the ICRC provides technical services to individuals on an ad hoc basis. One of the major examples of this type of humanitarian protection is the issuance of the Red Cross *titre de voyage* or travel document.

In a bureaucratic world, it is amazing what can be done if the proper form is filled out. Conversely, it is amazing what is opposed for lack of an administrative requirement. The ICRC has been able to get countless individuals out of some difficulty by providing them with a piece of paper—now widely accepted by states—on which the state can stamp a visa for one crossing of a specified boundary. Without this Red Cross travel document, which to some extent replaces a passport, a functionary of a state is frequently unwilling to let a person move across an international boundary. There is nothing on which to stamp the visa!

While the above analysis is slightly oversimplified, it is a fact that even when there is a political will to permit persons in danger or in some other need to move across an international boundary, there are technical problems to be overcome. The ICRC has sought to meet these technical problems with the Red Cross travel document.

The document originated during the closing days of World War I when a number of prisoners of war, who had been deprived of their official papers, were released but were unable to cross a boundary for lack of proper papers. Thus the origin of the titre de voyage was an extension of ICRC concern with prisoners of war. Once the document came into use, and was acceptable to states, the ICRC began to use it for civilians in need. A number of Jews were able to flee Nazi Germany through possession of this document and the willingness of states to accept it in lieu of an exit visa stamped into a German passport. A striking use of the travel document for civilians occurred at the end of World War II. The collapse of the Third Reich left a large number of workers, non-Germans deported to Germany by force, without the necessary papers to return home. The Red Cross travel document facilitated their repatriation.

More recently, the travel document has been useful to the humanitarian work of the ICRC in Uganda and Chile. In Uganda under the regime of Idi Amin Dada, a number of Asians were ordered out of the country by a certain date, and their rights—and papers—in Uganda were ruled void. Those Asians who had achieved Ugandan citizenship had no other documents permitting their entry into another country. Some of the Asians held British passports but were unable to enter the United Kingdom because of limits set on the immigration of certain categories of people. The situation, therefore, was that many individuals faced detention, and possibly worse, if they stayed in Uganda, but they were prevented from leaving because of the lack of proper papers necessary to enter another country. The problem was acute because of the ruthlessness of the Amin regime: possibly as many as 90,000 people had simply disappeared in Uganda between 1971 and 1974.[33] The ICRC, in conjunction with the High Commissioner for

Refugees, was able to help these individuals escape an uncertain fate through issuance of the Red Cross travel document, with the UNHCR subsequently negotiating the entry of these Asians into states willing to accept them. The task of the ICRC was basically supportive and technical.

Likewise in Chile after the 1973 coup, in addition to the Chileans detained and visited by the ICRC, there were a number of non-Chileans who desired—or felt compelled—to leave Chile but were unable to do so for lack of proper credentials. In many cases these non-Chileans were leftist Brazilians, Uruguayans, Argentines, etc., who became targets of the new military junta but who were unable or unwilling to obtain the necessary exit papers from their own governments. These individuals believed that if they went to their own embassy in Santiago for help, they would be either refused or arrested. While therefore coming under the legal jurisdiction of the UNHCR, these individuals still required exit and entry papers when the UNHCR was able to find an asylum state. The ICRC provided the necessary travel document.

In a small number of instances the issuance of the document has been controversial. It is a fact that the Red Cross *titre de voyage* played some part in the escape of certain Nazi officials from Germany after the war. Adolph Eichmann had one of the documents in his possession when he was seized in Argentina by Israeli agents. While the ICRC says it never has knowingly issued a travel document to war criminals or other fugitives from legitimate justice, theft of the documents and falsification of papers by others has occurred.[34]

The overall use of the Red Cross travel document has, without doubt, been beneficial to large numbers of individuals in need. Its use remains an important technical service provided by the ICRC. It is issued without the formal approval of the host state, but in no clandestine way.

In at least two other situations since 1945 the ICRC has provided technical services of a humanitarian nature. Under Article 16 of the Japanese Peace Treaty, the ICRC became a technical intermediary for distributing Japanese assets held in neutral countries to former detainees who had suffered undue hardship in Japanese detention places. While the sums involved were ultimately small, the ICRC was asked by the signatories to the treaty to make the determination of who was to get what.

Secondly, also after World War II, the ICRC was asked by the West German government to help in the payment of compensation to former detainees of the Third Reich who had been victims of pseudo-medical experiments. The requested task of the ICRC was to serve as a technical intermediary, principally with the Polish and Czech governments, with whom West Germany had no diplomatic relations at that time, in order once again to determine who was to get what.

These technical services provided by the ICRC, whether concerning the Red Cross *titre de voyage* or an indemnity program, illustrate the broad extent of ICRC ad hoc diplomacy and its varied nature.

AD HOC DIPLOMACY IN REVIEW

It bears repeating that ad hoc diplomacy has always been the central means of ICRC protection. Medical assistance and protection by Henry Dunant at Solférino preceded efforts to develop law for the wounded in battle. The subsequent concern of the ICRC with developing law has tended to obscure the central importance of ad hoc diplomacy. Some observers, and perhaps some legalists within the ICRC, believe that the primary task of the agency is to develop humanitarian law in armed conflicts. The fact of ICRC history is that ad hoc diplomacy has preceded legal development and indeed has been the background and foundation of legal developments.

The importance of ICRC ad hoc diplomacy is further enhanced by the historical fact that even when law has been written, its de jure application has not always—or even frequently—followed. The ICRC's protection efforts remain ad hoc because the parties involved refuse to accept, formally and officially, a role for the ICRC under law. This will become clear in later analyses. For example, ICRC relations with Israel with regard to protection in the territories occupied since 1967 remain ad hoc rather than de jure under the Fourth Geneva Convention—at least in the view of Israel, which in practice controls the situation.

While ICRC ad hoc diplomacy has historically led to the development of law and eventually to some ICRC diplomacy based on statutory law, there is no guarantee that this process will occur. Indeed, the probabilities regarding current ICRC ad hoc diplomacy are otherwise. That is to say, while ad hoc protection of prisoners of war preceded de jure protection in the history of the ICRC, nothing guarantees that current efforts to protect political prisoners will ultimately lead to de jure protection—and the probabilities are that such diplomatic practice will not result in an international convention on political prisoners.

For one thing, the concept of political prisoners is not a clear legal term permitting easy definition and consistent application. While there may be some controversy about who exactly is a prisoner of war, the complexities and ambiguities are much greater regarding who is a political prisoner. Moreover, the concept of political prisoner seems to states to pose more of a threat to their claims to domestic jurisdiction and freedom of decision-making. A prisoner of war is a foreigner in one type of factual situation—armed conflict. By contrast, a political prisoner may be a state's own national during situations of "normality." The inroad on state claims to jurisdiction are thus much greater.

If there are major problems in developing law to regulate political prisoners in the foreseeable future, the problems are even greater with regard to developing law to regulate the taking of hostages in hijackings and kidnappings.

Therefore much if not all of current ICRC ad hoc diplomacy is likely to remain ad hoc for the foreseeable future. Bits and pieces of what the ICRC has been doing in this area of its operations may fall under new statutory law. For example, some types of political prisoners may be entitled to prisoner-of-war status if certain supplements to the 1949 Geneva Conventions become law; guerrilla fighters in a civil war or a war of national liberation, heretofore regarded by the ICRC as political prisoners because of the demands of the challenged government, may receive legal protection if certain changes occur in the statutory law.

But in general a great deal of ICRC protection efforts will remain without precise legal basis. At the same time, there is some probability that the requests for ad hoc diplomacy will increase in both volume and type. As the ICRC becomes better known, as the units of the world political system become more interdependent, as the probability of conflict therefore increases, and as the need for neutral intermediaries increases in order to aid in the resolution and supervision of conflict, demands on the organization should increase.

Because of these changes in world politics, as well as problems in obtaining legal regulation, ICRC ad hoc diplomacy is likely to remain an important part of ICRC activity.

Nothing is certain in world affairs. The increasing political conflict could result in a decline in demand for ICRC activity, because the parties are so committed to political goals that they leave no room for humanitarian activity. Thus a government like that of Cambodia in 1975, or Iraq in the same year, is inclined to say to the ICRC: we have no humanitarian need; we do not need your services.

But these are situations where a party is in control of territory and events. It is likely that there will be many situations of prolonged conflict, where the parties do not control events completely. It is in these situations that an impartial actor takes on importance in an increasingly "politicized" world. While that process of politicization may limit or even exclude ICRC action on occasion, that very same process gives rise to a need for effective and impartial action where, for example, nationals are detained abroad or where there is a need for a party to justify its detention conditions to some source of criticism. Thus politicization can give rise to a need for a neutral intermediary and to impartial supervision, perhaps even more than to exclusion of humanitarian action.

5 Legal Development Efforts

The ICRC has sought to guarantee, through the development of international law, that certain humanitarian activity will occur (as noted in Chapter 1). Thus far the ICRC has focused its legislative efforts on law for armed conflict—viz., war. The result has been seven conventions, the last of which are the four Geneva Conventions of 1949. For over thirty years these four Conventions have constituted the bulk of international statutory law for war situations. ICRC legislative efforts have thus been successful—as measured, over time, by the adoption of law. Despite this success, ICRC legislative efforts in the 1960's and 1970's have been controversial. Success has been joined by criticism.[1]

LAW OF ARMED CONFLICT

Historical Traditions

The law of armed conflict, *jus in bello,* or law to regulate the process of war, is composed of several traditions (see figure 5.1). The ICRC has been responsible, historically, for the development of one of these traditions. Currently, the ICRC has assumed part of the responsibility for meshing these traditions into an effective and modern law of war.

Figure 5.1. Law in Armed Conflicts

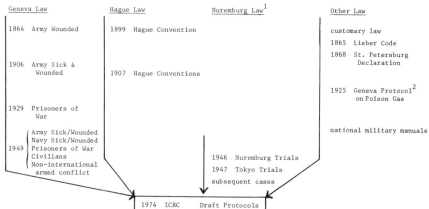

[1]Pertaining to violations of *jus in bello*.
[2]Considered by some to belong to Hague Tradition.

Henry Dunant and the ICRC focused on victims of wars, and this concern led to one strain of legal thinking called the Geneva traditions, or Geneva law, or Red Cross Law. The ICRC tried to secure legalization of its ad hoc activity in war situations, in order to guarantee humanitarian protection and assistance to victims of wars. This concern was well received by states, and seven conventions were concluded at Geneva between 1864 and 1949, with the ICRC serving as catalyst and drafting secretariat. The focus was war victims: wounded and sick military personnel (first two Conventions of 1949); prisoners of war (Third Convention); civilians (Fourth Convention); and victims of civil wars (Common Article 3 of all four Conventions).

During this same period, other legal developments occurred touching upon legal regulation of the conduct of wars. At the turn of the century at the Hague, Netherlands, conventions were concluded pertaining to neutral rights, methods of warfare, prisoners of war, etc. These diplomatic conferences were separate from the ICRC, and the law emanating from them was, accordingly, called the Hague law. There was an overlap between the subject matter of the Geneva and Hague traditions, not only because both explicitly regulated prisoner of war matters, but also because Hague regulations on aerial bombardment and other *methods* of warfare obviously affected *victims* of war—which was the major focus of the ICRC. Nevertheless it was argued, for purposes of distinction if not for accuracy, that Geneva law was concerned with victims and Hague law with the rights and duties of states. An accurate distinction was that the Geneva tradition had a watchdog—the ICRC—whereas the Hague tradition did not.

After World War II these two legal traditions were supplemented by a third, which can be called the Nuremburg tradition. This tradition, comprising the

Nuremburg and Tokyo trials of the late 1940's and subsequent cases, established among other things the principle of individual responsibility for violating the norms of the Geneva and Hague traditions. Whereas before 1945 the existing law was said to apply only to states as collectivities, the Nuremburg tradition formalized the principle that individuals as individuals could be prosecuted for violations of the law in armed conflict, even though the violations occurred in the name of the state.

For some twenty-five years after the Nuremburg and Tokyo trials, the Nuremburg tradition was controversial. Some said the principle of individual responsibility was not universal law but only victor's justice, practiced against the defeated but not the victorious. And the UN General Assembly failed to endorse seven tenets said to constitute the Nuremburg principles by the International Law Commission, an agency of the UN system.[2] In the 1970's not only did the U.S. move, to some extent, to implement the Nuremburg principle against some of its personnel in the Vietnam War, but also there was a move to write some of the Nuremburg principles into the draft protocols to the 1949 Geneva Conventions, which would confirm the Nuremburg tradition as valid public law.[3] While the legal status and the contents of the Nuremburg tradition remained controversial, there was growing reason to refer to it as another element in the modern law in armed conflicts.

Finally, in addition to the Geneva, Hague, and Nuremburg traditions, there were other sources of law producing modern jus in bello. There was the bulk of customary law on this subject. There were explicit conventions which seemed to be part neither of the Hague nor Geneva traditions, such as the 1925 Geneva Protocol on poisonous and asphyxiating gases. And there were national documents that seemed to be in a twilight zone between national law and emerging customary international law, such as the American, British, and West German military field manuals.[4]

All of this, then, constituted the origins of jus in bello. One of the reasons this body of law has been so little known is that it has been so disjointed. Another reason has been the distant origin of some of it. And a third reason has been vagueness.[5] It had been a long-standing ICRC view that it had responsibility for updating and clarifying only the Geneva tradition. By 1970 this view had changed. The ICRC, and others, became convinced that a review of almost all of jus in bello was required if the Geneva tradition was to be relevant to the armed conflicts of the last quarter of the twentieth century.

Modern Developments

The ICRC could hardly be unaware of deficiencies in the law of armed conflicts.[6] It was, after all, the ICRC which—for example—had sought access to French prisoners of war in Algerian hands, or had sought to assist civilians in Indochina. But while the ICRC was concerned about the weakness of jus in bello, and while ICRC efforts were made to draw attention to this weakness, it cannot be said that the ICRC was the only—or even major—catalyst in updating the law.

ICRC legal development efforts achieved results only when elements acting through the UN system took up the question of armed conflicts at the UN conference on human rights in 1968 in Teheran. The UN Teheran Conference, followed by reports by the UN secretary general and subsequent debates and resolutions by the UN General Assembly, had the effect of focusing attention once more on the victims of armed conflicts—and the means and methods of warfare that produced the victims. It was this concern for ''human rights in armed conflicts,'' expressed through the UN, that started the wheels rolling again for further development of jus in bello.[7]

Stimulated by UN developments, the ICRC intensified its efforts in the late 1960's to supplement the 1949 Conventions. Noting that the Red Cross Conferences had endorsed such efforts long before 1968, the ICRC sought to maintain its position as legal secretariat for law pertaining to victims of armed conflict. Although the Human Rights Division of the UN Secretariat was also interested in the question, after a period of some uncertainty about who was to do what a division of labor was agreed upon, and the ICRC was once again given the job of preparing for a diplomatic conference.

This endorsement of the ICRC as host for preparatory meetings and drafter of legal documents was strongly supported by the Western group of states, and some other states, that lacked confidence in certain aspects of the UN system. There was strong feeling among Western governments that the ICRC should once again be given this role of helping to develop law because of a desire to avoid, as much as possible, the ''politicization'' of the legislative process by the third-world majority in the General Assembly. Moreover, the ICRC was presumed to have expertise on these matters not found within the UN system.[8] Other states agreed for reasons of tradition, deference to the West, the ICRC's image of expertise, or apathy.

In any event a significant movement started in the late 1960's to improve the law in armed conflict, with the ICRC involved in an important way.

Strategy

At the outset of this legislative process a significant decision had to be made by the ICRC and other participants: what should be the basic form of law sought? Should one write a new convention or conventions? Should one revise the 1949 Conventions? Should one add protocols to those Conventions? If so, how many?

The ICRC was somewhat cynical about the intentions of states and thus believed the 1949 Conventions should not be directly altered. In those Conventions rested the cumulative efforts toward legal development of some ninety years. It had taken so long to get so much law on the books. The ICRC feared that if the 1949 Conventions were opened to revision, or were superseded by a new Convention, states would take either opportunity to reduce their legal obligations. If, on the other hand, one added protocols to those Conventions, then the 1949 law remained valid for all those not accepting the protocols, and for those points not covered by the new protocols. Thus to preserve what had been gained in 1949, the ICRC opted for protocols, which have the same legal effect as conventions.

The ICRC also believed the two-protocol approach was the most realistic. Thus it proposed one protocol for international and one for intrastate armed conflicts. It was the ICRC's view, buttressed by interaction with government officials, that most states would insist on a legal distinction between international and noninternational war. Some ICRC officials knew that such a distinction in situations like Indochina was difficult and perhaps impossible to make. But it was the ICRC's judgment that governments demanded that distinction in order to accept less regulation of their actions when dealing with what appeared on the surface to be domestic challenges. The ICRC accepted as a fact of life that the law in armed conflicts was structured not solely for the victims of those conflicts but because of state interests in "sovereignty" and "domestic jurisdiction."[9]

The ICRC believed it was better to get *some* law based on a two-protocol approach, than no law because of insistence on a one-protocol approach covering all armed conflict that would not be accepted by states. Like its applied protection and assistance, ICRC legal development efforts utilized the incremental approach. Small improvements, even if accompanied by distasteful elements, were preferred over the pursuit of large objectives that might meet total failure.

As for the number of protocols, the ICRC was content to stop at two, like many other participants, for fear of overloading the diplomatic conference. There was a concern expressed by the ICRC—and others—that if too many subjects were legislated at one time, the entire legislative process would collapse under the weight of controversy.

Such were the choices facing the ICRC at the start of the attempt to improve the law in armed conflict. They were not the decisions that made headlines, but they were crucial choices as far as the legislative process was concerned, and they were choices that would have future importance for individuals caught up in armed conflicts.

Needless to say, the ICRC alone did not make these decisions. But the ICRC had significant influence, difficult to measure precisely, in their making. The ICRC did have a reputation for legal expertise on these matters, and a number of states tended to defer to ICRC preferences regarding formulation of a legal instrument. Moreover, the ICRC was responsible for the early drafting of proposed instruments and the articles contained therein. Once formulated, the basic approach was changed in its broad outlines only with difficulty, even if specific articles were amended comparatively easily.

Of course not all parties agreed with ICRC preferences on these subjects.

Some believed it was a mistake to retain the 1949 Conventions untouched, either because those instruments were so complex or out of date. Some believed a one-protocol or mini-convention approach was preferable to the two-protocol approach, for the sake of simplicity and equal protection for victims of all armed conflict. Some wanted at least three protocols rather than two, with the subject of weapons covered in a third protocol.

Nevertheless, the ICRC based its strategy on majority sentiment, and legislative efforts in the late 1960's and 1970's occurred on the basis of two ICRC draft protocols, to be added to the four Conventions of 1949.

This ICRC strategy for legal development was thus conservative, in the sense of being cautious or prudent. The ICRC was seeking change without losing what had been gained in the past, as compared to risking some loss of old law in order to achieve new law. It was also conservative strategy in the sense of seeking to create the type of legal instrument that a majority could accept at the outset of the legislative process, rather than seeking an instrument desired by the minority but negatively viewed by the majority. Hence the ICRC sought new law on the basis of conventional thinking and a common denominator that could lead to universal acceptance, rather than pushing for a legal instrument viewed by some as highly controversial and likely to be rejected or to meet heavy reservations.

Those supporting the ICRC's stand on the shape of legislation argued that a conservative strategy was correct in the delicate matter of getting parties to accept regulation of situations involving violence. Law in armed conflict was said to be inherently a subject viewed with skepticism. Where a party was concerned enough about issues to use violence, it was argued that party was not likely to view restrictions on his employment of violence with great relish. Those criticizing the ICRC's stand argued that the outcome of the legislative process would be more law that was overcomplex and irrelevant to the situations it was supposed to regulate. It was said the law would be out of date when legislated. It was argued by some of these that only a simple instrument pertaining to all armed conflict would in fact be applied.[10]

As frequently is the case with these matters, there was disagreement as to what was, on the one hand, realistic, and on the other hand idealistic or legalistic. Was it realistic to be cautious and idealistic to be bold? Or was it realistic to be bold and legalistic to be cautious?

Tactics and Substance

In the past, the tactics of the ICRC in its legal development efforts can also be called conservative, although the substance of what it has proposed has not always been cautious or conventional.

It can be said that the ICRC has employed conservative tactics because it has not acted as an overt lobbyist so much as a drafting secretariat. In general it has not directly and overtly argued in favor of a specific law and worked for its adoption. Rather, the ICRC has tended to use the wording of draft articles and commentary on those articles to exercise indirect influence. The ICRC has tried to exercise influence informally at times, through such steps as private conversations with various delegates. But in general it has believed that its opportunity for direct lobbying is severely restricted by the determination of states to control the content of the law. While the ICRC is proud of its record in helping to produce the Geneva Conventions, and while some circles refer to those Conventions as Red Cross law, the ICRC likes to emphasize that the Conventions are state law, not its law.

A number of observers, especially in the West but also in the Third World, believe the ICRC has greatly underestimated its own potential for exercising influence in support of law for armed conflict.

For its part, the ICRC has believed that only on certain subjects can it intervene vigorously and overtly in the legislative process. It believes, as previously indicated, that most subjects must be left to states. On some subjects, particularly those related directly to Red Cross agencies, such as detention visits or provision of relief, the ICRC believes it has grounds for speaking out—although at the diplomatic conference on humanitarian law that began in 1974 it was the League and national societies that tended to be engaged in overt lobbying on these subjects, with the ICRC being drawn into this process by the initiative of other Red Cross actors. On a few subjects the ICRC itself has taken a strong and clear position, such as its role in supervising the law (covered below in some detail).

Precisely because the ICRC did have this view of matters and did therefore use conservative tactics in the late 1960's and 1970's, it is difficult to judge whether it had perceived matters correctly or, conversely, whether it had failed to take maximum advantage of its influence. It was true that some delegates desired a more active ICRC—a sentiment reflected in a Canadian's statement to this author: ''When the ICRC speaks, absolutely everybody listens; it should speak more.'' It was also true that League officials, along with officials from various national societies, had taken the lead on certain matters, had secured the cooperation of key states for what they wanted, and had successfully affected the two protocols. It was also observable that prior to the convening of the diplomatic conference the ICRC had not launched any major effort to get support from the national societies for an ICRC point of view on particular matters.[11]

On at least one major subject in the 1970's the ICRC did *not* pursue conservative tactics, but spoke openly and with vigor. The substance of its position, however, was conservative. This ICRC position was highly influential in the bargaining and debate at the 1975 session of the conference. The subject was the Protecting Power system, and the ICRC was strongly opposed to becoming an automatic supervisor of the law. It was willing to supervise only with the expressed and specific consent of a belligerent—not automatically. Despite strong urging by a number of states—e.g., Belgium and the Netherlands—the ICRC clung to its desire to act only in a situation where a fighting party gave its consent. This deference to state authority eventually was written into draft protocol 1.

The subject is important and merits detailed attention.[12]

The Protecting Power system as found in the 1949 law provides for the appointment of neutral states as Protecting Powers in order to help belligerents to implement the law. If these Protecting Powers or state-appointed substitutes are not appointed in a situation of international armed conflict, three options are open to the ICRC under the 1949 law. Either it can formally offer its services as a substitute for the Protecting Power, in which case the belligerent has a legal obligation to accept the ICRC's offer. Or the ICRC can offer its services not as a formal substitute but simply as a humanitarian agency that has certain "traditional humanitarian activities" to perform, to be exercised with the consent of the belligerents. Or the ICRC can offer to perform certain specific tasks such as "automatic" inspection of places of detention.[13]

In a noninternational armed conflict, the ICRC may offer its services to the parties, but they have no legal obligation to accept.

In the history of things since 1949, states have been clearly appointed as Protecting Powers in only two armed conflicts, the Suez affair of 1956 and the Goa incident of 1961. (In the 1971 war for Bangladesh, Switzerland was named a Protecting Power among the belligerents but was not a full Protecting Power in the view of India.) In all these cases, the ICRC continued to protect and assist individuals according to its traditional activities, despite some role for neutral states.

In all other situations of armed conflict, Protecting Powers have not been appointed to see that the Geneva Conventions are implemented. In this context, the ICRC has become an *unofficial* substitute for the Protecting Power. It has sought the implementation of the Conventions in the position of performing its traditional tasks. It has not in general offered itself as a formal substitute for the Protecting Power, a move which, according to legal theory, requires the state in an international armed conflict to accept that offer. Only in 1972, in dealing with Middle Eastern states, did the ICRC clearly offer itself as a full and formal substitute for a Protecting Power. There was, in the view of the ICRC, no affirmative response.

Against this historical background, the subject of the supervision of humanitarian law arose in the Geneva diplomatic conference that began in 1974. There was general awareness that the Protecting Power system had not been used as intended. But the subject of what change to make became highly controversial.

A number of states wanted the ICRC to be an *automatic* substitute for the Protecting Power where such was not appointed.[14] The ICRC overtly and strongly opposed this move, despite the argument that such a change would improve the implementation of humanitarian law. The ICRC strongly believed that it should not be thrust upon a state in a situation of armed conflict where that state might oppose a role for the ICRC. The ICRC was prepared to assume all the duties of a full and formal substitute, but only with the specific consent of the parties. A general consent, expressed through ratification of the treaty, would not suffice for the ICRC. It did not want to accept the role of automatic policeman. It preferred the role of voluntarily accepted legal adviser.[15]

This strongly held position by the ICRC in the negotiations weakened the movement for an automatic supervision of the law, for it was only the ICRC that stood any chance of being accepted as an automatic supervisor. The UN was unacceptable to many parties, and a representative of the UN Secretariat himself stated in a working group at the 1975 session that the UN should not assume that task. No other NGO besides the ICRC had consistently supervised the Geneva Conventions. It would be the ICRC or nobody.

Once the ICRC had stated its opposition to automaticity, and since the East European delegations were also strongly opposed to that concept, the Western and Third World states in favor of automaticity via the ICRC were left in a poor bargaining position. A consensus was finally reached, requiring states to consult with the ICRC about the appointment of Protecting Powers, and to accept the ICRC as a substitute for Protecting Powers; the ICRC would not offer itself unless the party agreed in advance to accept the ICRC or another impartial humanitarian body.[16]

In its arguments in 1974 about substitutes for the Protecting Power, the ICRC used overt lobbying; the substance of its position was deference to specific state consent. This outspoken demand for specific consent rather than automaticity in the operation of the substitute for a Protecting Power solidified the East European bargaining position, which became the controlling argument (as a general and nontechnical statement).

On other subjects, too, the ICRC has at times taken a highly active stand. The subject of legislation on weapons presents an interesting example. The ICRC has been intermittently active with regard to the weapons question. When active, the substance of ICRC lobbying has verged on the radical, so radical, indeed, that certain observers were led to question the political astuteness of the institution.

For much of its history, the ICRC regarded weapons as somebody else's business, unless there was an exceptional reason to view the subject otherwise. When the ICRC was getting under way in the 1860's, others were already at work on such subjects as the legal status of dumdum bullets and other weapons that might cause unnecessary suffering or have indiscriminate effects. And the ICRC had more than enough work to do in developing law for victims such as the wounded, the sick, the detained, the civilian in a war zone. Where there seemed exceptional reason to become concerned with the legal regulation or prohibition of some weapon, the ICRC did so. The institution supported efforts to ban poisonous and asphyxiating gases in the mid-1920's. But by and large the ICRC regarded weapons, along with methods of attack, as subjects not in the Geneva tradition.[17]

The development of atomic and nuclear weapons caused the ICRC to depart from its traditional orientation and directly approach the question of the legal status of certain weapons. The use of high-yield atomic or nuclear weapons in a large-scale war would render the Geneva Conventions meaningless, and the ICRC knew it.

In the mid-1950's the ICRC expressed clearly its changed approach to legal development efforts:

> The ICRC draws attention to the danger of the Geneva Conventions remaining inoperative if the belligerents are not limited in any way in their choice of weapons or methods of warfare. It had already asked, in its Appeal of April 1950, ''how blind weapons could spare hospitals, prisoner of war camps and the civilian population''?
>
> This concern about the means of waging war is not recent. It is true that, to begin with, and later when extending the Geneva Convention, the Red Cross endeavored to ensure the protection of certain categories of individuals, without attaching primary importance to the manner in which hostilities were conducted. The time has come, however, when it has to consider the dangers with which the victims with whom it is concerned, and non-combatants in general, are inevitably threatened, through the terrifying developments in the means of waging war.[18]

While the ''time had come'' for the ICRC to try to stimulate legislation on weapons, the time had not come for governments to respond positively to ICRC overtures on this subject. Part of the problem was that the ICRC seemed to be seeking a total prohibition on the use of weapons relied upon by the major states for their security. The key provision in the ICRC's *Draft Rules for the Limitation of the Dangers Incurred by the Civilian Population in Time of War,* presented to the International Red Cross Conference in 1957, was Article 14:

> Without prejudice to the present or future prohibition of certain specific weapons, the use is prohibited of weapons whose harmful effects—resulting in particular from the dissemination of incendiary, chemical, bacteriological, radioactive or other agents—could spread to an unforeseen degree or escape, either in space or in time, from the control of those who employ them, thus endangering the civilian population.
>
> This prohibition also applies to delayed-action weapons, the dangerous effects of which are liable to be felt by the civilian population.[19]

Any weapon with an uncontrolled radioactive fallout, for instance, would thus be prohibited from use. As such, this proposal came at a time when the Soviet Union had rejected the Baruch Plan for the control of nuclear weapons, put forward by the United States at the end of World War II, and had decided to seek nuclear parity with the U.S.; when the U.S. and its NATO allies had adopted the doctrine of massive retaliation based on nuclear weapons; and when China had decided to develop nuclear weapons.

That being the case, the ICRC's draft rules received perfunctory debate at the Red Cross Conference and nothing more. And that being the case, the ICRC returned to its previous orientation of legislating for victims without attention to the legal status of weapons and methods of combat. While it is not recorded in any document, there was widespread belief that the ICRC had been naive in its approach to the weapons question, had no real experts on the subject despite its consulting with experts,[20] and had damaged its image by its rather simplistic foray into the weapons subject.

It is probable that the ICRC itself drew some of the same conclusions, for after its lack of success in the mid-1950's it avoided the subject of means and methods of combat insofar as legislation efforts were concerned. In actual protection operations the ICRC was certainly concerned about means and methods of attack. In situations of armed conflict like Vietnam it raised the question of means and methods both publicly and privately.[21] But for some twenty years after the mid-1950's the ICRC developed no further proposals for any kind of weapons legislation. Indeed, when Sweden and some other governments sought to include legislation on specific weapons in the diplomatic conference of the mid-1970's, to a number of parties the ICRC seemed unenthusiastic—not only because of the fear of overloading the conference with controversial subjects, but also because of its earlier difficulties on the subject.

Sweden and other governments pushed for inclusion of the weapons question.[22] One of the primary concerns of these governments was napalm, and since the United States had used so much napalm in Vietnam, the primary objective of Sweden was to get the U.S. to agree to discuss weapons which might cause unnecessary suffering or have indiscriminate effects. This the U.S. agreed to do if the meetings were held under the aegis of the ICRC rather than the United Nations. Sweden agreed, and thus the ICRC became involved in the weapons question once again by virtue of this Swedish-American accord, to which the Soviet Union was added, and to which the ICRC assented.[23]

In the meantime, the ICRC had willingly produced a number of draft articles in its two draft protocols pertaining to methods of attack, in an attempt further to protect the civilian population. Thus the ICRC was certainly ready to undertake a legislative effort for the further protection of noncombatants, even if it had reservations about tackling once more the problem of specific weapons.

The ICRC did host meetings of government experts to discuss certain conventional weapons that might cause unnecessary suffering or have indiscriminate effects, did supply legal staff for those meetings, and did handle the publication of reports. But its role was a very quiescent one. It was ready to record a consensus and to facilitate negotiations among governments. But it had no in-house experts on the subject. It had not been out in the Geneva countryside shooting sheep with M-16 rifles to see if their projectiles had the same effects as dumdum bullets. In general the ICRC had little or nothing to offer as an expert lobbyist on the subject of weapons, but was simply a drafting legal secretariat.

Therefore, the ICRC's tactics in legislating humanitarian law for armed conflict have been generally conservative, although there is a difference in the initiative and assertiveness of the ICRC according to subjects being discussed. The issues on which the ICRC is highly active in a direct and overt way, such as the Protecting Power system, are few. The issues on which it is a moderately active lobbyist have been usually linked to its area of expertise in making prison visits and providing material and medical assistance, and are still relatively few in number. Its approach is usually indirect—the writing of draft articles and commentary. The issues—like the weapons question in the 1970's—on which the ICRC is a drafting secretariat, recording and formulating governmental consensus, are many.

It bears repeating that in legal development matters, the drafting of articles and the writing of commentary are points of leverage for the exercise of some influence, even if that influence is circumscribed by state policy.

On those issues where the ICRC does take a clear stand in support of specific law, the institution finds it difficult to do so and yet maintain an image of impartiality. Even if the ICRC is motivated by a concern for what it thinks is the best approach to humanitarian law, some party or another is likely to accuse it of being partial. This was the case in the 1975 negotiations on the Protecting Power system. Ironically, it was a number of Western delegations, normally supportive of the ICRC, that made representations to it urging a more neutral demeanor on the part of ICRC legal officials. Several Western delegations thought the ICRC was unnecessarily associating itself with specific Eastern European bargaining positions. These Western delegations were arguing that if the Eastern European states ratified the additional protocols as the West would like them to be formulated, without reservations, the East Europeans would be indicating, ipso facto, consent for the ICRC as automatic substitute; thus the ICRC would have its expression of consent. When an ICRC official associated himself with a Ukraine proposal requiring specific rather than general consent, a number of Western delegations became unhappy.

Overt lobbying by the ICRC is clearly a difficult process, even on subjects where states expect it to express its view. And on subjects where states expect the ICRC to have less reason to assert itself, overt lobbying is even more difficult. Some states still see the international legislative process as a process for *state* decision, even on humanitarian law in armed conflicts where the ICRC is accepted as a legitimate participant. ICRC participation has been primarily expected in the hosting of meetings, the drafting of articles, the writing of the commentary, the giving of legal advice when asked—the speaking-out on a few subjects.

The ICRC, however, has not made much effort recently to expand expectations about its legitimate role in legislative efforts and a legitimate conception of humanitarian impartiality. In particular, the ICRC has not worked closely with national societies in order to expand governmental perspectives on what the

ICRC should do. Many Red Cross officials attend diplomatic conferences as governmental officials—sometimes as head or assistant head of delegation. The ICRC has not consistently utilized this situation to produce governmental support for ICRC desires. Nor has the ICRC tried to suggest that impartial humanitarianism permits the taking of specific stands on the basis of pure humanitarian motivation, even if such a stand might lend support to a particular coalition of governments. After all, governments are familiar with such a conception of impartiality from the days of Dag Hammarskjöld at the United Nations, and many governments supported his conception of neutrality based on commitment to the principles of the Charter. The ICRC could try the same approach to impartiality, based on Red Cross principles.[24]

As for the substance of ICRC tactical stands, this varies considerably. As noted on the weapons question, the ICRC in the 1950's had a radical stand aimed at making all high-yield nuclear weapons illegal; by the 1970's this had changed to no concrete policy stand at all, but rather a general endorsement of legislative efforts against weapons that might cause unnecessary suffering or have indiscriminate effects. On the question of substitutes for Protecting Powers, the ICRC in the 1970's had a very conservative stand, refusing to support those states that wished to give it authority to supervise the law automatically. By contrast, in the 1920's the ICRC had itself proposed that it be given the authority, automatically, to appoint substitutes.[25]

The substance of the law of armed conflict is now immense, making it difficult to chart all ICRC tactical positions. Further research might well explore the question of whether the substance of ICRC decisions related to legislation is now more conservative than previously. On some subjects, such as law to regulate internal armed conflict, the ICRC has been more progressive than most states, as will be seen below.

LIMITS TO ICRC LEGISLATIVE EFFORTS

ICRC legislative efforts have always been linked to jus in bello, law in war. The ICRC has consciously chosen to avoid two other areas of legislation: (1) law pertaining to the start of war, and (2) civil rights legislation in times of peace.

Jus Ad Bellum

With regard to law for the start of war, *jus ad bellum,* the ICRC has consistently maintained its distance from that subject. It has consistently stressed the difference between jus ad bellum and jus in bello, for that distinction is fundamental to the ICRC's humanitarian protection and assistance efforts under law. Whatever the judgments about who started war and why, the ICRC argues that certain humanitarian values should be implemented by all to all.

Therefore the ICRC has tried to avoid all legal questions dealing with "just wars," aggression, self-defense, and intervention. There is a long line of philosophical and legal thought about jus ad bellum (see figure 5.2). But the ICRC has undertaken no legislative efforts on this subject. However much it may be dedicated to peace philosophically, its actions are linked to conflict; and its legislative actions are linked to armed conflict.

The ICRC has believed for some time, or perhaps been compelled to argue, that its work in jus in bello makes a contribution to peace indirectly. It has been argued that implementation of humanitarian law under conditions of reciprocity facilitates understanding among the conflicting parties and thus hastens an end to the conflict. The argument is that if the conflicting parties implement humanitarian law and cooperate with the ICRC, a basis is laid for a rapid return to peace. In broader context, it is also argued that cooperation among national Red Cross Societies on all sorts of programs improves international communication and understanding, thus making an indirect contribution to peace.

Somewhat cynically, it has been privately argued by some governmental officials that the ICRC has such an extensive view of humanitarian law in armed conflict that the ICRC and "its law" are getting in the way of the process of war. It would follow from this argument that the ICRC is making a surreptitious contribution to peace by so restricting parties in the conduct of war as to make war impossible as a viable means of state policy.

Whatever the merits of these arguments about the ICRC and peace, it remains a historical fact that ICRC legislative efforts have dealt with the process of war—armed conflict. Efforts to prohibit war or to regulate its commencement have been left to others.

The ICRC is under some pressure from elements within the Red Cross

Figure 5.2.   International Law and Violence

Law of armed conflict, or *jus in bello* (law regulating process of war)	Law of peace, or *jus ad [contra] bellum* (law regulating commencement of war)
Customary law and Geneva, Hague, and Nuremberg traditions of statutory law	"Just War" Doctrine League of Nations Covenant Kellogg—Briand Pact United Nations Charter Nuremberg tradition (pertaining to crimes against peace) UN debates and resolutions on aggression, and principles of friendly relations.[1]

[1] UN debates and resolutions have inferior legal status compared to treaty law and to events such as the Nuremberg Trials.

movement to alter its orientation. But it is extremely doubtful that the ICRC could retain an image of impartiality and yet take any meaningful and specific action on the peace-war question. While most people who are not barbarians are in favor of peace at the general level, the real question is, whose peace, specifically? The general commitment to peace breaks down into conflict over which form of peace, leaving what elites in control, over what territory. It is not very helpful to be "for peace in the Middle East." At the level of specific action one has to make a judgment about peace on whose terms: with or without the state of Israel, with or without a Palestinian state, with what rights for whom in the Suez Canal, etc. To take a stand on these judgments, the ICRC would destroy its acceptability as an impartial and humanitarian intermediary.

One can be against aggression in the abstract without much difficulty, but the real question is whether one can recognize it in a specific situation, differentiate it from defensive action, and take action to oppose it. The ICRC has wisely refrained from getting involved on these issues, for it well understands the difficulties inherent in specific choice.[26]

Now this stand against direct involvement in peace-war questions, however much it may be based on an accurate understanding of impartial humanitarianism, can lead to misperception and misunderstanding in the ICRC's legislative efforts. This occurred at the 1974 session of the Geneva diplomatic conference on humanitarian law. Certain individuals at the ICRC interpreted some non-Western proposals as the introduction of peace-war issues into humanitarian law. This was not the only view possible.

At that 1974 session, and before, there was debate on the issue of what was, in law, to be the definition of an international armed conflict. To know when the ICRC draft protocol on international armed conflict applied, that is to say, to know when it was to become the controlling law, one had to say what factual situation activated the law. The traditional law up to that time had used a geo-military definition of an international armed conflict. A certain level of violence, produced usually by states, had to be factually present, or regular troops of a foreign state had to enter the conflict, before the factual situation called for the application of the full international law of armed conflict.[27]

A large number of third-world states, and with lesser enthusiasm the socialist states, wanted to add an additional criterion to the definition. In addition to the geo-military criterion, these states wanted wars of national liberation, and wars against colonial, racist and occupying regimes, also to be included as international armed conflict. This additioanl part of the definition was opposed by most of the Western states, who argued, in part, that such a proposal was a "just war argument" which interjected principles of jus ad bellum into jus in bello. The leading Western states argued that the Third World proposal interjected subjective considerations about the cause of violence into what should be an objective judgment based on levels of violence and crossing of boundaries.

The ICRC's draft protocols used the Western rather than third-world approach. These draft protocols were heavily influenced by the active participation of Western legal experts in the long drafting process. For example, at the 1971 meeting of government experts, states from the North Atlantic-Western Europe area numbered 16; those from Latin America, 3; Africa, 4; Asia, 5; the Middle East, 5; and Eastern Europe, 6. Moreover, the "delegation" from Kenya was one man; that of the United States contained 15. Burundi sent 2 people; the government of Switzerland 7.

Now from the outset of the drafting process the ICRC had attempted to produce an international, cross cultural grouping of experts. In February of 1969, the ICRC had invited nongovernmental experts from 25 different states plus the UN. Only 9 of these were from the North Atlantic-Western European region. But the richer West sent more, better-trained people to all of the experts' meetings between 1969 and 1974. And in general the Western states took the process more seriously than others. The result was that the ICRC draft protocols were heavily influenced by Western views.

But while Western states were influencing the ICRC's draft protocols, with the willing participation of the ICRC, the more numerous third-world and socialist states were adopting resolutions in the UN General Assembly calling for liberation fighters to be considered as prisoners of war, for example. This "UN approach" to what was a prisoner of war entailed the judgment that a war of national liberation was an international armed conflict. It was introduced into the 1974 session of the conference on humanitarian law, as might have been expected. The same governments that had voted in the General Assembly were the governments attending the Geneva Conference. By calling the Geneva Conference a conference on humanitarian law, one did not change the views of governments on how they approached the issues.

Nevertheless, the ICRC's draft protocols failed to anticipate majority sentiment on a definition of an international armed conflict. The ICRC's draft article on the subject ignored the UN resolutions, except for a footnote offering a second-choice formulation which was far short of what the third world wanted. In general, the ICRC forgot the maxim that the driving force behind law was not logic but life's experiences. While it might be more logical—at least to the Western mind—to maintain the traditional definition, the new definition did not destroy humanitarian law but rather could result in the extension of that law.

The third world was not arguing that colonial, racist, and occupying regimes had no legal rights; rather, the argument was that these regimes had to apply the full international law of armed conflict even if the level of violence was not great or regular foreign troops had not crossed a boundary.

It was a "messy" definition that was desired by the third world, for it wanted a modified norm of justice to be added to the traditional geo-military norm. And it was subjective; after all, what was a war of national liberation—could the Kurds in Iraq qualify, or Eritreans in Ethiopia? And what about a racist regime: certainly South Africa would fit that label, but what about Uganda and Burundi? But for all its faults, it was not the kind of argument launched by North Vietnam, to the effect that its opponents had no legal rights (see below, note 28.) Thus the third-world position was not detrimental to humanitarian values.

It was politicians's law rather than lawyer's law, and since the ICRC's lawyers were not politicians they did not appreciate the third-world proposals very much. The ICRC's draft law on the subject was associated with Western arguments and was the focal point of a long wrangle at the 1974 session. The third-world position carried the day, and the ICRC was widely viewed as out of touch with political reality, although the ICRC never formally opposed the third world.

Third-world arguments that wars of national liberation are international armed conflicts may be bad law from the Western lawyer's point of view, but there is reason to query why the ICRC paid so little attention to the UN approach. (1) The old definition inherently worked to the advantage of South Africa and Rhodesia, since under the old definition, they did not have to pay attention to the law of international armed conflict with regard to opposition fighters unless violence escalated to a high level. Since a choice was inherent for the ICRC if it made a specific proposal (it had to come down for or against the law's applying to these regimes), the question can be raised whether it was diplomatically wise for the ICRC to do what it did. (2) The old definition was more restrictive of the field of humanitarian law than the proposed definition, and it can be asked if the ICRC should not have favored the broadest possible definition of a prisoner of war. (3) The old definition, too, was subjective, in that it did not specify what level of violence exactly had to be present for an international armed conflict legally to exist. The old definition was vague and thus subject to varying state interpretations based on self-interest. Since it was not a matter of departing from a specific norm that had been widely applied without controversy, it can be asked if the ICRC position were well conceived. (4) And since the new definition would probably not lead to profound changes in behavior in the future, the question can be raised as to whether the damage done to the ICRC's image in the third world and Eastern Europe was worth that damage. It was hard to conceive of, say, South Africa agreeing that its opponents in battle were indeed a national liberation movement entitled to the full protection of humanitarian international law. Thus one would continue to have competing legal arguments about the overall nature of the conflict (national liberation movement vs. domestic treason and subversion to be regulated by national law.) Since there would be no authoritative third party to make a binding judgment on the competing claims, the question can be asked whether the ICRC should have allowed itself to be associated with the Western position. The new law would not be automatically implemented in any event. (As the ICRC had done on other controversial draft articles, it could have formulated two drafts without giving a preference, letting states choose in the conference.)

Therefore, while the ICRC has been opposed to interjecting considerations of ''just war'' into legislative efforts for jus in bello, it does not follow that it is wise for the ICRC to oppose everything that Western governments call a ''just war argument.'' There are ''just wars'' and ''just wars.'' That is to say, while the ICRC could never accept the point of view articulated by North Vietnam in 1974 without destroying itself as an impartial and humanitarian intermediary,[28] the ICRC could indeed learn to live with the third-world definition of an international armed conflict.

The legislative process for international humanitarian law in armed conflicts, like other legislative processes, is a *political* process in the basic sense of that word. Legislation inherently entails a struggle to make public policy. The humanitarian lawyer, no less than other participants in the legislative process, must—if he is to be sophisticated—be aware of the necessity for policy choice and for an evaluation of the costs and benefits entailed in any choice.

Human Rights Law in General

The ICRC has also consistently tried to avoid not only jus ad bellum but also legislation pertaining to civil rights not in time of armed conflict. The ICRC has tried to draw a sharp distinction between humanitarian law in armed conflicts and other ''human rights'' law.[29]

With regard to ''human rights law in peace,'' there is a difference between ICRC legislative efforts and operational efforts. On the one hand the ICRC avoids such questions as whether the law under which detention occurs meets generally accepted criteria for legitimacy (assuming that judgment can be made) and whether judicial due process has been pursued. On the other hand the ICRC, operationally, is much concerned with protecting and assisting political prisoners and hostages. Therefore its avoidance of the *legal* issues outside the scope of armed conflict is accompanied by operational interest in all sorts of situations touching upon human rights in peace. Where there appears to be a violation of human rights not in time of armed conflict, the ICRC may very well be involved operationally in an effort to respond to the needs arising out of the violation. But it still avoids questions of causation and their attendant legal dimensions. (The avoidance of causation is similar to avoidance of jus ad bellum.)

This second self-limitation in the legislative efforts of the ICRC is, like the first, a product of experience in international politics. If the ICRC does not challenge the legitimacy of national laws and does not question their content, the ICRC stands a better chance of trying to help the individuals that may need help. If the ICRC raised the questions of whether administrative detention should exist at all, or whether habeas corpus can legitimately be suspended, or whether the taking of hostages is really necessary and permissible, the ICRC would lessen its chances of being able to help the people that need it. The ICRC gets to see the unsavory ''backyards'' of a number of regimes by skipping these legal questions.[30]

While the ICRC is frequently criticized for not extending its conception of protection far enough to challenge the national laws under which detention occurs, the ICRC maintains its conviction that it should continue with ad hoc diplomacy on certain subjects and skip the legal issues. The ICRC tends to see itself as a kind of humanitarian ombudsman on these matters, trying to improve the situation for individuals through private negotiation rather than formal legislation. It points to frontal attacks on alleged violations of human rights by the Council of Europe in Greece and the United Nations in South Africa, and the ICRC draws the conclusion that frontal, legal challenges to national law do not get far by way of improving things for the individuals in question.

Should there emerge a clear conception of political prisoner, should there emerge a political will to regulate internationally that type of individual, along with effective prohibition of the taking of hostages, the ICRC could remove its self-imposed limitation on legislative efforts. In the meantime, the ICRC does not think individuals will be much helped by raising questions in international law that constitute a frontal attack on governments' claims to domestic jurisdiction.

ICRC LEGISLATIVE EFFORTS: CONCLUSIONS

The ICRC has provided a valuable service in its legislative efforts since the early 1860's. Its efforts in this domain have led to greater humanitarian protection and assistance in armed conflicts for individuals, as will be demonstrated in the following two chapters. Its efforts have, in large part, both caused states to face questions in this area and made it easier for them to reach agreement on the questions.

Despite past achievements for the ICRC in its legislative efforts, the institution is facing, and will face, criticisms of its work in this domain. Some observers are already demanding a de-emphasis in ICRC legal development work—at least a de-emphasis on the development of *traditional* international law—viz., law based on national sovereignty (ultimate authority by the nation-state). This demand for de-emphasis results from two interrelated arguments.

Politicization

First of all, the legislative process for humanitarian law in armed conflict has been heavily politicized, even beyond the politics inherent in that process.

The legislative process is inherently a political process, in the sense that conferences to develop humanitarian law entail struggle to make public policy. This simple point, so evident to many observers and participants in the process, has not always been fully appreciated by some elements of the ICRC. These European-trained lawyers, some with philosophical orientations, have not fully appreciated the extent to which a legal choice even on humanitarian subjects entails a judgment about policy that can work to the advantage of some but not to others. Thus a norm regarding the rights of national Red Cross Societies to provide medical and material assistance in an armed conflict entails a judgment as to the extent of governmental control over domestic and foreign private agencies, and results in a struggle over whose view is to prevail. The making of humanitarian law is not one in which men of goodwill solely consider the needs of the victims of war, reaching agreement on the basis of humanitarian reason triumphant. It is a political process, first of all, in this basic meaning of "politics": whose view is to prevail, backed by what power and authority.

Beyond this inherent political element, the legislative process has been heavily politicized in that elements of realpolitik have been interjected directly into the process. States not only struggle because of disagreements over such things as extent of legitimate governmental control compared to rights of international organizations or transnational movements; they struggle also in an effort to strengthen the power of their group and weaken the power of an opponent.

India spent much of the 1974 session of the diplomatic conference trying to make law that would weaken the power of South Africa, Rhodesia, and Israel, among other things. These states would, in the Indian view, have to meet certain humanitarian norms regarding respect for civilians and combatants that might hamper or encumber their military efforts in dealing with "national liberation movements" struggling against colonial, racist, or occupying regimes.

At the 1975 session, India spent much time in opposing proposed law that might apply to it. Having been energetic in trying to make law that would apply to *others* and limit *their* domestic jurisdiction (through Indian support for the amendment extending the full range of the international law of armed conflict to wars of national liberation), the Indians then opposed almost all aspects of the entire second protocol pertaining to noninternational armed conflicts. The Indians were fearful that the second protocol would limit *them* in dealing with various violent situations in India.[31] The Indian position was not unique, shared as it was by many of the Afro-Asian delegations.

That a humanitarian legal conference in the mid-1970's should become emeshed in realpolitik was not surprising. At approximately the same time, UNESCO (United Nations Educational, Scientific, and Cultural Organization) was undergoing the same politicization. The Afro-Asian states were voting to bar Israel from certain rights, and "the North-West" was responding by curtailing its contributions to UNESCO. Thus the old distinctions between what was "political" and "nonpolitical" were breaking down. ICRC efforts to call itself nonpolitical and to say that humanitarian law was outside the political arena were efforts out of step with the tendency to use all organizations and meetings as weapons in realpolitik struggles.

That being the case, there were demands for the ICRC to "mothball" projected legislation, to wait for a more propitious time, or at least to seek legal development on a regional rather than global basis. In general, there was a growing belief that the long struggle to develop law in the 1970's was not worth the effort expended. The protocols, it was argued, would not be accepted by many parties because of certain articles produced on the basis of realpolitik considerations.

The ICRC, however, believed in incremental improvements and seemed willing to accept certain disadvantages along with a growth in the law. To the ICRC, imperfect law was the only law that existed.

Traditionalism

Criticism of the ICRC for helping to produce politicized law was accompanied by criticism for producing traditional law. The ICRC is a humanitarian NGO, but it has helped produce law that is heavily concerned with national sovereignty and domestic jurisdiction of states rather than humanitarian values. Thus the ICRC has been strongly criticized for helping develop traditional law based on the interests of nation-states, rather than transnational or supranational law based more decidedly on humanitarian values.[32]

For example, many states desired a second protocol pertaining to noninternational armed conflicts with a very "high threshold" of violence necessary for application of the protocol. That is, they wanted a protocol that would only be applied if some degree of territory were held for some time by the challengers in a noninternational armed conflict, or if sanctuaries for the challengers were present within the given country, or if some other relatively stringent requirement were met.

Now the ICRC wanted a second protocol permitting the international law of noninternational armed conflict to be applied more frequently rather than less; it wanted a "low threshold" of violence so that international humanitarian law and its protection would be as easily available to victims as possible. The majority of states preferred the high threshold, and if that becomes law, then the ICRC is expected to abide by that law after its coming into force, even though it was law fashioned to extend states' domestic jurisdiction and to reduce the field of application of humanitarian law.[33]

The ICRC does have the so-called right of initiative, and ICRC theory is to seek a legally guaranteed minimum level of protection and assistance while using its right of initiative to probe for governmental acceptance of humanitarian activity above and beyond the law. It is good theory. But in many cases a government will say to the ICRC that since the law does not apply, or since legal requirements have been met, the ICRC has no right to seek something further from the government. Thus the existence of the law of armed conflict can prove a barrier or an impediment to ICRC efforts.

The ICRC is both the benefactor and the victim of its association with the law of armed conflict. It benefits from its generally valued work with prisoners of war. But it pays a price for its reputation. If prisoners of war (or protected civilians) are not present, legally speaking, sometimes governments object when the ICRC seeks to enter a country.

Moreover, under both the 1949 Conventions and the projected two protocols, states have the last say on almost everything. There is no third party to the conflict authorized to make a binding legal judgment about when the law is to come into force for a particular situation, who is to resolve disputes in legal interpretation, and who is to insure that the law is supervised. This continuation of problems that have plagued all traditional international law for some time is viewed critically by a number of observers.

Therefore the criticism is launched that the ICRC should seek supranational law with a strong humanitarian content or no further law at all. The ICRC has not believed in direct challenges to claims to domestic jurisdiction and national sovereignty, finding it more practical to proceed according to what is acceptable to a majority of states. These two views have to be evaluated according to historical perspective: is the amount of good done through the traditional approach sufficient for its justification?

What might be added is that the ICRC's traditional approach to these matters is a form of humanitarian politics. The ICRC's stand on these subjects is a policy stand which increases or decreases the bargaining influence of other actors in the legislative process. Its refusal in 1975 to work in support of more authority for third parties in armed conflict undercut the influence of states like Belgium and the Netherlands and helped states like the Soviet Union. Just as nonintervention in a civil war in fact constitutes intervention in favor of the stronger party, so the ICRC's "nonpolitical" traditionalism in legal development has a political impact on the struggle to make the law of armed conflict, through support for those elements most committed to claiming national rights. The ICRC's approach may be more or less favored, depending upon one's reading of history. Nevertheless, the political element is there, regardless of the ICRC's position.

Summary

The ICRC and the status of international humanitarian law in armed conflicts is caught up in a twofold challenge on the basis of (1) failure of law adequately to reflect other values besides the preservation of governmental authority (such as humanitarian values), and (2) failure of law to permit nonstate actors to have extensive rights in the law (whether the ICRC or some other actor).

There is a general crisis in patterns of world authority.[34] The nation-state is no longer in full control of events, and patterns of world authority reflect that confusion. There is competition in patterns of world authority among nation-states, international organizations, and individuals. The ICRC, as a nongovernmental international organization, has believed it should operate only with state consent, and that the most realistic way of protecting and assisting individuals is through that approach. Thus its legislative efforts have been designed to modify traditional international law according to humanitarian values, but not challenge that traditional law. Present ICRC legislative efforts are based on deference to the nation-state as the most realistic humanitarian approach. That legislative effort, with its implications for obeying the law after it comes into force, has done much good for individual victims of armed conflict from the 1860's to the 1970's. Whether it is an approach that will suffice for the future is a different question.

6 ICRC Legal Protection: Combatants

The ICRC is better known for its attempted protection of one type of combatant—the prisoner of war—than for any other activity. Despite the fact that early ICRC humanitarian efforts were directed toward other individuals such as the wounded, and despite the fact that others besides the ICRC have been interested in prisoners of war, increasingly in the twentieth century the subject of prisoners of war has become widely regarded as a special domain of the ICRC.

In many situations since 1945 the ICRC has attempted to protect detained combatants by helping to insure that the captor treated his enemy according to certain humanitarian standards. In many of these situations there was disagreement whether the individual was really a detained combatant entitled to international protection or a common criminal. Even in the face of agreement that an individual had been a combatant, he did not always obtain the status of prisoner of war, because much of the violence since 1945 occurred in a factual setting not clearly and universally regarded as an international war. Some parties regarded the violent situation as a civil war or domestic instability. Legally speaking, prisoners of war are found only in international armed conflict. The ICRC has had a broad view of who is entitled to its protection. Other parties—both states and nonstate parties—have resisted this view at times. What has resulted has been humanitarian politics by the ICRC—the struggle to implement humanitarian values as public policy.

INTRODUCTION: THE BASIC PRINCIPLE

ICRC efforts to protect combatants are part of an historical concern stretching from at least the middle of the sixteenth century until today. Against a background of murder, slavery, and ransom of those captured in battle, there arose the idea that war should occur within a cadre of rules and that these rules should also pertain to those captured. From the early writings of Francisco de Vitoria (c. 1550) through the writings of eighteenth-century philosophers like Emmerich de Vattel and Jean-Jacques Rousseau, one can trace the development of the idea that the man who was captured should no longer be regarded as an active enemy. This intellectual development is well summarized by William E. S. Flory:

> During the latter portion of the 17th century through the 18th century, the leading major principle seems to have been humanitarianism. Although the principle was nebulous and indefinable in general, it frequently had a definite meaning when related to particular cases. Thus, the use of the principle appears to have aided in the growth of the rules that captors may not, except in very unusual circumstances, kill prisoners and that they must be freed after the war is over. The idea of human dignity and value came to be applied to the sphere of prisonership during the latter part of the period. This development is significant because it seems to involve a growth beyond an idea of generosity and sympathy on the part of the captor to the idea in embryo of human rights of prisoners.[1]

These humanitarian ideas pertaining to fighters, long written about by social and legal philosophers, and endorsed by the French revolutionary government in 1789, received their first governmental formulation in the American Civil War, when the Federal government published the Lieber code. An international effort to formally regulate the subject occurred at the Hague Conference in 1907. But it was the ICRC, after engaging in ad hoc diplomacy toward combatants in 1870 and 1914, that facilitated the adoption of extensive regulations—found first in the 1929 Geneva Convention and then in the Third Geneva Convention of 1949.

The basic principle of the 1949 Convention on prisoners of war is that a "benevolent quarantine" should be provided for foreign combatants placed hors de combat.[2] In that Convention, 143 rules were established, creating obligatory standards for the captor state pertaining to prisoners of war.

Also in the Third Geneva Convention of 1949, Article 3, pertaining to internal war, provided minimum and vague protection for "persons taking no active part in the hostilities, including members of armed forces who have laid down their arms and those placed *hors de combat* by sickness, wounds, detention, or any other cause." Therefore in noninternational armed conflict, combatants (and others) were to be treated humanely when captured, even though such fighters were not, officially, prisoners of war.

What began in the minds of intellectuals in about the sixteenth century has become extensive treaty law in the mid-1970's. The ICRC played a major role in translating these humanitarian ideals into international law from about 1870 to the present. Its efforts in relation to the Third Convention of 1949 are frequently of major significance in world affairs.[3]

MAJOR PROBLEMS

In the period since 1949, the ICRC (and other parties) have encountered five fundamental problems in trying to obtain the implementation of at least some part of the Third Geneva Convention: (1) the basic principle of the Convention has been rejected; (2) the basic principle has been ignored; (3) there has been disagreement regarding *when* the Convention applied; (4) there has been disagreement regarding *to whom* the Convention applied; (5) there has been disagreement regarding *by whom* the Convention is to be applied. While there have been many other specific problems, these have been the fundamental ones.

Rejection of the Principle

A rejection of the basic principle that a foreign combatant placed hors de combat should benefit from a benevolent quarantine occurred as soon as the principle was given its 1949 formulation. In the Korean War of 1950–53, both China and North Korea rejected the principle through their behavior. This rejection did not constitute illegality in the technical sense, for neither were parties to the 1949 Conventions at that time. (Controversy over the 1929 Convention was discussed in Chapter 1.) The ICRC, however, upon the outbreak of violence in 1950, requested that all parties involved apply the just-written Conventions even though no state had had time to adhere to them.

The response of North Korea to this ICRC initiative was at first ambivalent.[4] Initially that regime said it would apply the Third Convention; but as the fighting continued in the summer of 1950, North Korea refused to respond to further ICRC inquiries, and it never granted visas to ICRC representatives who were seeking to enter North Korean territory. Likewise China, when it entered into direct combat, refused to accept the ad hoc application of the Convention or to permit the ICRC to visit prisoners of war held by it.

Beyond the North Korean and Chinese rejection of ICRC visits to prisoners of war, which were mandatory under the Third, these parties rejected the basic principle of that Convention in actual practice. Whatever source one uses, it is clear that mistreatment and political indoctrination plus insufficient nutritional and medical care occurred in the prisoner-of-war camps run by the Chinese and

North Koreans. Apparently some improvements did occur toward the end of the war. There was never any third-party supervision.

As for South Korea and the United States, the latter being the command authority for ''United Nations forces,'' these parties accepted in principle the applicability of the Third Convention. While specific problems arose with regard to its implementation, in general it is fair to say that there was an effort in good faith to implement the Third in the South. There was, in addition, some de facto protection given by the ICRC to detainees in the South who were not prisoners of war. Not only was the ICRC given full rights of visitation under the Third throughout the South, but the ICRC also visited a number of civilian prisoners in the jails of South Korea.

Thus in the Korean War there was not a reciprocal acceptance of the basic principle found in the Third Convention. In this situation, the ICRC made continuous efforts to secure protection for POWs in the North. With regard to this ICRC effort, it can be argued that the ICRC made an initial faux pas in its diplomacy; for when the war broke out, the ICRC sent a cable to the USSR asking it to help in securing cooperation on protection matters from North Korea. At that time, however, the Soviet Union was disclaiming any responsibility for events in the Korean peninsula and certainly did not want to do anything that would make the North Korean regime appear to be a Soviet puppet. The USSR told the ICRC to contact the North Koreans directly.[5]

This démarche toward the Soviet Union was part of an ICRC effort to make contact with the North Koreans through every useful means. The ICRC also contacted China, and—in addition to sending representatives to Moscow and Hong Kong—had a representative in Peking. While the government in Peking was willing to grant a transit visa to the ICRC delegate, China was either unwilling or unable to assist that delegate in entering North Korea. Nevertheless, the ICRC had delegates ready and waiting on the periphery of North Korea should that state permit ICRC humanitarian protection.

Persistent efforts by the ICRC toward North Korea, and later China, efforts which continued through 1950 and 1951, were matched by persistent efforts to implement the Third Convention in the South. The lack of reciprocity did not result in an ICRC ''whitewash'' of detention policies in the South. The ICRC engaged in serious conflict with American military officials over prisoner-of-war treatment there. The friction reached crisis proportions in 1952 at the prisoner of war camp at Koje. For a time the ICRC was barred from the camp, and American military officials were highly critical of the ICRC for allegedly not considering the disruptive behavior of the prisoners.[6] For its part, the ICRC continued to insist strongly on changes in certain policies, changes which were finally made. Also, the ICRC had long been directly criticizing certain detention policies of the South Korean government. In letters to the government, the ICRC urged that beatings be stopped, better guards be hired; and in one letter the ICRC implied that the foreign minister had lied.[7]

The ICRC was aware that if it hoped to enter North Korea, it had to maintain an image of impartiality and independence from the West. While its overtures to the Soviet Union had not helped, beyond that point the ICRC had attempted to protect its image of impartiality. For example, it engaged in long discussions with United Nations officials over material assistance in the South. The ICRC was concerned that its cooperation with the UN in sending relief, at a time when "the UN" was leading the defense of the regime in Seoul, would make the ICRC appear to be an arm of the UN. Some degree of Red Cross autonomy was finally established.[8] The ICRC was also careful not to recognize the Red Cross Society in the South until it had reduced its claims to jurisdiction over all of Korea.[9] The quest for a neutral image was badly served by the ICRC's agreement to investigate charges of biological/chemical warfare; the ICRC accepted the American request for inspection without waiting for agreement to the inspection from China. China subsequently intensified its verbal attacks on the ICRC as being part of an imperialist conspiracy. Indeed, during the latter stages of the war China criticized the ICRC in such strong language over its radio network that the ICRC protested.

In sum, both North Korea and China, after an initial period of some ambivalence toward the Geneva Conventions and the ICRC, firmly rejected the humanitarian principle of the Third Convention especially—and rejected any supervisory role for the ICRC. This situation seems to have had the effect of causing the detaining authorities in the South to deviate at times from a strict application of the Third Convention.[10]

Moreover, the longer-term effects of the socialist rejection were also serious. The United States military began to teach its personnel that they had a duty to continue the struggle after capture. The United States code of conduct, while it was not American military law, was nevertheless vigorously taught. It suggested American military personnel had a legal obligation under American law to resist and harass their captors. This further undermined the basic principle that the struggle stopped upon capture. As such, the American code of conduct, like socialist policies of detention in Korea, constituted a vicious circle of rejection of the foundation of the Third Convention.[11]

Disregarding of the Principle

There is a difference between disregarding the basic humanitarian principle found in the Third Geneva Convention of 1949 and rejecting it. The difference is in the motivation of the detaining authority; the situation of the detainee remains the same.

In the Korean War, for example, there was a definite policy choice to ignore the ICRC and its requests for a system of humanitarian protection. In a situation like the Congolese Civil War of 1960–64, the problems stem from a different source. In that war the central government, while it indicated it would implement the humanitarian law of armed conflict, was generally ignorant of its technical content and provided no instructions to its armed supporters. Indeed, one of the problems in the Congo was the undisciplined behavior of the central army. If this was a problem with the central army, it was even more the case with the rebel bands that opposed that army, not to mention the actions of the white mercenaries fighting for the secessionist province of Katanga. The behavior of UN forces, largely drawn from other African states, was not clearly better. It was, after all, UN forces that killed the ICRC head of delegation and two other ICRC delegates, and permitted boxcars of prisoners to suffocate.[12]

Despite the fact, therefore, that a head of government or some other public official like the UN secretary general may give his assurance that humanitarian law will be implemented, in actual fact that law may be disregarded. In the particular case of the Congolese Civil War, a number of captured combatants were summarily executed and some detainees were abused, even though the greatest number of prisoners of war were probably held in adequate conditions and were visited by the ICRC. In wars like the Congolese, disregarding of humanitarian principles is seen in attempts to use the Red Cross symbol for military advantage and in military attacks on Red Cross installations—not to dwell on attacks on Red Cross personnel.

Controversy over Application

Even where basic humanitarian principles pertaining to prisoners of war are not overtly rejected or disregarded, the ICRC may encounter great difficulty in securing humanitarian protection because of disagreement and controversy over whether the law—or some part of the law—applies. The controversy basically centers on what is an international armed conflict and a noninternational armed conflict, and who is entitled to say when one or the other occurs.

Without writing a legal treatise on the subject, one can note several fundamental points. The Geneva Conventions do not provide any central, authoritative party to give a legally binding judgment as to when an international or internal armed conflict exists. The result is that the various actors are both claimant and judge with regard to legal argument, for all practical purposes. They can claim that war exists or not, and there is no party that passes definitive judgment on that claim.

This means that there can be a divergence of view as to what law should apply to a given factual situation: should the four Conventions apply, based on the view that the situation should be legally characterized as an international armed conflict; should Common Article 3 apply, based on the view that the situation is a noninternational armed conflict; should none of the Conventions apply, based on the view that the situation is one of domestic instability?

A divergence of view frequently occurs with regard to these choices, first of all because many situations are in actuality extremely complex. It is not always evident—even to disinterested or impartial third parties—what legal label should be appended to a factual situation. In the Vietnam War, academics and more sensible citizens of various countries argued at great length whether the situation was an international war between North and South Vietnam, a civil war within one Vietnam, or a civil war within South Vietnam with foreign intervention by North Vietnam and the United States, among others.

A divergence of view also exists because governments and other parties engaged in a conflict have vested interests in making a certain legal argument. They are more interested in using legal argument in the political-legal process of making and implementing policy than in the academic-legal process of correctly attaching a legal label to a factual situation. These parties are more interested in securing their policy objectives than in being consistent, orderly, and truthful.

Thus the government of Pakistan argued in early 1971 that there was no civil war in the eastern region—despite declarations of intent to secede and the existence of widespread violence. The Pakistani government claimed it was a matter of domestic instability falling outside the scope of the law of armed conflict, and the government initially refused entry to the ICRC. On the other hand, India regarded the situation at a minimum as one of civil war, if not a situation of genocide or a war for national liberation—both of which were, in the Indian view, international. The United States had realpolitik reasons for deferring to the Pakistani view, and the Soviet Union had similar reasons for agreeing with India.

The legal arguments in early 1971 regarding events in the eastern region of Pakistan were therefore diverse; the reasons for those arguments were as much political-legal as academic-legal; and the resolution of the competing arguments occurred through force of arms not through dispassionate judicial inquiry. Once the regular Indian Army intervened in behalf of the Bengali independence movement, all parties agreed that the entire Third Geneva Convention should come into legal force, as the situation had clearly become one of international armed conflict.

Also illustrative of this controversy over legal labels was the complete change in Portuguese legal claims toward African liberation movements. As long as it was Portuguese policy to retain territories in Africa, that government regarded those captured while struggling for self-determination in Guinea-Bissau, Mozambique, and Angola as detainees under Portuguese law. Many other parties, especially the black African states, regarded these individuals as prisoners of war engaged in an international armed conflict for national liberation. The ICRC was first permitted to visit these black detainees as political prisoners by voluntary grant of Lisbon, not as detainees protected by the law of armed conflict. But once a coup occurred in Lisbon and governmental policy was altered in favor of granting independence to these territories, Portugal viewed the detainees as entitled to the full protection of the Third Convention—and the ICRC was so informed.

The level of violence remained the same; the factual properties of the situation remained the same in all other respects (who was involved, and who was supporting whom). But Lisbon developed a new policy toward the future of the territories; this altered the controlling legal argument about the legal status of the detainees and the legal base of access for the ICRC.

While it is widely accepted that the ICRC can assert its view as to the legal protection that should be applied, parties frequently disagree with that ICRC view on the basis either of an honest difference in interpreting the facts or of a difference in priorities. The ICRC is interested in the welfare of individuals; a party to the conflict may be primarily interested in securing control of the government, or putting down a challenge to one's rule, among other things. Such priorities lead the conflicting parties to seek to reduce their obligations under law to a minimum in order to maintain their freedom of action.

Controversy over Individual Status

Even where a party accepts some part of the law of armed conflict and permits the ICRC to enter its territory, the ICRC encounters a problem in obtaining a satisfying definition of which individuals are entitled to what type of legal protection.

This has been a long-standing problem in the effort to protect individuals. During World War II, when the 1929 Geneva Convention on prisoners of war was legally binding, the warring parties had a tendency to restrict the definition of prisoners of war to the smallest possible realm. In particular, individuals not in official uniform and not directly and formally part of a regular military force were sometimes, perhaps even frequently, treated as spies and saboteurs rather than prisoners of war—viz., sometimes they were shot instead of being placed in a POW camp.

After the war, the ICRC responded by successfully urging that the 1949 Conventions include protection for these irregular resistance fighters.

In the post-1949 period, a major problem for the ICRC has been in securing adequte protection for guerrilla fighters. The problem is major because of the prevalence of guerrilla warfare and terrorism, and the concomitant decline of traditional conventional warfare between uniformed armies of warring states.

In major wars after 1949, such as in Algeria and Vietnam, where at least one of the major parties accepted some part of the law of armed conflict as binding, there remained the difficulty of classifying the guerrilla fighter. A great part of the problem was confusion over the legal status of the individual if the detaining authority captured him when he was not bearing arms or engaged in direct and violent hostility. If he were thought to be a sometimes-fighter for the Algerian National Liberation Front, or a nonfighting supporter of the Viet Cong, was he to be treated as a POW? Or as a civilian detainee under the Fourth Convention? Or as a protected person under Common Article 3? Or simply as a regular prisoner under the national law of the detaining authority?

On the basis of Algeria and Vietnam principally, the trend has been to categorize as prisoners of war—in addition to regular, uniformed military personnel—those individuals captured with arms ready for fighting (in French, *pris les armes à la main*). But this left undecided the legal status of unarmed individuals. And in some cases an armed individual was detained under national law for violating some gun law—or even for curfew or tax violation, depending on what charges were pressed.

In sum, despite the tendency to classify all armed combatants as prisoners of war even if they did not meet the archaic conditions of the Geneva Conventions (such as wearing uniforms and carrying arms openly), there was much controversy over the legal status of other detainees. There were charges that in places like Vietnam, Algeria, Malaysia, and the Philippines, for instance, the classification system of the detaining authorities was arbitrary in general and on occasion subject to great distortion.

Controversy over by Whom Applied

Only states are legal parties to the 1949 Conventions. But in much of the violence since 1949, nonstate parties have been major actors in the conflict. These independence or liberation movements and other versions of "private armies" have not been permitted to adhere formally to the law.[13]

Only in Africa have nonstate parties generally accepted legal obligation and permitted ICRC inspection of prisoner-of-war conditions. This was the case not only for the Biafran authorities in the Nigerian Civil War, but also for certain black liberation movements such as the National Front for the Liberation of Angola and the Popular Movement for the Liberation of Angola.

On the other hand, certain movements in Asia and the Middle East have explicitly rejected legal obligation. This was true of the National Liberation Front in Vietnam. And the leader of the Democratic Front for the Liberation of Palestine has been quoted as saying that Palestinian guerrillas are involved in revolution and revolution has no rules.[14]

Some movements, as the Algerian Liberation Front, have accepted legal obligation theoretically but have denied systematic third-party supervision of detained combatants.

The ICRC, in the context of the Vietnam War, argued that a nonstate movement was bound by the law because of adherence to that law by the established government. But this argument has not been widely accepted. Logically, if a movement challenges the existence of a government, it is not likely to accept the decisions of that government. Factually, movements have sometimes not wanted to restrict their actions by accepting legal limitations that work to the advantage of the government. Movements have seen terroristic attacks on civilians as necessary when the government possesses putative superiority in conventional military terms. Thus these movements have seen little self-interest in eschewing the taking of hostages and in similar action proscribed by the Geneva Conventions. Moreover, a terroristic-guerrilla war is frequently a war of movement without fixed sanctuaries within the target state. This makes it logistically difficult for the challenging movement to meet the humanitarian standards of detention required by the Geneva Conventions.

While established governments have been less than perfect in their adherence to humanitarian standards for the protection of prisoners of war, parties not widely recognized as governments have presented even more problems for the implementation of those same standards.

A double standard frequently exists. The government is expected to apply some part of the international law of armed conflict—at least Common Article 3 if not the entire four Conventions. But the challenging faction or movement seems to escape widespread censure for ignoring limitations on its actions. The ICRC does not endorse this double standard. But the fact remains that it has had difficulty in securing the cooperation of certain nonstate movements for the protection of fighters hors de combat. The double standard persists in fact, though opposed in humanitarian principle.

THE RECORD OF SUCCESS

Despite the five major problems noted above, the ICRC has helped in securing protection for detained combatants on a number of occasions since 1949.

First of all, the ICRC has frequently been successful in obtaining either a statement that the law of armed conflict applies, or a statement that the ICRC can visit individuals that somebody views as detained combatants. The ICRC likes to think it does not, technically speaking, pass judgment on the overall legal nature of a conflict. But an ICRC initiative in seeking application of international humanitarian law can result in a government's agreeing that some part of that law exists; this has the effect of putting a legal label on the conflict—at least from the point of view of that government. Thus it was an initiative by the ICRC in 1965 that resulted in the United States agreement to apply especially the Third Geneva Convention to the Indochina War—a move that was to characterize that conflict, for the American government, as an international armed conflict.

In some cases the established government has agreed with the ICRC that a noninternational armed conflict exists, as did the military junta in Chile after the 1973 overthrow of the Allende government, and as did France in the Algerian War. Some attention was also given to Common Article 3 in Guatamala (1954), Cuba (1959), Yemen (1962), and South Vietnam (mid-1960's).

In other cases, while governmental authorities refuse to accept an ICRC view that some part of the law of armed conflict is relevant, those authorities nevertheless permit ICRC visits in response to ICRC requests. In Northern Ireland, the British government permitted ICRC visits to administrative detainees (but not convicted persons) connected with the Irish Republican Army. To many, especially in the Republic of Ireland, these detainees were combatants. This was also the pattern in Kenya and Cyprus (1950's).

Therefore, the first point in the record of success is that the ICRC does frequently secure the promise of detaining authorities either to admit the applicability of law, or admit the ICRC to detainees, or both.

Secondly, the ICRC has gained access to detained combatants in the wake of the initial promise of cooperation from the detaining authority. Rare is the case where a governmental party admits that the law of armed conflict applies and then refuses access to the ICRC.

In only two cases has a party to a conflict argued that some part of the statutory law of armed conflict applied, then refused access to the ICRC for detainee visits. In Algeria and Vietnam, both the Algerian NLF and North Vietnam argued that an international war existed but refused systematic access to the ICRC. The NLF demanded that the French agree to its view before giving ICRC access, and North Vietnam argued that its reservation to the Geneva Third Convention exempted American flyers from POW status. In neither situation did the ICRC gain access. (Both cases are covered below in detail.)

In the Middle East in 1973, ICRC access to Israelis detained by Egypt and Syria was delayed but eventually gained.

It is still the general rule that the ICRC gains access to the combatant detainee once the detaining party admits that the law of armed conflict applies in some form. That was the case, in general, in Pakistan, Bangladesh, and India in 1971; in the Middle East in 1956, 1967, and 1973; in South Korea and South Vietnam; on the French side in the Algerian War; in El Salvador and Honduras in 1969; in Chile in 1973; in Cyprus in 1974; in Africa throughout the 1960's and 1970's in the black states and on the part of the black liberation movements. While this list of examples is neither exhaustive nor definitive, it does establish the general pattern.

The provision in the Geneva Conventions for the appointment of a state as Protecting Power has not been a barrier to ICRC access to prisoners of war. First of all, the general trend is that such states are not appointed. Where they are formally appointed as Protecting Power, as Switzerland was in the 1956 Suez affair, they do not interfere with ICRC traditional activities.

A third point of success is that after the law is accepted and/or the ICRC is admitted, eventually some of the substance of humanitarian protection is achieved as specified in the Third Convention or as outlined in Common Article 3. Over time the ICRC is able to get the detaining authority to accept much of the Third Convention. In an internal war regulated by Common Article 3, the ICRC reasons by analogy to the Third, while making allowances for the fact that an internal war requires some departure from the complete Third Convention.

It can be said that detaining authorities cooperate to some extent in improving conditions of detention over time. Housing, food, and medical care are usually improved, and systematic mistreatment is usually curtailed—although the time span involved can be lengthy. Rare is the authority that officially endorses torture, mistreatment, or poor conditions during the course of ICRC visits. (The case of France in Algeria is analyzed below.)

ICRC representations are important in securing improved treatment and conditions. Incompetent or sadistic guards are noted on the basis of prisoner testimony; their removal is urged when warranted. Detaining authorities are urged to correct overcrowding and other bad conditions, especially when likely to lead to violence. Material and medical assistance is provided by the ICRC when the detaining authority cannot. This need has been pronounced in some situations, as in the Nigerian Civil War, when the ICRC not only had to feed the Nigerian POWs held by the Biafrans but also had to feed the Biafran guards.

An extremely important aspect to the ICRC's protection activities is the work of the Central Tracing Agency. This administrative arm of the ICRC operates under rights guaranteed by the Third Convention in international armed conflict, and it has functioned in many noninternational armed conflicts as well. It has become such a useful thing that it is called upon to locate people all over the world on matters having little or nothing to do with armed conflict.

With regard to protection of prisoners of war, the Central Tracing Agency is absolutely essential for the ICRC. Once an individual is identified by the ICRC, his name and other basic information transmitted to the Agency in Geneva, and his state of origin notified of his capture, an important element of protection is placed in motion. Beyond that point, the detaining authority must—under law—accept responsibility for his welfare and provide him a benevolent quarantine until the end of the conflict. This initial, definitive identification is the key to subsequent protection efforts. That the identification process under the ICRC's Central Tracing Agency is widely regarded as definitive is a reflection of the fact that the CTA is the most efficient organization of this kind in the world—although some complain about its not being computerized. It has been practicing its trade for over a century, processed inquiries during World War II at a rate of between 50,000 and 100,000 per *day,* and has the capacity both to set up regional offices at a scene of a conflict and to teach the process to national Red Cross Societies. In the mid-1970's, its work in places like Chile and Cyprus was a sine qua non in ICRC protection.

In all of these matters, from identification and tracing, to inspecting a place of detention, to conducting an interview with detaining authorities and transmitting reports to officials in authority, the ICRC has developed a special expertise during the course of over a century of experience.[15] Its delegates have learned over time what tricks detaining authorities will try to use in order to hide a man. Conversely, they have learned to be wary of taking prisoner testimony at face value without a careful cross-checking of the allegations.

Of course the ICRC makes errors from time to time. An example of a technical mistake occurred after the war for Bangladesh. There was a disturbance in a detention camp run by India. An ICRC delegate conducted an investigation and sent his report to Geneva. He reported that Indian guards had unnecessarily used force which had resulted in the "murder" of several prisoners. Geneva headquarters failed to change the wording of the original report, and sent copies of the report both to Pakistan and India, as was customary. Pakistan, as might have been expected, found the report highly important and published its contents—as it had a traditional right to do. This action greatly embarrassed India, which subsequently asked the ICRC delegate to leave the country.

Nevertheless, the ICRC is widely regarded as the most effective and responsible inspector of detention places. Various proposals aimed at creating a United Nations or other agency for such inspection have never gotten very far for this reason. This is not to say that this situation will always exist. And it is not to say that in the past detaining authorities have always welcomed the ICRC with open arms—or open prison doors. But if a detaining authority wants—or feels pressured to have—international inspection of detention of prisoners of war, it has preferred the ICRC to Amnesty or a UN agency because of ICRC expertise and discretion.

CASE STUDIES

This record of expertise and discretion has been built up through the exercise of humanitarian protection in complex and trying situations. Three case studies will be examined that demonstrate this point: the Indochina War, French phase; the Algerian War; the Indochina War, American phase.

No three case studies can say everything about prisoners of war. All three case studies chosen are different from conventional wars such as have been fought between Israel and Egypt or between Pakistan and India. Examples of guerrilla wars have been chosen because of the prevalence of that type of violence since 1949 and because of widespread predictions of more of the same. Two of the case studies pertain to the same socialist regime in Asia; and an Asian socialist regime may have a rather extraordinary policy toward prisoners of war, not comparable to other types of regimes. With all these, and other, limitations to the use of these case studies, current ICRC efforts at protection of prisoners of war is well demonstrated by these examples.

Indochina War, French Phase

Factual Situation and Legal Policy.　When violence occurred between the French and the Viet Minh in Indochina after World War II in 1946, the ICRC made contact with both parties. The initial French response was that a role for the

ICRC was not needed. But as the violence increased, and as the number of French military personnel captured by the Viet Minh increased, the French changed their policy and permitted the ICRC access rights to detained combatants held in the south of Vietnam, without formally characterizing the overall nature of the conflict.

The policy of the Viet Minh under Ho Chi Minh was at first unclear. Viet Minh representatives initially indicated to the ICRC that some visits to detained personnel might be possible. There was no Viet Minh reluctance to deal with the ICRC delegates as far as talks were concerned, and the Viet Minh forces cooperated with the ICRC in implementing truces for the purpose of conducting these talks. In 1947, the ICRC carried out one visit to detained French military personnel—a visit that occurred by chance rather than by formal plan.[16] After that, the Viet Minh permitted no ICRC visits to any category of detainee. Viet Minh policy thus slowly evolved to a clear rejection of any ICRC protection.

ICRC Activity. As the French progressively attempted to create a noncommunist zone in the south of Vietnam rather than grant independence—as the former colonial power—to all of Vietnam, it found itself progressively involved in a major armed conflict. Despite that fact, the French never made any formal statement as to whether it was fighting an international or a civil war. Thus it was not clear whether the 1929 Geneva Convention on prisoners of war applied, or any other part of international law.[17] The ICRC, however, was quietly given the right to see all detained combatants held by the French; these numbered approximately 65,000 during the early 1950's.

In its dealings with French authorities, the ICRC both secured cooperation and ran into difficulties.[18] While an improvement in detention conditions was obtained, it would be fair to state that treatment in Vietnam by the French was very similar to what was to occur in Algeria. Because of this, there was friction between the ICRC and especially French military and civilian authorities in Vietnam. Because of that friction, ICRC personnel were withdrawn by Geneva, and Paris made changes in French personnel in the field. The situation for prisoners held by the French improved, but that is not to say that the situation was fully satisfactory by humanitarian standards. The French were short of resources. The French military did not give high priority to humanitarian matters. There was no great pressure generated from metropolitan France regarding detention matters. Few if any outside parties took note of the situation in the detention places run by the French.

In this context, it would also be fair to say that ICRC activity was not characterized by aggressiveness in humanitarian matters. For example, while the ICRC had a general right of access, the prison of Con Son was visited only twice during the 1947–54 period. There were few delegates in the region, and if the French had few resources and not much incentive to make major changes, there was some feeling among the delegates that there was no point to repeated visits.

The ICRC itself had limited resources, with continuing problems from World War II, new problems in Korea and the Middle East, and a lack of reciprocity from the Viet Minh.

As for ICRC activity vis-à-vis what had become the Democratic Republic of Vietnam, the one visit to French personnel had come about simply by chance. An ICRC delegate, in the process of holding talks with Viet Minh representatives in the field, had come across a small group of captured French. The delegate proceeded to interview the prisoners about their conditions and treatment and to submit a report to Geneva. Subsequently the ICRC made efforts to improve the diet of these prisoners, efforts which the ICRC later said were successful.[19] But the ICRC was not able directly to verify that alleged improvement.

Beyond these events of 1947, the ICRC tried to get letters to and from French detainees. It tried to arrange truces for the release and repatriation of sick and wounded, and other detainees. It sought to utilize the Central Tracing Agency to communicate basic information on French personnel to their families. These efforts, in behalf of some four to five thousand detainees held by the Viet Minh, were progressively met by rejection after the early period of indecisiveness in 1946–47. For example, at the 1954 battle of Dienbienphu, the Viet Minh forces rejected ICRC appeals for a truce in order to evacuate the dead and wounded, although it is possible that French medical helicopters had not been limited to strictly humanitarian missions.

After the defeat of the French at Dienbienphu, and their surrender not only of their forces but also of their plans for the south of Vietnam, French detainees were released by the regime in Hanoi. The ICRC was not permitted to assist in the disorganized and harsh release operation, which consisted basically of opening the gates of detention camps and letting the prisoners—in a weakened condition—make their own way to French lines. There is little doubt but that detention conditions were harsh, even as systematic physical abuse seemed absent. French nationals unaccounted for were never located or otherwise identified; and the ICRC was not permitted to enter North Vietnam after the war to trace those missing.[20] The ICRC was asked by Hanoi to help in the relocation of some former French Legionnaires who had defected to Hanoi during the war and who feared to return to French areas. The ICRC responded affirmatively and helped these individuals travel to states willing to receive them.

Conclusions.   In the French phase of the Indochina War, the ICRC had delegates on the scene and succeeded in making contacts with the parties concerned. It tried to achieve humanitarian protection for prisoners at a time when the violence in Indochina was overshadowed by other situations deemed more important in the major capitals of the world. The ICRC was long active in Indochina before the French and American publics, or many others, cared very much what was occurring there.

In its efforts to protect prisoners of war on both sides, the ICRC made some effort to construct an image of impartiality. For example, early in the conflict

Geneva explicitly cabled its delegates not to tarry in territory in the north controlled by the French; thus the ICRC attempted to establish an independence from the French and tacitly to respect Viet Minh claims to jurisdiction over the north. Five years before the Chinese were to attack the ICRC for being a lackey of Western imperialism, the ICRC was respecting the claims of a small socialist movement in armed conflict with France, in order to improve the possibilities of humanitarian protection of a reciprocal basis. ICRC use of the British Consulate in Hanoi to make inquiries about French personnel was not, however, a move to reduce the pro-Western image of the ICRC. On the other hand, the ICRC also sought out the Indian Red Cross as an intermediary.

In its efforts to protect and assist detainees in French-held areas, the ICRC was persistent enough to incur difficulties with French authorities. If the ICRC was not as persistent as some critics might want, it seems important to place humanitarian efforts in global perspective. Violence in Indochina was not regarded as terribly important in the late 1940's and early 1950's, beyond the political and military elites directly involved. Other major situations of violence were occurring. But there was no whitewash by the ICRC of the situation in the south. Very few cared what happened to prisoners of war in the south, and the ICRC did what it could. But not even the Viet Minh generated much attention on the subject of their detainees.

After 1954 and the end of the French phase of the war, the ICRC dealt with Hanoi on certain matters, although it was given the "cold shoulder" by the North Vietnamese delegation to the 1954 Geneva Conference on Indochina. In the early 1960's the ICRC was acceptable to Hanoi as an intermediary in the movement of Vietnamese from Thailand to North Vietnam. But from 1946 until the start of the American phase of the Indochina War, the ICRC was never accorded a major role by Hanoi.

As for French-ICRC relations, the Indochina War was followed immediately by the Algerian War. The latter was to be much more important than the former for those relations.

The Algerian War

Factual Situation and Legal Policies. From the early 1950's and especially after 1 November 1954, several Algerian groups, increasingly rallied around the National Liberation Front, sought independence from France. Terror and guerrilla warfare were means to this end, and the violence was often directed against elements of the Arab population as well as against the French army and colonizers.[21]

Notwithstanding this terrorism, the NLF argued that the four Geneva Conventions of 1949 should apply to the conflict, and much effort on the part of the NLF was directed to convincing third parties—and France—that it was a belligerent under international law. Progressively into the conflict, the NLF appeared to pay some attention to the precise norms of those Conventions, although compliance with those norms was decidedly far from complete. Also during that conflict, the NLF endorsed the applicability of Common Article 3 pertaining to internal war. Toward the close of the conflict, the NLF sent its accession to the four Conventions to the Swiss government, a move prompting critical statements from not only the French government but also the Swiss and the ICRC.[22]

Therefore the NLF position on the applicability of the Geneva Conventions, or a part thereof, was not consistent—nor was its attention to applying all or part of the law of armed conflict. Not only did summary executions and terrorism continue, with some diminution perhaps, but also the ICRC was denied systematic access to French personnel detained by the NLF. An effort by the ICRC in 1958 to visit certain French nationals was apparently blocked by France in order to avoid conferring status on the NLF,[23] but later and other visits were blocked by the NLF itself.

The ICRC did make one visit to French personnel in NLF hands. In February 1958, the NLF agreed to allow the ICRC to observe detention conditions at one place of detention. This incident was related to a question of greater importance to the conflicting parties: whether the NLF was powerful enough to hold its detainees within Algeria or whether it had to use Tunisian territory. And this question was related to another issue, that being whether the French were justified in conducting bombing raids on Tunisian territory. Thus the visit took place in the context of international criticism of the French for their bombing policies and French claims that the Tunisians were lending support to the Algerians. The NLF was trying to use that visit to demonstrate that French personnel were indeed held within Algeria, and the French were trying to counter that claim. The ICRC carried out the visit but did not try to establish whether the place of detention was a permanent site in Algeria or whether the prisoners had just been brought there for the purpose of being seen by the ICRC. No other ICRC visits took place under NLF auspices. The ICRC was called upon by the NLF and the "Algerian Red Crescent" to help in the release of French personnel from time to time, and the ICRC participated in these releases in the context of great publicity.

The French position on the applicability and implementation of the law of armed conflict was not totally dissimilar from that of the NLF. The French stand on applicability was only slightly more consistent, but there was an equally marked difference between what law was said to apply and what was done in fact.

The French government, in 1954 and 1955, characterized the situation as a problem of domestic law and order. Nevertheless, an ICRC mission to Algeria was authorized in 1955. Then in June 1956, the government said: "In conformity with Article 3 of the Geneva Conventions regarding armed conflicts not of an international character, which arise in the territory of one of the contracting parties, the International Committee of the Red Cross has offered its services to the French government. The French government authorized it to send a mission to Algeria.''[24] The government thus left the clear impression that it recognized the situation as one regulated by Common Article 3. Increasingly into the 1950's and early 1960's, the verbiage of the government, and even more importantly some actions of the military in the field, conveyed the impression that captured combatants were prisoners of war and that the NLF was a belligerent, although France never expressly said so. However, especially during the 1950's, French courts tended to view violent Algerians as common criminals; the situation became somewhat different only after 1961.

In general, therefore, France moved from the view that the Algerian conflict was an internal matter of law and order to the quasi-official view that it was an internal war, and finally to the de facto view that the conflict was an international war.

The gap was considerable, however, between recognition of the law which applied, and efforts to implement any law, aside from the law of the jungle. While the French did make some effort to classify their opponents into Reds (opposition fighters), Pinks (sympathizers with the opposition), and innocent citizens that might nevertheless require forced relocation, and while thus it can be said that the French did try, to some extent, to distinguish between combatants and civilians, it is also true that the French army used torture as an official policy. A section of the army viewed the Algerian conflict as part of a global revolutionary war, against which any means were permissible, even as the government in Paris was authorizing systematic ICRC visits to places of detention from 1957 until the end of the war.[25]

While, in sum, both parties took positions on the applicability of international law, largely with an eye to questions of status and political psychology, a war of terror and torture raged, with institutionalized brutality on an exceptional scale.[26]

ICRC Activity. The ICRC established contacts with the NLF, and additionally carried on talks with detained Algerian leaders such as Ben Bella in metropolitan France. The ICRC, however, was not able to effect any major changes in NLF policies; a special accord on humanitarian matters drawn up by the ICRC in 1958 was unacceptable to the NLF (and to France). The ICRC was able to obtain a small flow of information about detainees, in the form of letters from prisoners to their families.

As for ICRC-French relations, the dominant issue was torture and mistreatment of detainees as practiced by the ''Fifth Bureau'' of the French military command structure.

Allegations of torture had long plagued French efforts in Algeria. The government itself had created the Safeguard Commission as early as 1957 to investigate allegations of torture. Certain military and civilian officials had resigned to protest use of torture. Various religious groups in France had tried to publicize the issue. But it was not until an ICRC report was leaked to the press that torture as French military policy, tolerated by weak governments, came to an end.

On 5 January 1960, *Le Monde* carried a front-page exposé of French torture practices, based on a complete series of ICRC reports dating from 1959. The government compounded difficulties by trying to seize copies of the issue after it was already on the streets. What *Le Monde* reported, and was able to document through ICRC observations that went unchallenged by any public authority in France, was the following: detention conditions in two-thirds of the collection centers were unsatisfactory; in one internment camp which had existed for three years the situation was "disastrous"; torture occurred on a wide scale; the ICRC's delegates had witnessed "operational exploitation"; some detainees were "completely terrorized"; large numbers of Algerians had "disappeared"; prisoners had died for lack of medical attention; and so on *ad nauseam*. There was no doubt about the facts. The ICRC report of 15 December 1959 contained 270 pages covering 82 places of detention, with names and details.[27]

The French government, having unsuccessfully tried to seize issues of the paper, subsequently confirmed the accuracy of *Le Monde*'s articles. So did the ICRC when asked by the press. The government did not hold the ICRC responsible for the leak nor did it interrupt ICRC activities. With less than a dozen copies of ICRC reports in circulation, most close observers pointed the finger at disgruntled civilians in the government, although the point of leak was never definitively established.

The publication of the ICRC reports caused certain French officials to resign. Moreover, the "Fifth Bureau" was dismantled the month following publication. And torture as a policy ceased in Algeria. The results of publication were so clear and so conducive to an improvement in the situation for detainees that the ICRC undertook a review of its discretionary policies. The ICRC concluded that while this publication had been beneficial to detainees in Algeria, the ICRC should maintain its discretionary policies in order to maximize ICRC acceptability to all parties in the future.

During this public uproar about torture in Algeria, the ICRC continued its discretionary activities in metropolitan France. In addition to prison visits, the ICRC tried to mitigate the harshness of French judicial procedures vis-à-vis Algerians. It supported the movement to adopt a special penal code for Algerian detainees, which succeeded in 1961. And ICRC delegates followed detainees into court to observe trial procedure. Of special concern to some ICRC delegates was the problem of protecting detainees from pro-NLF lawyers. These lawyers, supposedly acting to defend detainees, had a tendency to argue that the individual was engaged in war and that in war killing occurs. Since French courts were not receptive to this argument as a valid defense for acts committed, the argument led to sure and heavy sentences. While the ICRC was concerned about this situation and its impact on the individuals, the organization was at a loss as to how to alter the situation.

But in general ICRC efforts had great impact on France in the Algerian War, perhaps the greatest impact of any ICRC activity in any war. This impact was not, however, completely of the ICRC's making. *Le Monde*'s exposé, in the context of an increasingly unpopular war, had a great deal to do with creating that impact.

The War's End and Thereafter. Under the Evian Accords of 1962 ending the Algerian War, France and the NLF agreed to a ceasefire and the release of prisoners of war within twenty days. The ICRC was named in the Accords as an intermediary in these matters, and the parties agreed to give to the ICRC the location of internment places and the names of detainees.

The French largely complied with these provisions, being anxious to terminate a long and lost effort. The NLF did not. Lack of NLF cooperation led the ICRC to make repeated efforts to gain information on, and admittance to, the detainees held by the NLF. The Algerian Red Crescent was a frequent go-between. Finally the ICRC made a public statement criticizing the NLF. While some prisoners were released to the ICRC, many were unaccounted for. The ICRC never gained access or satisfactory information. This situation led to friction between the ICRC and the Algerian Red Crescent.

In addition to concern over French military personnel, some 200 of which were never accounted for, the French were also concerned about the fate of many civilians in Algeria. These were not covered by the Evian Accords. In early 1963, after it was clear that the Algerian authorities had said all they were going to say regarding military personnel, the ICRC was asked to make a study regarding the fate of civilians. This request was by agreement of Algeria and France. Some 1,200 civilians of French nationality were unaccounted for in Algeria. In addition, many Harkis (Algerian-born Arabs who served with the French during the war) were missing.

The ICRC was accorded partial cooperation by Algeria for this inquiry. The study could only definitively account for about 25 percent of the missing French. (Of this portion, half were certified as dead; 15 percent were located in French prisons; 20 percent were otherwise located; and 15 percent remained unaccounted for but probably dead.) All the rest were totally unaccounted for. Of the Harkis, the ICRC reported that some 2,500 were detained by Algeria at the end of the war. (Algeria subsequently agreed to liberate them, but upon liberation about 5 percent were killed by the Arab population. So some were put in protective custody, and many were transferred to France.)

Beyond the subjects of military and civilian personnel, the ICRC also had extensive dealings with the Algerian Red Crescent immediately after the war. These two Red Cross agencies signed an agreement under which the ICRC agreed to promote the development of the national society in certain ways.

Despite wartime frictions, therefore, the ICRC was acceptable to the two governments, and to the Algerian Red Crescent, for certain postwar tasks. These tasks led to more friction, not only because the Algerians were uncooperative regarding military personnel but also because the French were uncooperative for a time regarding the distribution of material assistance. Given persistent differences of opinion between the ICRC and the Algerians, it is striking that the

Algerians permitted the ICRC to conduct the study on missing civilians—a sensitive subject involving both the use of terror by the Algerians and their detention policies.

In sum, in the Algerian War the ICRC found a situation similar in some ways to the Korean War and the French phase of the war in Indochina. There was not a situation of reciprocity between the parties concerning ICRC visits to individuals. Despite this fact, the ICRC did not whitewash the problems existing on the side it visited. Indeed, the work of the ICRC on the French side in the Algerian War, made known to the Western public as never before because of *Le Monde*'s exposé, no doubt enhanced the image of the institution as a thorough and responsible humanitarian organization. Some observers, however, might question the ICRC's silence in the face of the use of torture as a policy, not just as sporadic acts by individuals.

The ICRC's long involvement in the Algerian War and its aftermath was of some help to the ICRC when it found itself once again involved in an armed conflict in Indochina—this time in the American phase of that war.

Indochina War, American Phase

Factual Situation and Legal Policy.　　After the close of the French phase of the conflict in 1954, the struggle continued between forces under Ho Chi Minh and opposing forces using Saigon as a central base. The United States replaced France as the prime mover in the south. The United States never accepted the outcome dictated by the French phase, a fact not only demonstrated by the oft-cited example of Secretary of State Dulles's behavior at the 1954 Geneva Conference (he refused to shake hands with his North Vietnamese counterpart). U.S. refusal to accept a communist Vietnam was even better demonstrated by the covert intervention of the CIA against the military capability of North Vietnam before the ink was dry—so to speak—on the Geneva Accords.[28]

For almost ten years, between 1954 and the mid-1960's, this violent struggle attracted little public attention outside Indochina. For its part, the ICRC maintained one delegate in the area. The agency sought the application of Common Article 3 by the parties in Hanoi and Saigon, presumably on the view that the situation was a civil war within the one state of Vietnam. Such a view was supported by the logic of the 1954 Geneva Accords, which called for elections throughout the territory of Vietnam to determine the future of that area, and which did not explicitly mention or in any way recognize a second government in the south. ICRC efforts in support of Common Article 3 did not appear to be the most vigorous that could be imagined. Hanoi did not formally admit the relevance of that part of the law. There appeared to have been some attention to Common Article 3 by authorities in Saigon, at the prodding of Americans.[29]

In 1965, in the context of escalating violence, the ICRC wrote formal letters to the United States, the Republic of Vietnam (South), the Democratic Republic of Vietnam (North), and the National Liberation Front (Viet Cong), stating its views that an international armed conflict existed and asking the parties to accept legal obligations under the four Geneva Conventions of 1949.[30]

U.S. Response. After several months' delay, the United States accepted the view that the situation in Vietnam was an international armed conflict regulated by the 1949 Geneva Conventions. The U.S. response was consistent with American claims that North Vietnam was engaging in international aggression across an international boundary and threatening the existence of a legitimate regime in South Vietnam that had a right to individual and collective self defense. Thus the ICRC position was compatible with the basic American view of the war.

American decision makers saw certain problems in formally agreeing with the ICRC on the applicability of the 1949 Conventions, but the dominant thought in official circles was that the risks inherent in accepting that law were preferable to the risks involved in rejecting the ICRC's position.[31] An American rejection of that view not only would have weakened the basic American argument that Hanoi was engaging in aggression, but also would have exposed the American government to domestic and foreign criticism for ignoring law that logically should apply. The U.S. government was also concerned with reciprocity in implementing the laws of war. Therefore Washington instructed the American Embassy in Saigon to take the steps necessary to bring American policy into compliance with the Third Convention especially. When the embassy objected, Washington reaffirmed its decision. The embassy was also instructed to make an effort to bring Saigon's policies into line with this basic decision.

The United States started a search for a Protecting Power to oversee the implementation of the Geneva Conventions. The United States wanted to find a state to serve as a Protecting Power for both itself and North Vietnam, in order to facilitate rapid communication and mutual trust in humanitarian matters. But finding such a state acceptable to both was not easy. After considering France and other parties, the United States reached agreement with Egypt that that state would serve as the Protecting Power of American interests vis-à-vis North Vietnam. But Hanoi rejected the arrangement in the context of publicity from the Western press.[32] Finally, the U.S. asked the ICRC to take action under the Third Convention regarding humanitarian affairs in the South.

Other humanitarian issues confronted the Americans, requiring a legal opinion. In the late 1960's, there was widespread concern over the treatment meeted out to certain detainees once they were in the hands of the South Vietnamese. Some of these individuals had been captured by American forces. But it was American policy to turn over all captives to Saigon. In this situation, the ICRC approached the American government and called its attention to Article 12 in the Third Geneva Convention. This article states that the capturing power retains ''residual authority'' over those it captures, regardless of what power is actually in physical control of the detainee.

After some discussion within the Administration—in which there were differences of opinion between the White House and the State Department—the U.S. in 1969 reaffirmed its full residual responsibility for prisoners of war captured by it and turned over to the Saigon regime. But the United States refused to accept full residual responsibility for "civilian defendants" initially detained by the U.S. and then turned over to Saigon authorities for prosecution or detention under the law of South Vietnam. For these the U.S., under directives from the White House, accepted only residual responsibility under Common Article 3. This meant, in logic, that the U.S. recognized a civil war within an international war, and that in dealing with civilians rather than prisoners of war the Saigon regime had only to meet the vague standards of the Common Article.

In its reply to the ICRC on this question, the United States called attention to the lack of a legal basis in the Geneva Conventions for ICRC intervention in behalf of South Vietnamese civilian prisoners. The U.S. reply disagreed with the ICRC's contention that provisions of the Fourth Convention were relevant to this situation. The United States did say that the ICRC should be given access to civilian prisoners on the same basis as for prisoners of war. (Saigon authorities, however, did not agree to permitting ICRC visits to civilian detainees on that unconditional basis.)

The South Vietnamese Response.   The government in Saigon, under American pressure, also accepted the legal validity of the 1949 Conventions insofar as they pertained to international armed conflict, and especially to prisoners of war. The government had adhered to the 1949 Conventions in 1953. Virtually all regular North Vietnamese troops operating in the South were, upon capture and detention, classified as prisoners of war under the Third Convention as supervised by the ICRC. In addition, Viet Cong captured in battle were also so regarded legally. This latter protection went beyond the strict necessities of the technical meaning of the Third Convention, which requires, among other things, that combatants, in order to qualify for prisoner-of-war protection, wear uniforms and carry arms openly. This extension of the scope of the Third Convention was worked out by the ICRC and American authorities, and the Saigon authorities were "brought on board" by the Americans.

While problems occurred in implementing the Third Convention, that protection was extended to some 40,000 individuals during the American phase of the war, over three-quarters of whom were irregular combatants.

With regard to prisoners not viewed by Saigon as prisoners of war, Saigon claimed (as noted briefly above) that these individuals were a subject of domestic jurisdiction and therefore altogether outside the scope of the international law of armed conflict. This constituted a major controversy. There were allegations that the process of differentiating a prisoner of war from a "civilian defendant" was highly arbitrary.[33]

The North Vietnamese Response.   The government of the Democratic Republic of Vietnam had adhered to the 1949 Geneva Conventions in 1957.

At that time, like other socialist states, it had appended a reservation to Article 85 of the Third Convention. That reservation stated, in part, that the protection of the Third Convention would not be extended to those "prosecuted for and convicted of" crimes occurring prior to capture.[34] Before the American phase of the Indochina War, it had been ascertained what the Soviet Union had meant by its similar reservation. In an exchange of letters with the Swiss government, the Soviets had indicated their reservation did *not* vitiate the protection of the Third Convention *prior* to conviction for war crimes.[35] It was generally assumed that the North Vietnamese reservation meant the same, for to argue otherwise would negate the meaning of the entire Third Convention and would thus be logically inconsistent with adherance to that Convention.

Nevertheless, North Vietnam claimed that American flyers detained by it had committed a war crime by waging aggressive, imperialistic war and were thus not subject to the protection of the Third Convention under the terms of North Vietnam's reservation. Not only the ICRC but most legal scholars—at least the non-Marxist ones—disagreed with this interpretation.[36]

Now it can be fairly stated that North Vietnamese legal arguments were not always carefully considered. Hanoi's legal arguments for its reservation to the Third Convention were largely specious, a conclusion supported by careful legal scrutiny. Hanoi's legal arguments were also confused from the standpoint of the politics of law. The North Vietnamese response to the ICRC's 1965 letter constituted an essay on the alleged illegality of American entry into the war. Thus Hanoi's response refused to accept the widely recognized distinction between the process of war—with which the ICRC is concerned—and the start of war. Moreover, subsequent to North Vietnam's refusal to accept legal obligations with regard to the process of war, that regime protested to the ICRC alleged violations of precisely that law. Despite its rejection of the application of the Third Convention in the North, Hanoi requested application of the Fourth in the South. In transmitting North Vietnamese claims that American bombing violated parts of the Fourth Convention, the ICRC could not logically have entertained much hope about a positive response to those claims, in the light of Hanoi's flagrant rejection of the Third Convention.[37] In point of fact the ICRC was not able to generate a positive response in Washington or Saigon, despite the very real probability that certain American and South Vietnamese policies did indeed violate aspects of the Fourth Convention—especially American bombing.[38]

Thus the overall North Vietnamese approach to the law of armed conflict was inconsistent: it tried to select the parts of the law it wished to utilize in criticizing its opponents, and to reject that part that pertained to its own actions. While this tendency is not the monopoly of Hanoi, that regime's blatant inconsistency reduced the impact of its propagandistic and other, more legally legitimate, efforts with regard to the Fourth Convention. Moreover Hanoi's policy of rejecting the Third Convention meant that it would have great difficulty in raising the subject of conditions of detention in the South. In point of fact, Hanoi did not directly raise the question of detention in the South with the ICRC and seemed largely unconcerned about the fate of North Vietnamese and Viet Cong prisoners.

Be that as it may, in retrospect it is clear that Hanoi adopted a general policy of rejecting all legal obligations and systematic inspection related to prisoners of war. It has been argued that—legal arguments aside—Hanoi's actual behavior was not very different from that of its opponents concerning humanitarian issues,[39] although that seems difficult to substantiate.[40]

The NLF Response.   The Vietnamese National Liberation Front developed a different legal argument from Hanoi, but the practical result for the ICRC and for NLF-held detainees was the same. The NLF consistently pointed out to the ICRC that it was not bound by any part of the 1949 Conventions as it had not adhered to that body of law. While asserting that its detainees would be treated humanely, the NLF explicitly rejected any legal obligation of any kind. This policy position was articulated during 1965 and 1966. Indeed, by the end of the latter year the NLF had told the ICRC through three different contacts that the ICRC had received the final word on the subject.

ICRC Activity.   ICRC activity during the American phase of the Indochina War may be summarized under four headings: (1) the issue of American pilots held by Hanoi; (2) the issue of detainees held by Saigon; (3) the issue of American bombing in both North and South; and (4) the issue of detainees held by the Viet Cong.

1. American pilots held by Hanoi. When Lieutenant-Commander Alvarez became the first American military pilot to fall into North Vietnamese hands in 1964, it appeared that Hanoi—as in early stages of the French phase—did not have a firm policy on the subject of enemy prisoners of war. Third-party reports reached the ICRC indicating that Alvarez was being considered as a prisoner of war in law and in fact. The ICRC was able to get some family packages to him using the Cambodian Red Cross as intermediary. And North Vietnam itself released some information to the ICRC in 1965.

Increasingly, however, Hanoi developed the policy of silence, no legal obligations, and no ICRC or other systematic visits regarding American personnel. During the period 1966–69, during which Hanoi's policy became clear, the ICRC was very active diplomatically in trying to obtain access to the growing number of detainees in the North. Establishing contacts and learning Hanoi's position were not major problems despite the pro-Western image of the ICRC in the eyes of North Vietnam.[41] ICRC–North Vietnamese relations were carried on in Moscow, in certain Arab capitals, and at Paris. The Americans had their contacts at these and other places, and not only government officials but also American Red Cross leaders had conversations with various socialist and third-world parties. The problem in trying to protect individuals in the North was not ICRC image and difficulties in communication, but rather what was being communicated. Hanoi's policy of rejection of the Third Convention became clear in this period. Egypt was as unacceptable to Hanoi as the ICRC for supervision of law that was undesired.

The ICRC could achieve little primarily because Hanoi adopted a "hard line" with regard to detainees, coupled with selective release and repatriation of some personnel. Nine American pilots were released by North Vietnam during the war, either to further the antiwar movement in the United States, or to exert psychological pressure on the remaining pilots in the North, or to demonstrate the nature of detention in the North, or for some other reason. The ICRC was ignored by Hanoi in these release operations.

The ICRC received increased attention from the U.S. after 1969, because the subject of American prisoners of war in the North became more directly tied to bargaining on the basic issues of the war. The Nixon Administration, upon the recommendation of Secretary of Defense Laird, consciously decided to "go public" on the subject of prisoners of war. Thus the effort was made, 1969 to 1973, to exert public pressure on Hanoi to get a change in its policy on POWs— and to bring to the surface an issue on which the badly divided American public could agree. The American Red Cross was involved in this publicity effort. As a result, questions were raised in Congress as to whether the activities of the American Red Cross were proper.[42]

But as the American government tried to exert public pressure on Hanoi to release American detainees, Hanoi tried to turn the pressure against Washington by arguing that the American prisoners of war would be released when the Americans withdrew from Vietnam. If the Americans wanted the men so badly, all they had to do was leave.

The ICRC was drawn into this process of increased public attention to the POW question because the United States directed many proposals and inquiries through the ICRC. But the ICRC was unable to achieve any change in the situation. Indeed, the more the issue became public and tied to the core issues of the war, the less room there was to maneuver on humanitarian grounds.

In retrospect, it appears that the American decision to go public did cause Hanoi slightly to modify some of its policies on the detainees. There was an increase of information regarding who was detained, although this release of information became controversial. U.S. officials disagreed with Hanoi as to the accuracy of the information. For its part, the ICRC had no way to check the accuracy; and the information had been first given to other parties and only later to the ICRC. But despite the increase in publicity during 1969 and thereafter, there were no further releases, no access for the ICRC, and no change in North Vietnamese legal claims.

In 1973, the United States and North Vietnam, along with Saigon and the Viet Cong, signed the Paris Accords. As part of the Accords, American detainees were to be repatriated in return for progressive American military withdrawal from Vietnam. The ICRC was not involved in any of this, in deference to

Hanoi's wishes, although the U.S. sought to include the ICRC as an intermediary.[43]

Thus some 500 American military personnel were released without a role for the ICRC. As for their treatment and conditions of detention, it would appear that, in relative terms, their treatment was considerably better than was the case for American personnel held in North Korea, or for Algerians held by the French. There appears to have been some physical abuse, and psychological pressure was sometimes applied through solitary confinement and systematic deprivation of favors. On the other hand, some American prisoners indicated they had intentionally provoked their captors in order to challenge Hanoi's authority and to build morale among the prisoners.[44]

Throughout the 1960's and 1970's, the ICRC had done what it could in behalf of these individuals. It had sent its delegates around the world in an effort to make contacts with Hanoi's representatives, including sending personnel to mix with Indochinese communist circles in Paris. Some criticized the ICRC for turning the question into a legal issue too quickly and for issuing statements implying criticism of Hanoi.

2. Detainees held by Saigon. Alleged or real combatants taken prisoner in the South frequently suffered a cruel fate, certainly until the mid-1960's. During this period, it appeared to make little difference whether the Army of the Republic of Vietnam (ARVN) was the sole captor and interrogator, or whether American personnel were present or did the capturing. Although definitive proof is lacking, press coverage on the subject makes it apparent that summary executions, torture, mistreatment, and poor detention conditions did exist.

This press coverage, rather than action by the ICRC, accounts for the fact that from about 1965 the United States began to take steps to improve the handling of prisoners *taken by it or in its presence*. Washington officials, operating in a context of criticism of their policies in Vietnam, were embarrassed by many of the press reports and photos. It was not unknown for a story to appear in the American press and for Washington immediately to send a cable to its Saigon Embassy asking for investigation of the reported incident. It was in the mid-1960's, amongst this publicity, that Washington authorities began to prosecute American personnel for violations of the laws of war.[45] By the end of the Johnson Administration, the situation had vastly improved for those taken prisoner by the Americans or in their presence. Given the pervasive nature of the American military effort, this change accounted for better treatment for the bulk of combatant detainees in the South.

A persistent problem was *Saigon's* treatment of combatant prisoners. That regime had friction, not only with the ICRC, but with the United States as to how captured fighters were to be treated. When a problem arose, the ICRC not only dealt directly with Saigon but also sought to press the United States in an effort to get a change of policy by South Vietnam. Both in the Johnson and Nixon Administrations, it occurred that the ICRC would make a request to the U.S.

government regarding detainees in the South, and Washington would immediately send a cable to the Embassy in Saigon instructing it to try and secure the cooperation of Saigon officials. Secretary of Defense Laird was essentially correct when he said in 1970, "We have cooperated, and the South Vietnamese—we have insisted that they follow the rules—have cooperated with the International Red Cross on every occasion. Any recommendation which is made by them is implemented as rapidly as possible."[46]

In the last three to four years of the war, in the South the ICRC had complete access to those detained as prisoners of war under South Vietnamese authority. This meant that the ICRC was supervising the conditions of detention of some 40,000 persons, eight to nine thousand of whom were North Vietnamese regular military personnel. The situation for these 40,000 individuals was improved over a considerable length of time, although there were problems of varying importance and duration. For example, in 1970 there were still major problems of overcrowding and especially mistreatment at the large POW camp at Phu Quoc.[47]

In 1971, the ICRC was asked to arrange the repatriation of some of these prisoners of war to the North, as the U.S. and Saigon hoped to effect reciprocal action from Hanoi. The ICRC carried out the request, but no reciprocity was forthcoming—perhaps in part because American and South Vietnamese officials directed such publicity to the ICRC-supervised effort that it appeared to Hanoi as a propaganda stunt. In any event, controversy surrounded the repatriation scheme, with the ICRC implicated.

The major problem in the South was not prisoners of war but what Saigon called "civilian defendants". In the mid-1960's the ICRC, Saigon, and the U.S. had reached agreement on a definition of prisoners of war. While this went considerably beyond the requirements of the 1949 law, it left a large number of persons outside that definition who might reasonably be considered to be detained because of the conflict. For example, a nonfighting member of the NLF was not considered to be a prisoner of war but was, when captured, left to the mercy, such as it was, of Saigon. Therefore the ICRC agreed on a definition of prisoners of war, then sought access to the remaining "civilian defendants." The ICRC probably was too quick to formalize its access to prisoners of war, as this made access to civilians more difficult.

At one end of the scale of possible types of prisoners, there was a difference of opinion about who was a prisoner of war and who was a "civilian defendant." In the middle of the scale there was what the ICRC regarded as the political prisoner—the individual indigenous to the South and not a member of the Viet Cong, who was detained because the Saigon regime regarded his opinions or actions as a threat. At the other end of the scale, there was a difference of opinion as to who was, on the one hand, a prisoner of war or political prisoner, and, on the other hand, who was a regular civilian defendant under South Vietnamese national law. And in the case of, say, the individual arrested for violating curfew or carrying a concealed weapon, there was considerable question as to the accuracy of Saigon's decisions regarding which of the three categories of detainees he really was: prisoner of war, political prisoner, regular prisoner (see figure 6.1).

This confusing situation had long been of concern to the ICRC. After the Geneva Accords of 1954 but before American military intervention, the ICRC had been able to make some visits to what it termed political prisoners under the Diem regime. While these visits had no precise legal basis in international law, and while the access of the ICRC was never complete, still the ICRC saw a number of non-POW detainees held in the South—after 1958 and especially after 1966. Sometimes the ICRC managed to hold private talks with the prisoners, sometimes a governmental representative was present. The same general situation prevailed under governments subsequent to Diem.

In 1965, however, the Saigon governement closed off its jails and other civilian prisoner installations to the ICRC. The motivation for this move is difficult to establish. Perhaps it was an effort by the government to draw the line regarding ICRC supervision, since it was during 1965 that the ICRC gained formal access rights to prisoners of war. The ICRC was able to gain some access to "civilian defendants" the following year, and from 1966 to the 1968 Tet offensive the ICRC was once again able to see some non-POW detainees on an unsystematic basis and without general permission or "ground-rules." All visits to "civilian defendants" were suspended because of the disorder produced in the region by Tet.

In 1969, the ICRC received general permission from the highest levels of the Saigon government to visit "civilian defendants": the ICRC was to give one month's notice of the places it wanted to visit; no private talks were to occur with prisoners; and the prison at Con Son was off limits except for POWs. The ICRC did not reject this governmental permission "with strings" but set out to test the new system. Even under this governmental directive, the ICRC was refused access to certain places by local authorities.

Figure 6.1.   South Vietnam: Types of Prisoners[1]

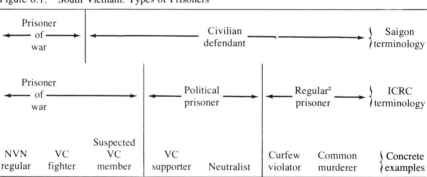

[1]Omits detention categories under Fourth Convention, as Saigon declared that legal instrument was not relevant.
[2]Or "penal law prisoner"; in French, "prisonnier de droit commun."

Then in 1970 controversy erupted over the prison at Con Son. The finding of the "tiger cages" by an American Congressional delegation, and the dramatization of the issue of mistreatment of civilian prisoners by the Western press, led eventually to a tougher bargaining position by the ICRC on the subject of its access to these prisoners.

First of all, Saigon, in an effort to counteract criticism, issued an erroneous statement saying the ICRC had visited Con Son and had certified that conditions were good. The ICRC immediately protested to the government and issued a statement saying it had been restricted to the part of Con Son containing prisoners of war; it had never been given access to the greatest part of the prison which housed the civilian prisoners.[48]

Second, and despite the false nature of the statement by South Vietnam, the ICRC seems to have felt embarrassed by not being better informed on the situation. The ICRC in Geneva had received detailed information from a private and reliable source concerning the situation at Con Son some years before the situation became public knowledge. It appears that the ICRC had not taken vigorous action on the basis of that information. Certainly the ICRC had not been able to ameliorate the situation regarding the tiger cages before the Congressional discovery.

Thirdly, the ICRC approached the Americans in an effort to gain some further access to civilian prisoners in the South. But the U.S. did not pressure Saigon effectively on the subject. The U.S. gave the ICRC little direct and effective support on the question of "civilian defendants," aside from assisting Saigon through goods, police training, and the building of newer prisons (the ICRC was given a look at some of the blueprints for comments).[49]

Fourthly, and most importantly, the ICRC tested a statement issued by the Saigon government at the time of the Con Son controversy. The government at that time said: "The Government of the Republic of Viet Nam is always prepared to assist qualified international institutions which may wish to make on-the-spot visits to its correctional institutions and prison camps." The ICRC found this statement to be without meaning. Between the Con Son controversy of 1970 and March 1972, the ICRC tried to resume its prison visits to civilian prisoners according to its standard rules of procedure—viz., general access, talks without witnesses, and repeated visits. These techniques are a counterweight to any effort by the detaining authority to use ICRC advance notice of visits in order to hide a prisoner from the ICRC.

But in March 1972, the ICRC took the unusual step of itself suspending visits to civilian prisoners in the South. The ICRC believed that the Saigon regime was attempting to manipulate the ICRC—i.e., trying to get it to continue its prison visits so the regime could say the Red Cross was present, while preventing the ICRC from doing any good for the prisoners. Saigon put so many obstacles in the way of the ICRC that after over a year of further efforts the ICRC reached the conclusion that the Red Cross symbol was being damaged without any corresponding benefit for the detainees. Therefore it quit.[50]

The ICRC made one subsequent visit to a place of civilian detention, at the request of Saigon, in order to help stabilize a riotous situation that was injurious to detainees. After the 1973 Paris Accords were signed but not implemented, the ICRC took the initiative to call the attention of the parties to the fact of nonimplementation and to offer its services in the implementation of the protocol dealing with prisoners.[51] This effort was unsuccessful. Except for these two efforts, the ICRC was finished with civilian prisoners in the South because of the 1972 withdrawal.

This meant that somewhere between 30,000 and 200,000 individuals were detained by Saigon, without international inspection, either because of some relation to the Indochina War or as political prisoners. The numbers were elusive because of the vagueness of categories of prisoners. (Did one consider as a political prisoner someone in the Chieu Hoi program—that is, someone who had allegedly fought for the VC but had rallied to Saigon's side and was kept in detention for political education purposes?) While the numbers were difficult to establish, there were few observers who though arrest and detention in Saigon's jails were anything but arbitrary and harsh.[52]

With regard to visits to civilian prisoners, the ICRC had found Saigon opposed, Washington not interested enough to generate effective pressure, and Hanoi and the NLF apparently accepting the situation as a fact of life.

3. American bombing. Legally speaking, the conduct of bombing operations, and whether such operations harm civilians rather than combatants, are issues separate from the issue of prisoners of war. Means and methods of war are supposedly regulated by the Hague Conventions, inter alia, and civilians are supposedly protected by the Fourth Geneva Convention of 1949, not the Third. Nevertheless, in the Vietnam War there was a logical connection between bombing and prisoners of war, and the ICRC was active on both issues. Therefore the subject of bombing is briefly included here.

The relationship between bombing and prisoners of war is well captured by S. D. Bailey:[53]

> The present state of humanitarian law has paradoxical results. The crew of a bombing plane may direct their weapons against a military target in a built-up area and, as an indirect consequence, may kill or injure tens or hundreds of thousands of "innocent" civilians. If the plane is later hit by anti-aircraft fire, the crew may eject or bail out, and then claim the full protection of the Hague and Geneva Conventions from those who may have survived the attack.

Surely a part of Hanoi's reasoning toward American pilots detained in the North was based on its view that the bombing was aggressive and indiscriminate—views repeatedly expressed to the ICRC and other parties. The ICRC no doubt perceived this relationship between POWs and bombing. Moreover, the ICRC was concerned about the impact of bombing on civilians in both North and South, and about the striking of medical and other nonmilitary targets.

For these reasons, and in the context of mounting concern over prisoners of war in the North, the ICRC wrote the United States in 1966 and thereafter to express its concern about American bombing policies.[54] There was no change in American policies. The Americans had felt for some time that they had taken steps to make their bombing as accurate as possible, including the use of approach paths that subjected American pilots to increased anti-aircraft fire for the sake of improved accuracy.[55] Noncommunist, eye-witness reports, however, indicated widespread destruction of schools, hospitals, and other nonmilitary targets in the North, and widespread destruction in the South.[56]

In the final years of the American phase of the war, the ICRC continued privately to express its concern to the United States. In 1972, the United States agreed with the ICRC to examine the possibility of creating neutral zones in the South which would be sanctuaries from bombing and other military operations. The United States asked the ICRC to get the other fighting parties to examine this idea and to see if it could be made acceptable to all. In return for the creation of the sanctuaries, the United States would ask that its opponents not conduct military operations in the zone and that, among other things, freedom of movement be maintained through the zone. The negotiation of the Paris Accords in 1973 superseded this limited diplomatic exchange.

American bombing policies, therefore, were not significantly altered from their military rationale for the sake of humanitarian concerns. This made ICRC efforts in behalf of American prisoners of war more difficult (although there is no evidence that Hanoi would have changed its policies toward POWs had American bombing policies been different). But like the use of free fire zones and search and destroy missions on the ground, American bombing policies helped to create a climate of opinion pervading the Vietnam War that made it difficult to focus strictly humanitarian interest on prisoners of war. Both bombing and prisoners of war became issues central to the bargaining over the future of Vietnam; thus they became predominantly issues in realpolitik, and their humanitarian dimensions receded.

4. Detainees held by the NLF. During the war, there was no legal obligation accepted by the NLF, and there was never any international supervision for the 60–90 American detainees held by the NLF at any one time. The same situation prevailed for other detainees.

While the NLF claimed that it treated its detainees humanely, and while in general summary executions and torture were not characteristic, nevertheless the very nature of a war of movement without fixed sanctuaries in the South meant that there would be great hardship for NLF detainees. The ICRC delivered some medical assistance to the NLF via Hanoi, and offered medical teams, which were rejected. For NLF detainees held in the South, detention did not appear to meet the standards of Common Article 3.[57]

Some detainees of the NLF were transferred to the North, generally by forced marches. While this probably resulted in improved conditions of detention, it also resulted in a lack of clear authority over the prisoners. The NLF did not admit to the transfer, and North Vietnam did not admit to knowing anything about such individuals. The problems of international supervision and accountability, already considerable, were magnified.

Sporadic releases occurred throughout the war for detainees under the NLF. The ICRC was not involved in any of these. At the end of the American phase of the war, numerous individuals allegedly captured by the NLF were unaccounted for.

ICRC Activity in Review.   In the early years of the American phase of the Indochina War—viz., in the mid-1950's—the ICRC was on the scene, doing what it could. The scale of its protection efforts was small, as there was little international concern for Vietnam at that stage compared to Hungary, Suez, and Algeria.

Some ICRC formal actions were carefully considered. Initial efforts to have Common Article 3 accepted were in keeping with the logic of the 1954 Geneva Accords—that is, that there was a civil war within the one state of Vietnam.

Likewise, the ICRC's recognition of two Vietnamese Red Cross Societies was reasonably well handled. While the entire question of recognition might have been delayed, it can also be argued that formal recognition was merited on humanitarian grounds, i.e., to improve the infrastructure for material and medical assistance. When the ICRC recognized the Society in the South in 1957, it stated that such recognition did not preclude the recognition of a Society in the North. And the ICRC quickly recognized the Society in the North when it applied for recognition shortly thereafter. ICRC statements in 1957 about recognition were a signal to Hanoi to seek recognition for its Society, a signal correctly perceived.[58]

The ICRC tried to establish an impartial image. The ICRC did offer material and medical assistance to all parties early in the conflict. More importantly, it sought independence from other Red Cross organizations in the South. When several national Red Cross Societies undertook material assistance programs that the ICRC thought were too closely linked to the aims of the government in Saigon, the ICRC disassociated itself from these efforts. The ICRC also displayed an interest in certain refugee and minority problems in the South that the South Vietnamese Red Cross and its supporters did not particularly like.[59] The ICRC also became increasingly assertive vis-à-vis South Vietnam on the question of "civilian defendants." But none of this ICRC activity had any noticeable impact on Hanoi's attitude toward the ICRC.

The above is not to say that the ICRC was perfect in its activity. In particular, some of its personnel in the South seemed openly pro-American, even as they appeared openly anti-Saigon. There were other personnel problems as well.[60] And it took the Con Son controversy to cause the ICRC to "get tough" with Saigon on the question of civilian prisoners. Moreover, whereas the ICRC added its voice to the protest against 1966 moves to try American pilots as war criminals in Hanoi, the ICRC did not add its voice to the protest against the murder of civilians at My Lai and other places in the South. It is argued by some that the two situations are not comparable, that an ICRC voice was not needed regarding My Lai, since steps were taken by appropriate national officials. Nevertheless, some observers believe the ICRC was too much concerned with a few professional fighters detained in the North and not concerned enough about large numbers of civilians endangered in both North and South.

In evaluating ICRC efforts in the American phase of the Indochina War, it is important to note the general view of the war emanating from Hanoi. It appears that the ICRC was rejected by North Vietnam on policy grounds, not primarily because of tactical mistakes or image. North Vietnam had a parochial, "just war" view of the situation. It was in the right; its opponents were wrong. Therefore its opponents had no legal rights. Furthermore, Hanoi recognized that prisoners of war were a useful bargaining weapon, and that every aspect of detention could be utilized in bargaining, despite the words of the Third Convention. Further, Hanoi was a relatively closed and highly nationalistic society and thus did not want foreigners investigating what occurred on its territory.

The clearest statement of North Vietnamese policy toward humanitarian questions occurred after the American phase of the war had ended.[61] At the 1974 session of the Geneva Conference on humanitarian law, the North Vietnamese delegation argued that the aim of "humanitarian" law should be to oppose imperialistic aggression as a war crime, that the separation of aggression and humanitarian laws of war was dated and unacceptable, and that the effort to balance humanitarianism with military necessity was "inadequate and dangerous" and "should be excluded." The intent of the North Vietnamese statement was implicitly to defend the idea of just war: the imperialistic aggressor is wrong and has no legal rights; all law should favor the "under-developed and ill-equipped peoples." Those struggling against imperialism are just, and law should reflect that value judgment. Thus there is no room for jus in bello, humanitarian law, and neutrality. There is only room for a blanket condemnation of imperialistic aggression. Given the North Vietnamese psychological framework reflected in this legal statement, it is no wonder that the ICRC was not acceptable to Hanoi.

The ICRC and humanitarian law were accepted to some extent by the United States for two primary reasons: as a government under law, the United States would have found it embarrassing to ignore the Geneva Conventions after it had claimed that Hanoi was engaging in international aggression; and the United States needed a respected international presence in that conflict since its own involvement was so controversial at home and abroad.

Saigon accepted the ICRC and accompanying law where the United States pressured it to do so. Where the United States did not generate effective pressure, as on the issue of "civilian defendants," Saigon did not respond affirmatively to humanitarian requests.

Combatants and the ICRC

It bears repeating that the Indochina War, both phases, and the Algerian War do not explain everything. Vietnam is not Bangladesh; Algeria is not Syria. These case studies do, however, demonstrate some of the basic problems and accomplishments of the ICRC as it seeks to protect combatants in the modern period of world politics.

In addition to the problems and accomplishments already noted, it can be said first of all that humanitarian protection and ICRC supervision may be asymmetrical, and it would seem that reciprocity is not at all the backstop to the laws of war that it has been pictured to be. Conflicting parties may accept legal protection and accept the ICRC less for reasons of reciprocity (though it may be hoped for in the future) than for reasons of law abidance and the need to offset criticism. (Some protection and ICRC access is reciprocal, as has been the case in the Middle East wars and in the wars for Bangladesh and Cyprus.) The ICRC has long argued that application of humanitarian law should not be governed by considerations of reciprocity. A good deal of behavior can be cited in support of that ICRC argument. The difference between argument and behavior does not seem so great. It is probable, however, that the moral motivation of the ICRC on this issue is not matched by fighting parties, who no doubt engage in asymmetrical protection and assistance for reasons of expediency.

Secondly, it bears repeating that the ICRC has great difficulty, like others, in matching the 1949 Conventions to factual situations like Vietnam and Algeria. In particular, the difference between a combatant who is hors de combat and a detained civilian is exceedingly difficult to establish in what is legally an international armed conflict, but one fought within one territorial unit. Trying to distinguish between persons protected by the Third and Fourth Conventions in an unconventional war, where suspected fighters may be nationals of the government being fought, is an insoluble problem for the standpoint of the wording of the 1949 Conventions. The ICRC was probably badly advised to emphasize the Fourth Convention in its dealings with Saigon concerning unarmed persons considered by that regime as its nationals. The ICRC would have been better advised to seek access to suspected fighters denied prisoner-of-war status, and to other persons, by (1) avoiding all legal labels; or (2) retaining an emphasis on Common Article 3, which applies simply to people detained by reason of events or conflict; or (3) utilizing an informal and broad definition of prisoner of war under the Third Convention. None of these approaches is free from problems, but the ICRC approach used in Vietnam—viz., an early and formal definition of a prisoner of war and then reliance of the wording of the Fourth Convention—gave Saigon authorities a traditional legal argument with which to block ICRC access to detainees denied prisoner-of-war status.

Thirdly, despite problems in its application, the Third Convention and prisoners of war have high standing among most regimes and in most conflicts. It is generally expected that the ICRC will have some role to play in their regard. The authorities that reject the terms of the Third Convention and the ICRC pay a price in terms of criticism from governmental and popular circles. There is thus an informal and "built-in" sanction at work in support of protection and assistance for prisoners of war. Widespread support for the concept of prisoner of war, and for third-party supervision of their detention, is both clear and clearly increasing.[62] The ICRC has played an important role in this process. Incumbent in this role, however, is the moral obligation not to permit the high standing of the Third Convention and prisoners of war to obscure the need for improved protection and assistance to civilians in a war zone—the subject of the following chapter.

7 ICRC Legal Protection and Assistance: Civilians

The ICRC has been concerned for the fate of civilians in a conflict situation for some time, even though the organization is better known for its work with prisoners of war (and even though the ICRC has recently been devoting more attention to the "first cousins" of prisoners of war—political prisoners). Stimulated particularly by World War I and the Spanish Civil War in the 1930's,[1] the ICRC had tried to develop international law for civilians in a war zone prior to World War II. That war interrupted plans for legal developments. It also confirmed the ICRC's belief that the civilian population in war was in need of improved humanitarian protection and assistance.

In World War II, the ICRC not only pursued its tasks concerning prisoners of war, but also sought to protect various civilian detainees (notably Jews in Germany) and to bring medical and material assistance to civilian victims of war. Assistance operations were massive compared to past ICRC statistics, although civilian relief was not distinguished from prisoner-of-war relief in Red Cross records.[2]

The ICRC's commitment to large-scale civilian assistance operations in armed conflict was further established by events in Palestine just after World War II. There, the first Arab-Israeli War produced over 500,000 refugees in need.

And in those days prior to the creation of UNRWA (the UN Relief and Works Agency) and the UNHCR (the UN High Commissioner for Refugees), the ICRC carried out an assistance operation over several years. From 1948 through 1950, the ICRC had responsibility for assisting an average of 450,000 Palestinian refugees through every type of assistance possible: food, clothing, housing, medical care, and schooling.[3]

Against this immediate background the Fourth Geneva Convention of 1949 was drafted and came into force. It might be more accurate, in the practical sense, to say that that legal instrument was drafted and became new law on the books, for the new law has not—as of the mid-1970's—been formally acknowledged as fully applicable in a prolonged conflict.

There have been at least two instances in which the conflicting parties formally accepted the applicability of the four Conventions as a body, but without extended fighting or control of foreign territory providing a test of the terms of the Fourth Convention: the Suez affair of 1956, and India's takeover of Portuguese Goa in 1961. There have been other instances in which some part of the Fourth Convention has been applied, on the basis of largely de facto rather than clearly de jure activity by the ICRC. For example, civilians were protected and assisted by the ICRC, to some extent, in the international armed conflicts occurring in Indochina after 1965, in the Middle East in 1967 and thereafter, in Asia in 1971, and in Cyprus in 1974.

There have also been occasions when the Fourth Convention has been applied to some degree in noninternational armed conflicts, even though its implementation is not mandatory. In the civil wars in the Congo and the Yemen in the 1960's, the ICRC (along with other Red Cross organizations) was active especially with regard to medical assistance.[4] At the end of the 1960's the ICRC was a major actor in the Nigerian Civil War as the principal coordinator of authorized humanitarian assistance on both sides of the fighting for most of the duration of the war. In the civil war in Jordan in 1970, the ICRC participated in a unified Red Cross relief mission in order to provide extensive medical and material assistance.[5] In Chile in the wake of the 1973 civil war, the ICRC provided rather extensive assistance to the families of those detained by the Chilean military government. (Beyond these examples of ICRC protection and assistance to civilians in armed conflicts, whether technically international or noninternational, there has been a whole series of ICRC efforts to help civilians in situations not generally recognized as being an armed conflict.[6])

The pattern that has emerged with regard to implementing the Fourth Geneva Convention for the protection of and assistance to civilians is this: despite the law on the books, efforts to help civilians in armed conflicts have been largely de facto rather than de jure; the pre-1949 and post-1949 situations have not been drastically different. Civilians have received some protection and assistance, but not because it has been legally guaranteed in detail.

PROBLEMS IN APPLICATION

The Fourth Geneva Convention of 1949, pertaining to civilians during the process of armed conflict and during occupation of territory as a consequence of armed conflict, has met three general types of difficulties. These problems in application have become problems confronting the ICRC.

1. The primary problem under the Fourth Convention, as noted in the preceding chapter regarding the Third, is the ability of states to avoid all or part of their legal obligations. This avoidance of the Fourth Convention, or parts thereof, takes three major forms.

a. Some fighting parties reject the Fourth Convention *in toto* by arguing that the geomilitary scale does not justify using the label of armed conflict. Thus the government of Iraq did not allow either the ICRC or the Swedish Red Cross to provide assistance to civilians in the Kurdish region in the early 1970's although both Red Cross agencies made separate overtures. Iraq did not admit the existence of an internal armed conflict regulated by Article 3 of the Fourth Convention, despite widespread violence and the supplying of weapons to Kurdish fighters by the United States and Iran.[7] The Iraqi government was intent on maintaining its claims to domestic jurisdiction, and it no doubt saw a Red Cross presence in Kurdistan as inconsistent with those claims. While the ICRC was allowed to visit Kurdish detainees in Baghdad, it was not allowed to enter Kurdistan to help civilians.

Likewise in Ethiopia, the ICRC was not permitted to enter the province of Eritrea, which in the 1970's especially was the scene of a war of secession, despite widespread reports of violence and civilian hardship. Indeed, the existence of civilian hardship seemed to be an important element in the government's efforts to deal with armed opposition.[8] If there was no food in the area of Asmara, the insurgents would be forced to move elsewhere, leaving that city to government control. In response to ICRC requests to provide assistance in the Asmara region, the Ethiopian government said there was "no emergency."

b. Some parties reject the Fourth Convention on the basis of some legal technicality, despite a factual situation called "armed conflict" or "occupation" by most parties. In 1962, when China took territory from India in their border war, China refused: to accept the applicability of the Fourth, to appoint a Protecting Power, or to permit the ICRC to see Indian detainees held by China. The Chinese argument was that, since diplomatic relations between China and India were not broken during the incident, there was no need for the Fourth or an intermediary. When the Indian authorities permitted the ICRC to visit Chinese civilians in detention, the Chinese criticized both India and the ICRC; China's argument was that its consular representative in the area should have had access to Chinese nationals.[9]

Similarly, the Turkish government played legal games in the 1974 violence in Cyprus. Turkey referred to its armed presence in Cyprus not as part of an armed conflict but as "intervention" under the Zurich Agreements of 1960—agreements giving to Turkey, Greece, and the United Kingdom responsibility for guaranteeing the security of the 1960 Cypriot constitutional order. While Turkey thus said that the Fourth Convention did not apply de jure, it permitted the ICRC (and other parties such as the UNHCR) to assist and protect civilians to some extent in the part of Cyprus it controlled. Paradoxically, while Turkey refused to accept the Fourth de jure, and refused to consider the ICRC as acting under that law, it insisted at times that an ICRC delegate head the UN convoy that brought material assistance to Greek Cypriot civilians found in the area of Cyprus under Turkish army control.

c. Even where parties do not reject the Fourth Convention, they may escape particular obligations on the grounds that the law is vague and that *they* are entitled to interpret the law. Most of the law of armed conflict is an attempt to blend humanitarian considerations with military necessity and state security. Many of the articles in that law achieve this blending only by including both of those principles, humanitarianism and military necessity, in a vague mix. This is certainly true of the Fourth Convention.[10]

As we shall see in the case studies that follow, the wording of the Fourth does not always make clear what Israel is obligated to do in the occupied territories (if we assume, along with the ICRC, that the Fourth should indeed apply), or what Federal authorities were obligated to do in the Nigerian Civil War. Given such vagueness as an uncontestable fact (as the price paid for getting the law on the books), it is not so surprising subsequently to find national decision makers—including courts—interpreting the Fourth Convention with a heavy emphasis on state security at the expense of humanitarian values.

2. A second major problem in securing the protection of, and assistance to, civilians has been the breakdown of the traditional distinction between civilian and combatant. It is a distinction which is, needless to say, crucial to that part of the Fourth Convention which seeks to regulate the process of violence (rather than occupation). The breakdown stems from two causes: industrialized-technocratic warfare, and terroristic-guerrilla warfare.

Industrialized-technocratic warfare was the stimulus that produced the Fourth Convention. "Aerial bombardment," as it was called, directed toward population centers in World War II as never before, was the basic stimulus to the Fourth Convention. Atomic bombing of Japanese cities merely confirmed the obvious. Long-range artillery is simply bombing without aircraft. There has remained a tension between the terms of the Fourth and the supposed military gains from the use of such methods.

Technically speaking, means and methods of warfare are not regulated directly by the Geneva Conventions, but rather by the Hague Conventions. As already noted, the Geneva Conventions are concerned overtly with victims, not weapons and strategy or tactics. But victims, on the one hand, and means and methods, on the other, are inseparable in fact and in logic. Thus it can be said that the Fourth Geneva Convention, along with the Hague Conventions, has tried to protect civilians from destruction not justified by military necessity. Attacks on civilians and civilian property are legally justified only in terms of military necessity, or in terms of incidental damage related to a permissible military target.

But industrialized-technocratic warfare has had two effects on these supposedly limiting concepts. First of all, industrialized warfare requires a civilian base to fight the war—workers in war-related industries. What had been viewed in the past as a noncombatant became as important to the battle as the soldier. Without the maker of guns, there could be no war. And, as a logical deduction from this state of affairs, the maker of guns became an important target for the opposing force. And the maker of tires. And the maker of butter. And the maker of everything else. Since the opposing force had both the desire and the means to attack the industrialized worker, and since rearguard morale was also a component of the war machine, the civilian was attacked.

Secondly, industrialized-technocratic warfare was difficult to control precisely. It was difficult to limit destruction to a military target even if defined narrowly. If North Vietnamese anti-artillery guns were located in the suburbs of Hanoi, could an American high-altitude bomber realistically be expected to knock out such guns without extensive damage to the surrounding civilian areas? On the one hand there were technocratic developments that showed some promise of making attacks more precise, such as laser beams used as weapons. On the other hand, there were *methods* of attack used by numerous states, such as saturation bombing, carpet bombing, boxcar bombing, and other imprecise methods. Relatedly, while there was a theory of limited nuclear war, there was also the reality of fifty-megaton warheads that made any distinction between civilian and military targets nonsense.

Industrialized-technocratic warfare, referring to both means and methods, increased indiscriminate attacks in fact. That it could be done from a distance—from miles up or away—made it psychologically easier to kill and maim indiscriminately both combatant and civilian.

The second main cause of the breakdown of the distinction between combatant and civilian is terroristic-guerrilla warfare. If industrialized-technocratic warfare makes it more desirable and easier to kill and wound en masse, then terroristic-guerrilla warfare makes it more desirable—if not easier—to kill and wound on a small scale, with a killed or wounded civilian being as good a target as anybody else. If the Americans in Vietnam could be criticized for their bombing-artillery practices, then so could the Viet Cong be criticized for their assassination of village chiefs friendly to Saigon, and other attacks on the civilian population (policies also pursued by the Americans through such things as the Phoenix program of political murder).

The core of terroristic-guerrilla strategy and tactics is to mesh the military operations with the civilian population: to hide one's fighters in the "sea of the people," and to destroy confidence in the established authorities by proving that no civilian is safe from attack anywhere. A bomb in the supermarket is as good as one in an army camp. The key goal is the psychological-political one of driving a wedge between the people and the authorities: the civilian is the key, not the soldier. The official combatant—the conventional soldier—was to be avoided, unless he could be isolated and attacked on terrorist-guerrilla terms. Terrorist-guerrilla strategy is also aimed at coercing support for its cause. The "rebels" in Algeria not only attacked French civilians and French settlers but also Arabs who had not rallied to the independence movement. Apathy was almost as detrimental to the cause as opposition. In either case, the civilian was a prime target in the struggle.

This strategy, in turn, gave rise to "counter-insurgency" strategy, whose effects on civilians were similar to the other side. Civilians were forcibly moved to isolate them from the enemy, and became the targets of pressure and coercion if they refused cooperation.

Therefore, in sum, a second reason for ICRC difficulty in securing the implementation of the Fourth Convention, which tries to limit abuses of power by a fighting or occupying party, is that neither established governments nor challenging factions tend to regard the civilian as some innocent bystander in the violence, to be protected and succoured by a humanitarian agency. The "innocent" civilian may in fact be part of the enemy, or in any event indistinguishable from the enemy.

Examples of the interplay between technocratic and terroristic warfare, and its debilitating impact on humanitarian law, are found in the preceding case study on the Vietnam War. The use of civilian suffering as a weapon in war is discussed in the case study of the Nigerian War, below.

3. A third problem in implementing the Fourth is not so much the nature of the international legal order (viz., the leeway given to the states to say whether they will or will not accept law), and not so much the nature of warfare (industrialized-technocratic and terroristic-guerrilla), but the psychology of the soldier—who frequently is not only the fighter but also the policy maker as well.

The "old-boy club" operates in favor of the Third Convention and prisoners of war. A detained, wounded, or sick combatant is, after all, like the victorious combatant in one respect. He is a fighter. At worst, he is a conscript that was compelled by his superiors to fight. He is, in the final analysis, worthy of protection and assistance either because of his manly virtues as a fighter, or because of his misfortune as a conscript.

But the civilian is frequently viewed as nothing: weak, sometimes old, perhaps female. In many cultures there is nothing there to command respect.

It is striking that in the 1971 War for Bangladesh, prisoners of war were protected and assisted in general, but civilians were raped, murdered, detained, or—if lucky—ignored by the three armies. The government of Pakistan went to the International Court of Justice in an attempt to secure protection and assistance for its prisoners of war in Indian hands, but that same government failed to show similar interest in the applicability of the Fourth Convention for either Indian or Bangladesh civilians detained by it. More to the point, India, while permitting extensive ICRC inspection of prisoner-of-war installations, refused to extend that permission to all detained Pakistani civilians.

Among even enemy soldiers there is sometimes a certain mutual respect—or perhaps mutual commiseration. This is lacking in some cultures between soldier and civilian. The result is that the civilian receives less protection and assistance.

According to the *New York Times Index,* that newspaper in 1973, with regard to the Arab-Israeli conflict, carried 32 references to the ICRC. Twenty-eight of those referred primarily to prisoners of war; 1 reference was to civilian problems. In 1974, the figures were 22 references to the ICRC and prisoners of war; and again 1 reference to civilian problems.[11]

GENERAL POSITION OF ICRC

When acting in relation to the Fourth Convention, the ICRC—as in its other efforts—tends to act discreetly and pragmatically. While it puts forth its own view of the applicability of the Fourth, it does not usually press that view in the face of opposition. It prefers pragmatic humanitarian work to legal arguments; and as long as the former exists, the latter is not emphasized. Indeed, the ICRC has refused to give a view, even privately, on the precise meaning of certain articles in the Fourth Convention, arguing that this determination was for states. This occurred, for example, in the conflict over Cyprus.

On occasion, the ICRC has taken public steps in defense of civilians in an armed conflict or in territory occupied as a result of armed conflict. ICRC attempts during a war to mobilize some sort of public pressure on conflicting parties to protect and assist civilians have not been notably successful. Inherent in any violent situation is a formidable barrier to such ICRC efforts: the tendency for all parties to accept a fait accompli. For example, in the 1974 war in Cyprus, there were numerous reports of death and hardship for civilians. Yet once the fighting subsided, most parties were so relieved at the cessation of violence that there was little desire to press for sanctions against any participant for violations of the law of armed conflict. Most parties wanted to maintain the calm and move on to peace negotiations. While understandable and perhaps even commendable, this attitude is a powerful incentive for the conflicting parties to do whatever they want to do while the fighting lasts.

In the midst of the 1973 war in the Middle East, the ICRC launched a number of public appeals to the parties, reminding them of their obligations under the Fourth Convention to protect and assist civilians. Particularly when Israel shelled Damascus, the ICRC made public appeals not only for all parties to respect the 1949 law, but even that the parties should respect the draft law that was then being proposed as a supplement to the 1949 law—draft law that would offer more extensive civilian protection but was not yet binding. When Israel refused to adhere to that appeal, the ICRC gave prominent publicity to the Israeli refusal.

The ICRC also offered to create a commission of inquiry to investigate all alleged violations of the Geneva Conventions in that war. Furthermore, the ICRC called on all signatory states to the Geneva Conventions to secure the Conventions' implementation in the Middle East.[12] All of these efforts had not the slightest observable impact on any party (aside from the fact that the Arab states, in the midst of the Israeli attack on Damascus, agreed to accept the provisions of the draft law on protection of civilians, an acceptance that was without military sacrifice for them).

The ICRC did thus "go public" during that 1973 war. The only thing it did not do was name specific names of those who had violated what law and where. Through its public statements, the ICRC attempted to draw the parties' attention to the legal issues, to force them to speak to those issues, to embarrass them when they refused to accept ICRC overtures, and to mobilize outside pressure on them.

The belligerents continued to do what they wanted to do, counting not only on the reluctance of outsiders to go to war to enforce humanitarian law, but also on the reluctance of nonbelligerents to make diplomatic overtures on humanitarian questions when realpolitik issues were at stake. Would the United States exert pressure on Israel in behalf of civilians in Damascus in the context of all the other issues at stake in the Middle East? Would the Soviet Union exert pressure on Syria in behalf of Jews living there?

War is such a big thing, and rarely fought for humanitarian causes! (Turkey did refer to its action in Cyprus as humanitarian intervention. India, with more justification, referred to its armed action in Bangladesh as an effort to stop genocide.) Thus it is difficult for the ICRC to influence states to adopt a humanitarian policy that the states themselves have little inclination to accept. It would appear that if there is not a pro-ICRC element with influence either within the government or within the populace, there is little the ICRC can do during the course of war to mobilize pressure for the protection of civilians. The condition that generated pressure on the French in Algeria and the Americans in Vietnam progressively to implement parts of the Geneva Conventions was the unpopularity of those wars with sectors of the political elite and larger populace. Even then, fighters seemed to benefit more than civilians.

CASE STUDIES

Out of the many attempts by the ICRC to secure protection and assistance for civilians caught in conflict since 1949, two situations stand out in importance, in addition to the Vietnam War (covered in Chapter 6).

In the territories occupied by Israel since 1967, the ICRC believes the Fourth Convention to have been put to its longest test. In the ICRC view, the situation has been one of occupation as a result of an international armed conflict, and the main subject of importance to the Red Cross under the Fourth Convention seems to be protection of civilians, with secondary attention to assistance.

In the Nigerian Civil War of 1967–70, the ICRC believes the Fourth Convention to have been extremely important for Red Cross assistance, despite the fact that the violence was a civil rather than an international war.

Territories Occupied by Israel, 1967–74

After the 1967 and 1973 wars in the Middle East, Israel controlled territory that had been under Arab jurisdiction previously. (The present analysis is not directed to the pre-1967 period.) For much of this Israeli-controlled territory, there was controversy over who had the legal right to what. For virtually all of it there was controversy over the nature and impact of Israeli administration. The ICRC was caught in the middle of these disputations, as it took a stand on some of the legal issues, sought to protect and assist civilians (and fighters) in Israeli-controlled areas beyond Israel's 1967 boundaries, and issued special publications on the situation.

Factual Situation and Legal Policy. Factually, there were two types of territory acquired by Israel in the armed conflicts of 1967 and 1973. There was area generally regarded as belonging to a state (parts of the Sinai regarded as Egyptian; parts of the Golan regarded as Syrian). And there was area whose legal status was more indeterminate (the West Bank and Jerusalem areas, variously regarded as Jordanian, British, United Nations, or *res nullius*—belonging to no one).

Legally, the ICRC believed that all of this territory fell under the terms of Article 2 of the Fourth Convention, which states, in part, "The Convention shall also apply to all cases of partial or total occupation of the territory of a High Contracting Party, even if the said occupation meets with no armed resistance." The ICRC position on the applicability of the Fourth was widely supported. The United Nations General Assembly and also the UN Human Rights Commission made the same interpretation.[13] Other circles of opinion, including Israeli and American ones not unfriendly to the state of Israel, came to the same conclusion.

The government of Israel stated that it wished to "leave open" the issue of the applicability of the Fourth to the territories in question. Israeli officials argued that the Fourth Convention only applied to occupied territory when a sovereign's control had been ousted through armed conflict; since Israel challenged the sovereignty of Jordan in the West Bank and Jerusalem areas taken by Israel, it therefore challenged the applicability of the Fourth to these areas—and did not formally accept the Fourth as applying to other territory either. Israel added, however, that it would apply the humanitarian content of the Fourth on a de facto basis; and it invited the ICRC to carry out its traditional humanitarian activity without regard to legal issues.[14] This legal position picked up some support from academic circles but was opposed by most states, as demonstrated by voting in the UN General Assembly.[15]

There were two reasons that the applicability of the Fourth Convention in the Middle East received so much attention. First, there was the realpolitik reason. A number of Arab and other parties believed that by avoiding de jure application of the Fourth Convention, Israel was trying to engage in what they termed "creeping annexation and imperialism."[16] Put less provocatively, this argument was that Israel—like Turkey in Cyprus—wanted a free hand to dispose of the territories in keeping with her definition of her national interest. In particular, Article 43 of the Fourth prohibited annexation of occupied territory. Israel had annexed eastern Jerusalem after the 1967 war, and some parties thought Israel intended to claim formal ownership over other parts of the territories as well. Israel denied that she was imperialistic, argued that the Holy Places in east Jerusalem were open to all and could be internationalized, and was prepared to enter negotiations on the disposal of the other territories in the context of an Arab-Israeli peace treaty.

The second reason for interest in the Fourth was humanitarian. Israel claimed that the impact of its administration in the territories was beneficial to the inhabitants: the death penalty, extant under Jordanian law, had been removed under Israeli law; there had been an improvement in socioeconomic conditions; etc. This Israeli claim received support from some scholarly circles.[17] An ICRC official was quoted as having said that Israeli administration was basically liberal.[18]

On the other hand, there were charges that the Israeli government was systematically violating the humanitarian rules of the Fourth Convention.[19] Some of these charges were based, in part, on ICRC prison reports apparently made available by Jordanian officials.[20] And the ICRC itself made public a long statement of concern about conditions and treatment in the territories in the *International Review of the Red Cross* (August and September, 1970).

Controversy over the specific norms of the Fourth Convention centered on at least eight issues:

1. Property destruction. Israel destroyed certain civilian properties in the territories, or refused their use to inhabitants and/or owners, in response to alleged subversive activity against Israeli authority. Israel argued that this was permitted under Article 53, which allowed demolition that was "rendered absolutely necessary by military operations." Israel also claimed that this policy of property destruction was permissible under Article 64, which allowed local law to remain in effect during occupation; and Jordanian law permitted such demolitions.

There was challenge to these Israeli interpretations on several grounds. There was debate as to the meaning of the words "absolutely necessary . . . military operations." And there was the further argument that such property destructions frequently took on the nature of a collective punishment, which was forbidden by Article 33 without any qualifications. There was also controversy about the facts surrounding demolitions—e.g., whether any subversive activity had in fact occurred, whatever the law.

2. Expulsions and forced transfers. Israel expelled certain people from the territories. At issue was Article 49, stating that "deportations of protected persons from occupied territory to the territory of the Occupying Power or to that of any other country . . . are prohibited, regardless of their motive." Israel argued that neither the letter nor spirit of Article 49 applied. Israel was not deporting in the technical sense but rather returning certain security risks to their colleagues; such a policy was said to be more humane than indefinite detention. It was added that the numbers involved were small, in any event.[21]

This Israeli position met opposition by those who insisted upon a strict application of Article 49, and who believed that Israel might be engaging in expulsions without adequate safeguards for the individuals in question, and/or on the basis of a desire to protect informants rather than detain or go to trial.

Israel also engaged in the forced removal of certain persons from parts of the territories. This is also prohibited by Article 49, unless "the security of the population or imperative military reasons so demand." In that event, the occupying power is responsible for the welfare of the persons so moved, and "The Occupying Power shall not deport or transfer parts of its own civilian population into the territory it occupies." An Israeli High Court decision held that in the Sinai, there was military reason for the removal of bedouin elements.[22] Israeli further argued that the introduction of fortified farms in the territories did not violate Article 49, since such institutions were partly military rather than fully civilian.

There were challenges to these Israeli positions. Some questioned the military necessity of certain forced movements, believing that the ground was being prepared for Jewish settlements of a civilian and commercial nature. There was also criticism of forced civilian transfers in east Jerusalem, which Israel regarded as under its law rather than the Fourth Convention.[23] And some believed that living conditions for certain persons forced to relocate from the Sinai were not adequate.

3. Judicial process. Israel was proud of the legal system it had instituted in the territories, in which Israeli military law was layered above civil law remaining from Arab administration. Israel believed individual rights were protected, and that the impact of military law was the same for Arab civilians as for Israeli military personnel.

There was at least one point of controversy over the judicial process in the territories. It was alleged that confessions were coerced and that courts did nothing to mitigate this practice. A controversial group charged the following:

> Almost all convictions in the Israeli Military Courts in the occupied territories are based on confession by the accused. In very many cases the prisoners deny their confession in court and complain of being coerced under torture. They describe

exactly the various methods of torture applied on them, sometimes even point out the evidence of torture in the courtroom and offer to be submitted to medical investigation to support and prove their complaint of torture under interrogation. In all cases there was no official *judicial* investigation of these complaints. Even in cases where an obviously incapacitated man with physical marks of torture appears before the court, the court of the Appeal Commission refuses investigations into the matter.[24]

4. Interrogation. Israeli high officials insisted that all detainees were humanely treated. They agreed to notify the ICRC of an arrest within eighteen days and to permit ICRC visits to detainees not later than thirty days after arrest. Such arrangements were probably permissible under Article 5 of the Fourth, permitting "loss of rights and privileges" for persons "definitely suspected of or engaged in activities hostile to the security of the [occupying?] State," including "rights of communication." Article 5 further stated that "such persons shall nevertheless be treated with humanity."

There were charges that coercion and torture did exist. An Israeli official was quoted as saying that psychological pressure and some rough handling did occur.[25] And parts of alleged ICRC reports were circulated which seemed to establish prima facie evidence of mistreatment, a conclusion also reached by Amnesty International.[26]

5. Conditions of detention. It was generally admitted that the conditions of detention could be a problem from time to time, owing to overcrowding in the wake of armed conflict or widespread arrest.[27] The controversy centered on the extent of material and medical deficiencies and their duration.

6. Administrative detention. Article 78 of the Fourth Convention permits administrative detention "for real and imperative reasons of security." There was some controversy over whether this phrase was being misinterpreted by Israel in order to avoid trials in which it might have to disclose its informants through judicial testimony. For its part, Israel emphasized that most detainees were eventually charged under law rather than held under administrative order.

7. International traffic. Israel was proud of its "open bridges" policy of encouraging contact across Middle Eastern boundaries. Israel and its supporters cited this traffic in persons as evidence of favorable Arab attitudes toward that administration.

On the other hand, there were charges that Israel refused to permit persons who could be considered as Palestinians to enter or reenter the territories. And others claimed that certain collective punishments, such as prohibition of movement into or out of certain villages suspected of subversive activity, interfered with the educational activities of inhabitants.

8. Assistance. Israel tended to regard international interest in medical-material assistance for the territories as part of an Arab campaign to discredit Israeli administration and cast doubt on the welfare of inhabitants of those territories.[28]

Others believed there was real need for assistance in parts of the territories, especially in the Sinai. At El Arish, for example, it was alleged that the Israelis had taken over the local Red Crescent hospital and curtailed the activities of indigenous doctors, without providing an adequate replacement and despite the prohibitions found in Article 57 especially.

ICRC Activity.   In the context of these controversies, of both a humanitarian and realpolitik nature, the ICRC faced difficult choices. It sought the full application of the Fourth Convention, even to the point of using strong diplomatic language by publicly deploring Israel's refusal to accept the Fourth de jure.[29] But the ICRC, in effect, seemed to accept the Israeli position that it and that government should agree to disagree on certain matters while working together on other matters. While the ICRC publicly deplored Israel's general legal position, it did not appear to push that point of view vis-à-vis Israeli officials, apparently believing that such an approach would do no humanitarian good and might even be counterproductive. This meant that the presence of the ICRC in the territories could be taken by some observers as evidence of adequate protection and assistance to civilians there. Indeed that precise claim was made by Israel and its supporters—as had been done by other parties in other situations.[30] But the ICRC appeared to some as an accomplice to illegal, inhumane, or simply controversial policies.

It is difficult to say exactly what has been transpiring in the territories on some of the eight controversial issues noted above. It is unlikely the ICRC would "deplore" Israel's refusal thus far to accept the Fourth de jure without valid humanitarian reason, unless the ICRC had become overconcerned with law per se or had lost a sense of impartiality from working with Arab populations. (The latter was unlikely, since the ICRC was also working with Israeli prisoners of war in Syria and Egypt.) Furthermore, that something seemed to be wrong in the territories—from a humanitarian point of view—can be surmised from special ICRC publications on the situation in the Middle East. While these 1970 publications directed criticism at Arab parties for failure to implement parts of the Geneva Conventions, the bulk of the publications' contents were directed at Israel.

If, for example, we take the issue of interrogation, we find the ICRC saying in 1970, "During the visits, delegates have sometimes met detainees whose bodies showed traces of, according to the prisoners, ill-treatment during interrogations . . . the visiting procedure laid down by the Israeli authorities no longer permitted it [the ICRC] to ensure that interrogation methods at variance with humanitarian law did not occur." (The visiting procedure referred to entailed denial of ICRC access during the first thirty days of detention.) From such an unusual statement in 1970, one can only deduce either that some humanitarian need existed with regard to interrogation, or that the ICRC wished to absolve itself of any responsibility in connection with interrogation controversies. In that the ICRC continued to make detention visits, one might be on safe grounds in concluding that a humanitarian problem did indeed exist. Questions could well remain, however, concerning its relative gravity.

If we also take the example of controversies surrounding the judicial process in the territories, it would seem that in the mid-1970's the ICRC was not in a position to have a definite view on judicial investigations into allegations of coerced confessions. While the ICRC is reported to have made a general study of legal issues arising under the Fourth, it had apparently not emphasized judicial issues in its applied protection in the territories. The ICRC had seemed to emphasize detention issues and social assistance (supervising and facilitating the international movement of persons), and had seemingly not engaged in widespread and systematic trial observation.

Therefore the controversies surrounding the eight issue areas would continue, not only because of conflicting legal interpretations but also because of both vague ICRC statements and no ICRC statements on certain of the issues.

The ICRC had long operated on the principle of interjecting a minimum degree of humanitarianism into a situation. There was little doubt but that such an objective was being achieved in the territories, compared to past occupations. The ICRC had played a useful role in reducing detention overcrowding and in providing Arabs a link with the non-Israeli world. But achieving some humanitarian progress left open the question of how the ICRC was to deal with Israel on other issues, such as Israel's denial of ICRC involvement in matters touching upon east Jerusalem, which Israel had annexed. And it was on this type of issue that ICRC was urged by Arab parties to exert itself, because such issues as annexation and forced movement of persons raised the question of "creeping imperialism" which was of so much concern to particularly the Arab states and the Palestinians. Strong ICRC language and special publications only fueled suspicions that something was wrong; the ICRC seemed caught between a desire to say something and commitment to its principle of discretion.

Israel had insisted that it and the ICRC agree to disagree. Israel's basic strategy toward issues arising under the Fourth was to set aside the points on which there was a difference of opinion and to concentrate on doing those things where Israel and the ICRC were in agreement. The ICRC, in accepting this position as a matter of fact, was able to promote a minimum degree of humanitarianism in the territories. But it was an achievement purchased at a price. And the ICRC did not seem entirely convinced that the price was right, even as it apparently felt it had to continue payments.

The Nigerian Civil War, 1967–70

There was also a price to pay for the ICRC in the Nigerian Civil War. The price of providing food to those dying in Biafra was increased friction and finally hostility with the established government in Lagos. What was demanded of the ICRC, if it were to continue its assistance operations, was that it become a

revolutionary humanitarian actor, willing to flaunt the expressed policy of a
government—a governmental policy largely in keeping with the Fourth Geneva
Convention. This price the ICRC was unwilling to pay.

Introduction.   In the mid-1960's, Nigeria was wracked by ethnic tensions
and political violence. Those in the Eastern Region, principally the Ibos, believed themselves to be the targets of discrimination and perhaps even genocide
within the federation of regions that was the state of Nigeria. Others in that state
believed the Ibos to have been socially and politically aggressive—in the violence, they were reaping their just rewards.[31]

The Eastern Region formally seceded in the spring of 1967, after large-scale
ethnic violence and a related series of governmental coups and countercoups. Lt.
Col. Odumegwu Ojukwu proclaimed the existence of the state of Biafra. General
Yakubu Gowon decreed a war of national unity in the name of the Federal
Military Government of Nigeria.

Thus there existed a civil war between an established government and a
secessionist movement. It was recognized as such by almost all other parties.
Only five states formally recognized Biafra as a state (Tanzania, Zambia, Gabon,
Ivory Coast, and Haiti). Those additional few parties actively supporting the
secessionist movement (like France and Portugal) never extended formal recognition but rather maintained relations on a de facto and often covert basis.

In this situation of widespread consensus on the nature of the violence, there
was no controversy over the minimum application of Common Article 3, pertaining to noninternational armed conflicts. One of the things that made the Nigerian
Civil War legally different, however, was that this minimum application of the
laws of war was superseded by an expressed willingness by both sides to apply
all Four Geneva Conventions. General Gowon was quoted as saying his government was "honour bound to observe the rules of the Geneva Convention [*sic*]."
Further, that government created a code of conduct for Federal troops which, it
was said, "must be read in conjunction with the Geneva Convention [*sic*]."[32]
Likewise, Ojukwu gave assurances that Biafra would follow the Conventions
too.[33]

This civil war, supposedly regulated by the Four Conventions of 1949, was to
be of tremendous significance to the ICRC. It was to become a test of the
relevance of those Conventions to a classic situation of civil war—classic in the
sense of having conventional actors and conventional means and methods of
warfare.

The war was also to become a test of the ICRC as manager of large-scale
assistance. The material and medical assistance delivered to the war area was to
become the largest ICRC effort since World War II. Each year of the Nigerian
War, on the average, the ICRC handled goods and produced services amounting
to about three times its normal yearly budget at that time. Moreover, in the
Nigerian assistance effort, unlike World War II, there was to be careful scrutiny
of assistance management after the fact.

Finally, the war was to be a major test of the ICRC as an actor in world affairs. The impact of the war on the ICRC went far beyond that of assistance management and involved such issues as the political sophistication of the ICRC and its overall operating effectiveness.

In fact, the Nigerian Civil War was to become more traumatic for the ICRC than Korea, Algeria, Vietnam, or any other armed conflict since 1945. Its position was to be more in the public eye than ever before. Consequently, the difficulties of the ICRC—both self-generated and encountered—were to be more penetrating in their impact.

Conversely, the ICRC's impact on the war was also seen to be more important than before.

The First Stage (June 1967–May 1968)   The first stage of the war, from its formal start to the Federal capture of Port Harcourt, was a period of leisurely involvement for the ICRC. At the start of the war the ICRC was preoccupied with the June war in the Middle East and its aftermath. And there was the escalating Vietnam War, among other problems demanding its attention.

In Nigeria the fighting started slowly after the formal statements of May and June 1967. It was not until Biafra lost control of Port Harcourt, in May 1968, and thereby lost its principal route for imported foodstuffs, that the humanitarian issues of the war became so salient.

During these first eleven months, the ICRC maintained good relations with both parties. Before the war had started, the ICRC had had a senior delegate, George Hoffmann, in the country. In the process of keeping himself informed during the time of tribal and partisan political violence, Hoffmann had obtained both an understanding of Nigerian politics and ready access to Nigerian leaders. His understanding of the overall situation was reflected in his judgement that major violence was likely and that the ICRC should use the island of Fernando Po (capital: Santa Isabel) in Equatorial Guinea as the base area for assistance— recommendations that were eventually implemented. His access to Nigerian-Biafran leaders was reflected in his quick trips to both Gowon and Ojukwu—in that order—when the war was declared, but before hostilities commenced.

ICRC relations with Biafra were excellent throughout this first stage. Ojukwu promised his cooperation with the ICRC on humanitarian matters, although from the very first he stipulated that no humanitarian assistance was to be flown into Biafra from territory controlled from Lagos. Thus the crucial issue of the symbolic value of Red Cross relief was posed by Ojukwu to the ICRC at the very outset. The ICRC proceeded to move a medical team into Biafra, along with a head delegate for that side of the war. That medical team was flown in with the permission of Lagos, from Santa Isabel directly to Biafra. A second team, replacing the first, was later sent to Biafra by boat from the Cameroons. A third replacement team went from Lagos to Santa Isabel to Biafra by air.

ICRC relations with Lagos during this stage remained good but were deteriorating by the end of the period. The relations had started on an excellent note, owing mainly to Hoffmann's careful policy of dealing with Gowon first and securing Gowon's permission for the first trip to Biafra. There was also endorsement of the ICRC from leaders in the Nigerian Red Cross, who were influential in the Federal government. Moreover, the ICRC was acting to improve Nigeria's military medical corps and was also beginning to provide material assistance to civilians on the Federal side.

But the basic tension in ICRC-Lagos relations appeared during this first stage of the war. Lagos had declared a total blockade on Biafra as of October 1967. While this effort was not very effective during the early part of the war, nevertheless the ICRC expressed its concern about the blockade's effects on the civilian population. This was seen by the "hawks" in the Nigerian government and army as meddling in Nigerian affairs. ICRC concern was especially resented since Biafran policy was to charge Lagos with intended genocide of the Ibo people. The hawks saw the ICRC as not only interfering but also taking Biafra's side.

Gowon was not a hawk, relatively speaking, and he and other "doves" were sympathetic—within limits—to ICRC concerns. Two ICRC flights to Biafra had been approved—one after the blockade had been declared. But the ICRC wanted to go further. The ICRC sought from both sides some general negotiated agreement on Red Cross assistance to Biafra. As this proved difficult to obtain, the ICRC sought some sort of permission from Lagos that it would not interfere with Red Cross planes flying into Biafra through Nigerian air space. The hawks, significantly controlling the Federal airforce as well as other bastions in the military, were opposed.

But on 9 and 11 April 1968, the ICRC and Lagos exchanged letters through which the ICRC was given a fly-at-your-own-risk "permission." Lagos said that if the ICRC persisted in trying to get assistance into Biafra by air, it could do so at its own risk. Moreover, Lagos said it would take all precautions to avoid incidents. The ICRC responded that the agency did indeed accept responsibility for the flights, but noted that Lagos had indicated no objection to the flights and would seek to avoid incidents.

This agreement of April 1968 was to acquire acute importance after the fall of Port Harcourt.

In summary of this first phase of the war, it can be noted that the ICRC had a small presence in the war zone. The figures in Table 7.1 are indicative of this situation.

The medical team in Biafra had proven so difficult to resupply, in the context of the Federal blockade, that it was withdrawn for a time. Only two ICRC flights had gone into Biafra, one in July and one in November. Along with medical personnel, these flights had transported a total of nine tons of material and medical assistance to the secessionist area. Relief was comparably small on the Federal side.

ICRC activity was not only small, but also quiet. In generated little controversy—none on the international scene and almost none within the war

Table 7.1. Non-African Personnel Employed by the ICRC in
Connection with Assistance

Year	Federal side	Biafra	Total
1967			
June	1	0	1
July	2	2	4
August	2	2	4
September	2	3	5
October	5	3	8
November	5	4	9
December	5	5	10
1968			
January	4	4	8
February	4	1	5
March	9	0	9
April	10	0	10

area, except for the important disagreement between hawks and doves on the Federal side.

The smallness and tranquility of the ICRC presence, which was almost totally concerned with assistance, were soon to end. The next stage was to be decisive—not for the war but for the ICRC. Red Cross assistance, and the hawk-dove split in Lagos, were to transform the ICRC position in the war into an international cause célèbre.

The Second Stage (May 1968–June 1969) The fall of Port Harcourt to the Federals made their blockade effective. Biafra's main channel for protein—Scandinavian dried stockfish—was closed. It was not long before kwashiorkor (acute protein deficiency) appeared in the secessionist area. Widespread death followed.

In the summer of 1968, various reports reached Geneva regarding the situation in Biafra. But hard facts and figures were difficult to come by, and the ICRC made no major effort to obtain those facts. All reports, however, confirmed a view held by the ICRC since early 1968: the situation in Biafra was very serious—and deteriorating.

In the wake of the April agreement, the ICRC had hired an American independent flyer, Hank Wharton, to get relief into Biafra by air. He did so at night, and between April and July the ICRC managed to get seventeen flights and 170 tons of assistance into Biafra. There were no ICRC personnel on the ground to handle distribution, which was left to Biafran authorities (including the army) and to the various church representatives in the area.[34]

This effort was decidedly inadequate, a fact "discovered" especially by the Anglo-Saxon press in July.[35] The Western press was aided in this discovery by the Geneva-based public relations firm employed by Biafra. Public concern in the West, especially in the Swiss, Scandinavian and Anglo-Saxon states, jolted the ICRC headquarters out of a "business-as-usual" attitude. Moreover the Scandinavian churches were constructing their own assistance operation, eventually called Joint Church Aid (JCA). Pushed by Western public opinion, and stimulated by the prospect of humanitarian competition, the ICRC rapidly began to take significant action. Death in Biafra became the ICRC's dominant, and perhaps only, concern in the war.

Toward the end of July, the ICRC went outside its regular cadre of personnel and appointed August Lindt as special ICRC delegate in charge of the Nigerian operation. Lindt was a former UN High Commissioner for Refugees and at that time was Swiss ambassador to the Soviet Union. His reputation was outstanding.

In August, the ICRC launched an appeal for money and goods through the Red Cross network. This was only the second such Red Cross appeal since the start of the war, and it helped to dramatize the situation in Biafra.

On the basis of this appeal and the ICRC's own resources, a crash program of emergency relief—mainly foodstuffs—was activated. The appeal did not stipulate what was needed or desired, and there was no overall assistance plan. The emphasis was simply on getting as much food and medical assistance into Biafra as possible. The results can be partially seen in Table 7.2.

ICRC personnel increased rapidly also, on both sides. In July 1968, the ICRC had no personnel in Biafra. In August, 15 were present, in September 80, and in October 103. Thereafter, the figure averaged about 80 (local employees not included).

On the Federal side, the figure was 21 in July, 80 in August, 210 in September, 244 in October, and a peak of 247 in January of 1969.

In July 1968, the ICRC financial picture showed the agency in the black. In September, the ICRC was running a deficit of 2,252 thousand Swiss francs; by November the deficit had grown to 4,932 thousand. That was approximately one-fourth of the ICRC's planned annual budget.

It was only under these financial pressures that the ICRC paused to evaluate its assistance effort.[36] From November 1968 on, and especially after early 1969, the ICRC had a more detailed idea of what it wanted by way of material and medical assistance and how it was going to pay for what it wanted.

The crash assistance program, despite its weaknesses in planning and funding, had saved lives in Biafra and on the Federal side. No one knows for sure how many. But while the ICRC did finally pause to evaluate its assistance program in financial and management terms, it never fully evaluated its overall strategy in the war. Indeed, there was no overall strategy, except to get food into Biafra. This, needless to say, caused problems.

The ICRC and Relief Negotiations.   The policy asserted by Ojukwu at the start—that no Red Cross relief was to come directly from Federal territory—was consistently maintained by Biafran authorities. The political symbolism of Red

Table 7.2. ICRC Flights into Biafra

Year	Number	Tons of goods
1968		
August	28	219
September	146	1,287
October	179	1,841
November	137	1,229
December	210	2,048
1969		
January	29	304
February	184	1,888
March	227	2,292
April	476	5,039
May	331	3,924
June	56	650
July	2	20
thereafter	0	0

Source: Swedish Royal Ministry of Foreign Affairs, *Sverige och konflikten i Nigeria 1967–1970*, Stockholm: Kungl. Utrikesdepartementet, 1970, p. 140.

Cross relief was to be a constant of the war: would that relief symbolize Biafran independence of Federal supremacy? Efforts to deal with this problem, during the second stage of the war, had two phases.

First, the ICRC acted alone in trying to reach a Biafran-Federal accord. There were two fundamental options for a relief operation: a surface route and some type of airlift. The former would be slower to mount but more economical in the long run.

The parties would agree on neither option.[37] The symbolic and psychological reasons for this disagreement were ever present, although rarely articulated.[38] To Biafra's desire to avoid even the appearance of Federal control regardless of the cost in Biafran lives, those authorities added other reasons. Certain proposed land routes allegedly interfered with Biafran military operations. Other proposals allegedly did not contain sufficient checks to insure that the relief food was not poisoned.

As for an airlift, there was only one choice insofar as a negotiated agreement was concerned—day flights—although there was room for choice regarding which Biafran airstrip was to be used. The ICRC proposed various forms of air corridors, as did Lagos. But Biafra alleged that these would present it with various unacceptable military risks.

It became clear that Biafra wanted the existing night flights to continue, as the relief planes provided a shield for the arms planes being flown by mercenaries and others. While the Nigerian airforce did not have great capability for night interception, whatever capability it had was further reduced by a reluctance to shoot down relief planes. Thus the gunrunners mingled with the foodrunners, as both they and the Federal pilots played hide-and-seek in the dark airspace over Uli and Umbilago airstrips. Biafra was unwilling to give up this nighttime shield, which was important to its military effort, even if a day airlift would bring in more guaranteed food.

Biafran counterproposals were rejected by Lagos on two grounds. Either the Biafran proposals were said to present Lagos with unacceptable military risks, or the proposals were seen as confirming the independence of Biafra from Federal control—which was precisely what Lagos was fighting to prevent.

In this latter regard, the key point was the nature of Lagos's supervision over the relief. Was it acceptable for the relief plane to touch down in Lagos or some other part of the Federal side before going into Biafra? Was it sufficient for a Federal official to inspect the planes somewhere outside Federal territory— perhaps at the ICRC staging base on Fernando Po island? Would both parties accept ICRC supervision alone, rather than (a) direct Federal supervision, or (b) supervision by some state or political international organization? On these points the parties never agreed.

Whatever the specifics of the proposals, whether for surface or air routes, each side was concerned primarily about the symbolic value of inspection.

The second phase of diplomatic efforts to reach agreement on the process of humanitarian assistance to Biafra occurred after early 1969 when the United States government became consistently and actively involved in relief negotiations.[39]

The United States had been supporting both the ICRC and JCA in logistical ways during the Johnson administration. The Nixon administration moved to enter negotiations directly by dispatching a special relief mission to the war area. While working closely with the ICRC on such matters as efforts to obtain concrete information on the situation in Biafra, the American mission and the ICRC reached agreement on a division of labor in the negotiations.[40] The U.S. would concentrate on a surface route for relief while the ICRC would pursue the subject of a daytime airlift.

The Americans believed that use of the Cross River was the best way to get large-scale relief into Biafra, with the foodstuffs off-loaded onto shallow-water craft from oceangoing vessels. This Cross River project was eventually "agreed to in principle" by both sides. But it was largely a meaningless gesture, as the parties subsequently refused to discuss specifics.

That project, like negotiations on flights, snagged on the issue of supervision. Biafra wanted a state to supervise the project. Lagos believed such a move would imply recognition of the independence of Biafra. The American mission was authorized only to seek to get relief into Biafra on a basis Lagos could accept. Thus U.S. policy was to do as much in support of humanitarian assistance as possible, but within the confines of not challenging Lagos's authority.

Therefore, in summary of relief negotiations, neither the ICRC in phase one, nor the ICRC and the United States in phase two, could get the two sides to separate humanitarian assistance from the issue of political images. More general negotiations through the Organization of African Unity likewise failed to lead to any agreement.

ICRC Friction with Lagos. To some extent the very ICRC interest in Biafra, by itself, created friction with Lagos—or more precisely created friction with the Federal hawks. There were some Federals who believed all foreign interest in the war, however expressed, to be an unwanted intrusion into Nigerian affairs. Various Federal officials publicly criticized the ICRC, along with the churches; and the ICRC was not permitted to operate in certain parts of Federal territory, despite the fact that Gowon had named the ICRC as the overall coordinator for humanitarian assistance on the Federal side.[41]

Gowon, obviously, did not have full control over the hawks, especially some military commanders. These latter tended to see the most humanitarian policy as the "quick-kill" approach: tighten the blockade, kick out the humanitarian agencies, and militarily terminate the secession as quickly as possible. It was argued that this was the really humanitarian thing to do, rather than allow the war to drag on. The problem was that the Nigerian military was slow in demonstrating its capacity for the quick kill.

To this inherent difference of view between the Federal hawks and the ICRC, other points of friction were added. There was the shielding of gunrunners by ICRC planes; although unintended by the ICRC, it was still a fact. There was the fact that the ICRC had asked Lagos to lift its blockade in the fall of 1967. There was the fact that the Federal military requisitioned some Red Cross aircraft for military purposes and that Lindt protested this action. There was the fact that the ICRC equipped a Biafran airstrip with radio and other electrical devices; although these were "neutralized," the Biafran military eventually took over the facility prior to its capture by Federal troops. There was the fact that the Federal airforce bombed not only civilian targets in Biafra but Red Cross installations as well—and Red Cross personnel were killed by Federal troops.

As if all this was not enough, the ICRC added to its troubles with Lagos through the attitudes and actions of its personnel.

First of all there was Lindt, a man much interested in the well-being of Africa, who came to the ICRC with an outstanding record as a diplomat. In the Nigerian war, Lindt was to get the ICRC airlift going, and thus saved many lives. However, he failed to understand African feelings in Lagos, and he made tactical mistakes. One author has summed up the conventional wisdom on Lindt thus:

> He was temperamentally unsuited to cope with the complex political subtleties of the crisis and the sensitivities of the belligerents. Lindt throught he could not only produce a mutually-agreed relief plan but also, it seems, act as a peacemaker and bring the war to an end where everyone else had failed. Here he came unstuck. He flitted tirelessly from side to side arousing everyone's suspicions and causing appalling confusion in his own Geneva office, rarely telling them where he was and sometimes disappearing for days at a time. He also tended to take the law into his own

hands and some of his negotiating techniques were closer to those of a nineteenth-century mill-owner handling the labour than those normally associated with an ambassador who had served his country in Washington and Moscow. "If he spoke to the Americans and Russians as he does to us," a Nigerian diplomat once complained to me after a particularly gruelling round of relief negotiations in Lagos, "it's a wonder that Switzerland is still around."[42]

Second, there were other Red Cross personnel in the field, both ICRC delegates and individuals on loan from national Red Cross Societies, who rubbed the Nigerians the wrong way. One of the problems was that Hoffmann, who had gotten along exceedingly well with the Federal leadership and the Nigerian Red Cross, had been transferred to Ruanda to work on a problem concerned with the protection of white mercenaries fallen into African hands. Surrendering mercenaries had requested an ICRC presence, and this was difficult to refuse. The ICRC was short of manpower, and despite Hoffmann's good record in Nigeria he was needed elsewhere. While in Nigeria, Hoffmann had maintained a "low profile" for the ICRC delegation in Lagos. After his departure, that delegation was seen by some Nigerians as acting too much like another white embassy—and without always understanding the local scene. That delegation had over half-a-dozen head delegates during the three years of the war; consistency was obviously lacking. Moreover, some of the lower-rank personnel in Lagos were not outstanding—temporary delegates on short leave (three to six months) from other Swiss jobs.

Third, there was the attitude of ICRC headquarters in Geneva. The pro-Biafran concern of Western public opinion, the efficient "selling job" of the Biafran public relations firm in Geneva, the tendency to try to compete with the pro-Biafran churches in getting relief into the enclave (a tendency encouraged by Lindt in the field), the lack of good reporting from the field on the Federal side combined with excellent reporting by the one head of delegation in Biafra after September 1967, all led the highest level of ICRC headquarters into a pro-Biafran position. It was a position recognized not just by sensitive Lagos but by various ICRC delegates as well. The fact that Ojukwu was "playing politics" with the relief issue was largely ignored. Also largely ignored was Gowon's flexibility in permitting some authorized flights into Biafra, in giving the fly-at-your-own-risk permission, and in disagreeing with his own hawks in pursuing negotiations on humanitarian assistance involving outside agencies.

To summarize ICRC friction with Lagos, it can be said that as the second stage of the war progressed, Lindt became the target of the Federal hawks. His success in getting the ICRC airlift going, and keeping it going despite political pressures,[43] contrasted with the inability of the Federal army to make the long-proclaimed final push. Lindt's abrasiveness, and his shuttling back and forth from side to side, contributed to friction and suspicion.

ICRC headquarters was too uninformed, and too much oriented to Biafra, to change the field situation. Messages were sent to headquarters, through Red Cross societies and governments, urging that Lindt be replaced and other changes made to bring about a more balanced ICRC impact. Without being fully aware of what it was doing, ICRC headquarters continued the unarticulated and unintended policy of revolutionary humanitarianism—getting relief into Biafra despite the unhappiness of the established government. ICRC headquarters did not officially say yes or no to this de facto policy; it basically deferred to events generated in the field.[44]

During this second stage, the ICRC was providing material and medical assistance to some 2.5 million individuals on both sides. The assistance program was going well administratively, especially on the Biafran side where duplication with the church groups and assistance to the military had been controlled. While there were some administrative problems on the Federal side (for instance, owing to the need to negotiate with other relief agencies rather than command and to get materiel into freshly captured areas quickly, and to inadequate control procedures), nevertheless the management of assistance was relatively good for a war situation.

The friction with Lagos, however, was to terminate that assistance program.

The Third Stage (June 1969–March 1970)   The friction between the ICRC and Lagos came to a head in June 1969. Lagos finally asserted its full rights. As a result, the ICRC finally decided to defer to Federal policy—at least formally.

On 5 June 1969, a Red Cross relief plane was shot down by a Federal fighter aircraft; pilot and crew were killed. The premeditated attack occurred at dusk, but in enough daylight so that eyewitnesses on the ground could distinguish the Red Cross symbol on the plane. The hawks had struck, in an effort to force the hand of the doves.

The response of the ICRC was to challenge the act publicly.[45] Now it was true that the plane was flying over Nigerian airspace in light, whereas the original permission of April 1968 had been understood to mean night flights. Also, that original agreement had been officially revoked in October 1968, at a time of pronounced Federal unhappiness with the ICRC. But at the time of that revocation, the ICRC had received private assurances from high Federal officials that the ICRC flights could continue without incident. That private understanding was continued into 1969. Indeed, days before the June 5 incident, the ICRC was again privately informed that its planes would not be attacked.[46] The ICRC followed up its challenging public statements with two flights into Biafra.

But then, not only did Gowon publicly assert Nigerian domestic jurisdiction over all its airspace at all times, also the American government privately told the ICRC that the Federal airforce intended to use its newly attained night interceptor capacity.[47] This information turned out to be incorrect, but at the time it was the factor that caused the ICRC to terminate further unauthorized flights to Biafra.[48]

The shooting incident, and the possibility of further incidents, caused the ICRC to pay closer attention to the Fourth Geneva Convention and its Article 23:

Each High Contracting Party shall allow the free passage of medical and hospital stores and objects necessary for religious worship intended only for civilians of another High Contracting Party, even if the latter is its adversary. It shall likewise permit the free passage of all consignments of essential foodstuffs, clothing and tonics intended for children under fifteen, expectant mothers and maternity cases.

The obligation of a High Contracting Party to allow the free passage of the consignments indicated in the preceding paragraph is subject to the condition that this Party is satisfied that there are no serious reasons for fearing:

(a) that the consignments may be diverted from their destination,

(b) that the control may not be effective, or

(c) that a definite advantage may accrue to the military efforts or economy of the enemy through the substitution of the above-mentioned consignments for goods which would otherwise be provided or produced by the enemy or through release of such material, services or facilities as would otherwise be required for the production of such goods.

The Power which allows the passage of the consignments indicated in the first paragraph of this Article may make such permission conditional on the distribution to the persons benefited thereby being made under the local supervision of the Protecting Power.

Such consignments shall be forwarded as rapidly as possible, *and the Power which permits their free passage shall have the right to prescribe the technical arrangements under which such passage is allowed.* [Emphasis added]

The ICRC finally took into account that the established government in a civil war, voluntarily applying the Fourth Convention, probably had the legal right to set the terms of inspection for relief flights into the secessionist area.[49] Attention to this factor, in the context of the ICRC's image as a law-abiding actor, caused the ICRC officially to reject revolutionary humanitarianism. The new president of the ICRC went to Lagos in a personal effort to improve relations. In this diplomatic effort, arranged with the help of the United Kingdom, President Naville formally acknowledged that the ICRC would not undertake unauthorized flights. In return, among other things, Lagos eventually permitted five ICRC flights into Biafra. The ICRC maintained its "airforce" for some time after that, at considerable cost, but the ICRC airlift was finished.[50] In the meantime, Lindt was declared persona non grata by Lagos, and the ICRC's role of relief coordinator on the Federal side was also terminated by Lagos.

These actions did not completely finish the ICRC as far as the war was concerned. Visits to prisoners of war continued, although the numbers involved were small. ICRC medical and relief teams stayed in Biafra, receiving their supplies primarily from the churches.

JCA, after carefully watching the ICRC experience in June, decided to resume night flights. JCA successfully did so, thus once again proving the incapacity of the Federal airforce to enforce the blockade in the air at night. JCA had never wanted to contend with the issue of legality in Lagos's eyes, believing that its revolutionary humanitarianism took precedence over neutral humanitarianism based on law.

The ICRC, for its part, continued one aspect of revolutionary behavior. It transferred some of its stocks from Santa Isabel to the "French Red Cross" flying into Biafra from Libreville, Gabon. This airlift by the "French Red Cross" was in fact operated by the French government through the embassy in Libreville. It was an operation with no formal connection to the ICRC and no authorization from Lagos. The ICRC, in late 1969, however, used an unofficial delegate in Libreville to coordinate ICRC operations with that airlift, to maintain contact with ICRC teams in Biafra, to maintain rapport with Ojukwu, and finally to help evacuate ICRC teams in early 1970 when the Biafran resistance collapsed.

Officially, the ICRC continued to seek a negotiated agreement between both sides in support of day flights. Biafra was still opposed, except on terms that Lagos did not accept. At one point the ICRC threatened to start day flights without a negotiated agreement, but strong opposition from Biafra curtailed the move in that direction.[51]

When the war ended, the ICRC was not permitted to bring assistance into the Eastern Region, nor were other non-Nigerian parties. Several officials of the ICRC were permitted by the Nigerian authorities to enter the former secessionist area to observe conditions there. In March, 1970, the ICRC closed its Nigerian office.

Conclusions.   As a test of the laws of armed conflict, the Nigerian Civil War, like all wars, was inconclusive. ICRC protection efforts went without controversy, except for limited discussion about flying out prisoners of war to a neutral state. In fact, protection matters were forgotten at times, in the concern for assistance.

As for assistance and the Fourth Convention, the ICRC for a long time tended to ignore the exact wording of Article 23, as did everyone else. The general feeling within the ICRC was that, while Article 23 permitted the state which allowed relief to pass its territory the right to set the technical terms of passage, in order to insure certain interests, that right did not extend to the right to engage in genocide.[52] And there was some acceptance within the ICRC, perhaps subconsciously, of the Biafran claim that Lagos was engaging in genocide. President Naville turned to a cautious interpretation of the terms of Article 23 in July of 1969, although he was later persuaded to be assertive about possibly flying relief to Biafra without a negotiated agreement, and the ICRC remained assertive about getting goods into Biafra via the "French Red Cross."

The Nigerian experience had the effect of focusing subsequent legal development efforts on changing Article 23 to guarantee civilian relief, and the Canadian government—which had withdrawn some of its logistical support for the ICRC during the Nigerian War—eventually made some efforts to get parties interested in a separate relief convention.[53]

Thus as far as legal assistance under the Fourth Convention was concerned, Article 23 was first bypassed by the ICRC, then cautiously adhered to, and then became subject to revision efforts.

The second test provided by the war, that of the ICRC as assistance manager, led to a mixed—if more definite—conclusion.

In assessing assistance needs, certainly the early record of the ICRC was poor. It did not have firm information about the situation in Biafra, it did not get that information, and its appeals in August 1968 did not specify what was needed. The result was that national Red Cross Societies sent some goods that could not be used.[54] Once the ICRC established a consistent presence in Biafra, as was the case from fall 1968 to the end of the war, assessment improved. But the peak of starvation was the summer of 1968, and the ICRC was largely uninformed and unprepared for the dimension of that need.[55]

The collection of goods was not bad, beyond the period of open-ended appeals. An independent audit of ICRC assistance operations after the war concluded that there had not been excessive stockpiling and that goods were reasonably protected from loss, damage, or theft during storage.

As for distribution, on the Biafran side the ICRC record seemed better than the churches, at least insofar as avoiding duplication of services and insuring that relief was not diverted to military purposes. From the time of the start of the big ICRC airlift in September 1968 to its curtailment in June 1969, it is difficult to see how the ICRC's Biafran distribution scheme could be improved, given the prevailing conditions. On the Federal side, some question can be raised about distribution: not only because kwashiorkor reappeared on the Lagos side in early 1969, but also because some 3,700 tons of assistance went unaccounted for (possibly well used, but still unaccounted for).

Finally, insofar as assistance management is concerned, the ICRC's record in evaluating its performance and planning for the future must be rated only fair to poor. It did authorize an independent study of its tactical management, but another study that was to deal with an analysis of ICRC policy in the war disintegrated without official conclusions or significant findings. Thus while the managerial aspects of ICRC performance were reviewed, how those managerial tasks related to the larger question of ICRC policy pertaining to assistance in armed conflicts was a question never formally or officially answered. Indeed, the question ceased to be posed. ICRC archives on the Nigerian experience remain unorganized and unstudied, except for the quasi-official Hentsch publication.

The third test—that of the ICRC as actor in world affairs—likewise leads to conclusive answers, *insofar as this one case study is concerned*. The judgment is inescapable that, in general, the ICRC was politically unsophisticated in the Nigerian War. Neither its headquarters nor its head of operations in the field understood why there was so much friction with Lagos. Neither fully appreciated the extent to which Ojukwu bore responsibility for creating difficulties over humanitarian relief. There were ICRC individuals who understood well the political situation, like Hoffman, and Head Delegate Jaggi in Biafra, and Head Delegate Bingami in Lagos after Lindt's departure. But in general the ICRC was "taken-in" by Biafra's well-oiled propaganda effort, with pro-Biafran Western public opinion also playing a role. The ICRC was also easily manipulated by the British government.[56]

It is not to be forgotten that the ICRC did, in late summer 1968, get going very quickly once it decided to act. It did save thousands of lives in the war. And while JCA may have flown in more tons of relief, not to mention demonstrating to the ICRC that an airlift was possible,[57] nevertheless the ICRC contribution was considerable.

The point remains, however, that probably not two people within the ICRC's policy-making council knew that in Nigeria at peace, some 400—500 people per annum died of kwashiorkor. That is to say, there was in Nigeria in the late 1960's a death baseline of that magnitude. Moreover, it was normal African practice, given a shortage of food, to let the children do without first. They were unproductive at the moment and easily replaceable. A delegate like George Hoffmann knew all this, but the Assembly of the ICRC did not. And therein lay the difference in how the two evaluated reported figures coming out of the war, not to mention statements emanating from the Biafran side.

Starvation is starvation. But the ICRC, which has traditionally chosen to act on the basis of negotiated agreement, must do one of two things. Either it must stick to the negotiated-agreement approach, carefully evaluating who is using the starvation issue as a weapon in realpolitik. Or it must discard negotiations in favor of revolutionary humanitarianism—in this case, a response to starvation regardless of the desires of the conflicting parties. (A compromise measure for the ICRC would be to retire to the sidelines if a negotiated agreement could not be obtained, but to encourage various national Red Cross Societies to do what they thought best. While this is not a perfect solution, emphasizing as it does the fragmentation of what is supposed to be a unified movement, it is a solution permitting some Red Cross response to starvation while preserving the traditional image of neutrality of the ICRC.)[58]

In the Nigerian War the ICRC never really decided whether it was to be a revolutionary or discretionary humanitarian actor. Therein lay its basic problem. This problem existed because the ICRC as an institution had no clear conception of strategy, a weakness which in turn stemmed from lack of continuity in personnel (both in Lagos and within headquarters) and a lack of coordination between headquarters and the field.

The specific manifestation of this basic problem was assertiveness toward Lagos without full understanding either of Lagos's concerns or the ICRC's own position. This assertiveness was perhaps personified by Lindt, but it was present even after his departure from the scene. As the war moved to a close, despite all that had happened in the past and despite advice from insiders and outsiders to use a "low-profile" or "soft-sell" approach to Lagos, the ICRC presented Lagos with a long list of what that party should do by way of assistance in the secessionist area after the war.

While ICRC motivation was commendable, it is still true that the ICRC had learned nothing about dealing with the Federals. For example, the Federals would not even use Uli Airport after the war, as it had become the symbol of relief to Biafra. And here was the ICRC, that had flown into Uli, telling Lagos what it should do after the war, instead of offering its help in doing what Lagos wanted to do.

A humanitarian motivation is no substitute for political sophistication.

8 The ICRC Administrative Process: Organization, People, Money

An analysis of the ICRC's administrative process meets many obstacles, and for that reason the analysis presented here must be regarded as tentative rather than definitive—a first step rather than the final word.

One obstacle is the lack of literature on the subject to serve as a point of comparison. There is almost nothing written on the internal workings of the ICRC by outsiders, primarily because meetings and records are regarded as confidential by the ICRC. The little that has been written by ICRC officials or ICRC consultants is not always oriented to broad questions of administrative policy. A second obstacle is the complexity of the ICRC. There are different levels of decision-making, different divisions within the professional staff, different functions and roles. A generalization about one level, division, or function is not necessarily valid for another. A third problem is that the ICRC is a small institution greatly affected by personalities; this increases difficulty of analysis of administrative process over time. Fourthly, and probably most importantly, the ICRC is very much in transition as this is being written. ICRC administrative organization was altered in July 1973. Thus an analysis of pre-1973 administration is of diminished relevance; an analysis of the post-1973 period is somewhat premature.

There remains a need, however, for some understanding of the inner work-ings of the ICRC. A discussion of what the ICRC is trying to do in world affairs would not be complete without some discussion of how it organizes itself for that activity and how it manages its resources. A limited and tentative discussion is better than no discussion at all.

ORGANIZATION

Until the early 1970's, the ICRC administrative process was dominated by a collegial body and its president. This body was called the Committee (Comité) and consisted of up to twenty-five Swiss citizens coopted by the Comité itself. The president of the Comité was also president of the ICRC, and frequently he was a very powerful—even dominant—figure. Often he was president, prime minister, and party secretary rolled into one. In certain cases he was a philosopher-king as well since he had the opportunity, and sometimes the inclina-tion, to pronounce upon the meaning of Red Cross principles. Max Huber was among the most well known of these strong presidents (president 1928–45), at least outside the House, but Leopold Boissier (president 1955–64) among more recent presidents was also viewed as a very influential figure. Such presidents and their activist colleagues on the Comité recognized no limits on the scope of their decisions. Once interested in a matter, they could consider the slightest tactical detail of ICRC activity. Therefore in the post-World-War-II period, as indeed before, the diplomatic position of the ICRC was largely the product of decision by the Comité, frequently led by strong presidents.

Two further things can be said about ICRC decision-making in general, prior to the early 1970's. First, while the Comité was the dominant element in that decision-making, there was also periodic and extensive deference by the Comité to the delegate in the field. This characteristic stemmed from weak communica-tions, and it was the delegate *sur place* rather than the Geneva headquarters that really knew what was going on in places like Ethiopia and Spain in the 1930's.[1] Much the same was true during World War II, especially in Russia and Asia. But even more recently, when the ICRC had its own radio network and access to modern communications systems, the idea persisted within the Comité that it was the man in the field who knew best what to do, at least until some ill-defined point. Thus in addition to periodic activism by the Comité, there was also periodic deference to the man *sur le terrain*.

Second, it appears that the Comité was, in general, more conservative than the ICRC delegates in the field. This has been documented, as noted earlier, for the history of ICRC work with political prisoners.[2] It probably holds for other subjects as well, although proof is lacking at present. With regard to political prisoners, it is clear that individual delegates committed the ICRC symbol to certain actions, and that the Comité was hesitant to endorse and support that expansion of activity. At least on this one subject the Comité can be said to be conservative, in the Burkean sense of being cautious about engaging in change and undertaking something new.

The ICRC administrative process that existed until the early 1970's can thus be summarized as one of centralized conservatism along with decentralized activism. A major problem in this process increasingly was identified in the late 1960's and early 1970's. This major deficiency had an external and internal aspect.

Major Problem

The basic problem was that the entire process of decision-making within the ICRC was amateurish.[3] Decisions were being made in the Comité on a broad range of subjects by nonspecialists in humanitarian law and diplomacy. Members of the Comité were professors, lawyers, retired politicians and civil servants, doctors, bankers, businessmen, etc., the overwhelming number of whom had never served in the field. The ICRC was dealing with professional politicians, professional civil servants, professional soldiers, and in some cases professional terrorists. And yet its general decisions were being made largely by nonprofessionals in humanitarian matters.

Moreover, as the demands on the ICRC increased and as the ICRC took up new initiatives, the ICRC found itself with more activity of a more complex nature. Even traditional activity became more complex because of the changed nature of world affairs. The 1949 Geneva diplomatic conference consisted of sixty states, mostly Western. Twenty-five years later the conference to supplement the 1949 law consisted of over 120 states, mostly non-Western. Non-Western policies dominated the 1974 session of that conference. Moreover, "liberation movements" and international organizations were also active at that conference. Hence the ICRC, in carrying out its traditional work of trying to help develop humanitarian law, faced an increasingly complex situation.

Both with regard to "old" and "new" activity, therefore, increasingly there was strong feeling that the Comité was not fully capable of handling this complex and varying subject matter of global extent. The problem reached to the very fundamentals of ICRC organization. The work load that was demanded and the expertise that was required were viewed as simply too much for the part-time humanitarians in the Comité. They usually came to ICRC headquarters in Geneva periodically while away from their first careers. Given this situation, it was not particularly surprising for an observer to uncover various complaints about the Comité's awareness, political acumen, and general competence.

The awareness of a major problem was found within the House and also outside the ICRC in both Red Cross and governmental circles. Some serving within and under the Comité, as well as many interacting with the ICRC, came to the same conclusion. There had to be a major change in the organization of the

ICRC if humanitarian protection and assistance were to be practiced effectively in the last quarter of the twentieth century. To borrow a phrase from Walter Bagehot, many saw the Comité as more dignified than effective.

External Aspect.   The external aspect of the basic problem was that in recent years the Comité had developed little consistent strategy, or basic sense of direction, in ICRC work. Either because of a tendency to defer to the delegate in the field or for some other reason, the Comité qua collegial body had failed to examine systematically a whole series of questions. Whether with regard to improving relations with non-Western parties or maintaining standards among national Red Cross Societies, the Comité was largely silent. The ICRC's diplomatic position was not so much the result of consciously made strategy or general policy but rather the result of several steps taken in the midst of some pressing need and lacking a clear objective. A classic case was that of the dispatch of a delegation to Pakistan at the time of the 1971 turmoil without advance consultation with the Pakistani government. The delegation was refused entry into that country. Because of such events, the ICRC was viewed by some parties as cautious in general but prone to precipitous involvements. Once involved, the ICRC seemed sometimes to act without concern for long-range considerations. ICRC involvement in the Nigerian War fitted this pattern exactly: the ICRC was slow to respond to events in that country, but when it did become involved the ICRC lacked a long-term strategy for dealing with Lagos. In fact, the Nigerian affair really demonstrated the utter inability of the old Comité-dominated system to function at all. The Comité finally recruited an outsider, Mr. Lindt, to direct ICRC affairs in Nigeria-Biafra, agreeing to his demand for a carte blanche in policy matters.[4]

Internal Aspect.   The internal aspect of the basic problem was that the management of the ICRC was as unsystematic as its external moves. If the ICRC lacked a strategy on many questions, likewise it lacked effective internal management. There were at least three deficiencies in this regard.

1. Decision-making was not fully coordinated within the House; the levels of decision-making were not integrated.[5] This lack of integration pertained to three levels.

First, the opinion of the lower-ranking delegate in the field was not, in general, systematically obtained. It was only in the late 1960's that any move was made in this direction. Prior to that time, the Comité—while deferring initially to the man sur place—frequently failed to solicit his opinion when the Comité plunged into the affair in question.

Second, there was not systematic coordination within the various sectors of the Geneva headquarters. In particular, the two main action sectors, Operations and Law, proceeded in a largely independent manner. The Operations Department, frequently dealing with legally ambiguous situations and sometimes led by men who did not regard international law as entirely helpful to humanitarian values, proceeded pragmatically. For its part the Legal Department was largely oriented not to field situations but to developing legal materials, and to the development of the meaning of Red Cross principles and doctrine. There was, progressively until 1975, and by comparison with events in the 1940's, no tight meshing of field experience with legal development; nor a meshing of the law on the books with field situations (see Chapter 5).

The third lack of integration pertained to the highest levels of the ICRC. It appears to be the case that different elements within the Comité in more recent years did not always follow the same policy. While one individual or faction seemed to be pursuing one line of diplomacy, other individuals or factions seemed to be acting in a different direction. Much of this diversity transpired through informal contact. Thus it is difficult to prove not only what policy was, but when countervailing power was exercised. But the Comité has not given the appearance of unity and consistency since perhaps the latter years of the presidency of Samuel Gonard (1964–69).[6] At these three levels, then, there has not been integration of ICRC decision-making.

2. Furthermore, the ICRC has not had the most systematic and analytical budgetary and financial procedures. In the past it has been difficult if not impossible to determine what has been spent on particular tasks—e.g., the protection of political prisoners. This has made difficult both policy review and policy planning. And neither government officials nor academics—and perhaps not even ICRC officials—were sure how much a particular ICRC operation cost— e.g., the airlift of material-medical goods into Biafra, calculated either per ton or per capita.[7] Lack of a sufficiently detailed budget, and lack of adequate fiscal controls during an operation, compounded the problems brought about by lack of integration in decision-making. Indeed, the two went hand in hand.

3. A third problem of internal management was that the ICRC before 1973 lacked procedures designed to benefit from the past. The ICRC was an institution much concerned with precedent but with a poor memory of its own past. At one and the same time the ICRC was frequently wary regarding the long-range implications of a current action but also ignorant of the contents of its own archives. There were no procedures designed to make use of the ICRC's rich diplomatic history to the benefit of current policy. There has not been a systematic review of past situations and difficulties to see what can be learned for the future.[8]

These three interrelated problems of amateurism, lack of strategy, and lack of systematic management under the old Comité-dominated administrative system led to major changes for the ICRC, commencing in the late 1960's and formalized in the early 1970's. As of July 1973, there is a new overall organization for the ICRC.

(It might be noted that "intelligence-gathering" does not appear to have been a major problem in the past, or at present. ICRC officials claim, and there seems little evidence to the contrary, that the institution is reasonably well informed about alleged violations of fundamental human rights from newspaper sources and NGO and individual petitions. There may have been a Western orientation in past "intelligence sources." But a clipping service covering *Le Monde* and the *International Herald Tribune* would seem to provide at present as much or more "non-Western" information as non-Western sources themselves. Of course it remains exceedingly difficult for any transnational actor or intergovernmental organization to establish facts in places like the People's Republic of China or the Soviet Union.)

New Structure

The new formal structure can be depicted as in figure 8.1. This new structure and its accompanying "internal regulations" are intended to systematize, rationalize, and professionalize ICRC administration. The new regulations stipulate that the Assembly's jurisdiction is restricted to fixing the doctrine and the general policy of the ICRC and to exercising the topmost supervision over the entirety of ICRC activities.[9] At first glance this does not appear to be much of a restriction. But *general conduct* and *direct administration* is expressly given to the new Executive Council headed by its own president (whom I shall henceforth call the executive director to avoid confusion with the president of the

Figure 8.1. Formal Structure of the ICRC, after 1973

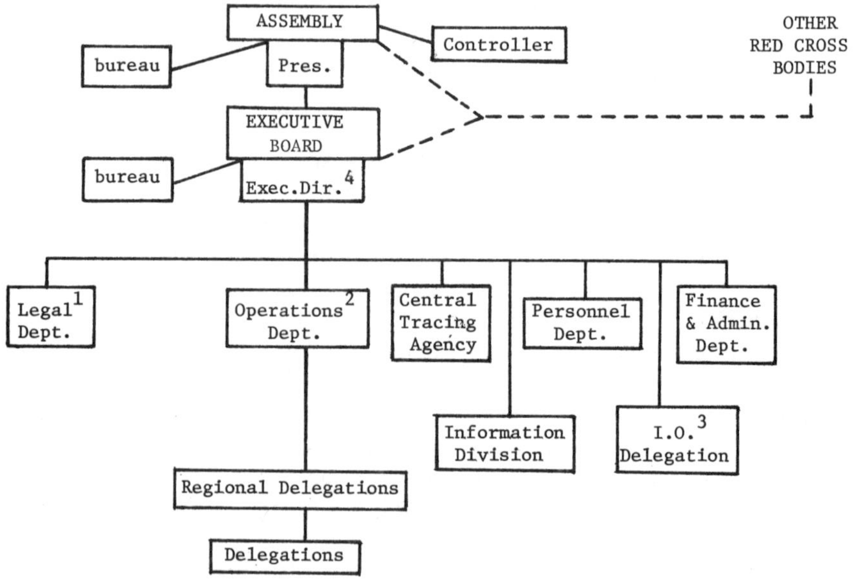

[1]Officially the Department of Law and Principles.
[2]Composed internally of geographical bureaus and support offices.
[3]Officially the Delegation to International Organizations.
[4]Officially "President."

Assembly). While the Assembly remains the "supreme" organ of the ICRC, having the final say on general matters including financial matters, the responsibility for day-to-day affairs is given to the Council. Thus the Assembly has strategy and financial control, but the Council has both policy and tactics, including the formulation of the draft budget.

Further, under the Executive Council but not showing on official administrative charts is "la Direction," made up of the heads of the major departments (composed at the time of writing of the directors of Law, Operations, Personnel, Administration and Finance, and the head of the Tracing Agency). Thus there is a group, in addition to the Council, outside the Assembly and responsible for the coordination and administration of specific policy and tactics. It is made up of professional ICRC diplomat-administrators. While the members of the Council can be amateurs or not, members of the Direction are all professionals. It is the group with the most fully informed overview of ICRC affairs; it reports to the executive director.

Some of these changes might appear semantic, with new names looking like new titles for old bodies. The Executive Council looked somewhat like the old President's Council, a sort of "little Assembly" that had existed as the old president's main working group. And there has been a secretary general in the past, as well as a Direction.

What was important about the 1973 changes was the authority of the executive director, and under him of the Council. The changes were more real than semantic, for the director and Council had immediate authority over whatever arose in ICRC affairs, within the financial and strategic guidelines as might be laid down by the Assembly. The Council only reported to the Assembly ex post facto; it did not have to seek specific guidance before acting. Moreover, the Council had the direct advice of the professional staff.

Beyond semantics and formal, legal changes, there was a shift in power toward the professional side of the House and away from the Assembly. There was also an upgrading of Personnel and Administration, as the directors of these two departments were added to the Direction. And the head archivist was sometimes informally added to the Direction to improve continuity with the past. All of these changes were intended to professionalize and systematize ICRC activity.

This new structure has already given rise to an embryonic administrative process that shows signs of functioning as intended. For example, on the question of political prisoners the ICRC has pulled together virtually all of its middle- and high-ranking officials who have knowledge or experience on the subject. A series of meetings among these officials led to a series of draft policy statements, which were sent eventually by the Council to the Assembly. The Assembly then approved them as the official strategy of the ICRC on the subject. Likewise the budgetary process is being initiated by the financial-administrative staff experts, working in close coordination with the other departments and their geographical and functional sectors. Drafts are then compiled by first the Direction and then the Council, and finally an official draft is submitted by the Council to the Assembly for formal approval.

Some of these processes did start under the ancien régime, but the new organization has encouraged and formalized the trends. Insofar as one can judge after a very short period of observation, the new organization seems to be promoting the objectives desired. Not only has a brake been applied to Assembly involvement in tactical matters, but also there has been greater integration in ICRC decision-making. A striking change, brought about less by organizational impetus and more by personnel shifts, is an integration between Operations and Law. Officials in the Legal Department are being required to have field experience, and those in Operations are being required to represent the ICRC at some legal meetings, among other changes.

There are some problems under the new system, and three of some importance can be identified already:

1. There is the problem of the two presidents. The problems were so evident that in 1976 the ICRC shifted back to a one-president system, with Alexander Hay as president of the ICRC, the Comité, and the Executive Board. It is still instructive to review the problems, for future reference. Since the president of the Executive Board (my "executive director") was charged with directing specific policy-making and implementation, the president of the Assembly was reduced to handling reflective and representational functions (and the executive director was expressly given some of the latter). In short, there was an executive division of labor, with the Assembly president getting less power and authority. This could have been a workable division. But it is doubtful that many men of outstanding capabilities would have been drawn to the presidency of the Assembly as it existed. It was no secret that the first executive director, Roger Gallopin, had been more central to ICRC affairs than the first Assembly president, Eric Martin. And it was no secret that the latter had been less than fully satisfied with his position, wanting to do more but circumscribed by the new authority pattern. Any system with two presidents contains the seeds of competition and confusion unless one is reduced to the position of a figurehead. One can note that under the Fifth French Republic, that is, since 1958 in France, there is, with each change in the Presidency, some question as to the division of labor between president and prime minister. When it is established that a Pompidou or a Giscard d'Estaing does indeed intend to continue in the Gaullist tradition of a strong president, then the prime minister is reduced in importance. Likewise with the ICRC, there is some continuing question as to the interplay between president and executive director.

2. There is still the problem of the "two Assemblies." There is the real Assembly and there is the "little Assembly" or Executive Board. And there is the Direction in addition. The reason for even having an Executive Board is not entirely clear. If a collective group is needed beyond the Assembly, the Direction is by far the more capable group. Moreover, the Executive Board can draw, and

has, on amateurs rather than professionals. Of the seven members in 1973, five were amateurs. Slight changes in 1974 did not alter the fact that some of the characteristics of the old Assembly were carried over in the new Board. So the reason for having that Board was hard to define, unless it were viewed simply as a transitional device to build support within the House for the new organization. The real "cabinet" for the "prime minister" (executive director) was the Direction. And there was some evidence that that latter group was spending a great deal of time preparing for and answering the questions of a largely amateurish Board.

3. Last but not least there is the problem of the Assembly's role. It is difficult for the Assembly to play a meaningful role in ICRC affairs if it is cut off from day-to-day policy and tactics. Moreover, the difference between strategy and policy is not always self-evident. It is likely that the professional staff will adopt very broad definitions of not only what is policy but also what is tactics. Staff aggrandisement would leave the Assembly with a narrow definition of strategy; moreover, Assembly strategy would tend toward artificiality—and the Assembly would tend to become a rubber stamp—if it were cut off from day-to-day affairs. Like the British House of Commons, the Assembly may have the final, formal say both on general policy and financial policy, but that does not necessarily mean having an independent impact on matters, as a collective body.

There has been, since July 1973, some confusion as to the proper role of the Assembly. For example, in the late summer and early fall of 1974 there was evident confusion over what was strategy compared with policy and tactics. The ICRC had agreed to host a conference of government experts on the subject of conventional weapons that might cause unnecessary suffering or have indiscriminate effects. The matter of invitations to the conference was controversial, primarily because of the then-contentious issue of what to do with the Provisional Revolutionary Government of South Vietnam (PRG). The PRG had not been admitted to the 1974 session of the Geneva diplomatic conference and had not been recognized by all governments. Yet some governments strongly wished that delegation to be invited. The Assembly took jurisdiction over the invitation question. Some observers and participants did not think the subject pertained to strategy; others were concerned with the outcome—the PRG was not invited, by vote of governments. (There did not, however, seem to be any major "diplomatic fallout" from this incident.) The point to be made here is that there was some confusion and disagreement as to who should do what within the ICRC.

The Assembly is still in search of its proper and constructive role. Under the new regulations, the Assembly is authorized to make use of consultants, "Swiss or foreigners," and it is possible that the Assembly could use such individuals to make studies for it that would allow it to exercise a critical review of ICRC policy and tactics as conducted under the Executive Board. Such a process could lead to a useful system of checks and balances as well as to an independently considered strategy of some practical use. As of the mid-1970's, the Assembly was concerned with a search for even more basic things, such as the best interval for meetings. It had tried once a month and once every two months, as well as every six weeks for a two-day session. Clearly the Assembly was in search of itself.

All of these organizational issues were under continuing and almost continuous review by the ICRC in the mid-1970's. The study that led to the 1973 change was followed by the study director's final report for the Joint Committee for the Reappraisal of the Red Cross in the summer of 1975. The ICRC itself had internal studies under way in conjunction with both of these outside studies. If the ICRC had not yet found all of the right answers for its organizational needs, it had certainly made an effort to get the right questions raised. As in the past, much will depend on the new president, Mr. Hay.

PEOPLE

In the mid-1970's the ICRC was in the process of changing not only its organization but some of its policies relating to personnel. Other policies not yet changed were being debated.

The Issue of Nationality

A perennial issue was the all-Swiss nature of the ICRC. The Assembly (which I will henceforth use as a term to cover the old Comité as well) had considered the issue on at least three occasions since the mid-1860's.[10] The question was widely discussed in the early and mid-1970's, although not formally debated by the Assembly.

The Assembly has always been all-Swiss; this characteristic has been required under ICRC regulations. As for the rest of the ICRC, it has been basically all-Swiss; most of the important officials have been Swiss. Strictly speaking, some ICRC delegates have been non-Swiss—French in particular. The non-Swiss delegates probably amount to fewer than one percent of the permanent staff throughout the history of the institution. More recently, some of the permanent staff at Geneva have been non-Swiss. In the early 1970's the ICRC employed some 55 non-Swiss out of a permanent staff of approximately 225. When the custodial and strictly service personnel are removed, one is left with about 10 percent of the permanent staff as non-Swiss. There was no important policy-making position held by any in this group. Thus for all intents and purposes one could say that the ICRC was wholly Swiss.

There have been many demands for a change in this situation, as well as many defenses of it. The demands arise especially when ICRC affairs do not appear to be proceeding smoothly. There are ideological demands, stressing the need for different schools of thought in the work of the ICRC. There are representational demands, stressing the need for a broader membership in response to a multinational, multicultural environment. Most of these demands for change argue that the acceptability of, and awareness by, the ICRC would be improved by the presence of non-Swiss somewhere within it.[11]

As for the acceptability of the ICRC by states and other parties for humanitarian protection and assistance, the Red Cross study director, a Canadian, concluded that the acceptance or rejection of the ICRC was not because of the Swiss nature of the ICRC but because of the functions to be performed. It was the function of protection or assistance by a third party in a conflict situation that was unacceptable when rejection occurred, in his judgment. This is also the ICRC view.

There are not many historical situations that can be used to test fully this view. On the basis of at least one situation the study director's view is proven correct. During World War II the ICRC was seeking, unsuccessfully, complete access to Jewish concentration camps in Nazi Germany. At one point the ICRC drew up a list of six names of prospective ICRC delegates and asked the German government to choose which it would find acceptable for camp visits. Four of the six were Swedish. The German government found all six unacceptable.[12]

It is the opinion of the Red Cross study director, after a three-year study on many subjects, that the all-Swiss Assembly is an asset to ICRC work because that body is widely associated with responsible and conscientious activity. In his view this image facilitates ICRC acceptance. The study director did find a need for improved openness and awareness by the Assembly but thought that this should be achieved through changed attitudes and the use of foreign consultants rather than through changed membership.

Beyond Assembly membership, the Red Cross study director was inclined to favor the use of non-Swiss as well as Swiss in certain ICRC tasks, such as activity associated with diplomatic conferences. Many Swiss professionals in the ICRC were less than enthusiastic about this, especially since personnel in the Law and Operations Departments were being increasingly used interchangeably. Many of the professionals thought the ICRC should remain Swiss to avoid problems of establishing equitable geographical representation and a possible decline in discretion. Frequently one heard the argument that the Swiss staff had proven its ability and should not be altered. On the other hand one also heard the argument that the number of qualified Swiss staff members was definitely limited. Supporters of this position pointed to ICRC difficulties in Chile after Allende, among other things, arguing that a lack of qualified people caused the ICRC to use nonprofessionals in key positions in the field, with less than satisfactory results.

The issue of the all-Swiss nature of the Assembly and/or staff is not likely to be answered by a formal move toward inclusion of non-Swiss as official members, at least for the near future, because both the Assembly and the Executive Board are opposed. The ICRC has clearly stated that it will *not* seek a monopoly over Red Cross personnel in the administration of Red Cross *assistance,* even in conflict situations, but will share administration with personnel from the League of Red Cross Societies—which draws its people from various national Red Cross Societies. (This leaves open the question of who should *direct* this administration of assistance.) Thus the ICRC will only seek a monopoly over personnel engaged in Red Cross protection. The ICRC is strongly committed to using Swiss personnel for detention visits and other delicate diplomatic matters. The ICRC has accepted the idea, in the abstract, of foreign consultants. Their use is explicitly approved in the 1973 internal regulations. But as of 1977 the ICRC has not used such people to any significant degree.

If ICRC effectiveness is generally perceived to be adequate or even improving, demands for change in nationality will diminish. But the demands will not disappear. Large-scale protection efforts will strain ICRC capability, and simultaneous involvements of this nature have occurred and will continue—e.g., wars in Nigeria and the Middle East in 1967, major involvements with political prisoners in Chile and Indonesia in 1975. Moreover, ICRC personnel have been basically not only Swiss but also white, male, Christian, and bourgeois. This leaves ample ground for criticism from certain viewpoints—e.g., nonwhite, female, Marxist, and third-world.

Some further commentary helps clarify the ICRC personnel situation.

Personnel Management: Recruitment, Training, Evaluation

1. The Assembly.   For the first sixty years of ICRC history, the Assembly was made up only of citizens from Geneva. The extremely closed nature of the ICRC was demonstrated by the wording of the *International Review of the Red Cross* in 1931: "Horace Micheli had his place in the Comité marked in advance, his father, Louis Micheli of the Right Bank, having been member of the Comité."[13] Recruitment by cooptation was gradually extended beyond prominent Geneva families to other prominent persons in Switzerland. Since the 1920's, attention has been directed toward counteracting or balancing the Geneva influence with a Swiss-German influence (which is the numerically dominant element in Swiss life). From 1923, which saw the first Assembly member who was not from Geneva, the Assembly has had more non-Genevois than Genevois. But in the mid-1970's both the executive director and the president were from Geneva. (President Hay is a Genevois.) There have been only some half-dozen females on the Assembly since 1863; and all Assembly members have been Caucasian.

The social base of the Assembly has been middle- or upper-class. There are no detailed sociological studies of Assembly membership. However, a bourgeois or upper-class standing has been necessary since Assembly members serve as a gesture of charity, there being no salary. (Only three Red Cross paid professionals have ever been coopted into the Assembly.) The social base of the Assembly can be inferred from the careers represented therein. From 1863 to the early 1970's, we find among the first 98 names: 37 lawyers, 19 doctors, 8 military men, 6 bankers, and a smattering of others such as politicians and men of letters.[14] If we take the Assembly as of 1 July 1974 we find: 4 ex-politicians or government officials; 3 doctors; 3 businessmen, 2 academics; 2 career Red Cross workers; 2 union leaders; 1 lawyer; 1 judge; 1 social worker. In more recent times the Assembly has consciously tried to obtain as members union representatives and others whose views could be said to differ from the mainstream of thought within the Assembly over the years. Put less delicately, the Assembly has tried to obtain some members from social strata supportive of liberal rather than conservative views.

As for the age base of the Assembly, it has been somewhat advanced. In the history of the Assembly the age at date of entry has varied considerably, with the youngest coopted at twenty-five and the oldest at seventy-four. If we consider the period 1 January 1950 to 1 January 1974, the average age at time of cooptation was just over fifty-three. If we take the average age of the Assembly as a whole at a given point in 1950, it was sixty; in 1960, sixty-four; in 1970, sixty; and at the start of 1974, again sixty.

The longevity of Assembly membership is considerable. Again for the period 1950–1974, with 1974 members excluded, the average tenure was 17.6 years; including 1974 members it dropped to 13.4. There is no great turnover of Assembly members. From 1950 to 1970, 41 different persons served on the Assembly, although up to 25 could serve at a given time. Nineteen of those 41 still served as of mid-1974. Thus only 22 had left the Assembly in almost a quarter of a century. (Under the 1973 rules as amended, Assembly members are elected to renewable four-year terms up to seventy-two years of age, extendable to seventy-five by special vote. After two terms, reelection must occur by two-thirds rather than simple majority vote.)

Given the social base of the Assembly, its age, and its longevity in terms of individual service, it would be reasonable to infer a conservatism in its intellectual disposition. This has been confirmed by the history of Assembly handling of the subject of political prisoners, as noted previously.[15] While other analyses are lacking and while most records pertaining to Assembly deliberations remain restricted, everything known from economics and sociology points to the fact that a middle- or upper-class, middle-aged group, drawn from "the establishment" of a wealthy country, and serving without pay (a reflection of affluence), would be conservative in the Burkean sense.

This conservatism in intellectual disposition can, of course, be viewed as good or bad depending upon one's personal convictions. Many governments appear to like ICRC conservatism, as most governments are not eager to see a nongovernmental organization concerned with humanitarian affairs play a large and active role in world affairs. Governments in general are greatly concerned about their independence of action and prestige, ergo favoritism for a cautious ICRC.

On the other hand, some observers of world affairs believe the ICRC to be too cautious in humanitarian matters, overly deferent to governments at the expense of human rights and welfare. Moreover, some observers believe the ICRC's conservatism has made it unsympathetic to certain human-rights problems and unacceptable to certain parties. Thus, in their view, true impartiality in ICRC activity has been impeded by the conservative disposition of the Assembly. One American scholar, as noted earlier, described the ICRC as made up of individuals more anticommunist than American businessmen.[16] And even within the ICRC staff there is some feeling that ICRC relations with certain regimes— i.e., the Castro government—did not develop "normally" because of Assembly antipathy toward those regimes. In such matters it is extremely difficult to prove impartiality. Many attitudes of influential ICRC officials—and especially their motivations—are not documented.

It is clear that Assembly members are drawn from the Swiss establishment. It is not absolutely clear whether this pattern of cooptation has led to a conservatism basically constructive or detrimental to ICRC activity. Jean Pictet, vice president of the Assembly, has stressed that humanitarian law hinges on its being acceptable to actors in world affairs.[17] This is a thesis supportive of legal conservatism, as the ICRC, in the last analysis, would have to follow legal opinion rather than lead it. In fact, the ICRC has tried to develop humanitarian law according to the lowest common denominator—viz., it has promoted law that could be universally accepted. Such an approach avoids radical or provocative legislation that might be accepted immediately by some and later by others. Conservatism aside, recent patterns of ICRC cooptation apparently have produced Assembly members nationalistic and ethnocentric.[18]

2. The Staff The ICRC professional staff is made up of paid employees who are not members of the Assembly. In a very small number of cases the dividing line between Assembly member and staff is not clear. In one instance, the individual is a member of the Assembly, a member of the Executive Board, and employed by the ICRC. In several other cases individuals are members of both Assembly and Board, but not paid a salary by the ICRC.

Leaving aside these individuals, one can say that the ICRC professional staff has three elements. There is the permanent staff, which in the early 1970's numbered around 225. There is the temporary staff, made up of individuals employed for short periods (say, six months to three years) but with no guarantee of continuing employment. These numbered around 30–35 in the early 1970's. And finally there is the occasional staff, hired for very short periods in response to crises. These might be termed quasi-professional. This number fluctuates wildly. During the Nigerian War the ICRC employed some 375 people beyond planned permanent and temporary staff. For the war in Bangladesh the comparable figure was 325. For the shorter wars in the Middle East involving fewer people the figure was approximately 65.

The permanent staff is not initially "recruited" by the ICRC. Individuals hear about the ICRC from relatives and acquaintances and apply to the institution. In a small country like Switzerland, and for a small institution like the ICRC, this haphazard process still accounts for three times as many applications as there are openings in an average year. But nonrecruitment fails to guarantee the quality of applicants, even if numbers are sufficient for planned activity. About 60 percent of the permanent staff have university training and degrees of some type.

The age of the permanent staff member when he joins the institution in that capacity is almost thirty-three, on the average. As of January 1974, the average age of the ICRC permanent staff was forty-one. Since there was no difference between males and females in this regard, and since most of the important officials are males, as compared with a female secretarial corps, it can be said that the average age of ICRC permanent delegates and other important officials is about forty-one also. This is young by Western governmental standards. And in mid-1975 both the director of Operations and the Director of Law were under forty. If we consider the average age of the permanent staff assigned to Operations, we find the figure of thirty-five and a half as of January 1974. Also, some delegates having rather high-level contact with government officials in the field are not from the permanent but rather from the temporary staff. The average age for the latter category is even younger than the permanent staff, which means that the average age of ICRC delegates in the field is under forty.

Longevity on the staff varies without evident pattern, except for one. There is a large group of newcomers, and there is a smaller but still distinguishable group of "old-timers." Currently there is not a large group of "intermediate-timers." Over one half of the permanent staff had served for six years or less as of early January 1974. These newcomers included both delegates and others. Beyond this group, the next peak in the chart of years of service occurred at the other end of the spectrum. About 16 percent of the permanent staff had served for more than sixteen years; 13 of these had served for more than thirty-three years. The average number of years served on the staff as of January 1974 was a little over eight for permanent staff members.

The members of the permanent ICRC staff are, in general, paid competitive salaries, by Swiss standards, at the lower ranks. However, ICRC salaries are taxable, whereas salaries for civil servants of the international organizations found in Geneva are not. Also, many Swiss firms pay a salary for a "thirteenth month of the year"; the ICRC does not. At higher levels, ICRC salaries are not competitive by Swiss standards. The staff assigned outside Geneva, however, receives travel allowances and a per diem of a competitive nature, which brings the total financial support up considerably. The ICRC is trying to match the pay scale of the Swiss foreign service. Already the lower-ranking staff member serving in the field does quite well for himself financially. But the financial picture is quite different for the older ICRC officials, especially those posted at headquarters. In sum, the ICRC official is paid an almost-competitive salary compared to Swiss functionaries and at an inferior rate compared to United Nations functionaries.

Training of delegates was almost nonexistent until the late 1960's and early 1970's. Before that, training occurred "on the job." In the early 1970's efforts were made to give some formal training in Geneva, primarily through lectures and above all simulation. Experienced delegates posed situations likely to be met in the field, requiring potential delegates to cope with the situations. This training lasted for a few days only, and emphasis remains on "on the job" training. The unwritten rule seems to be that a delegate needs close supervision for some four to six weeks before he can be expected to make detention visits or deal with government officials on his own. Where a delegate operates within a large delegation, and thus where mistakes can be counteracted relatively easily, supervision is sometimes shortened. Where a delegate operates largely on his own, say a regional delegate individually responsible for a dozen situations or so, supervision and training are extended. Errors of judgment in such situations are extremely difficult to counteract, and thus rarely are new delegates assigned to such posts. But under the impact of crisis the norm of careful supervision is sometimes honored more by its breach than by its practice, and training is sometimes cut to a minimum. Those *given* sensitive missions are almost without exception experienced officials. On the other hand, a sensitive situation can arise anywhere quickly, including in the zone of inexperienced, quickly trained, and unsupervised delegates put into the field in rapid response to conflict.

The evaluation of delegates by superiors with a view toward promotions and transfers appears to have been less than fully systematic. In the past, and in noncrisis times, this was not a major problem. The institution was small, the number of individuals to be evaluated likewise not very great, and most served at Geneva a good part of the time. With expansion of activity, the use of "temporary" personnel, and the trend toward regional delegations or offices, the importance of systematic evaluation increases. Some elements within the ICRC are aware of this, and moves are under way to standardize the evaluation process. Heads of delegations or subdelegations make personnel reports, but there has not been cross-checking of these reports by officials dispatched from Geneva. Moreover, debriefing sessions do not always occur for terminated or transferred delegates. The creation of a new Department of Personnel should help to correct some of the personnel deficiencies continuing from the past.

As for the temporary and occasional staff, much of what has been said about the permanent staff applies to the other two categories as well. As already noted, the temporary staff is younger than the permanent staff, and usually comes directly from university studies—with the exception of medical personnel who usually have two years or so of practice. In the past, over half of the occasional staff served only once under the aegis of the ICRC, but this figure is declining somewhat. The ICRC has not maintained a complete file on temporary and occasional personnel, which is striking given the obvious uses to which such information could be put during times of rapid expansion of personnel. Changes are under way to correct this deficiency.

The Image of ICRC Personnel. The Assembly and staff, taken together or separately, present an image to outsiders based on empirical and ascriptive traits. The empirical traits are relatively easy to identify. From the preceding paragraphs, one can conclude that the Assembly member is typically Swiss, white, male, relatively old, a "white-collar" career man, with little experience in the field but with some longevity in viewing humanitarian matters from Geneva—albeit periodically rather than consistently. The prototype of the staff member is Swiss, white, male, relatively young, university-educated, with several years' experience in humanitarian matters.

The ascriptive traits are more elusive, existing subjectively in the experience of the outsider. It is suggested here, however, that many outsiders have found two fundamental sets of ascriptive factors in dealing with ICRC personnel.

First there is the "honesty-integrity-responsibility" syndrome. A number of public officials and citizens hold the image that if the ICRC says something it must be so; if the ICRC does something it is done responsibly. As a previous ICRC president expressed it to this writer, the bourgeois nature of the ICRC may have created certain problems but it nevertheless guaranteed a certain honesty and integrity in Red Cross work. Whatever else may be said about the ICRC, there is virtually no empirical support for any argument that would find intentional realpolitik maneuvering or some intentional, covert, nonhumanitarian purpose in ICRC activity. While there are deficiencies in ICRC effectiveness, as is true of every institution, there is little support for any argument that would find gross irresponsibility toward individuals or authorities in ICRC work. ICRC officials have been widely viewed as trustworthy and conscientious.[19]

Second, there is the "secretive-aloof-closed" syndrome. There is no doubt but that numerous persons have, on the basis of personal experience, found ICRC personnel to be suspicious of, and reserved toward, outsiders. To a considerable extent that image is the result of the nature of ICRC work. Discretionary protection and assistance, demanded by public authorities and occurring in situations of conflict and tension, are not conducive to a completely open diplomatic style. However, a number of observers find ICRC personnel secretive to a dysfunctional extent. That is, the degree of secrecy exercised is held to extend beyond what is required for ICRC activity, even to the point where it proves detrimental to humanitarian action. It has been argued that the ICRC has held itself so aloof from UN proceedings and other diplomatic intercourse that it has lost a certain contact with political reality which has inhibited the agency's effectiveness.[20] It has also been suggested by some that the ICRC has been woefully weak in explaining, in analytical terms, what it is doing in the world. Red Cross and governmental personnel, not to mention educated publics, have little knowledge of the ICRC. And if the ICRC is not known it cannot be supported. One Nigerian army officer expressed his belief that this was part of the ICRC's problems in the Nigerian War. He himself, a graduate of the British military academy, Sandhurst, had never heard of the ICRC until the start of the Nigerian War. He found his colleagues on the Federal side fearing the actions of the ICRC largely out of misunderstanding. And the Red Cross study director, on the basis of his inquiry and experiences, found a need to "open the windows" at the ICRC.

Influential elements within the ICRC are trying to maintain what is beneficial in the ICRC's image and to reduce what is detrimental. One of the reasons most elements in the ICRC are opposed to the introduction of non-Swiss into Assembly membership or staff positions is the belief that Swiss nationality has produced the "honesty-integrity-responsibility" syndrome in the ICRC's image. On the other hand, while not admitting that excessive secrecy and aloofness are the product also of Swiss nationality, certain elements within the ICRC are trying to increase contacts with outsiders, improve external communications, and differentiate between a diplomatic secret and a statement needed to build support or to explain analytically.

In sum, the ICRC in the mid-1970's was directing more attention to personnel policies than probably ever before. Studies were being made by the new Department of Personnel, and changes were in process. The issue of nationality was being carefully examined, even if major change on that issue remained unlikely. What all of this meant for the future image of ICRC personnel was difficult to say, except that the "honesty-integrity-responsibility" syndrome should be enhanced by a more rational and systematic personnel policy.

MONEY

In the early 1970's the ICRC started using a tripartite budget. The "permanent" part of the budget was funded by "regular" donations from governments, national Red Cross Societies, and such other sources as ICRC investments. This permanent sector of the budget was intended to finance the minimum core of ICRC activity—that which was fully planned and had to be done.

The "temporary" part of the budget was funded by the Swiss federal government, with a maximum guarantee of five million Swiss francs. This temporary sector was intended to cover unusual expenses that might, nevertheless, be planned. For example, personnel costs that could not be met by the permanent budget but which seemed especially important, such as two regional delegates in Africa, were covered by this temporary sector.

The "occasional" part was funded by special, ad hoc contributions and was directed to emergency situations—usually associated with violence, mostly in the form of armed conflict. It was an unplanned sector of the ICRC's budget, usually constructed ex post facto as an income-expenditure tabulation.

Beyond these three sectors of the ICRC budget, there was a special collection among the Swiss people which was used strictly to finance material-medical goods distributed by the ICRC as assistance. This collection accounted for only a small part of goods distributed by the ICRC, most goods being donated by governments, international organizations (especially the Common Market), or national Red Cross Societies, and therefore not purchased with ICRC funds.

There were other, minor parts of the budget as well.

The intent of this tripartite budgetary structure was to put ICRC financing on a firmer basis by: guaranteeing the funding of a minimum core of activity, permitting improved planning for that core, and coping with expanded needs and crises as rationally as possible. Even the "permanent" or regular budget, however, was not funded by any system of assessment, either on governments signatory to the Geneva Conventions or on national Red Cross Societies. These "regular" donations were not fully regular but were pledged voluntarily by various parties. In some states the governmental contribution had become a part of national (municipal) law and thus indeed was regular—until the law might be changed. For example, U.S. government contributions to the ICRC for a long time were made at the discretion of the Executive from general contingency funds, but in 1973 ICRC funding was written into the Foreign Assistance Act by the Congress.

Facts and Figures

The ICRC planned budget (permanent plus temporary) is tiny compared to governmental expenditures, but in the early 1970's that budget was much larger than ICRC budgets of twenty years ago (The ICRC publishes the figures in its *Annual Report*). In 1974, the ICRC planned budget of about $8 million (20 million Swiss francs figured at slightly less than $0.40 per franc) was less than what the American Red Cross spent that year on first aid programs alone. The ICRC planned budget was also slightly smaller than the regular budget of the UNHCR. On this small financial base the ICRC was trying to protect and assist individuals around the world as routine activity. Small as it was, that 1974 ICRC budget was almost five times greater than the ICRC's 1950 budget, and almost six times greater than the 1960 budget. It should be kept in mind, however, that major crises are handled by the ICRC outside the planned budget. Some recent figures are listed in Table 8.1.

From these figures one can see two things, in addition to observing, in part, how the ICRC's financial records are kept. First, one can see the steadily increasing planned sector of the budget during the 1970's, which continues the more dramatic increase occurring over the past quarter of a century. Second, one can see the vast fluctuation in occasional expenditures. In 1972, for example, the ICRC had great involvement on the Indian subcontinent which required expendi-

Table 8.1.   Recent ICRC Budgets and Expenditures

	Planned budgets (not actual expenditures)			Additional expenditure	
	Permanent	Temporary	Total	Occasional	Special
1975	16,380,770	6,079,530	22,460,300	n/a	n/a
1974	14,923,515	4,418,785	19,342,300	n/a	n/a
1973	15,040,632	4,424,773	18,979,624	over 17 mil.	n/a
1972	14,894,622	4,788,282	19,682,904	over 15 mil.	ca. 2.5 mil.
1971	11,600,000	5,100,000	16,700,000	under 1.5 mil.	ca. 2.0 mil.
1970	9,084,000	6,532,000	15,616,000	under 2.3 mil.	ca. 2.2 mil.

Source: ICRC, *Annual Report,* 1970–75.

tures met by contributions listed in the occasional column. In 1973 there was war in the Middle East, which again necessitated unplanned expenditures to be met from unpledged funds.

Because of greatly expanded ICRC activity, ICRC budgets have become deficit budgets. This situation is not entirely new to the ICRC. But deficits have become chronic for the institution as of the mid-1970's. In 1970 the ICRC deficit was over 2 million Swiss francs, a large sum relative to the totals involved. Extraordinary contributions in the mid-1970's, from Switzerland the United States particularly, temporarily alleviated the deficits, but the constant shortfall in income remained.

Income Pattern

We have already noted the funding of the temporary budget by the Swiss government, the occasional budget by ad hoc contributions, and the special collection by the Swiss people.

As for the permanent budget, Switzerland (government and Red Cross) has been contributing about 50 percent of that total each year. The second largest contributor has been the United States. In 1974 the U.S. government jumped the level of its support from $50,000 to $500,000, which now represents about 20 percent of the Swiss contribution. Most of the rest of the ICRC permanent budget has come in recent years from fifteen industrialized nations, mostly Western. In order of size of contribution (1974) they are: West Germany, Sweden, France, Great Britain, Canada, Australia, Denmark, Japan, Italy, the Netherlands, New Zealand, Finland, Norway, Austria, and Belgium. This pattern of income means that only about 600,000 Swiss francs in the permanent budget come from all the nations in the world not mentioned above.

It is quite evident, therefore, that ICRC income for the permanent budget is largely Western or Western-aligned. The larger picture is the same. If we take governmental and Red Cross contributions to the ICRC in 1973, we find the following breakdown:

Western Europe & North America	89.10%
Latin America	.69
Eastern Europe	1.30
Africa (sub-Sahara)	1.27
Arab nations	1.38
Asia	2.52
Others	3.73
	100.00%

If it is evident that the ICRC is funded by Western parties, it is also evident that governments are the most important contributors—although this has not been the case always. If we look at income for the planned budget plus the Swiss collection we find the figures listed in Table 8.2.

Having noted the Western, governmental nature of contributions to ICRC budgets, one can make some observations about who does *not* give to the permanent budget. Oil-exporting nations (government and Red Cross society) do not contribute much, relative to their wealth. In 1973, for example, neither the Algerian government nor the Algerian Red Crescent gave *anything*. The government of Saudi Arabia gave nothing, and its Red Crescent a paltry 2,000 Swiss francs, which was slightly less than the amount given by the Venezuelan Red Cross. Iran (government and society) did give over 55,000 Swiss francs, and Kuwait's government gave 50,000. But these sums are small relative to the wealth of these nations and relative to other contributions. By comparison, Poland (government and society) gave 45,000 Swiss francs in 1973, or only 5,000 less than Kuwait.

The socialist nations in general, however, contribute only around 1 percent of the ICRC's permanent budget. The Polish level of contribution is not matched by any other socialist nation. In 1973 several socialist nations (government and society) gave nothing: North Korea, Cuba, Mongolia, Byelorussia and the U-kraine (legal fictions to be sure); and the Provisional Revolutionary Government of South Vietnam (not then in full control of claimed territory). The Soviet

Table 8.2.   Planned ICRC Budgets (in 000's of Swiss trancs)

Source	1950	1960	1970	1973
Governments	5	1.320	4.643	16.344[1]
Red Cross Societies	237	405	738	929
Swiss Public Collection	920	624	883	804
Income on investments	126	428	720	1.123
Other	850	887	983	1.836[2]

[1]Includes extraordinary contributions of 4 governments.
[2]Includes extraordinary contributions from 2 Swiss entities for special purposes—viz., to purchase books and to build ICRC annex.
Source: ICRC, *Annual Report*, 1950–73.

government gave nothing, and the Soviet Red Cross Alliance gave 16,250 francs—a figure topped by both China and Thailand, among others.

Third world donations generally were low to nonexistent, no doubt largely because of the precarious economic situation for most of them. Of the 32 nations contributing nothing to the ICRC's permanent budget in 1973, 22 were found in Africa and Asia, and probably 19 out of that 22 would be generally considered on the bottom rungs of the world's economic ladder.

By and large the same income pattern is found with regard to ICRC occasional budgets covering unplanned, emergency situations. That income is basically from Western governments. If the emergency situation occurs in the non-West, say in the Middle East, then a non-Western party may make a significant contribution. Also, certain socialist parties have made significant "occasional" contributions for the ICRC's work with political prisoners and their families in Chile. But the overall pattern of total ICRC income remains overwhelmingly Western.

When a government other than the Swiss government is relatively generous toward the ICRC, like the American government, this gives the ICRC the headaches of its pleasures. While the ICRC is pleased to have such resources, it becomes worried about its image of independence and impartiality. Thus the ICRC has recently undertaken a more systematic effort to obtain income from neutral and non-Western sources, particularly from the oil-exporting nations. The results of this effort are yet to be seen.

Expenditure Pattern

It is not always easy to tell from the public documents how the ICRC has spent its income, as noted previously. This difficulty does not stem from any duplicity on the part of the ICRC but rather from how it has kept its books in the past. While it has been clear what general purpose the money has gone for, and through what department, it has not always been clear exactly what function or task was executed.

It is only in recent years that the ICRC has been able to provide information on expenditures by function. From one set of figures it is easy to see that pragmatic activity—applied protection and assistance—has been the major element in ICRC expenditures. "Operations" constitutes the biggest chunk of ICRC expenditures:

1972	Regular budget	Total spent
Legal development—dissemination	13.03%	11.45%
Operations	52.96	46.52
Administration—education	34.01	29.87
Material—medical assistance	—	12.16

These figures from 1972 represent the general pattern of expenditure in recent years. The ICRC has rather consistently spent about four times as much on *directly* trying to help persons as indirectly trying to help them through development and dissemination of international law. Expenses for this direct work through the Operations Department usually go for such things as salaries of delegates in the field, their travel, and their supporting staff (much of which is often recruited locally).

It is not presently possible to say how much has been spent by the ICRC over time on different categories of persons without extensive and special research. Even with that effort, answers to certain questions are lacking. During World War II, for example, no records were kept which would have distinguished between prisoner of war and civilian, insofar as the value of transmitted goods was concerned. Likewise, in the past there were apparently no records kept that would allow one to differentiate financially among political prisoners, civilian detainees under the Fourth Geneva Convention, individuals in need of help from hijackings, families of political detainees, and so forth.

This type of analysis will probably be available in the future, as the ICRC improves the details of its budgets and fiscal controls. For example, if we look at the 1975 budget, we find two significant increases in expenditure, categorized by task. The ICRC planned to increase expenditures significantly for political prisoners and also ICRC relations with national Red Cross Societies. Spending for the former activity was projected to be up over 40 percent, and for the latter activity up almost 52 percent. The overall planned budget for 1975 was to be up some 16 percent over 1974 levels, with dissemination of law to be the only activity below 1974 levels (down about 6 percent).

Despite the planned increase in funding for politicial-prisoner activity, the thrust of the 1975 planned budget was still on conventional activity—viz., activity associated with the Geneva Conventions—as compared to extraconventional work. The latter was seen to be less than half as costly as the former. Of a planned budget of some 22.5 million Swiss francs, over 10.5 million was directed to conventional operations and legal work, with only about 3.2 million devoted to specifically extraconventional help. The rest was taken up with information, public relations, administration, etc.

One of the stark facts about ICRC expenditures was their unpredictability. In the three years of war in Nigeria, 1967–70, the ICRC out of its "own" funds spent 162.5 million Swiss francs according to one estimate (approximately $54.2 million). In addition, the material-medical goods donated by others and transmitted by the ICRC could be valued at around 138 million Swiss francs. The expenditures charged directly to the ICRC, while definitely small in relation to the amount spent on killing people in that war, were nevertheless, on a yearly average, about three times the ICRC total budget for those same three years. The normal scope of ICRC activity could be dwarfed by one situation. Similarly, although on a smaller scale, for the one year in which the ICRC had full access to political prisoners in Greece in 1969–70, the price tag for that operation alone was about 254.5 thousand Swiss francs. While, again, that figure is small relative to governmental expenditures, that figure is large relative to the ICRC budget for Operations or political-prisoner protection. Similar comparisons and conclusions can be drawn from the costs to the ICRC arising from emergency situations in Cyprus, the Indian subcontinent, and the Middle East.

In sum, the financial base of ICRC activity was a problem throughout the period under study here. The dominant attitude of the ICRC toward financing seemed to be that financial means should not determine activity. Rather, perception of what was needed to protect and assist individuals was the dominant factor in ICRC activity. It was assumed the means to carry out the activity would be found. This meant deficit budget planning and frequently a sizable shortfall of income. But the ICRC seemed to be trying to cope financially with expanded work of an unpredictable nature in as rational a way as possible. While questions might be raised about ICRC fund-raising efforts, certainly the budgetary process and fiscal controls were being handled in a way superior to the past.

CONCLUSIONS ABOUT THE ADMINISTRATIVE PROCESS

It bears repeating that the ICRC, administratively speaking, is very much in transition in the mid-1970's. It also bears repeating that what has been said in this chapter is admittedly only a first step, and an incomplete one at that, in understanding the internal workings of the ICRC.

Much of the ICRC, as of the mid-1970's, was caught up in a spirit of self-evaluation and change. The first fruits of that evaluation could already be seen in the new structure for the House. Increased attention to structural, personnel, and budgetary matters was evident.

Not all elements within the ICRC were completely happy with the entire trend of change. It would be natural for some elements in the Assembly to be concerned about the apparent decline in influence of that organ. It could be expected that some of the stronger exponents of Swiss nationalism within the ICRC might be wary of moves to use foreign consultants or in other ways to make the ICRC a more open institution. And some circles within the ICRC in the mid-1970's seemed to wish for less activity, conducted on a surer if smaller financial base. Some thought the ICRC was getting too big in its ambitions and acting too much like a public authority rather than a private humanitarian institution.

These and no doubt other reservations about ICRC change were articulated by important ICRC officials, but the direction of change seemed to be away from their opinions. The ICRC seemed to be in the process of professionalizing and systematizing itself in response to the demands made upon the institution. The

Nigerian War was perhaps the crucial factor in pushing the ICRC into accelerating change. In that war the ICRC found itself in the world spotlight—and also found its policy-making and management system lacking in certain respects. The result was a clearer push for acceleration of the changes already beginning.

In the mid-1970's it was interesting to observe that the ICRC was the one organ in the International Red Cross that was frequently evaluated by standards normally applied to governments and intergovernmental international organizations. When one raised the question, "did the ICRC have a policy on issue X," or "did it conduct itself well in situation Y," sometimes the answers were not entirely positive—as in the Nigerian War. But implicit in such evaluations of the ICRC was the fact that many expected the institution to operate with the same external and internal efficiency as a public authority. That expectation was testimony to the importance of the work of the ICRC. Administratively the ICRC was trying to make the adjustments to meet that expectation.

9 Conclusion: The Tradition of the Past and the Challenges of the Future

Arising out of a specific situation in 1859—the Battle of Solférino—the ICRC evolved in Darwinian fashion: from conflict to conflict it responded to particular humanitarian needs, then retained much of its pattern of action in the future; by the mid-1970's it had grown increasingly complex.

AN OVERVIEW

The ICRC has indeed become unique in world affairs. As I suggested in Chapter 2, Max Huber was correct when he wrote that various parties in world affairs "look to it for things that are asked of no other private organization in all the realm of international relations." The ICRC has become, in fact and in law, a quasi-public authority, such has been its utility to states and peoples. Not only has the ICRC been unique. The scope of its activity has also been impressively large, pertaining to both war and peace, diplomacy and material-medical assistance, law and alegal pragmatism. On the basis of this unique and wide-ranging activity the ICRC compiled a reputation unsurpassed and perhaps unequalled by most NGOs and IGOs (intergovernmental organizations). The ICRC has been proud of the tradition of the past, and with considerable reason.

After World War II and especially during the 1960's, however, the ICRC experienced considerable difficulty. The milieu in which it had operated changed in several important respects. The structure of violence changed, toward an increasing importance of unconventional war. The structure of power changed, toward a decreasing importance for the West. International institutions proliferated and interest in subjects of transnational import, including humanitarian affairs, increased. In this post-1945 period and especially during the 1960's, the ICRC was slow to adapt to many of the changes affecting the institution. Without doubt the ICRC was tardy in adjusting to the importance of non-Western influences, whether one refers to its dealings with Nigerian and Bangladesh authorities or to legal development efforts. Without doubt the ICRC was tardy in adapting to other NGOs and IGOs active in the humanitarian field, including even other Red Cross actors. And the ICRC was criticized for adhering to legal concepts alleged to be outmoded and inadequate for the regulation of violence.

As a result of both delayed adaption on its part and criticism of its position on complex subjects—criticism that might or might not be refuted—the ICRC encountered a difficult decade in the 1960's. In the view of those interacting with the ICRC or following its affairs closely, the reputation of the ICRC was tarnished, although its image remained relatively good among the attentive public and other nonspecialists in humanitarian law and diplomacy.

The interplay of a highly regarded diplomatic history with increased criticism means that the ICRC faces a challenging future. Without question the ICRC has proved itself useful in the past. But also without question, the ICRC has been less than fully effective in the modern period. Thus the central question for the ICRC as it enters its second century is can the institution restore its superb reputation through effective humanitarian protection and assistance? Such a restoration of image would not, or should not, be for reasons of pride but for reasons of further service to individuals in need.

THE TRADITION OF THE PAST

The uniqueness of the ICRC is demonstrable. While there are many agencies concerned with human rights and humanitarian affairs, and while many share certain concerns with the ICRC, none of these other agencies has done quite what the ICRC does. No other agency has gotten inside places of detention on as systematic and wide-ranging a scale as the ICRC, even though the ICRC's systematic reach is far from complete. No other institution has been asked to perform such a wide range of intermediary duties, from providing good offices in hijackings to supervising the international movement of a variety of types of persons. No other institution has served as a drafting secretariat for the law of armed conflict, although other organizations have contributed to that process. No other institution has been expected to take such wide-ranging humanitarian action in armed conflict, and no other organization has been given specific legal rights, in those war situations, to do precise things—e.g., visit certain detainees. (This range of activity has been outlined in Chapter 2; the variety of action under ICRC ad hoc diplomacy is evident especially in Chapter 4).

The broadness of ICRC activity is as noteworthy as its uniqueness. Some criticism of the institution is probably guaranteed by the very scope of activities undertaken, and by their difficulty. The ICRC is a small organization struggling against a wide array of apparently intractable problems. At a general level one can say that the ICRC has pitted itself against some very formidable forces: the inhumanity and destructiveness of war; the ruthlessness of elites whose security is perceived to be threatened; the terrorism of factions who feel so deprived that they endorse a philosophy of the "end justifies the means"; the callousness with which conflicting parties evaluate and manipulate a situation of starving civilians.

At a more specific level of analysis one can note some of the complex issues faced by the ICRC: how to identify a "prisoner of war" in unconventional warfare; how to differentiate combatant from civilian; how to regulate internal war; how to identify a "political prisoner"; how to depoliticize material and medical assistance; how to promote agreement within a multicultural, multiracial, and multi-ideological Red Cross movement which encompasses national societies of different economic levels.

If we look at the *cahier des charges* or check list for action of an ICRC delegate in the field, say in Africa, we find an agenda impressive in scope and seemingly requiring a "Renaissance man" for its execution. The ICRC delegate in Africa in the early 1970's was to: (1) visit prisons (prepare for the visit, make the visit, write the report, make follow-up contacts, supervise assistance within the prison); (2) distribute ICRC books, films, and tapes to various parties; (3) prepare and execute assistance operations outside prisons (gather relevant information, submit reports to Geneva, distribute and oversee small-scale assistance); (4) develop contacts with liberation movements and opposition groups; (5) develop and maintain relations with personnel from the League of Red Cross Societies; (6) maintain full contact with the Geneva headquarters; (7) provide an information service to governments and national Red Cross Societies, as well as to publics; (8) relate to ICRC legal development work (keep abreast of that work in general, provide explanations to interested parties, provide the ICRC legal delegation with relevant comments from field experience).

All of this was to be done frequently in places where the ICRC delegate and his symbol were unknown by most, where the climate and geographical conditions were inhospitable to rapid and sustained work, and where communication systems of all types did not exactly operate according to Swiss standards of efficiency.

To execute these duties ICRC officials have needed knowledge in many fields: politics, diplomacy, law; management, penology, psychology; languages, cultures; morality, philosophy, and religion.

Given the skills needed, the duties to be performed, the specific and general problems to be overcome or at least faced, it is remarkable that the ICRC has been able to construct such a highly regarded reputation. Perhaps, in all truthfulness, the ICRC's image has been the product of general impressions rather than close scrutiny of its actions. It is quite conceivable that in the past the ICRC benefited in some ways from a general lack of interest in, and knowledge about, what the institution was doing. In a climate of ignorance and low expectations, any types of humanitarian accomplishment might seem highly commendable. And it is possible that some of the more current criticism of the ICRC arises because of increased interest in what the institution does and in increased expectations as to what the agency should achieve.

Be that as it may, the tradition of the past left the ICRC with a good reputation, albeit recently tarnished. Of course respect for the ICRC has varied. At a general level of analysis, that respect has varied according to geopolitics. The most favorable attitudes have been Western. High regard for the ICRC in the West is typified by the statement of former United States Attorney General Ramsey Clark, when giving Congressional testimony on the situation in Chile after Allende:

> The more people that visit prisons, the better the prisoners have to be treated. Single trips can cause problems for prisoners, we know that. But the ability of the International Red Cross to visit prisons is awfully important in every country. Our country needs to open those things constantly [with foreign governments]. . . . If an outfit like the International Red Cross can't get in, you know it just makes you very doubtful that there is any hope for decent treatment.[1]

Noteworthy in these hearings was not just the former attorney general's failure to distinguish between the ICRC and the larger Red Cross movement (a confusion discussed in Chapter 1). More importantly, these hearings demonstrated the perceived importance of ICRC visits as a guarantee of "decent" detention conditions. When the Chilean junta suspended ICRC visits, this alarmed certain elements in Congress, who believed the suspension signified serious problems in Chilean prisons. And it appeared that the Executive Branch, supportive of the junta, took steps in behalf of a resumption of ICRC visits; the Executive certainly took steps to reassure Congress that the suspension was temporary.[2] It is evident that ICRC visits were highly regarded by both Congressional and Executive circles. And it is suggested here that this favorable attitude toward the ICRC has prevailed in most of the West—at least the industrialized, democratic West.

In the third world, respect for the ICRC can be extrapolated from cooperation with ICRC activity; there has been a considerable amount of both. ICRC detention visits are widespread in both Latin America and Africa, and the ICRC has had significant non-Western cooperation in wars in the Middle East and South and Southeast Asia.

It has been obvious that the ICRC's reputation is weakest in the socialist alliance (the philosophical reasons for this were discussed in Chapter 2, the financial evidence was presented in Chapter 8).

Beyond the level of general attitudes toward the ICRC, attitudes which have varied according to geopolitical criteria, it can be said that views of the ICRC have also varied according to *what* exactly the agency tried to do, and *how* it tried to do it. Insofar as ICRC functions and functional roles are concerned, the ICRC has been most highly regarded for its protection efforts. With regard to Red Cross assistance, there has been growing feeling, shared by the ICRC itself to some extent, that increased participation in assistance operations should be afforded the League of Red Cross Societies and the national societies. Moreover, within the function of protection, the roles of helping to develop and apply the law of armed conflict have been more widely favored than some aspects of the role of ad hoc diplomacy. This latter role of trying to help political prisoners, inter alia, has been regarded by ultranationalists as an unwelcome attempt to interfere in domestic affairs (discussed in Chapters 3 and 4).

How the ICRC has pursued its humanitarian activity has also produced different views. On this subject the differences of opinion have not followed geopolitical lines. Virtually all governments have favored the ICRC's policy of discretion—whether Western, third world, or socialist. Of course in a given situation some governments have wanted the ICRC to protest publicly the action of an adversary. But in general most governments have been happy with ICRC restraint, especially when it was a matter related to a government's own territory.

On the other hand, the "how" of ICRC operations has received some criticism from other NGOs and IGOs. Many of these other actors in world affairs have adopted a completely or partially confrontational approach in dealing with governments, and they have been critical of the ICRC for being overly cooperative toward governments. NGOs like Amnesty International have not shied away from public confrontations with governments when the situation was perceived to warrant such tactics, and these groups have sometimes been critical of the ICRC for not doing the same.

The ICRC has consciously chosen a particular place on the spectrum in the pursuit of humanitarian objectives. Considering the available options, its style of action can be referred to as impartial humanitarianism, as compared to international humanitarianism and revolutionary humanitarianism. One can illustrate as follows.

Revolutionary humanitarianism	International humanitarianism	Impartial humanitarianism
JCA	Amnesty/FAO	ICRC/UNHCR

Impartial humanitarianism can be thought of as proceeding on the basis of consent given by public authorities, with little or no criticism in public of their behavior. Examples of practitioners of this style of action are the ICRC and the UNHCR. *International humanitarianism* can be conceived of as proceeding on the basis of both conflictual and cooperative styles, depending on majority opinion and/or the givens of a particular situation. While cooperation between humanitarian actor and public authority is welcomed, the international humanitarian actor does not hesitate to engage in public denunciations if the situation seems to warrant or if majority opinion is in favor of such action. Most humanitarian NGOs and IGOs, including most UN humanitarian actors, are found in this area on the spectrum. *Revolutionary humanitarianism* is characterized by an operating style that takes incountry action which disregards the wishes and legal claims of public authorities. Thus Joint Church Aid (JCA) took action in the Nigerian Civil War that flaunted wishes and claims by Lagos. The most extreme form of this style of action is armed intervention by states, in the name of humanitarianism, against the wishes of a public authority.

Within this overall conceptualization it becomes clear that the ICRC has preferred cooperation even with "evil" regimes to a public protest or denunciation that would deprive it of access to individuals in need. The ICRC has adopted "a morality of choosing the lesser evil—often requiring a measure of accommodation with heinous regimes amounting almost to complicity."[3] While this has been generally favored by governments, it has been a style of action sometimes criticized by other actors (see the case study of Greek political prisoners, Chapter 3).

Despite all the variation in attitudes toward the ICRC, whether those attitudes are considered at a general level and according to geopolitics, or considered according to ICRC function and style, it can be said that the tradition of the past left the ICRC widely respected. Relative to other organizations, the ICRC has been perceived in general as appropriately executing a broad range of activity, frequently of a unique nature.[4]

THE CHALLENGES OF THE FUTURE

The ICRC built its reputation in war, in cooperation with nation-states, and in Christendom (meaning the cultural area of Western Europe in which there was a sharing of some basic values drawn from Christianity). This threefold description of the past milieu of the ICRC no longer describes its modern milieu. And therein lies the origin of important challenges to the ICRC in the future.

1. The structure of violence has so changed that it is increasingly difficult to distinguish peace from war, or, phrased differently, even to determine—factually or legally—when war exists. The change in the structure of violence has been twofold: toward constant planning for, and intermittent threat of, nuclear war; and toward increased use of guerrilla and terroristic war. The first change has not proven a practical problem for the ICRC; since an all-out nuclear war would prove any humanitarian restraint meaningless, the ICRC has ignored the subject (aside from a brief and abortive foray into the subject, covered in Chapter 5).

It is the second change in the process of violence that has raised practical difficulties for the ICRC. For one thing, it is no longer clear exactly *when* the ICRC is supposed to act. The ICRC had long oriented itself to war. Now that that category of conflict is not so clear, the ICRC has lost a benchmark useful in directing its activity. And where there is not complete agreement that there exists a situation of armed conflict, international or internal, consensus in support of ICRC action has also proved elusive. What were the appropriate regulatory standards in the Algerian and Indochinese Wars (see Chapter 6)? What was the ICRC entitled to do in these and other conflicts, and what could it persuasively ask the conflicting parties to do? Where was the generally recognized dividing line between a government's realm of exclusive responsibility and the realm of international obligations? Changes in the structure of violence around the world negated much of the utility of humanitarian law (meaning the international law of armed conflict) and made the activity of the ICRC more difficult to carry out. The ICRC found itself increasingly in uncharted waters, dealing not with legally identifiable "prisoners of war" and "civilian detainees" but with "persons detained by reason of political events" who might be, legally, common criminals under municipal (national) law. The scope of attempted ICRC activity increased in its pursuit of protection and assistance for individuals in need as a result of political conflict, but the consensus in support of ICRC action did not increase in proportion to the need.

2. The nation-state was joined on the world stage by a baffling array of actors (discussed in Chapter 2)—IGOs, NGOs, liberation movements, secessionist movements, mercenary armies, terrorist groups of obscure origin and of shadowy lines of responsibility. In the past the ICRC, like other agencies in the Red Cross movement, had viewed itself as a supplement to the services of the nation-state. All Red Cross agencies initially saw their mission as one of temporary and emergency action in the context of a hiatus in state services. But increasingly the ICRC found it had not just one public authority to deal with. It was not just the state the ICRC had to answer to and contend with. Other public and quasi-public authorities took a keen interest in the ICRC's activity—public authorities like the United Nations, Council of Europe, Common Market, Organization of African Unity; and quasi-public authorities (international interest groups) like Amnesty International and the International Commission of Jurists. Indeed, in certain situations relatively unorganized public opinion came to exer-

cise an influence on the ICRC, and in turn the ICRC felt a need to speak to those attentive publics (e.g., European and North American public opinion in the Nigerian War).

In sum, the ICRC was caught up in the fundamental change toward a sharing of influence and even authority among different types of actors in world affairs. The nation-state, while still the most powerful and authoritative of actors, was only one among many. The ICRC could not be a "handmaiden" to states and yet escape criticism from other types of actors. Moreover, the ICRC could not assume that these other actors would respect the ICRC's monopoly or priority of action in certain areas. The UN secretariat and certain UN committees were much interested in the development of humanitarian law. Amnesty was much interested in the protection of, and assistance to, political prisoners. Religious organizations, the UN Disaster Relief Office, and the League of Red Cross Societies were all interested in material-medical assistance. The ICRC, in short, increasingly found it had many authorities to deal with, many interested actors to contend with, and on occasion many publics to answer to. Some of these parties were not terribly deferential to nation-states' claims to national sovereignty or domestic jurisdiction.

3. The Western domination of world affairs had obviously changed, in a time of third-world control of the UN General Assembly, price-setting cartels by oil-exporting nations, and victories by non-Western parties in the Indochina and anti-Portuguese wars. It was not only that the influence of the West had declined in voting, economic, and violent terms. It was also that traditional Western ways of thinking about subjects had lost some of their compelling nature. Man was not so much viewed as an atom, surrounded by rights, moving toward happiness and self-fulfillment through personal achievement. Increasingly he was viewed by influential Western observers as part of some larger group—whether class, party, nation, or global mass; increasingly endangered by environmental limitations and exhaustions; perhaps heading toward austerity if not destruction.[5]

None of these changes in voting, economics, violence, or thinking was complete; and the West and its traditional concepts remained influential in all these categories of endeavor. But the direction of most of these changes was away from the conception of the individual found in early ICRC history. Group survival seemed to be taking precedence over legal and procedural respect for individual rights. Traditional humanitarian considerations seemed to be losing out to security strategy and to economic and environmental considerations. In general, elements in the West seemed to be adopting non-Western attitudes.

Because of these changes—in the structure of violence, the increased competition for influence and authority among different types of actors, and shifts in the global distribution of power (with power defined broadly to include the power of ideas as well as the power to vote and fight and set prices)—there was no certainty that the ICRC would be as useful in 2075 as it had been in 1975, if one could assume the arrival and continued existence of the twenty-first century.

All manner of institutions have, of course, come and gone. As Charles Reich wrote in *The Greening of America:* "All of the other machinery we use becomes obsolete in a short time. A social institution, which is, after all, only another type of machinery, is not necessarily immune from the same laws of obsolescence. The ideas or principles of society might remain valid, but the means for applying the principles could lose their effectiveness.[6] And as was written in another context: "Many organizations today are simply charming memorials to problems which no longer exist; some of them are in practice engaged in building pyramids to their own memory."[7]

At first glance the ICRC might seem to be headed for extinction, or at least marginal relevance, through failure to make the changes needed to keep pace with a changing environment. Internal problems were evident (Chapter 8), impeding adaptations. Levels of decision-making were not integrated; budgetary planning and fiscal controls were deficient; lessons were not drawn carefully and systematically from its past; attitudes of secrecy and aloofness were not countered. These internal problems led to external policies, or perhaps just an external series of steps, that were inconsistent in their rate of success.

The Nigerian situation was the most difficult for the ICRC, which compounded the considerable inherent difficulties by failing to adopt a central strategy and by failing to insure an equitable understanding of the Lagos position (see Chapter 7). Troubles was also encountered in the war for Bangladesh, where the early diplomatic faux pas toward the Pakistani government (see Chapters 1 and 8) was followed by management difficulties (not all goods could be properly accounted for, much to the consternation of donors like the Common Market and the U.S. Agency for International Development); and there was competition among the ICRC, League, and Bangladesh Red Cross. There were other "impurities" on the ICRC record as well, such as the choice of, and behavior of, certain ICRC officials in South Vietnam, which did not endear the ICRC to the authorities there.[8] The external record of the ICRC in the 1945–75 period was indeed uneven, due in significant degree to ICRC internal problems occurring in a context of rapid change.

At second glance and upon closer observation, however, there was cause for some optimism about the future utility of the ICRC. By the mid-1970's an attitude of self-evaluation and willingness to make changes was evident at the institution (see Chapter 8). The basic organization of the House had been altered in an effort to increase professionalization as a means to improved effectiveness. Budgetary planning and fiscal controls had been improved. Personnel training was receiving increased emphasis. Younger officials were being placed in key staff positions. And in general there was a willingness on the part of many ICRC officials critically to examine certain traditional assumptions, such as the assumed impartiality of the Assembly as usually composed.

The result of these internal changes was an improved external record. There was very little, if any, criticism of the ICRC in the war in Cyprus: it entered the conflict area quickly despite difficulties in communications, it did its traditional tasks effectively, and its image was such that it was asked to lead UN convoys bringing assistance to civilians. When violence escalated in Angola, the ICRC was present, informed, and active through its newly established delegate for southern Africa. When violence escalated in Argentina, the ICRC was present, informed, and active through its newly established office in Buenos Aires. Therefore the external record of the ICRC in anticipating, and responding to, conflict situations was improved, within the limits of financial ability and the cooperation of public authorities.

In the past there had been a time lag between perceptions of the ICRC's image and perceptions of its actual capability. As of the 1960's the ICRC was perceived by many to be more effective than it really was. On the other hand, in the mid-1970's it is probable there is another time lag: this time between perceptions of ICRC problems and deficiencies, and perceptions of steps undertaken to deal with them. Unperceived by many outsiders—this is understandable, since it is difficult to know what is occurring within the ICRC—important ICRC officials were making an effort to adjust to the institution's changed milieu. The spirit of self-evaluation had proceeded to the point of ICRC cooperation with the publication of an account critical of the ICRC's actions in Nigeria, based on internal documents (see the end of Chapter 7). There were still ICRC officials who defended the status quo uncritically, such as the official who told this writer in 1975 he saw no reason for change within the ICRC. And there were still ICRC staff members given to secrecy and aloofness. But the dominant attitude at the ICRC in the mid-1970's was one of critical examination and change.

Whatever the precise future direction of changes in types of violence, relationships among institutions, and the position of the West, there was every likelihood that "emergency situations," violence, and detention would be prevalent. Thus there would be a continuing need for ICRC protection and assistance as it had been generally known. But the ICRC would have to build support for its activity, and to get that support the ICRC would have to demonstrate efficiency in dealing with unconventional war, different types of actors in world politics, and non-Western parties and ideas.

The kinds of changes needed to improve the effectiveness of the ICRC will be better comprehended through critical examination of three fundamental challenges to the institution in the future.

The Challenge of Self-identification

It is perhaps strange to raise the question of self-identification for an institution over 100 years old. But it is not clear, either "objectively" or in the eyes of the ICRC, whom the ICRC represents or should represent. The ICRC may be said to have an identity crisis. And this affects what it does and how it does it.

1. Does the ICRC represent the mainstream of Swiss thinking on humanitarian affairs? Is the ICRC answerable only to the Swiss establishment? If not, then what is the implication for recruitment policies, composition of the Assembly, and linkages with other circles of opinion? Another way of posing the question is to ask if the ICRC is supposed to be a Swiss deus ex machina, appearing out of Swiss "neutrality" in time of crisis carrying the Red Cross symbol, only to return to the haven of that "neutrality" when the crisis is past, leaving the rest of the Red Cross movement to carry on without the ICRC? An important subsidiary question is its relationship with the Swiss government, especially when and if it enters the United Nations? Is the ICRC too closely linked to the Swiss government, not because that government seeks to control the ICRC—which it does not—but because the ICRC is overinfluenced by the very same attitudes found in Swiss governmental circles—attitudes more concerned with governmental rights and law than with humanitarian values per se? And will a Swiss government voting and negotiating in the United Nations compromise or reduce ICRC impartiality and effectiveness?

2. Does the ICRC represent all or part of the leadership of the Red Cross movement? Rather than being a Swiss deus ex machina, should the ICRC see itself as a more integral part of the Red Cross movement, relating more closely to the League and national societies, paying more attention to rational divisions of labor based on putative efficiency, seeking to maximize the potential of the movement as a whole rather than of only the ICRC? Has the ICRC been too much concerned with its own independence, to the extent that it has weakened Red Cross protection and assistance? Has the ICRC succumbed to the pursuit of self-glorification and been guilty of institutional jealousy like other bureaucracies, at the expense of individual needs in the world? If it be agreed that the ICRC at times has been intellectually isolated and overaloof, can this be countered by greater ICRC participation in and leadership of the Red Cross movement? In sum, is there such a thing, in practical terms, as ICRC independence within a context of interdependence with the rest of the Red Cross movement?

3. Does the ICRC really represent mankind, as some of its spokesmen have said from time to time? If the ICRC does represent mankind, is this more than a slogan—is there some practical significance to the claim? Does this claim imply that certain procedures are needed to insure the introduction of the views of mankind, in all their variety? Are advisory councils needed, or non-Swiss consultants, with some regard for geographical, ideological, and racial distribution? What procedures exist to insure that facts and opinions are obtained beyond Western sources? Are ICRC information services capable of relating to a broad spectrum of audiences? Is there a Western bias in ICRC operations?

The ICRC, in determining who it really is or wants to be, does not have to choose one identity to the total exclusion of others. It is possible to have concentric circles of representation and responsibility, or, phrased differently, to have a hierarchy of responsibility. But the ICRC needs to come to terms with exactly who it is and represents, as that choice should imply certain subsequent choices with regard to what it does, and how.

The Challenge of Evaluating Law

Related to the challenge of self-identification is the challenge of evaluating international law. In the future the ICRC will be called upon to justify its legal orientation—especially if the ICRC represents mankind and/or the International Red Cross. Two of the three functional roles of the ICRC have been legally oriented: helping to develop international law, and helping to apply it. There are increasing numbers who believe that even international "humanitarian" law (the international law of armed conflict) is used frequently to block humanitarian values. In a survey of the meaning and application of Common Article 3 from the 1949 Conventions, dealing with internal armed conflict, one author suggests that "the traditional categories of internal conflicts to which the laws of war apply reflect more deference to the supposed jurisdictional competency of national sovereigns than concern for the human rights of those caught up in the struggle."[9] The argument is echoed.[10] (See also Chapter 5.) Thus the law is said to exist primarily to embody such concepts as national sovereignty and domestic jurisdiction, rather than to promote humanitarian conditions for individuals.

Therefore the ICRC will be asked to justify the time and effort that go into legal development efforts, as well as to evaluate the practical humanitarian benefit stemming from the law and its application. There will be many who will want to place emphasis on ad hoc diplomacy, viewing consideration of legal factors as only a necessary evil. The argument that humanitarian law provides a guaranteed minimum threshhold of humanitarian behavior, while sound in theory, is not likely to be accepted uncritically by those familiar with the way states use legal claims.

Likewise the ICRC will be asked to defend in more general terms its contribution to preservation of the nation-state system of law in world affairs. In trying to develop humanitarian law and act within its guidelines, the ICRC has contributed, in fact, to the favor shown to nation-states, who are the only legal entities fully recognized in that law. Also, in saying that prison reports belong only to states, again the ICRC is buttressing a social organization that is increasingly being challenged or at least asked to share authority with other organizations. In the past it was practical for the ICRC to be almost completely cooperative with states, for states were the only authorities that really mattered. But in the future it may be practical, in pursuit of humanitarian goals, *not* to be completely deferential to nation-states. What is at issue is an evaluation of the social organization best able to promote the needs of individuals—whether those needs be security, economic, or humanitarian.

Such an evaluation requires a careful judgment of the law that endorses state supremacy. A humanitarian agency like the ICRC will be increasingly asked why it is so deferential to the nation-state system in world affairs when that very system produces so much destruction and suffering for lack of a regulatory mechanism, and when states are left free to be so inhumane to their own nationals. Insofar as the ICRC elects to pursue a legal orientation in part of its activity, it will certainly be asked *what kind* of law it is helping to develop and apply.

The Challenge of Moral Choice

Related to the above two challenges is the challenge of moral choice. The ICRC has pursued a morality of discreet incrementalism, which has been labeled above "impartial humanitarianism." The institution has avoided public disagreements with public authorities in favor of being discreet; and it has sought to improve bad conditions through incremental steps rather than through one "do or die" effort. Thus in the war in Indochina the ICRC did not publicly protest or otherwise dramatize bad conditions in detention centers in South Vietnam covered by the Geneva Conventions. The ICRC made discreet overtures that, over considerable time, had the effect of helping to improve those conditions.[11]

In the future the ICRC will be asked to define and defend its estimate of the reasonable length of time during which detention conditions and other subjects should remain a secret matter. For how many years should the ICRC observe beatings by guards and torture before some nondiscreet action is taken for the benefit of the suffering individuals? If, over time, discreet overtures do not lead to substantial change, is some other type of action by the ICRC justifiable? Phrased differently, how can the ICRC morally justify discretion in a situation in which improvements do *not* occur over time? Should the ICRC ask the individuals in need if they approve of some dramatic action by the institution? Should the ICRC proceed on its own to dramatize the situation in certain cases?

In part, what is at issue is the moral worth of the ICRC's "one more blanket theory" (see Chapter 3). In the past, as long as the ICRC could see some incremental improvement in some conditions—as long as it could bring in one more blanket to a prisoner—it would remain on the scene and act in a discreet way. But is this highly individualistic morality, which focuses on small improvements for one individual or one group of individuals, comparable or superior to group ethics? If blankets can be brought to 100 political prisoners under the regular prison authorities, but the ICRC is prevented from visiting 25 prisoners held by the military and allegedly tortured, is the ICRC morally justified in providing the blankets but being discreet about not being allowed to see the "security prisoners"? Does such an approach by the ICRC permit the manipulation of the institution, in that its concerns are channeled into a focus on trivia while fundamental human rights go unprotected?

Is it possible that some departure from discreet incrementalism, in certain situations, would in fact lead to a greater humanitarian good for the greatest number of individuals? Is it possible that ICRC efforts would take on increased effectiveness and be viewed more seriously if the ICRC withdrew more consistently from certain situations, as it did from visiting political prisoners in South Vietnam in 1972? Or more consistently took such vigorous action that it was asked to leave by authorities? Or more consistently protested publicly certain situations, as it did with regard to the use of gas warfare in the Yemeni Civil War in the 1960's and with regard to the situation in the Middle East in the 1970's?[12]

These moral choices will be complex, as are all moral choices when related to factual situations. But the ICRC will be asked by close observers of its activity whether it has made the choice most beneficial to persons in need, and whether that choice was made on practical humanitarian grounds rather than on abstract dislike of entering into conflict with a public authority. The morality of practical help will be increasingly difficult to define but must be faced nevertheless.

SUMMATION

Out of facing these three challenges will emerge the core strategy of the ICRC in the future. Who the ICRC represents and to whom it answers, what it does—especially in relation to legal considerations—and how it proceeds—especially in the context of moral choice—will determine the fate of ICRC activity in the coming years (insofar as the ICRC can affect its own fate).

There is likely to be continuing need for the ICRC, if its answers to the basic challenges noted above are well suited to the milieu of the institution. The complexity of violence, the complexity of the institutional landscape, the complexity of the international climate of opinion will certainly make life difficult for the ICRC. But none of these factors necessarily negate the utility of the ICRC. Even a Kissinger-like emphasis on security strategy at the expense of civil-political rights, and an emphasis on economic and environmental survival, will not necessarily rule out a role for the ICRC. Individuals will continue to suffer from a variety of "man-made conflicts" and will be in need of third-party assistance and protection.

The ICRC should have a continuing role in helping to respond to these needs for two primary reasons. First, the institution has been concerned with fundamental human rights rather than with civil-political rights or socioeconomic rights. That is to say, the ICRC has tried to see that basic human dignity is achieved through the absence of torture, mistreatment, degrading living conditions, and insufficient nourishment. It has not been centrally concerned, but rather only marginally concerned, with civil-political rights like access to legal counsel and right to habeas corpus, and even less with socioeconomic rights like right to strike and to minimum wage. Thus differences over civil-political and socioeconomic rights can continue without interrupting the ICRC's traditional concerns. Even if India, say, decides that civil-political rights must be curtailed in the interests of national security, harmony, and economic welfare, third-party supervision of detention can continue as in the past. Likewise, even if authoritarian coercion is necessary to respond to environmental limitations or catastrophes, a third-party humanitarian presence can be introduced into the situation.

Secondly, and relatedly, the ICRC should have a continuing role because of its having chosen an intermediate or indeterminate idea of humanitarian protection. The ICRC has sought to deal with an emergency situation in which individuals may suffer; it has left to others the determination of the cause of the emergency. Thus the ICRC has been more like a fire department than a police department. The cause of the fire is of less concern than putting out the flames. This does not imply that determination of the cause of human suffering is unimportant, or that those who cause it should not be punished, or that preventive measures should not be taken in the future. But the ICRC has left those matters to others. In traditional Red Cross jargon, the ICRC has chosen charity rather than justice as its central concern. In a world in which, internationally speaking, the police are absent and the courts easily bypassed, there should be a continuing role for the ICRC. If final or total solutions are unobtainable, the utility of intermediate solutions should be enhanced.[13] If arson cannot be determined, there is still need of a fire department to put out the flames.

The ICRC, in its continuing concern with fundamental human rights and with its intermediate conception of its tasks, is indeed a fragile and weak institution. Its weakness as well as its utility were well demonstrated by the situation in Angola in the fall of 1975. In the context of a bloody civil war there was civilian malnutrition and starvation in the northern region of that country. Religious organizations were aware of the problem but could not get assistance where it was needed. The ICRC was knowledgeable about the situation and had started an airlift of material-medical relief with over thirty persons involved—an action under way for some two weeks before it became general knowledge. But the magnitude of the problem seemed too great for regular ICRC operations. The ICRC wanted the United Nations to take over the airlift, but the UN was unable to respond for various reasons. Most governments were uninterested in the humanitarian problem, as they feared antagonizing one of the three parties in the internal war—all of whom were receiving foreign arms and other aid. The conflicting parties themselves were fearful that humanitarian involvements might affect realpolitik and partisan politics. Help to the particular individuals in need might lead to increased popular support for one of the conflicting parties.[14] So there the ICRC was, on the scene, prepared for an initial and small action, but unable to cope by itself with the situation in its entirety.

The weakness of the ICRC, compared especially to the power of nation-states and armed movements, is simply a fact of life, as true in the future as it has been in the past. This situation of weakness imposes two obligations on the ICRC. First, as Fouad Ajami wrote, initially with regard to the Middle East: "That words are the weapons left for the more humane elements . . . is a depressing statement about political power and those who hold it throughout the world. But the weak can hardly afford to be choosy; they must use the weapon at their disposal, regardless of how weak and ineffective it may turn out to be.''[15] Thus the ICRC faces the obligation to continue the struggle for humanitarian values, weak though it is.

Second, the ICRC has the obligation to maximize the power stemming from weakness. As the world becomes increasingly politicized, as more people hold governments responsible for more things, as attacks on governments and government officials increase, and as governments suppress opposition out of insecurity, the ICRC has the obligation to maintain and enhance its image of impartiality in a context of realpolitik and partisan politics.[16] In a highly politicized world, impartiality becomes a strength, as there is increased need for actors free from suspicion of participation in realpolitik and partisan politics. If the ICRC can enhance its impartiality, this impartiality—while initially a weakness since the ICRC is cut off from governmental alliance—can be turned into a strength. The ICRC is too weak to be feared, which is the ultimate source of its strength. But the ICRC has the obligation consciously to develop the strength that stems from this weakness.

Thus the ICRC will need a central strategy to enhance its impartiality and to make that impartiality most effective in support of humanitarian values. It will need to consider systematically who it is, what it does, and how it proceeds. For it will be acting in situations not very well marked by contemporary international law, among a variety of actors, in a world less and less influenced by traditional Western thought. Traditional ICRC assumptions are not likely to be fully applicable to a changed and changing milieu.

Paradoxically, perhaps, the development and application of ICRC impartiality is a political process. Impartial protection and assistance require policy and an awareness of that policy's impact on exercises of power and the structure of international relations.

The ICRC has a rich tradition of humanitarian service on which to draw in facing the challenges of a complex and changing world. Its symbol is still respected widely, and there is much experience recorded in its archives. Given the changes already in process within the institution, and given a reasonable amount of wisdom and luck in its future decisions, the ICRC can be expected to improve its efficiency in humanitarian protection and assistance. Further, through well-considered participation in the Red Cross movement, the ICRC could make some small contribution to the global integration of peoples through promotion of understanding and cooperation on humanitarian matters. In the long run, if such a time span exists, the ICRC might even make some contribution indirectly to a more peaceful world. It has long sought a more humane one.

Postscript

It may be useful to set out some personal comments on one view of the ICRC in the future. No doubt these personal observations reflect the questions raised in the preceding chapter. And perhaps the opinions offered here have already appeared in an implicit way in earlier discussions. Be that as it may, it seems at least honest to set them out here in candid form.

WHO THE ICRC SHOULD BE

I believe that the ICRC should be, in the future, the leader of a global transnational movement active for the benefit of mankind.

It seems to me that the ICRC in the past has been over oriented to the Swiss establishment. As a result, its approach to humanitarian affairs, commendable in many ways—not the least of which has been sincere motivation—has been too conventional (by Swiss mainstream standards). The institution's personnel have been drawn from too narrow a social base. In particular the Assembly needs not only less conservative, middle-class, "white-collar" types; it needs some radical humanitarian thought. The ICRC has been dominated by the type of thinking found in the Swiss Department of Politics (the equivalent of the Foreign Office or State Department), and is badly in need of systematic communication with circles of other opinion: nonwhite, non-Western, even radical opinion in order to obtain, at a minimum, a more complete understanding of issues, options, and implications of action. It is quite possible that the entry of Switzerland into the United Nations could be a good thing for the ICRC. On the one hand, such an entry could force the ICRC to loosen its ties with the Swiss government, in order to maintain ICRC impartiality when compared with a government voting and negotiating in the UN. On the other hand, it might lead to increased ICRC understanding of global events, through some contact with a more involved, better-informed Swiss government.

In part because of this past symbiosis between the ICRC and the Swiss establishment, the ICRC has appeared at times to consider itself more Swiss than Red Cross, and has been unnecessarily aloof from participation in the Red Cross movement. ICRC independence from the movement has been dysfunctional, to some extent, to Red Cross protection and assistance. The ICRC has been in the movement but not fully of the movement. In particular it has not—in the past— perceived the valuable role of national Red Cross Societies in legal development, application of law, and ad hoc diplomacy. The ICRC has not encouraged national societies to lobby their governments for humanitarian purposes—lobbying which, if necessary, can be considered apolitical since it is not motivated by favoritism in partisan politics. The ICRC has not encouraged national societies to play an active role in the teaching of humanitarian law. Nor has the ICRC tightly coordinated with them legal development efforts or provision of assistance to detainees. Use of the potential of the movement to secure maximum protection and assistance has not been considered until very recently at the ICRC, much less tried. Likewise the ICRC and the League have been competitors as much as partners. The fault for this situation does not lie entirely at the door of the ICRC. In my view, this competition should be resolved by the emergence of a changed ICRC as the sole leader of the Red Cross movement; the League should be the assistance coordinator for the movement. The ICRC has broad diplomatic experience and capable professional staff; the League is a focal point for national societies in collection of assistance and grassroots distribution. The two Geneva institutions could be connected by a Red Cross Relief Bureau, cochaired by an ICRC and a League official. The ICRC designate could assume leadership in "man-made conflicts," and the League designate could direct assistance otherwise. A jointly provided skeleton staff could exist under the Relief Bureau. Further, it seems evident that the ICRC needs an advisory council made up of representatives from national societies, with due regard for equitable geographical representation on the Council. The Red Cross Conference and League itself are too large to contribute effectively to policy formulation. Moreover, the Conference is too emeshed in realpolitik, owing to governmental presence and influence, and the League secretariat too critical of the ICRC for reasons of self-interest, for Conference and League opinions to be highly respected by the ICRC.

To be sure, the Red Cross movement qua movement will never be a tightly integrated global lobby and administrative actor. Neither the American Red Cross nor the Soviet Red Cross Alliance, for example, has shown any enthusiasm for taking instructions from Geneva. Both, like other national societies, are enmeshed in the point of view reflected in the statement of an American Red

Cross official: "We would never do anything to embarrass the American government." But between total fragmentation because of nationalism and total unity there is room for increased cooperation among parts of the movement: similar views of a rational division of labor are widely shared.

Finally, the ICRC *can* make a legitimate claim to representing mankind, but it needs to ensure that under that slogan there does not exist a purely Swiss or purely Western view of humanitarian action. To have that claim respected, the ICRC must act so that conflict in Cambodia is on a par with conflict in Cyprus. The institution should take one just as seriously as another. Moreover, the ICRC must be aware of, and seek to counteract, anti-Swiss and anti-Western feelings.

This challenge has been brilliantly analyzed by the African political scientist Ali A. Mazrui.[1]

> If one were to select three factors about contemporary Africa which are likely to bedevil the work of an organization like the Red Cross, one would be tempted to choose the following:
> Firstly, the fact that Africa is a highly politicised continent.
> Secondly, the fact that African politics have, in the last five years become, to some extent, militarized.
> And, thirdly, the fact that African history so far has been such that purely humanitarian motives are often suspect.
> . . . .
> Considering then, that Africa is a highly politicised continent, an organisation like the Red Cross which works best in conditions of political neutrality is immediately faced with major problems. How can the work of the Red Cross, in a situation which involves deep political divisions, be adequately regarded as politically neutral? Is not the act of neutrality itself a political decision in certain situations?
> . . . .
> [In the Nigerian war] Africa was testing afresh the viability of a movement of the kind, committed to political neutrality, yet seeking to operate precisely in those areas which are highly politicised and indeed often militarised. In the words of Colin Legum: "The I.C.R.C.'s troubles in Nigeria brought to light how badly out of touch the organization was with the feelings of the Third World which was not inclined to accept uncritically the policies determined by a group of Europeans, however lofty their motives."
> . . . .
> Within the kinship system Africans know a level of human compassion and human obligation which is not even comprehensible to the western mind. The idea of a tribal welfare system, within which voluntary service and hospitality is extended to the indigent, the disabled, and the aged, provides a striking model of the instinct of social fellowship in man. We all know of distant relatives we support, distant cousins who have a share in our salaries, distant kinsmen who can call upon us as guests in our houses for days, sometimes for weeks.
> And yet it seems as if the very fact that we have a highly developed sense of responsibility towards our own kinsmen, a much more developed sense than is discernible in western society, has resulted in diluting our capacity to empathise with those

that are much further from us. The growth of individualism in the West has curiously enough resulted both in reduced collective responsibility within the immediate society and increased capacity to empathise with man much further away, even in other lands altogether. The western individualist would be reluctant to contribute to the support of a distant cousin who finds himself in dire financial difficulties; and yet that same western individualist would be capable of rising to the occasion when news of a natural catastrophe in Pakistan or Chile reached him. With the African it is the reverse. He is much more moved by the day to day problems of a distant kinsman, than by a dramatic upheaval in a remote part of the world.

. . . .

More recently, there have been incidents since Africa's attainment of independence which have been defended on humanitarian grounds by the West, when in fact issues of racial solidarity on the part of the whites were discernible. A controversial example concerned the white hostages which were held by Congolese rebels in 1964 in their confrontation with their central government. . . . The hostages were later rescued by Belgian troops . . . [using] American planes in the process of this venture. Much of Africa was indignant. But the West justified the Stanleyville operation on grounds that it was a humanitarian act.

. . . .

But were the Americans and the Belgians really putting their humanity first and their nationality and racial identity second in that actual operation? Conor Cruise O'Brien, the former United Nations representative in Katanga, pointed out the relative indifference of European and American opinion towards Congolese suffering as contrasted with the indignant compassion which was aroused on behalf of white prisoners. O'Brien suggested that the ''humanitarian'' sensitivity displayed in the West at the time of the Stanleyville rescue operation was, in fact, little more than an instance of racial solidarity. He indicated that Africa's own indignation against the operation had the same source as Western self-righteousness in its regard—the main difference was that Africans lacked the power to send in paratroopers to rescue black victims from their oppressors in Dixie and South Africa.

. . . .

It is partly because of incidents of this kind, reinforced by the whole doctrine of the white man's burden in history and the place of humanitarian legitimation for imperialism, that the very term humanitarianism is sometimes suspect in the eyes of African nationalists. The Red Cross, as a movement ultimately predicated on the viability of the humanitarian impulse, has to grapple with this heritage of Africa's history.

If it succeeds over the years in ultimately restrengthening and reactivating the humanitarian impulse in the African, without putting too much damage on the tradition of kinship obligations, the movement of the Red Cross would have played a part in one of the most important social transformations in the African continent.

The importance of the ICRC's understanding non-Western attitudes will be accompanied, for the foreseeable future, by the fact that support for the ICRC will continue to be from the West. It is that area that, relatively speaking, is most interested in human rights as the ICRC would define them.[2] Nevertheless, the ICRC's action must indeed represent mankind if the institution is to claim to do so. The ICRC needs to open itself to increased contact with, and understanding of, others. And it must be prepared to cooperate more with other institutions rather than regarding them as interlopers into an ICRC monopoly. During the Indochina War, some ICRC officials were privately critical of Amnesty International for its suggestion that it might go to Hanoi to see detained American flyers. Rather than criticize that idea, it seems to me the ICRC should actively promote it if the ICRC itself is prevented from supervising detention conditions.

The self-view actually prevailing at the ICRC in past years, implicitly rather than officially, has failed to maximize Red Cross humanitarian protection and assistance, and at times has failed to promote humanitarian action, more broadly defined. What is required for change is an attitude of openness and cooperation on the part of the ICRC, not secrecy and aloofness. The ICRC's identity and subsequent action has to be defended on the basis of effectiveness, not on the basis of withdrawal into past traditions. In many ways the ICRC's record can be defended on its merits, ,without defensiveness. Even the undemocratic nature of the ICRC can be defended; many democracies have nondemocratic elements—such as courts—which serve well the needs of society and are regarded as an important check against the tyranny of the majority. The ICRC can be a respected leader of the Red Cross movement and a respected actor for the benefit of mankind if it does in fact seek to maximize humanitarian protection and assistance rather than extolling Swiss nationalism or the prestige of the agency per se.

THE ICRC'S EVALUATION OF LAW

Certain ICRC officials, lawyers and law professors among them, have allowed an instrumental view of international law to become a pursuit of law in and for itself. Pragmatic ICRC concern via ad hoc diplomacy historically led to an effort to use law to set a minimum floor of humanitarian behavior in armed conflicts. But states took that effort in support of ''humanitarian law'' and used it for defense of state interest in independent and exclusive state action. Along the process, the ICRC contributed to these problems by becoming proud of its record in promoting legal development, proud of its position as a drafting secretariat, proud of its position in the resulting law. The ICRC became reluctant publicly to acknowledge or criticize the antihumanitarian uses to which states put humanitarian law.

Others at the ICRC, however, have acknowledged privately the difficulties inherent in the ICRC's legal orientation. It seems to me that this bodes well for the future. Like them, I would argue that Geneva law has its uses and that on balance it is a good thing, but also that its instrumental nature must be kept in mind. Where that law does not promote humanitarian values, the law should be deemphasized.

The Geneva Conventions are useful as a background condition, against which one can make appeals for decent treatment in armed conflicts. The law is thus a backdrop useful for settlements "out of court" favorable to humanitarian values. Also, Geneva law, as a consensus statement about the nature of humane conduct in war, is a useful device through which to socialize actors into adopting more humane attitudes toward "enemies."

But the utility of Geneva law should not be overstated. It is rarely interpreted by courts. It rarely is applied formally, automatically, and without exceptions. And it frequently is used to block humanitarian action. The ICRC's association with the Geneva Conventions is not always a good thing for humanitarian pursuits. When the ICRC presented itself to British authorities in both Kenya and Northern Ireland, those authorities were initially reluctant to permit ICRC detention visits for fear of lending support to the argument that those situations were armed conflicts of some type—and thus subject to international regulation—rather than British internal matters. Appeals to international humanitarian law necessarily raise ahumanitarian questions about jurisdictions. And the very existence of international humanitarian law as it is now constituted tends to propagate an "internal" or "domestic" zone of jurisdiction where third parties are denied access. Yet much humanitarian need exists in this "internal" or "domestic" zone.

It can be argued in the last analysis that the world would be worse off without the Geneva Conventions than with them. I think that is probably true. As Telford Taylor has written, "If it were not regarded as wrong to bomb military hospitals, they would be bombed all of the time instead of only some of the time."[3] No doubt some inroads on death, destruction, and suffering have been made by the existence of the Conventions.

But the ICRC should acknowledge that the state sovereignty written into Geneva law is not always a good thing from the humanitarian point of view. State sovereignty arose as an idea in defense of human rights and in pursuit of human welfare. The state was argued to be supreme because presumably it could do more things for the individual, in comparison with feudal barons and other local and disjointed authorities. But in an era when many individuals question the willingness or ability of the state to provide social justice, among other things, to its nationals, there is no reason for a humanitarian agency like the ICRC to elevate the idea of state sovereignty into a religious tenet through its support for humanitarian law.

In the modern period it is difficult to understand why the ICRC has been so reluctant to limit the exercise of state sovereignty by refusing to assume the position of automatic supervisor of the Geneva Conventions, especially when a significant number of states themselves were willing to confer broad authority on the institution. The result of the ICRC's refusal to accept that authority has been to condemn the law to lack of effective supervision, to forego an opportunity to put pressure on a state to act in full compliance with humanitarian standards, to undercut the efforts of those states trying to improve the law's effectiveness, and to give rise to suspicions—especially on the part of some third-world actors—that the ICRC wanted to pick and choose its areas of operation rather than having to operate automatically and without favoritism. Compared with these considerations, the ICRC's reasons for refusing to supervise automatically state behavior in armed conflicts pale into insignificance.[4]

What is therefore suggested here is paradoxical. First, the ICRC should move to make Geneva law more effective and more oriented to human needs rather than state interests, when the two values are divergent. The ICRC should have no interest in the development of law primarily for state interest, but concentrate instead on its humanitarian content. This means, for one thing, that the ICRC could conceivably on occasion oppose any legal development on the grounds that the cure was worse than the disease. For example, the ICRC could have opposed legal development according to the two-protocol approach and insisted on a one-protocol approach or nothing at all, on the ground that only a one-protocol approach would be effective in protecting human rights (these issues were discussed in Chapter 5). Whatever the precise issues and judgments, in general the ICRC, in close cooperation with national Red Cross Societies, should lobby more overtly and vigorously for a "humanitarian law" more humanitarian in content. The ICRC could set up a separate administrative arm for the automatic supervision of the law, thus increasing its effectiveness. And it could set up a quasi-independent ICRC agency, similar to the Tracing Agency, to become an automatic official substitute for a Protecting Power. The separateness of such an agency would allow ICRC ad hoc diplomacy to continue without unnecessary entanglement in legal controversies.

Second, the ICRC should move to make as much of its work as possible alegal. This "delegalization" process would counteract certain claims by states—viz., that the law did not apply, that the law only required X but not Y, that use of the law led to implications about the overall nature of the situation that the state wished to avoid. In many situations an ICRC alegal, purely humanitarian approach might produce considerable humanitarian results. Geneva law should be regarded as a necessary evil and a last resort, useful in some but not all situations.

In sum, the ICRC should seek to bypass all legal issues whenever possible and return to its original pursuit of meeting humanitarian needs on a pragmatic basis, utilizing ad hoc diplomacy. When compelled by states to invoke legal considerations, the ICRC should struggle to insure that the development and application of Geneva law is indeed for humanitarian purposes and not just for state interests per se.

International law in general is in a state of flux. Parts of the law have collapsed and are no longer effective. Other parts of the law are being changed. New concepts and new authorities are in competition. This legal confusion cannot provide the ICRC with clear guidelines in the near future, and thus the ICRC needs to free itself from as much of this confusion as possible. When it becomes involved in legal matters, the ICRC should seek to remove the confusion clearly in favor of humanitarian protection and assistance. More development of traditional law does not necessarily favor this end.

THE ICRC'S EVALUATION OF MORALITY

What I have called above "impartial humanitarianism," meaning a distinctive style of action, has its uses in a world increasingly characterized by realpolitik and partisan politics. The ICRC, unlike many other humanitarian actors, but like the UN High Commissioner for Refugees, has utilized a long time-perspective in its activity. Both of these organizations have sought to achieve the greatest good for the greatest number on the basis of a long time span, rather than on the basis of immediate action in one context that might be so controversial as to exclude action in future situations. Impartial humanitarianism, relying as it does on discreet incrementalism for improvement in the human condition, requires a sizable time span for the charting of progress.

The ICRC has done much good for individuals using this style. The question the ICRC must answer in the future is *not* really whether it should entirely change its style and become either an international or revolutionary actor (as those concepts were used in Chapter 9). With other humanitarian actors engaging in confrentational statements and/or provocative action against public authorities, there seems little reason for the ICRC to emulate them completely. Precisely because other actors like Amnesty or JCA exist, the ICRC has reason *not* to adopt their style.

The question the ICRC really must answer is, where is the boundary delimiting impartial humanitarianism? Can the ICRC, for the sake of individuals in need, be a little more bold in its statements and actions? Can the ICRC, utilizing a reputation based on a past pattern of activity, do more for individuals in a certain context without jeopardizing its future work? It is my belief that the ICRC can move its particular version of impartial humanitarianism "one more notch" toward international humanitarianism—it can engage in increased publicity on a selective basis. It is my judgment that, properly executed, such a style of action will both accomplish more and will find support in the circles of world opinion interested in humanitarian values.

Now publicity in itself is not always a good thing for the ICRC. Its record of public dialogue, of a conflictual nature, with Nigerian authorities did not enhance the stature of the ICRC and did nothing to promote humanitarian endeavors in the Nigerian Civil War.

On the other hand, when the ICRC has sound reason to be dissatisfied with a party's attention to humanitarian affairs, when a party is not displaying a determined effort—over time—to rectify violations of fundamental human rights, some increased use of publicity would probably be widely supported, and in such a way that the ICRC's future utility to individuals would not be endangered. In certain situations public authorities need the presence of the ICRC as much as the ICRC needs the cooperation of those authorities. All of the advantages do not necessarily lie with the detaining, or occupying, or belligerent party. There is a good probability that certain regimes will learn to live with a more assertive ICRC—perhaps even respect a more assertive ICRC—for fear of the consequences of an ICRC departure. A controversial situation, as the United States found in Indochina or as Israel found in the occupied territories, may be utilized to maximize humanitarian values, as the regime in question may be amenable to further humanitarian steps because of fear that an ICRC public statement or even withdrawal might be forthcoming. The ICRC, motivated strictly by a desire to promote humanitarian goals, and thus acting according to the tenets of impartial humanitarianism, might on occasion violate the consent barrier, or might redefine the consent barrier so as to reduce the area of action in which state consent is respected. What is ultimately at issue is whether the ICRC is doing all for individuals in need that can be done, taking into account the ICRC's well-considered desire to be of use to individuals in the future. It is suggested here that the ICRC can indeed do slightly more.

ICRC folklore has it that an ICRC delegate dealing with an authority should always be on the verge of becoming persona non grata. This is good theory. The historical record shows, however, very few delegates being recalled to Geneva at the request of a public authority. The record also seems to show very little probing by Geneva in the recent past of the boundary of acceptance by those authorities. What they will and will not accept does not appear to have been carefully considered. And in a long time perspective, it may even be to the credit of the ICRC to be asked to withdraw from a situation. The decision of the Greek government not to renew the 1969 contract with the ICRC no doubt enhanced the ICRC's reputation over time, especially with the democratic government that followed the junta.

There is another relevant point. The climate of opinion concerning international interest in human rights has been changing. There is increasing interest in human rights on a global scale, even if that interest is not sufficiently strong to guarantee that violations of fundamental human rights are successfully countered (see Chapter 2). One consequence is that, as one member of the ICRC Assembly has written, "All the players on the world stage, and the Red Cross is one of them, are thus liable to be in the public eye and approved or criticized and disapproved at any time and anywhere for what they do or fail to do. The activities of the International Red Cross can no longer be carried out discreetly."[5] Another consequence is that, if the ICRC does not respond to some of the aspirations of some circles of opinion—like IGOs, other NGOs, and attentive publics—it is going to lose the support of these groups. Increasingly it is not just governmental opinion that the ICRC must respond to, but other informed opinion as well.

In the last analysis, the ICRC must make a difficult judgment about when the climate of opinion permits it a more assertive defense of human rights—assertive behavior that, because it is carefully considered and executed, improves a particular situation and also moves the international consensus in support of human rights one more step forward. A cautious, ''discreet incrementalism'' has served the institution well in the past. No doubt in many situations in the future it will be an appropriate style of action. But if it is true, as has been said at the ICRC, that the institution's discretion is its best trump (*atout,* in French), it is also true that a trump, to be effective, must be played.

The threat and actual use of publicity, when the ICRC is on firm moral grounds and when the form of publicity is well designed, will cause the ICRC to be supported by important elements in world affairs and to be taken more seriously. It will thus be a move, existing in the background, that will promote a productive conclusion in the more normal process of discreet negotiations.

FINAL THOUGHTS

For all of its recent difficulties, and for all of the criticisms directed at it, the ICRC has done much good in the world. Once admitted on a systematic basis to detention situations particularly, the ICRC can provide useful services to both detaining authority and detained individuals.

For the detaining authority the ICRC can become an independent administrative arm, allowing the central authorities to learn what is occurring in ''the boondocks.'' Most central authorities have difficulty keeping track of what occurs at lower ranks, because of either the primitive nature of the bureaucratic structure or the size of sophisticated structures combined with a quest for independence through obfuscation by those lower ranks. In either case the ICRC can become a useful humanitarian ''GAO'' to the central authorities—inspecting and reporting on what is occurring in penal and military departments.[6] In such a role, the ICRC can also interject new ideas based on its global experience (e.g., do newspapers in a prison really jeopardize a regime's security? ICRC experience suggests they do not). And the ICRC tends to raise the forgotten questions (such as when administrative detention should end, or why the administrative detainee should be treated according to criminal standards when he has not been convicted of any crime).

In improving the administration of detention and making it more responsible to central authorities, the ICRC is really working for the individual—even though there is a pay-off to the central authorities. Moreover, the ICRC provides the detainee with an important psychological boost by serving as a link with the outside world. And the ICRC's tracing service, combined with systematic interviews without witnesses, is a deterrent to the disappearance and mistreatment of individuals. Further, in less developed administrations, and in emergency situations, the ICRC is an important source of material-medical assistance.

There is, therefore, a valuable humanitarian role for the ICRC to play in the future. Its ad hoc diplomacy should be its core activity, as it was originally. This activity may become applied legal protection and assistance in those situations where parties admit the applicability of the law of armed conflict. And, to a lesser extent for the foreseeable future, some humanitarian gains may be recorded through legal development, perhaps on a regional basis.

To maximize the impact of this activity, the ICRC needs to enhance its image of impartiality and to promote its effectiveness through careful consideration of its strategy, policies, and tactics.

The ICRC is too weak to be feared, and that is the source of its strength. But, paradoxically, the ICRC needs to strengthen itself by facing the challenges of identifying who it really is, and what its evaluation of international law and its morality of action should be. This strengthening should occur within the confines of impartial humanitarianism, although there will be differences of opinion about the implications of that style of action. No doubt the ICRC will be accused from time to time of participation in realpolitik and partisan politics, for, as already noted, "one man's humanitarianism may be another's political maneuvering; and even the ICRC has been accused of favoritism."[7] Thus there will be no easy answers for every situation encountered by the ICRC, and certainly no set recommendations for every situation can be offered here.

But the ICRC should struggle to push to the maximum the welfare of those individuals it has elected to try to protect and assist, without losing its utility in the future. This is the meaning of humanitarian politics for the ICRC. No doubt the ICRC would agree without reservation with this goal. Choosing the most effective way to reach that goal is the basic challenge of the future.

Appendix A
Recognition of New National Red Cross Societies

To become a member of the International Red Cross, the applicant Society must satisfy the ten conditions for recognition listed below, and submit a request for recognition to the International Committee of the Red Cross, together with all relevant documents, in particular the following:

    (a) an authenticated copy of the governmental decree granting the National Society recognition in conformity with Condition No. 3 below;
    (b) a copy of the Statutes of the Society in force;
    (c) a copy of the latest report on activities.

The request for recognition must contain a statement in which the Society undertakes to comply with any conditions for recognition which may not have been the subject of statutory provisions.

CONDITIONS FOR THE RECOGNITION OF NATIONAL RED CROSS SOCIETIES

(Drawn up by an ad hoc joint Commission of the International Committee of the Red Cross and the League of Red Cross Societies, and approved by the XVIIth International Red Cross Conference, Stockholm, 1948)

Source: Appendix A is quoted verbatim from the *International Red Cross Handbook* (Geneva: Red Cross, 1971), pp. 332–33.

The Society shall:

(1) Be constituted on the territory of an independent State where the Geneva Convention for the Amelioration of the Condition of the Wounded and Sick of August 12, 1949, is in force.

(2) Be the only National Red Cross Society of the said State and be directed by a central body which shall alone be competent to represent it in its dealings with other members of the International Red Cross.

(3) Be duly recognized by its legal Government as a Voluntary Aid Society, auxiliary to the public authorities, in particular in the sense of Article 26 of the I. Geneva Convention of 1949, or, in States which do not maintain armed forces, as a Voluntary Aid Society auxiliary to the public authorities and acting for the benefit of the civilian population.

(4) Be an institution whose autonomous status allows it to operate in conformity with the fundamental principles of the Red Cross, as formulated by the International Red Cross Conference.

(5) Use the title and emblem of the Red Cross (Red Crescent, Red Lion and Sun), in conformity with the Geneva Convention.

(6) Be so organized as to enable it to deal effectively with the tasks incumbent upon it. Become prepared in time of peace for wartime activities.

(7) Extend its activities to the entire country and its dependencies.

(8) Not withhold membership from any of its nationals, whoever they may be, on grounds of race, sex, class, religion or political opinions.

(9) Adhere to the Statutes of the International Red Cross, share in the fellowship which unites its members—the National Societies and the International bodies—and keep in close touch with them.

(10) Honour the fundamental principles of the Red Cross as defined by the International Red Cross Conferences: impartiality; political, religious and economic independence; the universality of the Red Cross and the equality of all National Societies; and be guided in all its work by the spirit of the Geneva Convention and the Conventions which complete it.

Appendix B

Agreement between
the International
Committee of the
Red Cross and the
League of Red Cross
Societies for the
Purpose of Specifying
Certain of Their
Respective Functions
(Signed on
25th April, 1969)

PREAMBLE

The respective functions of the International Committee of the Red Cross, foun-der body of the Red Cross, and of the League of Red Cross Societies, world federation of the National Societies, both of which are constituent bodies of the International Red Cross, are, in their principles, established by Articles VI (for the International Committee) and VII (for the League) of the Statutes of the International Red Cross.

Nevertheless, the International Committee and the League have deemed it advisable to complete these Statutes with certain specific provisions for the purpose of defining insofar as possible the respective spheres of activity of the two Institutions which, while cooperating closely, remain independent. These provisions are the subject of the present Agreement, which has the character of a friendly understanding.

In this Agreement, the International Committee and the League have sought to harmonise their respective activities, in cases where the functions of both bodies are or might be exercised simultaneously, so as to ensure the unity and effectiveness of Red Cross work. They have also sought to avoid, in their relations with the National Red Cross Societies, any overlapping and confusion which might arise from the similarity of certain of their activities.

The International Committee and the League furthermore consider that, should it be impossible to find a solution for unforeseen problems in the Statutes of the International Red Cross or in the present Agreement, they should be solved on the basis of the general principles underlying the Statutes of the International Red Cross and the present Agreement. In particular, Red Cross action should always be primarily concerned with the interests of the persons to be helped and with safeguarding the fundamental and permanent principles of the Red Cross. Moreover, should unforeseen circumstances require some degree of adaptation, such adaptation should be examined by joint agreement, taking into account the situation and, where necessary, the particular character conferred upon the International Committee by its right of initiative confirmed by the Geneva Conventions.

Accordingly, it is hereby agreed, between:

The International Committee of the Red Cross in Geneva, represented by Messrs. Jacques Freymond, Vice-President, and Jean Pictet, Member and Director General,

on the one hand,

and

The League of Red Cross Societies represented by Messrs. José Barroso-Chavez, Chairman of the Board of Governors, and Henrik Beer, Secretary General,

on the other,

that:

I. Relief actions of National Societies for the civilian population

ARTICLE 1

Definition   Under the present Agreement, relief actions for the civilian population shall comprise not only all material assistance (foodstuffs, clothing, pharmaceutical products, shelter and money) but also the assignment of personnel of all categories. The term "civilian population" shall also include refugees and displaced persons.

ARTICLE 2

Red Cross action in the event of a conflict

In countries where there is an international war, civil war, blockade or military occupation, the ICRC, in virtue of the functions of a neutral intermediary devolving on it under the Geneva Conventions and the Statutes of the International Red Cross, shall assume the general direction of the Red Cross international action.

If, in these countries, as a result of special circumstances or in the event of a natural disaster, the League is, at the request of a National Society, called upon to give assistance to the civilian population of its country, the ways and means of the intervention of the League as well as its cooperation with the ICRC and the National societies concerned shall be defined from case to case in accordance with Articles 5 and 6 of the present Agreement.

When the intervention of a neutral intermediary is not or is no longer necessary, the ICRC shall reach agreement with the League with a view to associating it with the relief action or even handing over to it the entire responsibility.

ARTICLE 3

Red Cross action in peacetime

In peacetime the League shall coordinate the relief actions of National Societies on behalf of one of them, cooperate in distributions and direct the action when asked to do so by the beneficiary National Society or when circumstances require.

If a conflict arises in a country where the League is carrying out the above-mentioned activities and the intervention of a specifically neutral intermediary becomes necessary, the League shall propose that, in liaison with it, the ICRC assume these functions, in accordance with Articles 4 and 5.

ARTICLE 4

Method of cooperation

When the ICRC and the League are called upon to cooperate in the field of relief to the civilian population, the necessary machinery shall immediately be established, both in Geneva and the territories concerned, to ensure maximum efficiency and unity in the action of all the members of the International Red Cross: ICRC, League and National Societies.

As each situation will inevitably present different conditions, the respective spheres of activity of the ICRC, the League and National Societies in the territories concerned should be clearly laid down, from case to case, by the coordinating body provided for in the next Article.

ARTICLE 5

Coordinating
body

The ICRC and the League shall each appoint two delegates and two deputies, who should at all times be able to meet without delay and who shall have the task:

(a) of informing each other on the approaches made to their Institutions and on the conduct of the actions under way. The communications addressed by National Societies to one of the Institutions and which concern the other within the terms of Articles 3 and 3 shall be passed on to it without delay;

(b) of taking—in accordance with the Statutes of the International Red Cross and the principles of the present Agreement—all the necessary decisions to ensure an immediate intervention of the Red Cross and the speedy conduct of relief actions;

(c) of entrusting the execution of a given action to one of the two international Institutions without, however, excluding—if this seems advisable—a joint action, the ways and means of which should then be clearly defined.

The fact that a National Society submits a request to the ICRC or the League or spontaneously donates relief to them shall not change the distribution of the tasks between the two Institutions.

National Societies shall be regularly informed of the decisions taken in accordance with the above-mentioned provisions.

ARTICLE 6

Appeals

As a general rule, the appeals with regard to a relief action shall be launched to National Societies by one of the two international Institutions which, by virtue of Articles 2 and 3, is responsible for the action. There may also be joint appeals.

ARTICLE 7

League Field
Delegate

If in the event of a conflict a League Field Delegate is on the spot or is sent out at the request of a National Society, he shall carry out his duties vis-à-vis this Society in consultation with the ICRC delegation.

II. First aid

The promotion of this activity shall fall within the competence of the League.

III. Legal assistance for foreigners

The promotion of this activity shall fall within the competence of the ICRC.

IV. Training of medical personnel and preparation of medical equipment of National Societies

The promotion of this training and preparation shall fall within the competence of the ICRC and the League. The two Institutions shall coordinate their activities in this field.

V. Protection of civilian populations against certain effects of war

The protection of civilian populations by a development of international law shall fall within the competence of the International Committee.

This shall also apply to the practical measures to be taken in the event of an armed conflict (such as limitation of the dangers of war, evacuation, safety localities and open towns, transmission of complaints).

The promotion of the technical preparation of National Societies (civil defence) shall fall within the competence of the ICRC and the League. The two Institutions shall coordinate their activities in this field.

VI. Studies concerning the Geneva Conventions

It shall be the task of the International Committee to interpret the Geneva Conventions, to comment upon them from a legal standpoint and to establish model agreements, laws of application and similar documents.

VII. The Red Cross as a factor in world peace

In this sphere, which is of interest to the whole Red Cross movement the two Institutions shall as in the past endeavour to adopt a common attitude and to coordinate their activities.

VIII. Recognition of newly-formed or reconstituted National Societies

The recognition of New National Societies shall be pronounced by the ICRC while their admission to the League shall be decided upon by the latter. As these two operations are based on the same conditions they should be harmonized.

Consequently, these operations shall be preceded by a joint examination of the files to determine whether and, if so, to what extent the Society satisfies the said conditions. The circular issued by the International Committee to announce its recognition of the newly-formed Society shall mention the examination carried out in conjunction with the League. Similarly the League Secretariat shall draw the attention to this examination when it proposes the admission of the new Society.

If after detailed examination there should remain a divergency of opinion as to the fulfillment of any specific condition for recognition or admission, the Standing Commission shall be consulted.

IX. Structure and activities of National Societies

The two Institutions shall continue to study jointly the Statutes, structure, organization and activities of National Societies and, if applicable, to make the recommendations required.

X. Protection of the integrity of National Societies

The League and the International Committee may act jointly or separately in this sphere. In the latter case, the two Institutions shall consult each other.

XI. Relations with international institutions

In their relations with the United Nations and the other international institutions, the ICRC and the League shall continue to take counsel together with a view to adopting, if possible, a common attitude so as to maintain the unity and independence of the Red Cross.

XII. Covering of the administrative expenses of the Standing Commission

The International Committee and the League shall each continue to be responsible for one-half of the administrative expenses incurred by the Standing Commission.

XIII. Amendments to the Statutes of the International Committee and to the Constitution of the League

Neither the ICRC nor the League shall amend its Statutes or Constitution on a point related to their respective spheres of competence without giving the other an opportunity to express an opinion on the contemplated amendment.

XIV. Liaison between the governing bodies of the International Committee and the League

As a complement to Article VIII of the Statutes of the International Red Cross it is anticipated that representatives of each Institution should be invited to meetings of the governing bodies of the other whenever a question of common interest is being discussed. Representatives so invited may take part in the discussions, but shall not be entitled to vote.

At their joint meetings the two Institutions shall regularly keep each other informed on the broad outlines of their respective activities.

In addition there shall be regular contacts between those in charge of the various sectors of activity, in particular relief and information.

The two Institutions shall inform each other on the missions they are planning and on the important visitors they receive.

XV. Interpretation of the Agreement and cooperation

Whenever there might be a conflict between the spheres of competence or a need to interpret the present Agreement, the two Institutions shall determine with all speed which one of them shall assume responsibility for the action or shall reach agreement on the ways and means of possible cooperation. In the latter case, they shall continue to consult each other during the whole duration of the action, both at the headquarters of the two Institutions and in the field.

XVI. Application of the Agreement

The present Agreement, which replaces the Agreement concluded on 8th December 1951, shall come into force as soon as it has been ratified by the International Committee and by the Board of Governors in the name of the League and the National Societies.

The withdrawal of one of the Parties to the present Agreement cannot in itself be considered as affecting the friendly relations uniting the two Institutions. In such an eventuality advance notice of at least six months should be given.

Done and signed in two copies, at Geneva, on 25th April 1969.

For the League
of Red Cross Societies:
José Barroso-Chavez
Henrik Beer

For the International Committee
of the Red Cross:
Jacques Freymond
Jean Pictet

Appendix C
Political Prisoners and Law

Global, regional, and national law—taken together or separately—fails to give us a clear legal definition of "political prisoner." This is unlikely to change, not only in the near future but thereafter as well.

GENERAL INTERNATIONAL LAW

In all of general international law, the most specific agreement pertaining to political prisoners was a bilateral agreement between the ICRC and the government of Greece in 1969.[1] Under the terms of this agreement, the ICRC was granted, for one year, access by right to all places of detention in Greece where were held persons who were accused of political delicts as defined in Greek law, or who were classified as administrative deportees (that is, detained under administrative orders on Greek islands). While the scope of the agreement was generally clear, there being little difficulty in determining what individuals were thereby covered, the bilateral and so far unique nature of this agreement limits its significance in providing a definition of political prisoner that is globally valid.

There is a type of general international law that has been more widely accepted in the practice of states, that refers to political crime, and that provides interpretation by national courts of what "political crime" means. This is the extradition treaty, which regulates the return of an individual from the state-in-possession to the state-in-pursuit, except for those who have committed political crime. These political fugitives—or potential political prisoners—may be given political asylum by the state-in-possession. Unfortunately, national court interpretation of these treaties, as well as diplomatic practice, does not tell us precisely what is a political crime and who is a potential political prisoner.

There is no extradition treaty that defines political crime.[2] Moreover, national judicial traditions vary in attempts to define political crime among the different nations, and within the same nation at different times in history. Many courts agree that a "pure political crime" is one in which a person commits a crime with the expressed intention of destroying or changing the government by illegal means. Thus an attempt to blow up Parliament is considered by many an example of a pure political crime.[3] The major problem for courts has been how to characterize mixed crime: crime that has both "political" and "common" elements. How is one to view bank robbery—a common crime—when "political" factors are also present? Different courts have used different approaches to this question. At times some courts have tried to fathon the predominant motivation of the individuals. At other times other courts have raised the question of whether the mixed crime was incidental to a political struggle—i.e., was the bank robbery part of an ongoing struggle for political power among organized groups? Other courts at other times have tried to assess the impact of the mixed crime: was the major impact "political" or not, in the eyes of the court?[4]

The problem has been that courts have followed the conventional wisdom that has existed at a particular time and have defined political crime according to what the Executive Branch, if not the people, wanted. When individual anarchists seemed to plague the Anglo-Saxon countries, Anglo-Saxon courts raised the standard of participation in an organized movement. Only those committing crime directly or incidentally related to a struggle among organized groups could be said to have committed political crime. Thus only these types were eligible for asylum as political fugitives. Individuals who were not part of a group who committed crime, whatever their motive, were common criminals, to be returned through extradition for regular prosecution.[5] Likewise, Swiss courts, which had long emphasized the motivation of individuals in determining political crime, altered that approach when individuals from Yugoslavia hijacked a plane to Switzerland. The motivation of the individuals was not "political" in the sense of trying to discredit the Tito regime; the individuals wanted to change their personal situation. By traditional Swiss judicial standards, these individuals had *not* committed political crime and thus were subject to extradition back to Yugoslavia under the Swiss-Yugoslav extradition treaty. But Swiss Courts granted political asylum under the political crime clause of that treaty, using arguments that one writer has called "ad hoc" and "political."[6]

In sum, extradition treaties are widely used in international law, refer explicitly to political crime, refer implicitly to political fugitives who can be considered potential political prisoners, but do not provide us with a consistent definition of who these individuals are. The trend in court interpretation is that those who illegally seek to change the government, or those who commit common crime with the intent to make an impact on governmental policy, are political criminals. But there has been much vacillation on these points.

It is relevant to note that extradition treaties pertain only to the fugitive—the individual who has escaped factual control of the state which seeks him. Hence law follows factual possibilities in regulating what states will allow to be regulated. Extradition treaties do not attempt to regulate an individual under the factual control of the state that seeks to punish him.

Another type of general international law—refugee law—is similar in that it also seeks to regulate the individual who has escaped factual control of the pursuing government. But whereas extradition treaties treat the political fugitive as one who has committed political crime, refugee law treats the political fugitive as one who has fled a well-founded fear of political persecution. The key variable for refugee law is not prospect of political prosecution but prospect of political persecution.

The 1951 Refugee Convention defines an international refugee as one who:

> As a result of events . . . and owing to well founded fear of being persecuted for reasons of race, religion, nationality, membership of a particular social group or political opinion, is outside the country of his nationality and is unable or, owing to such fear, is unwilling to avail himself of the protection of that country.

Therefore if an individual fears persecution and is thus unwilling to submit to the laws of his national government, he can seek international protection and assistance from the United Nations High Commissioner for Refugees. If the High Commissioner's office finds the fear of persecution to be well founded, the individual is legally classified as an international refugee under the Convention, and the state-in-possession becomes legally obligated not to return the refugee to his original state.[7]

Refugee law and extradition law reflect the two dominant legal schools of thought about what constitutes a political fugitive—the potential political prisoner: one who is the target of political persecution, or one who has committed political crime.

Now the idea of political crime, under extradition treaties, arose because of the view that all governments shared an interest in prosecuting those who challenged governmental security—and that such prosecution could never be considered persecution. But the original purpose was turned upside down. The treaties came to provide for the nonreturn of those regarded as security threats to government. In a world of ideological conflict, there arose the idea of not returning the individual who had threatened the security of an enemy. And in a multicultural world, there arose varying views of what was legitimate prosecution for a security threat, and what was persecution stemming from an exaggerated sense of security needs.

The 1969 ICRC-Greek Accord, dealing not with fugitives but with individuals under the control of the punishing state, bypassed the persecution-prosecution distinction. An individual viewed by the Greek government as a threat to the state—directly or indirectly—fell under the jurisdiction of the agreement, whether indicted or detained by administrative order. The ICRC was not called upon to judge whether the government's detention was prosecution or persecution; this judgment the ICRC consistently seeks to avoid.

There are similarities between this 1969 agreement and the 1973 Paris Accords on the future of Vietnam. The "Prisoner and Detainee" protocol to these accords, patterned on the 1954 Geneva Accords, also seeks to reach into a state and to regulate detainees under the control of a punishing state. With regard to the territory of South Vietnam, this protocol states:

> The term 'civilian internees' is understood to mean all persons who, having in any way contributed to the political and armed struggle between the two parties, have been arrested for that reason and have been kept in detention by either party during the period of hostilities.

The protocol goes on to state that even if an individual has been tried and sentenced under national law, but falls under the terms of the protocol, he shall be returned to the other party according to the rest of the protocol.

While the wording of the protocol is not as clear as legal scholars would want, the intent was clearly to regulate those individuals detained by the authorities in Saigon as well as by the Provisional Revolutionary Government (Viet Cong), whether these individuals had taken armed action or had been involved in the struggle in some other way. There was no attempt to raise the distinction between prosecution and persecution.

The meaning of the protocol cannot be judged through observation of its implementation, for it was not implemented.[8]

It can be noted at this point that individuals detained in connection with a civil war have been theoretically regulated by Common Article 3 of the 1949 Geneva Conventions. This article is noteworthy because it is the most widely accepted piece of international law under which states agree to treat their own nationals in conformity with international standards. To be sure, these community standards have been "affectionate generalities."[9] Precise obligations have been lacking. But at the Geneva Conferences on Humanitarian Law in Armed Conflicts in the mid-1970's, legislation has been proposed that would more precisely regulate those "detained by reason of the conflict." The commentary on this subject, written by the ICRC, indicates that such legal wording would pertain not only to conventional forces, but to guerrillas, terrorists, and even noncombatants who are alleged to have some role in the noninternational armed conflict.[10] Should this draft legislation become law, many political prisoners in a civil-war situation would be covered, but without use of that exact term. Hence the trend in the law of armed conflict is similar to the 1973 Paris Accords and the 1969 ICRC-Greek Accord: political prisoners would be governed by the law, but vague terminology would be employed—terminology that did not raise the prosecution-persecution distinction.

And as long as we are speaking of legal theory, we should note that under the Nuremberg Principles, it is an international crime—a crime against humanity— to commit:

> Murder, extermination, enslavement, deportation and other inhuman acts done against any civilian population, or persecutions on political, racial or religious grounds, when such acts are done or such persecutions are carried on in execution or in connection with any crime against peace or any war crime.[11]

Hence according to this Nuremberg Principle (number six), political persecution and inhumane actions against the civilian population become international delicts when part of aggressive war or a war crime (e.g., a violation of the laws of war). It is relevant to our inquiry to note the subject matter supposedly regulated. But it is not reasonable to expect much actual implementation of legal protection under Nuremberg Principle six. Application of this principle depends upon an accompanying finding of a crime against peace (e.g., waging an aggressive war) or a crime of war (e.g., taking no prisoners). Given the difficulty in making an authoritative decision in these matters, it is not reasonable to expect much, if any, actual legal protection for political prisoners in connection with an international armed conflict.[12]

What we find in all of this general international law is attempted legal regulation for persons detained in relation to some sort of political conflict; lacking are consistent wording and clear interpretations. Even where international law has been extensively interpreted by national courts, the resulting understanding of political crime in relation to extradition is badly jumbled. Since 1945, there has been increasing attention to individuals detained in connection with political conflict, and the more violent the conflict the greater the attempt at international legal regulation. This is borne out by the 1973 Paris Accords, Common Article 3 of the 1949 Geneva Conventions, and the Nuremberg Principles. But the 1951 Refugee Convention and the 1969 ICRC-Greek Accord cover situations of lesser violence. Under some law the commission of political crime is controlling for obtaining international legal protection, with political crime being defined as an attack against the security of the government. Many courts look to the motivation of the individual as a controlling variable. In other cases, it is the governmental view which is controlling: if the Greek government in 1970, or the Saigon government in 1974, or a party to the new law of armed conflict pertaining to civil wars regards an individual as a threat to the government, then such an individual falls under the law in question. On the other hand, in the refugee law and the Nuremberg Principles, it is persecution, inter alia, which triggers legal protection—persecution as defined by some third party.

Beyond this confused point, we can look to two further sources of law: regional international and national law. What we find is more oblique references to political prisoners. We also find more confusion.

REGIONAL INTERNATIONAL LAW

Among many pieces of international regional law for Western Europe, there is the 1951 European Convention on Human Rights. This Convention not only establishes regional standards for human rights but also creates supervisory machinery. Under Article 15, many of these human rights standards may be abrogated during times of "war or other public emergency threatening the life of the nation." As a result of this article, the European Commission has had to deal with several cases in which the right of a government to detain individuals under special laws, and to treat individuals in an unusually severe way, has been challenged by parties to the Convention. While the Convention makes no mention of political prisoners, the individuals in question have been commonly referred to as political prisoners. This was the case when British detention was challenged in Cyprus in the 1950's, when Greek detention was challenged in the 1960's, and when British detention was the subject of litigation in the 1970's in Northern Ireland. In all three cases the ICRC was visiting the detainees as political prisoners.

In the two cases involving the United Kingdom, there was no clear-cut legal judgment as to whether Britain had violated the Convention. The Cypriot case was settled out of court, and while the case concerning Northern Ireland drags on there is widespread opinion that the regional institutions will avoid a definitive judgment and wait for other forces to settle matters. In the Greek case, the Council of Ministers made a judgment that Greece had, among other things, invoked Article 15 without justification and had employed torture as an administrative practice (see Chapter 3). Sanctions were not imposed.

These cases out of regional international law, as well as others arising under the European Convention, do not speak directly to the question of what is a political prisoner. Indeed, the practice under the Convention indicates that human rights can be protected to some extent without recourse to the term. Yet the attempts to implement the Convention also indicate that individuals are detained for dubious reasons and treated severely, even in the Western democracies; that the regional supervisory machinery works slowly and incompletely; and that while this regional law has been accepted by some dozen and a half states, it is not necessarily the best approach to the problem of protecting individuals from their own governments. Even with this regional law, the ICRC has remained active in the region visiting political prisoners.[13]

While regional international law sheds virtually no light on the question of what is a political prisoner, national law sheds a glimmer here and there, but the overall impression derived from a comparative examination is one of darkness.

NATIONAL LAW

A number of national constitutions or national penal codes have set aside sections in which a security or "political" crime is defined.[14] Thus these national laws run parallel to extradition treaties in implicitly considering as a political prisoner one who has illegally threatened the security of the government. This legal practice, however, is on the decline. While the idea of political crime was written into national law by the European states in the nineteenth century, and extended to their colonies, this practice has been almost erased in the twentieth century. There are few constitutions and/or penal codes that make reference to political crime in the sense of illegally attacking the government. For obvious reasons there are no national provisions defining political prisoners in terms of governmental persecution.

Now in addition to national laws defining political delicts in terms of the threat to governmental security, at least in the past, one can also discover what may be called sociopolitical crimes in the laws of a few Latin-American states. At times, Peru, for example, has had a section of its laws classified as governing crimes against the social structure of the state—i.e., violation of land reform laws.

Other states in Latin America, such as Chile and Uruguay, have special laws for a "state of siege," which is a situation short of civil war but not a situation of normality. A state of siege may be invoked for reasons of economics as well as violence. Special laws apply, and detention under these special laws is different from normal detention. Some observers refer to detainees during a state of siege as political prisoners.

Almost all national constitutions contain some sort of "emergency clause" during which exceptional detention practices, such as the suspension of habeas corpus, are permitted.[15]

Beyond these "special" laws, most of which directly relate to state security, there are other laws whose application is said to constitute persecution. Typical of this type of national law is the one linked to indirect or long-term security. The Soviet Union has a law making it a crime to defame the nation. Greece has had a law making it a crime to undermine the morale of the armed forces.

Moreover, any national law can be used to persecute, and thus the types of national law giving rise to charges of persecution are beyond tabulation. This is because almost any law, ostensibly legitimate in the sense of being within the accepted realm of governmental regulation, can be used for ends which are not generally accepted. Tax laws can be implemented against only members of an opposition political group. Traffic laws or housing codes can be implemented only against selected groups. A former attorney general of the United States made it clear that law enforcement officials use the law in this way:

> There is enough play at the joints of our existing criminal law—enough flexibility—so that if we really felt that we had to pick up the leaders of a violent uprising, we could. We would find something to charge them with and we would be able to hold them that way for a while.[16]

It is not only under prospect of "violent uprising" that law is used to detain suspected individuals, regardless of the original intent of the law; and it is not only "for a while" that suspected persons are so detained.

This is the major reason that national law provides so little insight into the definition of a political prisoner. The Saigon Government, fearing that Mr. X is either pro-Viet Cong or simply neutral, detains him under a provision of national law requiring all citizens to register currency transactions with a governmental agency. Subsequently the government can argue that Mr. X is simply a common criminal who has violated regular national law, and the government has the prima facie evidence of the nature of its legal charge to back it up. There is no overt evidence of persecution, and a security law is not involved.

A political prisoner, therefore, may be one detained for a security offense, or simply as a result of persecution stemming from realpolitik or partisan politics, but the law, in general, does not tell us which is which, or how to distinguish either from other categories of detention.

Appendix D
1969 Accord between the ICRC and the Greek Government Pertaining to Political Prisoners

VISITS TO PLACES OF DETENTION IN GREECE

The International Committee of the Red Cross has just concluded an agreement with the Greek Government under the terms of which the delegates of the International Committee are authorized to visit Greek political detainees and are allowed greater facilities to assist detainees' families.

Since May 1967 the International Committee of the Red Cross has visited a number of detention centres in Greece, but the authorizations granted its delegates were concessions without any obligation.

We give below the text of the agreement which places these activities on the basis they were previously lacking.

AGREEMENT BETWEEN THE GOVERNMENT OF THE KINGDOM OF HELLAS AND THE INTERNATIONAL COMMITTEE OF THE RED CROSS

The Government of the Kingdom of Hellas and the International Committee of the Red Cross, resolved to serve the cause of humanity and justice, have agreed as follows:

Visits to Administrative Deportees

ICRC delegates and their accompanying interpreters shall have access to all places where administrative deportees are permanently or temporarily held, namely: camps for deportees, places of temporary detention pending transfer, infirmaries and hospitals.

Visits shall be subject to the same conditions as heretofore and as set forth in previous reports.

Visits to Persons Accused or Condemned and Detained by the Judiciary

The delegates of the International Committee of the Red Cross and their accompanying interpreters shall have access to all prisons and other premises within the country where persons accused of or condemned for political offences are detained.

Visits shall be subject to the same conditions as heretofore and as set forth in previous reports.

Visits to Police Stations

The delegates of the International Committee of the Red Cross and their accompanying interpretors shall have access to all police stations where people are temporarily detained pending preliminary enquiries into political offences, so that they may form a personal opinion on the state of the premises and the conditions of detention.

Enquiries

The delegates of the International Committee of the Red Cross may, when so requested by families, ask the police authorities for information concerning persons arrested and detained whenever the families themselves have been unable to obtain such information direct from the authorities. The information requested shall, in particular, concern:

—the place of detention,

—the general nature of the offence,

—detention conditions,

—facilities for visits by members of the family or by the ICRC delegates.

Family Interviews

The International Committee of the Red Cross may continue to receive detainees' relatives to exchange family news.

Welfare of Detainees' Families

The International Committee of the Red Cross may undertake one or more welfare work projects for the benefit of the indigent families of persons who, for any reason whatsoever, have been detained for more than two years.

All such activities will be undertaken in association and co-operation with the Ministry of Social Welfare and the Hellenic Red Cross.

Assistance shall consist of the provision of clothing, food and pharmaceutical products. A large part of such supplies shall be purchased locally.

The International Committee of the Red Cross may, through the relevant authorities, also provide indigent families which have not so far been able to visit their detained relatives with travel tickets to enable them to do so.

ICRC Delegation Organization

The delegation shall have offices for its secretariat and for the purpose of interviewing families. The appointment of the delegates of the International Committee of the Red Cross and office staff shall be subject to the agreement of the relevant authorities.

The Government of the Kingdom of Hellas shall assign a senior civil servant as "liaison officer" with the International Committee of the Red Cross. The delegation shall apply to him to settle routine problems which may arise during the mission of the International Committee of the Red Cross and to arrange any meetings which may be required.

Statements and Publications

No statement or publication concerning the foregoing and the ICRC mission in general shall be made without prior consultation between the Government of the Kingdom of Hellas and the International Committee of the Red Cross.

The International Committee of the Red Cross will, for its part, issue from its headquarters in Geneva periodical press releases giving the names of places visited, the dates and conditions under which the visits were made (interviews without witnesses, etc.), the names of the delegates, and mentioning that reports on the visits will, as customary, be made to the detaining authorities.

These press releases will give no appreciation on detention conditions and the treatment of detainees.

News of other activities of the International Committee of the Red Cross in the country will also be given in these releases.

Reports on Visits

As usual the reports on visits shall be sent solely to the detaining authorities. The Government of the Kingdom of Hellas will abstain from issuing any publication of a part only of the reports or from making any public statement on extracts of the reports.

As in the past, and in keeping with customary practice, the International Committee of the Red Cross and its delegates shall not from any judgment on the reasons for internment and detention.

Application and Duration of the Agreement

The present agreement shall become effective on 3 November 1969. It shall be valid for one year thereafter. It shall be tacitly renewed from year to year unless cancelled by one of the contracting parties.

Appendix E
ICRC Statement on the Nature of Its Visits to Detention Places Involving Prisoners of War

THE ICRC AND THE PROTECTION OF PRISONERS OF WAR

Before the existence of the Red Cross and the Geneva Conventions, any soldier fallen into enemy hands was entirely at his captor's mercy. Now the Third 1949 Geneva Convention relative to the treatment of prisoners of war—recognized by 133 States—clearly lays down how he must be treated during captivity.

In order for prisoners of war to be protected effectively, their treatment must be open to supervision. It is for that reason that Article 126 of the Third Geneva Convention authorizes Protecting Power representatives to go wherever prisoners of war are held. The delegates of the ICRC have the same prerogative.

How do ICRC delegates carry out a visit to prisoners of war? What does their report cover? What use is made of that report?

Source: ICRC, *The ICRC in Action: Information Notes* no. 1926 (18 January 1973): 1–3.

The visit procedure includes a preliminary talk with the camp commandant, a general visit in the company of representatives of the authorities, talks in private with prisoners, and a final discussion with the commandant and his staff.

The preliminary talk enables the delegates to establish confidence and explain the nature of their visit which is in no way an inspection or an enquiry. Its purpose is to provide relief and comfort to prisoners of war and to help the detaining authorities to discharge their treaty obligations.

During the initial contact with the commandant, the delegates note the figures and the details of the camp organization, which are included in their report: number and nationality of prisoners, appropriations for food, medical staff, family visits, mail, deaths, escapes, transfers and other information which varies from case to case.

The general visit of the camp, usually with the commandant or his adjutant, should permit the delegates to see all premises occupied by the prisoners and to form an idea of the material conditions of captivity. They examine the general appearance of the prisoners of war, the degree of occupation of their quarters, the sanitary facilities available to them, the kitchen, and so forth. The doctor-delegates give their attention to the medical facilities, the running of the hospital or infirmary, and the prisoners' state of health. During this tour of the camp, the delegates interview prisoners. Their right to talk in private with the prisoners is laid down in the Third Geneva Convention.

The delegates discuss with the prisoners' representatives and also with prisoners of their own choosing. They may interview any prisoners wishing to make personal requests. In the course of these talks, the prisoners describe detention conditions and air their complaints.

Although delegates are in no position to carry out a thorough investigation into serious incidents arising out of friction between prisoners and guards or among the prisoners themselves—and such incidents do sometimes cause deaths or serious injuries—they can record the prisoners' version of the events and in some cases conduct a medical examination.

During the final interview—the last phase of the visit—the delegates convey their impressions to the commandant and ask him for his comments and explanations. They endeavour to settle problems on the spot, wherever reference to higher authority can be avoided.

Where incidents have occurred, the commandant's version—like that of the prisoners—will be included in the delegates' report to the ICRC. If the event was sufficiently serious, the delegates demand that the Detaining Power institute an official enquiry, in accordance with Article 121 of the Third Convention, and report to the ICRC.

The delegates' report on their visit, containing information supplied by the authorities and by the prisoners, as well as the delegates' own findings, is sent to the ICRC for scrutiny and forwarding to the Detaining Power and the prisoners' own Government.

If a government wishes to publish reports, it must publish in full, without any change, all reports on a series of visits, and not merely isolated reports. The ICRC has always strongly deplored the use of its reports in disputes which cannot but disserve the persons which the ICRC seeks to protect.

Notes

INTRODUCTION

1. Jacques Freymond, "International Red Cross and Peace," *International Review of the Red Cross* no. 638 (February 1972), p. 72. See also Freymond, *Guerres, Révolutions, la Croix-Rouge* (Geneva: Collection HEI Presses, 1976).

2. James E. Bond, *The Rules of Riot* (Princeton: Princeton University Press, 1974), p. 133.

CHAPTER 1

1. The official history of the ICRC, covering events to 1912, is by Pierre Boissier, *De Solférino á Tshoushima: Histoire du Comité International de la Croix-Rouge* (Paris: Plon, 1963). There is no English edition.

2. Max Huber, *The Red Cross: Principles and Problems* (Geneva: ICRC n.d.).

3. Hans G. Knitel, "Les Delegations du Comité International de la Croix-Rouge", *Etudes et Travaux de l'Institut de Hautes Etudes Internationales,* No. 5 (Geneva, 1967). Lyman C. White, *International Non-Governmental Organizations* (New Brunswick, N.J.: Rutgers University Press, 1951). *Yearbook of International Organizations* (Brussels: Union of International Associations, biennial).

4. For a brief survey of attitudes toward the ICRC, see Richard Magat, *As Others See Us: Views on Red Cross* (Geneva: Red Cross, 1975), pp. 42–45; staff paper, *Red Cross at National Level—A Profile* (Geneva: Red Cross, 1975), p. 63 and passim.

5. Oran Young, *The Intermediaries: Third Parties in International Crises* (Princeton, N.J.: Princeton University Press, 1967), p. 109.

6. See one of the few analytical books on the ICRC written by an insider, Jacques Moreillon, *Le Comité International de la Croix-Rouge et la protection des détenus politiques* (Lausanne: L'age d'homme, 1973).

7. See David P. Forsythe, "The Red Cross as Transnational Actor," *International Organization* (Autumn 1977), for further analysis on this point.

275

8. G. I. A. D. Draper, "The People's Republic of China and the Red Cross", in Jerome Alan Cohen, ed., *China's Practice of International Law: Some Case Studies* (Cambridge: Harvard University Press, 1972), p. 346.

9. Ali Sinjari, Member of the Central Committee of the Democratic Party of Kurdistan and the envoy of the party in Europe, "Report To The International Committee of the Red Cross and the League of Red Cross Societies", n.d. [spring, 1974], mimeo. Obtained from ICRC.

10. See Draper, "The People's Republic of China and the Red Cross."

11. Mao's government did give a transit visa to an ICRC delegate to enter China in order to travel to North Korea during the early 1950's. But the Chinese did not otherwise help the ICRC in its unsuccessful effort to enter North Korea. In general, Chinese attitudes toward the ICRC throughout the 1950's and 1960's were discourteous in the extreme.

12. Henri Coursier, *La Croix-Rouge Internationale* (Paris: Presses Universitaires de France, 1962), p. 69, and Huber, *The Red Cross,* p. 54.

13. "The Twenty-Second International Conference of the Red Cross . . . considers that if the statutes of a National Society cease to be in conformity with the conditions of recognition and admission, that Society will expose itself to re-examination." XXIIᵉ Conférence Internationale de la Croix-Rouge, Teheran, Novembre 1973, *Résolutions* (Geneva: ICRC) p. 5 [unofficial translation of the French text by the author].

14. This point is made in the reports by the Joint Committee for the Reappraisal of the Red Cross.

15. For a personal account of ICRC involvement in the Spanish Civil War and other involvements in the 1930's and 1940's see Marcel Junod, *Warrior Without Weapons* (London: Jonathan Cape, 1951).

16. See E. H. Beuhrig, *The UN and the Palestinian Refugees* (Bloomington: Indiana University Press, 1971); and David P. Forsythe, "UNRWA, the Palestine Refugees, and World Politics, 1949–1969," *International Organization* 25, no. 1 (1971): 26–45.

17. See *International Red Cross Handbook,* 11th edition (Geneva: ICRC, 1971).

18. Resolutions of the Conference do not create legal obligation for states attending and voting at the Conference. As for the authority of Conference resolutions within the Red Cross movement, the statutes of the International Red Cross state, "The International Conference shall have power to take decisions within the limits of the present Statutes, make recommendations and express wishes [Art. 2, 1] . . . It may assign mandates to the International Committee and to the League . . . [Art 2, 3]" But those statutes also state (Art. 6, 1), "The International Committee of the Red Cross is an independent institution, governed by its own Statutes." Therefore "Red Cross law" is confused on the legal status of Conference resolutions. Conference resolutions appear to have limited impact on anyone's behavior.

19. Statutes of the International Red Cross, Art. 10, 2.

20. Ibid., para. 4.

21. ICRC, *The ICRC and the Hungarian Crisis* (Geneva: ICRC, 1957).

CHAPTER 2

1. Bond, *The Rules of Riot,* pp. 186–87.

2. U.S. Congress, House, Committee on Foreign Affairs, *American Prisoners of War in Southeast Asia, 1971,* 92nd Cong., 1st Sess., 1971, p. 421.

3. Jean Pictet, *Red Cross Principles* (Geneva: ICRC, 1956); and Jean Pictet, *The Doctrine of the Red Cross* (Geneva: ICRC, 1962).

4. In addition to Pictet, *Red Cross Principles,* see Huber, *The Red Cross.*

5. See Huber, *The Red Cross,* in the French version, containing a chapter not found in the English: *La Pensée et L'Action de la Croix-Rouge* (Geneva: ICRC, 1954), pp. 306–8. Huber finally tends to use the two as synonymns. Cf. Pictet, *Principles.* Huber at one point suggested that "neutrality" was not a very useful term to use in conjunction with the Red Cross (*The Red Cross,* p. 63). The reader will note that the present author avoids that term in reference to Red Cross philosophy.

6. ICRC writing on neutrality does not mention the conception of neutrality held by Dag Hammarskjöld, which holds that neutrality applies to motivation. If an action is undertaken on the basis of a motivation directed toward principles rather than power advantage, for Hammarskjöld it was neutral

action. His principles were those of the UN Charter. This thinking could be applied to Red Cross principles as well. For a concise review of Hammarskjöld's thinking, along with citations of the relevant literature, see Leland M. Goodrich, "Hammarskjöld, The UN, and the Office of the Secretary-General," *International Organization* 28, no. 3 (Summer 1974): 467–83.

By comparison, some writers apparently assume that Red Cross neutrality means having a balanced impact. See, for example, Thiery Hentsch, *Face au blocus: La Croix-Rouge Internationale dans la Nigeria en guerre* (Geneva: Hautes Etudes Internationales, 1973).

Still others appear to say that what is neutral is what is agreed upon as not affecting power struggles. See especially Jean Pictet, *The Principles of International Humanitarian Law* (Geneva: ICRC, 1967) Cf. his *Red Cross Principles.*

7. This is clearly demonstrated in a short, thematic history of the Red Cross; see Ian Reid, *The Evolution of the Red Cross,* Background Paper No. 2 (Geneva: Joint Committee for the Reappraisal of the Red Cross, 1975).

8. For example, it is argued that Red Cross humanitarianism should lead to an attack on the evils that cause suffering, to "prevent" them and have them "eliminated." Just how this position is reconciled with the ICRC's not raising questions about the causes of detention but only the conditions of detention is not very clear.

One Red Cross commentator argued that "neutrality . . . never determines [Red Cross] behavior towards the human beings who suffer." How this position is reconciled with the ICRC's acting on the basis of the consent of public authorities, and *not* acting when that consent is not given, is not very clear either.

9. This was a clear finding of the Joint Committee for the Reappraisal of the Red Cross. See Donald D. Tansley, *Study Director's Final Report: An Agenda for the Red Cross* (Geneva: Red Cross, 1975). It is a characteristic long true of individuals in the Red Cross movement. See Huber, *The Red Cross,* pp. 65–66.

10. A public authority can be a state or a legal divison within a state, an international organization, or a de facto public authority such as a liberation movement in actual control of people or territory. Thus the Ian Smith regime is a public authority in Rhodesia, whatever its position in British or international law. The National Liberation Movement of South Vietnam was a public authority in much of South Vietnam during the Indochina War, whatever its legal status. The UN Organization in the Congo was a public authority during much of the Congolese Civil War.

11. See Evan Luard, "The Origins of International Concern over Human Rights," in Evan Luard, ed., *The International Protection of Human Rights* (London: Thames & Hudson, 1967), pp. 7–21.

12. The clash between state claims to jurisdiction over individuals and the claims of international organizations is well treated in William D. Coplin, "International Law and Assumptions about The State System", *World Politics* 17, no. 3 (1965): 615–34.

13. See William Korey, "The Key to Human Rights—Implementation", *International Conciliation* no. 570 (November, 1968); and Vernon Van Dyke, *The United States, Human Rights, and World Community* (New York: Oxford University Press, 1970).

14. See Roger S. Clark, *A United Nations High Commissioner for Human Rights* (The Hague: Nijhoff, 1972), especially at pp. 150–51 and the literature cited there.

15. A concise overview of the European institutions is found in Council of Europe, "Note on the Results Achieved under the European Convention on Human Rights 1953–1972," B (72) 99, Oct., 1972. Regarding the Inter-American Commission, see Anna P. Schreiber, *The Inter-American Commission on Human Rights* (Leyden: Sijthoff, 1970). For a global perspective, see John Carey, "The International Legal Order on Human Rights," in C. E. Black and Richard Falk, eds., *The Future of the International Legal Order,* vol. 3 (Princeton: Princeton University Press, 1972).

16. Jacques Freymond, "The International Committee of the Red Cross at Work", *International Review of the Red Cross* no. 98 (May 1969): 231.

17. See ICRC, *The ICRC and the United Nations* (Geneva: ICRC, 1951). Cf. Robert Riggs, *US/UN: Foreign Policy and International Organization* (New York: Appleton-Century-Crofts, 1971), pp. 64–65; and Sydney D. Bailey, *Prohibitions and Restraints in War* (New York: Oxford University Press, 1972), p. 131.

18. ICRC relations to the UN and other international organizations are similar to the Swiss government's relations: technical cooperation while avoiding debates and the taking of instructions. See Hans Haug, *Les Rélations de la Suisse avec les Nations Unies* (Berne: Paul Haupt, 1972).

19. On the utility of UN peacekeeping as an intermediate action, see Lynn D. Miller, *Organizing Mankind: An Analysis of Contemporary International Organization* (Boston: Holbrook Press, 1973), p. 132.

20. Pictet, *The Doctrine of the Red Cross,* p. 5.

21. Comité International de la Croix-Rouge, *L'Activité du CICR en faveur des civils détenus dans les Camps de Concentration en Allemagne, 1939–1945* (Geneva; CICR, 1947).

22. This section first appeared in slightly different form in my article, "The Red Cross as Transnational Actor." The footnotes have been removed and it is reprinted by permission of the publisher of *International Organization.*

23. Huber, *The Red Cross,* p. 168.

CHAPTER 3

1. Thomas St. G. Bissell, "The International Committee of the Red Cross and the Protection of Human Rights," *Revue des Droits de l'Homme* no. 1 (1968): 255–74.

2. *Saturday Review/World,* 15 June 1974, p. 19.

3. The most definitive work on this subject to date is Moreillon, *Le CICR et détenus politiques.* The only criticism of this book is that, with the benefit of hindsight, the ICRC's efforts toward political prisoners are made to appear more calculating and systematic than the actual history of that involvement reveals.

4. ICRC figures, obtained through interviews, and see also *Neue Zurcher Zeitung,* 31 March 1974, p. 6.

5. Claude Pilloud, "Protection of Political Detainees," statement to the panel on humanitarian problems and international law of the American Society of International Law, 15 October 1970, mimeo.

6. One who has some understanding of a situation from other sources can piece together fragments of information from the ICRC's publications. But if one has little or no information on a situation, ICRC publications are of little use in clarifying what is occurring. Exceptions to this ICRC policy of releasing little specific and clear information are covered subsequently.

7. The types of reasoning in support of requested access used by the ICRC, and the responses of governments, are reviewed in Moreillon, *Le CICR et détenus politiques.*

8. Amnesty International estimates that at least 65 states tolerate or officially use torture; see Amnesty International, *Report on Torture* (New York: Farrar, Straus and Giroux, 1975).

9. See especially the analytical report, Great Britain, Parliament, *Papers by Command,* 4887–4929, "Report of the Committee of Privy Counsellors appointed to consider authorized procedures for the interrogation of persons suspected of terrorism," March 1972, pp. 1–23.

10. Jacques Freymond, "Face à la guerre totale," 1973, mimeo (my translation).

11. T. R. Gurr, *Why Men Rebel* (Princeton: Princeton University Press, 1970).

12. While the literature on Indochina is voluminous, two works have influenced this analysis: Frances Fitzgerald, *Fire in the Lake: The Vietnamese and the Americans in Vietnam* (Boston: Little, Brown, 1972) and John T. McAlister, *Viet Nam: The Origins of Revolution* (New York: Knopf, 1969).

13. U.S. Congress, House, Committee on Foreign Affairs, *The Treatment of Political Prisoners in South Vietnam by the Government of the Republic of South Vietnam,* 93rd Cong., 1st Sess., 13 September 1973.

14. U.S., Department of State, *Human Rights in the Republic of Korea,* Special Report no. 5, September, 1974.

15. *New York Times,* 26 December 1973, p. 12.

16. *International Herald Tribune,* 7 August 1974, p. 4.

17. Great Britain, "Privy Counsellors report."

18. See Riggs, *US/UN,* p. 54.

19. Classic examples are: "Study of the right of everyone to be free from arbitrary arrest, detention and exile," UN Doc. E/CN.4/826/Rev.1 (UN Sales No. 65.XIV.2, 1974, and "Study of the right of arrested persons to communicate . . . ," UN Doc. E/CN.4/996, 23 January 1969. Both of these documents were excellent studies; both were buried under governmental apathy.

20. The UN Commission on Crime Prevention and Control has produced the UN Standard Minimum Rules for detention. The Commission is not empowered to supervise the implementation of the rules, which are supposed to govern national penal institutions. It is clear states do not pay much attention to the rules. United Nations, General Assembly, *Supplements,* ''The Standard Minimum Rules for the Treatment of Prisoners in the Light of Recent Developments in the Correctional Field,'' (A/Conf. 43/3), 1970.

21. The Inter-American Commission on Human Rights was particularly active in trying to protect political prisoners in the 1965 violence in the Dominican Republic.

22. Keith Legg, *Politics in Modern Greece* (Stanford: Stanford University Press, 1969), pp. 226–45. See also U.S. Congress, Senate, Committee on Foreign Relations, ''Greece: February 1971,'' a Staff Report, 4 March 1971.

23. Margaret Papandreou, *Nightmare in Athens* (Englewood Cliffs, New Jersey: Prentice-Hall, 1970), p. 261.

24. ICRC press release no. 869, 20 November 1967.

25. See James Becket, *Barbarism in Greece* (New York: Walker & Co., 1970).

26. *Look,* ''Government by Torture,'' 27 May 1969.

27. The Council of Europe is a grouping of some dozen and a half Western European states who have sought to promote such things as human rights on a regional basis. A Convention on Human Rights was adopted and opened for signature in 1951, with provision for a Commission on Human Rights as a first agent for implementation. This fact-finding and conciliation body can report either to the European Court of Human Rights created by the Convention, or to the Committee of Ministers, a group made up of the foreign ministers of the states that ratify the Convention.

For a concise and excellent overview of the Council of Europe and the Greek case, see Virginia Leary, ''The Greek Dictatorship, Human Rights, and the Council of Europe,'' paper presented to the Annual Convention of the International Studies Association, Toronto, 1975, mimeo.

28. Red Cross personnel were killed and injured in the Italian attack. See Junod, *Warrior Without Weapons.*

29. This ICRC report was leaked to the Council of Europe, most probably by individuals in the Greek government. See ''The Greek Case,'' *Yearbook of the European Convention on Human Rights, 1969* (The Hague: Nijhoff, 1972).

30. This ICRC report was also made public and is reproduced in Becket, *Barbarism in Greece.*

31. Ibid. Some said the ICRC was ''soft'' on the torture question. Junta leaders were later tried on torture charges; some were convicted by Greek courts. Press reports of the implementation of the accord ard found in: *Jerusalem Post,* 22 November 1970, p. 1; and *The Manchester Guardian,* 15 April 1970, p. 4.

32. ''The Greek Case,'' *Yearbook of the European Convention, 1969.* Under the terms of the Convention, a party may withdraw from the Convention, but that withdrawal does not take effect until six months have elapsed. Moreover, according to the treaty, a statement of intention to withdraw cannot be used to avoid legal obligations under the Convention. Thus, according to the prima facie meaning of the Convention, Greece could not escape litigation by withdrawing, since the litigation instigated by the Scandinavians pertained to events occurring while Greece was still bound under the law.

Beyond the actions of the Council of Europe, the European Common Market (EEC) froze certain arrangements and negotiations with the Greek junta but did not seek to change those matters precisely regulated by law. See Van Coufoudakis, ''The European Economic Community and the 'Freezing' of the Greek Association, 1967–1974,'' paper presented to the Annual Convention of the International Studies Association, Toronto, 1975, mimeo.

33. U.S., Department of State, *Greece: U.S. Policy* (Washington, D.C.: Government Printing Office, 1970, 1971).

34. See Legg, *Politics in Modern Greece.*

35. An unnamed official in the Greek government was quoted by the *New York Times* (9 November 1970, p. 1), as saying the ICRC had been helpful to the public image of the junta in foreign circles.

36. ''Where the age-old antagonism between freedom and tyranny is concerned we are not neutral. But other imperatives impose limits on our ability to produce internal changes in foreign countries. Consciousness of our limits is recognition of the necessity of peace—not moral callousness. The preservation of human life and human society are moral values, too.'' Henry Kissinger,

"Statement on U.S.—Soviet Relations," statement made to Senate Foreign Relations Committee, Department of State, *Special Report no. 6*, n.d. [1974], p. 3. Of course the outcome of this reasoning is exactly the same as the outcome of the first approach—disregard for specific and "pure" humanitarian concerns in favor of "security affairs." Roger Davies, a former assistant secretary of state, said with regard to American policy toward Greece that the question of NATO took priority over human rights in Greece; see *New York Times*, 15 July 1971, p. 5. The Kissinger approach is thus a more sophisticated version of the first approach.

37. Maurice Cranson, *What are Human Rights* (London: The Bodley Head, 1973), p. 85.

CHAPTER 4

1. This factual information on numbers of hijackings was compiled by Mr. Kim Hobson, a student at the University of Nebraska, using U.S. Congress, House, Committee on Foreign Relations, *Aircraft Hijacking*, 91st Cong., 2nd Sess., 1970; and *New York Times*, 1970-73.

2. Prior to the 1971 Montreal Convention on the Suppression of Unlawful Acts Against the Safety of Civil Aviation, the Civil Aeronautics Board of the U.S. government contacted the ICRC through the American Red Cross and asked for ICRC support for the tough anti-hijack language then being proposed. The ICRC refused to become involved in lobbying for new anti-hijacking law, believing such activity fell outside its proper scope of action.

3. This and other statements of fact in this section are drawn from an ICRC statement to a group of journalists, meeting informally in Geneva on 12 May 1972, as recorded by the ICRC. See also ICRC press communiqué no. 1130, 10 May 1972; and *New York Times*, 9 May 1972, p. 1; 10 May, p. 1; and 14 May, p. 4.

4. *Journal de Genève*, 28 July 1970, p. 1; *La Suisse*, 8 August 1970, p. 1.

5. *The Jerusalem Post*, 14 August 1970, p. 1; *The Beirut Daily Star*, 14 August 1970, p. 1; *Al Ahram*, 14 August 1970, p. 1 (translation by Swiss government).

6. Interviews, IATA officials, Geneva.

7. *The Congressional Record*, September, 1970, S15170.

8. Interviews, IATA officials, Geneva.

9. *New York Times*, 7 September 1970, p. 1; 8 September, pp. 1, 16, 17, 23.

10. *New York Times*, 9 September 1970, pp. 1, 15, 18, 19.

11. *New York Times*, 8 September, loc. cit.; 11 September, pp. 1, 14, 15.

12. *New York Times*, 10 September 1970, pp. 1, 16, 17; 11 September, *op. cit.*

13. *New York Times*, 10 September, loc. cit.

14. *New York Times*, 11 September, loc. cit.; 12 September, pp. 1, 10.

15. *New York Times*, 12 September, loc. cit.; 15 September, pp. 1, 16.

16. *New York Times*, 14 September 1970, pp. 1, 24, 25; 16 Sept., p. 18; 17 Sept., p. 1.

17. *New York Times*, 24 September 1970, pp. 1, 18; 27 September, Sec. VI, p. 1.

18. William B. Quandt, et al., *The Politics of Palestinian Nationalism* (Los Angeles: University of California Press, 1973), pp. 124–26.

19. *New York Times*, 8 September, 1970, loc. cit., 19 September, 1970, pp. 1, 6.

20. *New York Times*, 26 September 1970, pp. 1, 2; 28 September, p. 16; 29 September, p. 18; 30 September, pp. 1, 17.

21. *New York Times*, 30 September, pp. 1, 17.

22. The difficulty for the ICRC is discussed by Jacques Freymond, "The International Committee of the Red Cross in the International System," *International Review of the Red Cross* no. 641 (May 1972), p. 274. The difficulties for the ICRC in the Athens affair are discussed in the same article at p. 272.

23. For example, the PLO disclaimed credit for some hijackings by Palestinian splinter groups. The Soviet Union and other states like Egypt and Syria voted for anti-hijack measures at the United Nations.

24. For criticisms of ICRC personnel, see *New York Times*, 13 September 1970, p. 29; and 10 September, p. 17.

25. See James D. Cockcroft et al., *Dependence and Underdevelopment* (Garden City: Double-

day, 1972), pp. 129–31; Maria Esther Gilio, *The Tupamaros* (London: Secker and Warburg, 1972); anonymous, *Nous Les Tupamaros* (Paris: François Maspero, 1971).

26. *New York Times,* 1 August 1970, p. 1.

27. In Alain Labrousse, *Les Tupamaros: Guerilla urbaine en Uruguay* (Paris: Editions du Seuil, 1971), at p. 1972, it is alleged that Mitrione confessed Fly worked for the CIA. This is highly controversial.

28. The communications network of the Tupamaros is analyzed in *New York Times,* 27 September 1970, p. 11.

29. See Robert Moss, *Urban Guerrillas* (London: Temple Smith, 1972), pp. 217–39.

30. *Korean Herald,* 10 May 1974, p. 1.

31. See *Facts on File* 22 No. 1149 (1—7 November 1962): 385—86.

32. *New York Times,* 28 July 1967, pp. 1 ff. There is no evidence that the leak came from the ICRC. Press reports concerning use of poison gas dated back to 1963, at least; see the *New York Times,* 9 July 1963, p. 7, which refers to an article in the *London Daily Telegram.* From 1965 there were numerous reports, including statements by high American and British officials confirming the use of gas by Egypt. See the statement by Prime Minister Harold Wilson, quoted in the *New York Times,* 1 February 1967, p. 20. The controversy reached a crescendo in May, June, and July of 1967. For ICRC publications, see: press release no. 824 (31 January 1967), 829 (2 June 1967); *Information Note* no. 91 (8 February 1967); *Review* (February and June); and *Annual Report,* 1967, pp. 16–17.

33. Hal Sheets, "Uganda's Continuing 'Reign of Terror,' " *International Herald Tribune,* 7 August 1974, p. 4.

34. See further Gitta Sereny, *Into That Darkness: From Mercy Killing to Mass Murder* (New York: McGraw-Hill, 1974). This account argues that the ICRC did not check carefully enough when issuing Red Cross travel documents, especially those made available to persons recommended by the Catholic Church. See pp. 291, 314–17, and esp. 277: "I believe that as far as the International Red Cross is concerned, it was entirely due to the organization's not being equipped to carry out the rigorous individual screening that would have been required to deal with this complicated problem. This however is an explanation, not an excuse. It was obvious that the problem would present itself, and precisely in the place where it did—the International Red Cross office in Rome. That office ought, therefore, to have been enabled to cope with it."

CHAPTER 5

1. This chapter must be indeterminate in nature because of continuing efforts to supplement the 1949 Convention. Moreover, it should be noted that this chapter does not purport to be a legal treatise covering the content of the law of armed conflict but is, rather, a study of the *process* of legislating humanitarian law in armed conflicts.

2. See S. D. Bailey, *Prohibitions and Restraints in War* (London: Oxford University Press, 1972), and Telford Taylor, *Nuremburg and Vietnam* (Chicago: Quadrangle Books, 1970).

3. The case of Lt. James Calley was the most publicized, but there were many more. See, e.g., Peter D. Trooboff and Arthur J. Goldberg, *Law and Responsibility in Warfare: The Vietnam Experience* (Chapel Hill: The University of North Carolina Press, 1975).

4. Dietrich Schindler and Jiri Toman, *The Laws of Armed Conflicts* (Leiden: Sijthoff, 1973).

5. The chaotic nature of jus in bello has been long recognized. See J. L. Kunz, "The Chaotic Status of the Laws of War and the Urgent Necessity for their Revision," *American Journal of International Law* 45 (January 1951): 37–61.

6. Particular problems in applying the 1949 law to prisoners of war and protected civilians are covered in subsequent chapters.

7. In addition to Bailey, *Prohibitions and Restraints,* see CICR, "Ráffirmation et Dévelopement des Lois et Coutumes Applicables dans les Conflits Armés," Rapport présenté par le Comité International de la Croix-Rouge, Geneva, May 1969, especially at p. 20. And G. A. I. D. Draper, "The Ethical and Juridicial Status of Constraints in War," *Military Law Review* 55 (1972): 169.

8. ICRC's arguments in behalf of its role are found in CICR, "Réaffirmation," pp. 31—33. R. R. Baxter notes that the ICRC responded with "alacrity" to UN action in this field, "Humanitarian Law

or Humanitarian Politics," *Harvard Journal of International Law* 16, no. 1 (Winter 1975): 1-26. For examples of Western support of the ICRC compared to the UN secretariat, see George Aldrich, "Human Rights in Armed Conflict: Development of the Law," *Department of State Bulletin* 86 (1973): 876-77; and R. R. Baxter, "Perspective: The Evolving Laws of Armed Conflicts," *Military Law Review* 60 (1973): 99-111.

9. See F. Siordet, *The Geneva Conventions of 1949: The Question of Scrutiny,* (Geneva: ICRC, 1953), p. 34: "The Diplomatic Conference was not a meeting of jurists only. It was not concerned with purely scientific law to be treated on purely academic grounds. . . . But the enunciation of . . . principles came from plenipotentiaries who, as the representatives of sovereign States, were equally conscious of their duty to protect their countries' sovereignty."

10. See Jacques Freymond, "Confronting Total War," *American Journal of International Law,* 62 (1973): 672-75. (This is an English-language, published version of the work cited in Chapter 3, n. 10.)

11. While the ICRC was certainly in touch with other Red Cross leaders, the ICRC did not seek to lead a lobbying effort on the basis of the Red Cross movement as a whole. Indeed, it engaged in competition with other Red Cross agencies and officials. There was competition within the movement especially on the rights of the League and national societies as found in the draft protocols. In one sequence, the latter agencies secured acceptance of their point of view at a meeting of governmental experts; but the subsequent ICRC draft wording on the articles in question did not reflect that point of view; thus the League and national societies resumed their lobbying, not only on governments but also on the ICRC. Agreement was finally reached. It was clear the ICRC had tried to write that portion of the draft protocols from its own highly individual perspective, rather than from the perspective of the Red Cross movement as a whole.

12. See David P. Forsythe, "Who Guards the Guardians: Third Parties and the Law of Armed Conflict," *American Journal of International Law* 70, no. 1 (January 1976): 41-61, for a more complete and more technical discussion.

13. In the mid-1970 debates on automatic supervision of the law, little attention was paid to the fact that the ICRC had accepted the role of *automatic* supervision of detention conditions under both the Third and Fourth Conventions of 1949. ICRC spokesmen certainly made no reference to this point.

14. See Conference Document CDDH/56, 16 September 1974, "Comparative Table of Proposals and Amendments," pp. 23-29. (Conf. Docs. are available from the ICRC.)

15. The clearest expression of this ICRC position is found in ICRC, *Draft Additional Protocols: Commentary* (Geneva, October, 1973), p. 13. This position was rearticulated in Working Group A of Committee I in the 1975 session of the diplomatic conference.

16. See Conf. Doc. CDDH/284, 12 April 1975, "Committee I Draft Report," pp. 8-15, for a concise overview of negotiations on this subject, with reference to relevant documents.

17. For a review of this subject see Hans Blix, "Current efforts to prohibit the use of certain conventional weapons," n.d., mimeo, and Hans Blix, "Modernizing the laws of armed conflicts—present issues and approaches," n.d., mimeo. Cf. ICRC, *Draft Rules for the Limitation of the Dangers Incurred by the Civilian Population in Time of War* (Geneva: September 1956), pp. 17-21.

18. Ibid., p. 17.

19. Ibid., Article 14, p. 12.

20. There were no East Europeans among the experts consulting with the ICRC on the weapons question. This was because governments attended or not according to whether they had voted or not for the motion calling for a study at the Red Cross Conference.

21. It is not widely known that the ICRC took up the question of American bombing on several occasions. See ICRC, *Annual Report, 1966,* p. 16; *1967,* p. 21, and *1972,* p. 40 (French edition).

22. Blix. "Current efforts."

23. The ICRC, as was its custom, sought to rationalize its involvement in terms of resolutions of the International Conference of the Red Cross. See ICRC, *Weapons that may Cause Unnecessary Suffering or Have Indiscriminate Effects: Report on the Work of Experts* (Geneva, 1973), paras. 2, 5.

The clothing of interstate agreement in the verbiage of Red Cross resolutions is even more pronounced in ICRC, *Conference of Government Experts on the Use of Certain Conventional Weapons, Report* (Geneva, 1975), para. 1.

24. See above, Chapter 2, n. 6, for a discussion of Red Cross impartiality compared to Hammarskjöld's conception of his neutrality.

25. See Siordet, *Geneva Conventions,* p. 12. At the 1929 Diplomatic Conference the ICRC formally proposed the following: "The Contracting Governments, in case of war, shall mandate to the ICRC the mission of appointing roving Commissions, composed of citizens of neutral States, whose duty it shall be to ensure that the belligerents make regular application of the provisions of the present Convention."

26. The ICRC has recently tried to formulate its relation to the peace issue anew. ICRC, "Report to Belgrade Peace Conference," 1975, mimeo, p. 8. This traditional ICRC argument is largely unpersuasive, if only because the Conventions are rarely implemented to mutual satisfaction and thus rarely a point of good relations, but rather usually become points of controversy in interstate relations. It might be more credible, at least on historical-empirical grounds, to suggest that the connection between the ICRC and peace is that the ICRC creates a spirit of peace in the minds of protected persons through its protection and assistance work with individuals.

27. For a full treatment see David P. Forsythe, "The 1974 Diplomatic Conference on Humanitarian Law: Some Observations," *American Journal of International Law* 69 (1975): 77—91. Technically speaking, all that is required for the application of the law of international armed conflict is, in the words of an ICRC legal official, "two states and a shotgun." Nontechnically speaking, that application in practice has been dependent upon not only the military crossing of some interstate boundary (if only by pellets from a shotgun), but also a high—but unfixed—level of violence. The USSR and the People's Republic of China have been shooting across a boundary from time to time, but no attention has been paid to the Geneva Conventions because the level of violence (meaning sustained scope) has not been high.

28. See David P. Forsythe, "Law, Morality, and War After Vietnam," *World Politics* 28, no. 3 (1976): 450–72. In 1974 North Vietnam argued, in effect, that humanitarian jus in bello had to discriminate in favor of the guerrilla fighter who was struggling against imperialism, and that the traditional neutrality or impartiality of the Geneva tradition was pernicious. See further, Conf. Doc. CDDH/41, 12 March 1974, p. 5 and passim.

29. See Pictet, *Principles of International Humanitarian Law.*

30. Freymond, "The ICRC at Work," p. 232.

31. See, for example, Conf. Doc. CDDH/I/SR. 28, 17 March 1975.

32. See the recent writings by Jacques Freymond, for example the articles in the *Gazette de Lausanne,* 6 & 7 March 1974.

33. Analysis of Protocol Two is too complex for extended discussion here. What was approved by the 1975 session of the Geneva Diplomatic Conference was much less than what the ICRC wanted, but there was an increase in specific regulations for conflicts similar to the Spanish Civil War. But the scope of that protocol fell short of the scope of old Common Article 3 from 1949. Thus there was an increase in legal detail, purchased at the price of restricted legal coverage.

Some ICRC officials are optimistic that the new Protocol Two will not prove a barrier to broad and frequent application of humanitarian rules, and that if insurgents hold one city and apply the protocol to a hospital therein, the government will be obliged also to apply the protocol. The survey of state practice with regard to old Common Article 3 by James E. Bond (*The Rules of Riot*) does not lend support to that optimistic view. Nor do events in Ethiopia in the 1970's support an optimistic view of governmental attitudes toward humanitarian rules in internal war. The Ethiopian government has not permitted the ICRC to enter the northern part of that country despite prolonged violence and many deaths. See further Forsythe, "Law, Morality, and War."

34. See Coplin, "International Law and Assumptions about the State System."

CHAPTER 6

1. William E. S. Flory, *Prisoners of War: A Study in the Development of International Law* (Washington: American Council of Public Affairs, 1942), pp. 159–60.

2. Michael Walzer, "Prisoners of War: Does the Fight Continue after the Battle," *American Political Science Review* 63, no. 3 (September 1969): 777–86.

3. The word "supervision" is used here in the nonlegal sense and refers to ICRC efforts to help apply law, whether as an official substitute for the Protecting Power, by carrying out specific tasks, or performing unspecified activity. See above, Chapter 5.

4. ICRC, *Le Comité international de la Croix Rouge et le Conflit de Coreé,* vol. I, 26 June 1950–31 December 1951 (Geneva: ICRC, 1952). See also William L. White, *The Captives of Korea* (New York: Scribners, 1957), pp. 3–12, 23. On prisoner conditions and treatment, see U.S. Congress, House, Committee on Foreign Affairs, *Prisoners of War in Korea,* 85th Cong., 1st Sess., 27 May 1957; Great Britain, ministry of Defence, *Treatment of British Prisoners of War in Korea* (London: HMSO, 1955). See further the relevant literature contained in U.S. Army, "Prisoners of War Bibliography" (The Pentagon, March 1972, mimeo.), and especially Albert D. Biderman, *March to Calummy* (New York: Macmillan, 1963).

5. ICRC, *Le Conflit de Corée.*

6. See White, *Captives of Korea,* pp. 197–99. The ICRC was publicly criticized by General Mark Clark.

7. ICRC, *Le Conflit de Corée,* esp. p. 165.

8. Ibid., p. 218.

9. See above, Chapter 1.

10. Walzer, "Prisoners of War."

11. The ICRC was excluded from any role at the end of the war. The League and various national Red Cross Societies—especially the Indian—were centrally involved in the armistice negotiations and care of unrepatriated prisoners of war. See William H. Vatscher, Jr., *Panmunjom* (New York: Praeger, 1958); and James Avery Joyce, *Red Cross International* (London: Hodder and Stoughton, 1959), p. 203.

12. Donald M. McNemar, "The Post Independence War in the Congo," in R. A. Falk, ed., *The International Law of Civil War* (Baltimore: Johns Hopkins Press, 1971), pp. 259–68; *New York Times,* 3 October 1961, p. 3; 9 December 1961, p. 1; 18 December 1961, p. 3; 24 December 1961, p. 10. See also the literature contained in John Norton Moore, ed., *Law and Civil War in the Modern World* (Baltimore: Johns Hopkins Press, 1974), pp. 609–10.

13. See Michael Riesman, "Private Armies in a Global War System: Prologue to Decision," in Moore, ed., *Law and Civil War,* pp. 252–303.

14. George Habash, quoted in the *New York Times,* 11 September 1970, p. 15.

15. For the specific procedure of an ICRC visit, see ICRC, *The ICRC in Action,* no. 192, 19 January 1973, pp. 1–4. See also *International Review of the Red Cross,* no. 157 (April 1974), pp. 191–93. See Appendix E, below.

16. *International Review of the Red Cross* (1947) 1:95, 2:814.

17. Jean Siotis, *Le Droit de la guerre et les conflits armés d'un caractère non-international* (Paris: Pichon et Durand, 1958), pp. 178–79.

18. Siotis, *Le Droit de la guerre.* The present analysis is also based on interview findings in Geneva and Paris.

19. *International Review of the Red Cross* (1947) 2: 814.

20. On treatment in the Viet Minh camps, see: Bernard Fall, "Communist POW Treatment in Indochina," *Military Review* (December, 1958); Grand d'Esnon et M. Prestat, "Endoctrinement des prisonniers de guerre dan les camps du Viet-Minh," *Revue des forces terrestres* no. 6 (October 1956), pp. 31 ff.; Bernard Fall, *Street Without Joy* (Harrisburg, Pa.: Telegraph Press, 1966); Michael Veuthey, "La Guerilla: Le Probleme du traitement des prisonniers," *Annals d'Etudes Internationales* (1972), p. 124; George Armstrong Kelley, *Lost Soldiers* (Cambridge: MIT Press, 1965), pp. 87–90.

Regarding post-Dienbienphu events concerning prisoners and missing, see: Alan B. Cole, *Conflict in Indo-China* (Ithaca: Cornell University Press, 1956), p. 258; Pierre Girard-Claudon, "Les Prisonniers de guerre en face de l'evolution de la guerre" (Ikesis, Dijon, June 1955); and Robert R. Randle, *Geneva 1954* (Princeton: Princeton University Press, 1969).

21. A concise and excellent review of legal issues arising from the Algerian War is found in Eldon Van Cleef Greenberg, "Law and the Conduct of the Algerian Revolution," *Harvard International Law Journal* 11, no. 1 (Winter 1970): 37–72. Cf. Algerian Office–New York, "White Paper on the Application of the Geneva Conventions of 1949 to the French-Algerian Conflict," 1960, mimeo; and M. Bedjaoui, *Law and the Algerian Revolution* (Brussels: International Association of Democratic Lawyers, 1961). See also Siotis, *Le Droit de la Guerre.* Siotis had some access to ICRC records.

22. Greenberg, "Law and the Algerian Revolution," pp. 64–66. The ICRC, while welcoming the move by the provisional government, in effect chided the Algerians for their search for status at the same time that violations of humanitarian principles and law continued.

23. Ibid., p. 68 and note 143. See also Falk, ed., *Law of Civil War*.

24. Greenberg, "Law and the Algerian Revolution," p. 50, quoting "White Paper."

25. See *Ibid*. p. 54, and the literature cited at note 86. See also Edgar O'Ballance, *The Algerian Insurrection, 1954–1962* (London: Faber and Faber, 1967); David C. Gordon, *The Passing of French Algeria* (New York: Oxford University Press, 1966); and Yves Courrière, *Le Temps des leopards* (Paris: Fayard, 1968).

26. See especially Jacques Duquesne, *L'Algerie, ou la guerre des mythes* (Paris: Bruges, 1958); and Peter Paret, *French Revolutionary Warfare from Indochina to Algeria* (London: Pall Mall Press, 1964), p. 66 and passim.

27. *Le Monde,* 5 January 1960, p. 1. See also *Le Monde,* 6 January, p. 2; 10 February, pp. 1, 2; 12 February, pp. 2, 4.

28. New York Times, *The Pentagon Papers* (New York: Bantam Books, 1971), pp. 53–65.

29. Major General George S. Prugh, Judge Advocate General of the American Army, indicated, in a letter to this author dated 14 April 1975, that in the early stages of American involvement in Vietnam U.S. officials sought to persuade South Vietnamese officials to apply Common Article 3. In the view of Prugh, "the standards of Article 3, GPW [Geneva Prisoner of war Convention] were generally met. This is not to say there was anything like perfect compliance. This was a period of particularly vicious fighting, and there was little charity on the battlefield. But considering all the circumstances, including the uncertainties of GPW applicability and the necessity to teach and train restraint in the face of atrocious acts by the opponent, a remarkable high standard of compliance was achieved by ARVN [Army of the Republic of Viet Nam] and the RVN authorities."

30. *International Legal Materials* 4 (1965): 1171.

31. This and other statements of fact not general knowledge found in this case study are based on unimpeachable sources, combined with interviews, obtained in Washington, D.C., during 1972–75.

32. Speculation in the *New York Times* in early November, 1965, was both accurate and apparently damaging to the effort to reach agreement among Washington, Cairo, and Hanoi. At one time or another, Washington seriously considered, as a Protecting Power, Morocco, Senegal, Rumania, Poland, Canada.

33. See Alexander Casella, "The Politics of Prisoners of War," *New York Times Magazine* (28 May 1972), p. 26; Freymond, "Confronting Total War"; and Alfred Hassler, *Saigon, USA* (New York: R. W. Baron, 1970).

34. 274 United Nations Treaty Series 340.

35. Jean Pictet, ed., *Commentary on the Geneva Convention Relative to the Treatment of Prisoners of War* (Geneva: ICRC, 1960), p. 424.

36. See especially Howard S. Levie, "Maltreatment of Prisoners of War in Vietnam," in R. A. Falk, ed., *The Vietnam War and International Law* (Princeton: Princeton University Press, 1969), 2:361–97; and his "The Geneva Conventions and the Treatment of Prisoners of War in Vietnam," in ibid., pp. 398–415.

37. Most of these approaches were not publicized, and the reasons for this are discussed by Freymond, "Confronting Total War," pp. 677–78. References to ICRC actions regarding American bombing are found in ICRC, *Annual Report,* 1966, p. 16; 1967, p. 21, and 1972, p. 40 (French edition).

38. See, among others, Raphael Littauer and Norman Uphoff, eds., *The Air War in Indochina* (Boston: The Beacon Press, 1971); and two sets of hearings on the effect of bombings, one in May 1970, and another in April 1971, by the U.S. Congress, Senate, Judiciary Committee, 91st Cong., 2nd Sess., and 92 Cong., 1st Sess. See also a staff report by that same Committee, "Refugee and Civilian War Casualty Problems in Indochina," 28 September 1970.

39. Keith D. Suter, "The Work of the ICRC in Vietnam: An Evaluation," *Instant Research on Peace and Violence* 4, no. 3 (1974): 121–32.

40. David P. Forsythe, "The Work of the ICRC: A Broader View," *Instant Research on Peace and Violence* 5, no. 2 (1975): 108–16.

41. Raymond S. Eaton, Senior Vice President of the American Red Cross, was quoted as saying Hanoi had "deep concerns that the International Committee of the Red Cross is a pro-Western organization and would therefore not do this [supervise the Third Convention] properly." *Atlanta Constitution,* 21 August 1972, p. 8-a.

42. When the Nixon Administration did go public after 1969, the American Red Cross was utilized to help mobilize public opinion in support of governmental policy. This led to questions in Congress as to whether the American Red Cross was acting responsibly. Thinly veiled criticism arose

because of the nature of the material that national Society was supporting and endorsing—i.e., an allegedly incorrect and inflammatory article in *Reader's Digest.* See U.S. Congress, House, Committee on Foreign Affairs, *American Prisoners of War in Southeast Asia, 1971,* 92nd Cong., 1st Sess., March 23 24, 25, 30, 31; April 1, 6, 20, 1971, especially pp. 90–92. By contrast, the Johnson Administration, while seeking the implementation of the Third Convention in the North, had accepted the detention of American POWs as a wartime fact of life. Former Secretary of State Rusk said, if one wanted the POWs back, one could stop the war (interview, Athens, Georgia, 12 July 1972). Thus the Johnson Administration had not "gone public" on the question of American POWs and had not strongly sought their release, anticipating that such an effort would have given Hanoi more reason to tie POW treatment and release to American withdrawal from the South. (The Johnson Administration had "gone public" briefly on the POW question in 1966 in an effort to head off war crimes trials then feared to be imminent in Hanoi.) For an overview of American use of publicity related to POW treatment and release, see Jon M. Van Dyke, "Nixon and the Prisoners of War," *New York Review of Books,* 7 January 1971. See also Laird testimony in U.S. Congress, Senate, Committee on Foreign Relations, *Bombing Operations and the Prisoner of War Rescue Mission in North Vietnam,* 91st Cong., 2nd Sess., 24 November 1970, pp. 30–31.

43. Frank A. Sieverts, statement to the Congress, 31 May 1973, reprinted in *News Release: Department of State,* 13 June 1973, p. 4.

44. On detention conditions and treatment, see the testimony by former American detainees contained in Zalin Grant, *Survivors* (New York: Norton, 1975). On the other hand, on the subject of provocative behavior by Americans, see House, Committee on Foreign Affairs, *American POWs* (1971). See especially the analyses by Seymour M. Hersh, reprinted at the end of those hearings.

45. See further Trooboff and Goldberg, *Law and Responsibility in Warfare,* and Taylor, *Nuremburg and Vietnam.*

46. Senate, Committee on Foreign Relations, *Bombing Operations,* p. 35; see also p. 36. This statement appears to pertain especially to prisoners of war. U.S. activity in behalf of what Saigon called civilian defendants appeared to be much less, protestations by various American officials notwithstanding.

47. Under court order the American Executive released ICRC prison reports pertaining to the South, after the war was over. See *The Washington Post,* 22 June, 23 June, 23 July, 1975 for an overview.

48. For one account, see the *International Herald Tribune,* 10 July 1970, p. 2; and 15 July 1970, p. 4. The same thing happened again in 1973. The Saigon press agency Vietnam Presse released a story saying the ICRC had approved detention conditions for communist prisoners, based on a deliberate misrepresentation of ICRC visits and reports. The ICRC challenged that action publicly. See *International Review of the Red Cross* no. 152 (November 1973): 592.

49. The State Department officially argued that it was interested in the subject but that it was an internal affair for Saigon and that conditions were not so bad. See U.S. Congress, House, Committee on Foreign Affairs, *The Treatment of Political Prisoners in South Vietnam by the Government of the Republic of South Vietnam,* 93rd Cong., 1st sess., 13 September 1973, especially pp. 58 ff. The fact remains that, despite the building of new detention places, the U.S. had known of bad conditions in Saigon's jails since at least 1963 and had not effected a general improvement in the basic situation. See *New York Times,* 25 July 1970, p. 11.

50. ICRC, *Annual Report, 1972,* p. 43. ICRC efforts to gain permission for visits from the highest levels of Saigon's government, in the absence of American officials, are covered by the *Christian Science Monitor,* 30 July 1971, p. 2.

51. ICRC, *Annual Report, 1973,* p. 28.

52. See above, n. 33. Official classification rules are discussed by Bond, *Rules of Riot,* p. 153.

53. Bailey, *Prohibitions and Restraints in War,* p. 75.

54. See above, n. 37.

55. Interview, Dean Rusk, Athens, Georgia, 12 July 1972. See also John Norton Moore, *Law and the Indochina War* (Princeton: Princeton U. P., 1972) "Postscript on the Pentagon Papers."

56. Out of the vast literature on this subject, see, for example, the books analyzed by Ralph K. White in *Nobody Wanted War: Misperception in Viet Nam and other Wars* (Garden City, New York: Doubleday, 1970), pp. 52–53.

57. See above, n. 44.

58. The sequence of facts is presented in *International Review of the Red Cross* (1957), pp. 111, 245.

59. A vague reference to this subject is found in ICRC, *Annual Report, 1969,* pp. 35—36. By reading between the lines, one can discern that the ICRC was independently interested in the conditions of the montagnards who were being forced to relocate under governmental programs.

60. The personnel problems are alluded to by Freymond, "Confronting Total War."

61. Conf. Doc. CDDH/41, 12 March 1974, especially pp. 4–5.

62. See further Forsythe, "Who Guards the Guardians."

CHAPTER 7

1. A concise overview of ICRC efforts to help civilians is found in CICR, *Rapport du CICR sur son activité pendant la seconde guerre mondiale* (Geneva: ICRC, 1948), 1: 710–14. On the Spanish Civil War and the ICRC, see the book by the ICRC chief delegate, Marcel Junod, *Warrior Without Weapons.*

2. In addition to *Rapport,* see CICR, *Inter Arma Caritas: L'Oeuvre du CICR pendant la seconde guerre mondiale* (Geneva: ICRC, 1947).

3. ICRC, *The International Committee of the Red Cross in Palestine* (Geneva: ICRC, 1948).

4. ICRC, *Congo Medical Relief* (Geneva: ICRC, 1961).

5. CICR, *Rapport final sur l'operation de secours en Jordanie* (Geneva: ICRC, n.d.).

6. See the *Annual Reports* and the *Review* for brief descriptions of civilian assistance in places like the Brazilian Amazon. And see, in general, David J. Holdsworth, *The Present Role of Red Cross in Assistance* (Geneva: Red Cross Joint Committee, 1975).

7. *New York Times,* 2 November 1975, p. 14.

8. *New York Times,* 2 November 1975, p. 26.

9. Jerome Alan Cohen and Shao-chun Leng, "The Sino-Indian Dispute over the Internment and Detention of Chinese in India," in Cohen, ed., *China's Practice of International Law: Some Case Studies* (Cambridge: Harvard University Press, 1972), pp. 268–320.

10. "And the gravest failures [in implementing the Fourth] would spring not from individual lawlessness or depravity but from high policy of belligerent States. Military necessity and the needs of security are a legal excuse at many critical points in the Convention, for departures from its high principles." Julius Stone, *Legal Controls of International Conflict* (New York, Rinehart & Co., Inc., 1959), p. 692.

11. In 1973, of the 28 references primarily to prisoners of war, 4 references also entailed some reference to relief problems in general; 1 entailed a reference to civilian needs in passing; and 3 entailed some discussion of legal problems in general. In 1974, in addition to 27 references to prisoners of war and 1 reference to civilians, there was 1 reference to the general legal situation, including some attention to civilian problems. (Other categories of references to the ICRC used by this author were "miscellaneous," "unclear," "relief.")

One can surmise from this type of research that *New York Times* correspondents were not much interested in civilian protection and assistance, or, the ICRC did not generate much interest in these subjects, or both.

12. ICRC press releases nos. 1170, 1171, 1173, 1174, 1175, 1176, 1180, 1181, 1182, and 1189.

13. An overview is found in Nigel S. Rodley, "The United Nations and Human Rights in the Middle East," in John Norton Moore, ed., *The Arab-Israeli Conflict, Vol. II* (Princeton: Princeton University Press, 1974), pp. 419–44. Rodley makes clear why Israel refused to cooperate with both General Assembly and Human Rights Commission investigations. This lack of cooperation, plus ICRC discretion, makes noncontroversial information on the situation in the territories difficult to obtain. The reader, I hope, will appreciate this difficulty as he reads this case study, as well as the difficulties for analysis produced by the continuation of the situation at the time of writing.

Various viewpoints are easily found in the *UN Monthly Chronicle.* See for example, the January 1973 issue, pp. 88–90; February 1974, pp. 32–36; and January 1976, pp. 30, 101.

14. See especially Meir Shamgar (Attorney General of Israel), "The Observance of International Law in the Administered Territories," in Moore, *Arab-Israeli Conflict,* pp. 371–89. See further, Shabtai Teveth, *The Cursed Blessing: The Story of Israeli Occupation of the West Bank* (London: Weidenfeld and Nicholson, 1970).

15. Allan Gerson, "Trustee-Occupant: The Legal Status of Israel's Presence in the West Bank," *Harvard International Law Journal* 14, no. 1 (Winter 1973): 1–49. Legal scholars appear to differ on

this point. Stone, *Legal Controls,* does emphasize the importance of a relationship between sovereigns for determining when the law of occupation applies (p. 694). On the other hand, Morris Greenspan, in *The Modern Law of Land Warfare* (Berkeley: University of California Press, 1959), emphasizes that "Military occupation is always a question of fact" (p. 213; see also p. 219 and 155–56 for the same point.)

16. Interviews with Arab officials, Geneva, 1972–75. The law of occupation, composed primarily of parts of the Hague Convention of 1907 and of the Fourth Geneva Convention of 1949, has had as one of its major functions that of distinguishing between occupant and sovereign; see Stone, *Legal Controls,* p. 727. Since Israel avoided the title of occupant, Arabs saw this as a step on the way to claiming Israeli sovereignty over at least some of the territories.

17. See Julius Stone, "Behind the Cease-Fire Lines: Israel's Administration in Gaza and the West Bank," in Moore, ed. *Arab-Israeli Conflict,* pp. 390–418; and Morris Greenspan, "Human Rights in the Territories Occupied in Israel," *Santa Clara Lawyer* 12, no. 2 (1972): 377–402.

18. Greenspan, in ibid., p. 400. See also an observation by Michael Walzer, political philosopher at Harvard. "In general, the Israeli occupation has been liberal in its policies, decent in its day to day operations, and economically progressive. . . . There is, nevertheless, no such thing as a good occupation. The people of the West Bank do not want to be ruled by Israel, and so the Israeli presence is almost by definition repressive." *The New Republic,* 17 April 1976, p. 12.

19. See M. Burhan W. Hammad, "The Culprit, the Targets and the Victims," in Moore, ed., *Arab-Israeli Conflict,* pp. 361–70. See also W. J. Mallison, Jr., "The Geneva Convention," *The Arab World* (January 1970): 16–22.

20. Ibrahim Al-Abid, *Israel and Human Rights* (Beirut: Palestine Liberation Organization Research Center, 1969), pp. 74–77, 87, 119–20. The Research Director thanks, among others, "the Red Cross and Red Crescent Societies in Amman." The ICRC has never officially denied that the printed exerpts were parts of authentic ICRC prison reports.

21. Stone, in Moore, ed., *Arab-Israeli Conflict,* puts the number of persons deported at 71, as of 1 April 1970 (pp. 408–9).

22. The case was Sheikh Suleiman Hussein Uda Abu Hilo & Others, Petitioners, v. State of Israel & Others, Respondents (H.C. 302/72). See further *The Jerusalem Post,* 27 May 1973, and 29 May 1973. The Court's opinion was criticized by certain Israeli circles as giving an unnecessarily broad definition to military necessity.

23. See *International Herald Tribune,* 21 April 1975, p. 4.

24. Adnan Amad, *The Shahak Papers* (Beirut: Palestine Research Center, 1973), p. 18. A concise description of the permissible judicial system permitted in occupied territory is found in Greenspan, *Modern Law of Land Warfare,* pp. 256–57.

25. *New York Times,* 23 August 1974, p. 1. Other Israeli officials denied this.

26. Above, note 20, and Amnesty, *Report on Torture* (New York: Farrar, Straus and Giroux, 1975), pp. 231–34.

27. Stone, in Moore, ed., *Arab-Israeli Conflict,* p. 411. Stone is generally sympathetic to Israeli claims and practices.

28. Embassy of Israel, "Policy Background—President Sadat's 'Moderation and Statesmanship': A Closer Look," Washington, 15 April 1975, mimeo.

29. ICRC, *Annual Report (1973),* p. 6.

30. With regard to activity by the UN Human Rights Commission, Israel argued that the ICRC was already active on questions related to the Fourth Convention. See UN Doc. E/CN.4/1016. Stone, in Moore, ed., *Arab-Israeli Conflict,* p. 415, cites ICRC presence in the territories in refutation of criticisms of Israel. Likewise the government of Chile, when embroiled in controversy over UN investigation into detention practices, took out a large advertisement in the *New York Times* on 19 October 1975 (p. 43), pointing out that "The constant activity of the International Red Cross merits special mention. It has continuously visited the detention establishment in Chile and has been able, as its reports recognize, to converse privately with everyone in it deemed advisable."

31. For background information see John Hatch, *Nigeria, The Seeds of Disaster* (Chicago: Henry Regnery Company, 1970); Joseph Okpaku, *Nigeria: Dilemma of Nationhood* (New York: The Third Press, 1972); and Samuel U. Ifejika and Arthur Nwankwo, *The Making of a Nation: Biafra* (London: C. Hurst and Co., 1969).

32. A. H. M. Kirk-Greene, *Crisis and Conflict in Nigeria* (London: Oxford University Press, 1971), 2: 456.

33. Hentsch, *Face Au Blocus*, p. 27. ICRC, *Annual Report*, (1967), p. 38.

34. *The Nordchurchaid Airlift to Biafra 1968–1970: An Operations Report* (Copenhagen: Nordchurchaid, 1972).

35. The 12 July 1968 issue of *Life* seems to have triggered the awakening of American public opinion. The British press had devoted major attention to the Biafran situation earlier; see *Daily Telegraph,* 10 May 1968 and 5 July 1968.

36. Hentsch, *Face au Blocus* develops the theme that it was only under financial pressures that the ICRC developed an overview of what it was doing in the Biafran War. See especially pp. 138–43.

37. In addition to Hentsch and Kirk-Greene, *Crisis and Conflict,* see Suzanne Cronje, *The World and Nigeria: The Diplomatic History of the Biafran War 1967–1970* (London: Sidgwick & Jackson, 1972), for detailed coverage of relief negotiations.

38. Biafra's political-psychological approach to humanitarian relief was apparently discussed candidly with certain parties, including British diplomats. See John de St. Jorre, *The Nigerian Civil War* (London: Hodder and Stoughton, 1972), p. 245.

39. Gene Dewey, "United States Domestic Influence on Foreign Policy Decision-Making–The Nigerian Relief Case," paper prepared for seminar at the Geneva Graduate Institute for International Studies, Summer Session 1973, April, 1973. Dewey was a high official in the U.S. Mission to Nigeria.

40. At the prodding of the U.S., the ICRC undertook an effort to make a statistical-economic report on the situation in Biafra in the spring of 1969. There was great unhappiness in Washington with the result of this effort. See further St. Jorre, *Nigerian Civil War.*

41. The Federal commander in the Western region, Col. Benjamin Adekunle, was a particularly outspoken critic of the ICRC; he refused permission to ICRC delegates to operate in his sector for a considerable length of time. See Kirk-Greene, *Crisis and Conflict,* and St. Jorre, *Nigerian Civil War.* The chief ICRC delegate in Biafra was reported to say that he had sent some 50 reports to Geneva regarding Nigerian bombing of hospitals where he had personally verified no military target in the area. *Tribune de Genève,* 25 March 1969, p. 3.

42. St. Jorre, *Nigerian Civil War,* p. 243.

43. In the fall of 1968, Spanish Guinea received its independence as Equatorial Guinea. The newly independent government subsequently ordered the ICRC to cease its flights into Biafra from the Equatorial Guinean island of Fernando Po. There appear to have been two reasons for this. One was pressure from Lagos. The other stemmed from the domestic politics of the new state. The new government, meeting in the city of Santa Isabel on Fernando Po, was non-Ibo, while the population on Fernando Po was basically Ibo. The government appeared insecure and afraid of the Ibos in the population. Thus, in part, it acted to thwart the ICRC airlift into Ibo Biafra. The United States, UN Secretary General U Thant, and other parties made overtures to the new government to allow the ICRC to resume its airlift. The government finally consented, but the ICRC flights from Fernando Po had been suspended from late November 1969 until early 1970. In the meantime, the ICRC started an airlift from Cotonou, Dahomey.

44. It is significant that Jacques Freymond, acting president of the ICRC during most of the Nigerian Civil War, later wrote that one of the major organizational problems of the ICRC was lack of coordination—both between field and Geneva, and among offices at Geneva. See his "Le Comité international de la Croix-Rouge dans le systéme international," *Révue International de la Croix-Rouge* no. 641 (May 1972): 277–82.

45. Public exchanges between Geneva and Lagos are reprinted, in part, in Kirk-Greene, *Crisis and Conflict.* Some ICRC delegates were advising their superiors to avoid the tendency to reply publicly to every criticism in the Nigerian press.

46. In April and May 1969, ICRC pilots began flying earlier in the evening in order to get in extra "nighttime" flights—both to get food to Biafra and to "score points" in the competition with JCA. Also, it was widely believed the MIG fighters of the Federal airforce were lacking parts and thus were not fully operational. Thus some relief planes were even *landing* in daylight in Biafra.

As for Lagos's withdrawing permission formally but giving the ICRC private assurances regarding flights, see Hentsch, *Face au Blocus,* p. 154 regarding October 1968.

47. Ibid., pp. 182–83; Cronje, *World and Nigeria,* p. 137.

48. It should be mentioned that a factor contributing to ICRC problems was the action of Count Carl Gustav von Rosen of Sweden. Formerly a pilot for the churches, associated with the Swedes who were active in support of the ICRC as well as JCA, von Rosen made a military attack on the Federals with his small "airforce" in the spring of 1969. This demonstrated the weakness of Federal

air defenses. It also infuriated Lagos over the role of foreigners supporting Biafra. Coincidentally or otherwise, it was a plane donated to the ICRC by the Swedish Red Cross that was the victim of the 6 June attack.

49. The word "probably" is employed because the interpretation of the law is not clear at this time, given the lack of applications of the Fourth Convention to civil war situations.

50. Some of the criticism directed against the "high life" or "night life" of Red Cross personnel under contract to the ICRC stem from this period. It is important to distinguish between personnel on loan to the ICRC from national Red Cross Societies, sitting on Fernando Po with nothing to do; and on the other hand, regular (or temporary) Swiss ICRC delegates in Nigeria-Biafra.

51. Therefore, even after the shooting incident and the negotiations conducted by President Naville in July, the ICRC still considered being a revolutionary neutral—one who might act without belligerents' consents. Since the ICRC agreed with Lagos not to do this, then threatened to do it toward Biafra, then did not do so, it contributed to its image of not having a consistent strategy.

52. See Pictet, *Le Droit humanitaire et la protection des victimes de la guerre* (Leiden: Sijthoff, 1973), p. 63.

53. At the Geneva diplomatic conference in the mid-1970's on supplementing the 1949 Conventions, much attention was paid to the question of humanitarian relief in an armed conflict, largely because of the Nigerian events.

54. See St. Jorre, *Nigerian Civil War,* pp. 239–40.

55. Lindt, in August 1968 at the peak of starvation in Biafra, said ICRC efforts there were still "purely symbolic." *Tribune de Genève,* 15 August 1968, p. 3. One of the themes in Hentsch, *Face au Blocus,* is the slowness of the Red Cross movement to act regarding assistance; then, when it does act, it does so through public appeals which direct public attention to the conflict; but with public attention attracted, the conflicting parties tend to become rigid in their policies. Thus by the time the Red Cross movement is ready to provide assistance in a conflict, the parties may be unwilling to view that relief in strictly humanitarian terms. See Hentsch, pp. 234–40.

56. See Hentsch, *Face au Blocus,* pp. 192–95. The British government, subjected to domestic criticism for its tilt toward Lagos, arranged an ICRC-Lagos meeting and then made its own interpretation of the results. The image of the ICRC was used to deflate criticism of the government, for the government suggested certain ICRC actions would be forthcoming which, in reality, had no prospect of developing.

57. See, *The Nordchurchaid Airlift,* pp. 9–11. And see Morris Davis, "Audits of international relief in the Nigerian Civil War: Some political perspectives," *International Organization* 29, no. 2 (Spring 1975): 501–12.

58. This is, after all, what the ICRC did covertly with regard to the French Red Cross, after the ICRC had been forced to the sidelines by Lagos. It is also what the ICRC did in Burundi in the context of tribal strife, when it withdrew to protect its neutral image but did not contest the involvement of the League of National Red Cross Societies for the distribution of Red Cross relief, even though that relief was not permitted in all parts of the country and thus there was no guarantee that it would be impartially distributed, as under ICRC supervision.

CHAPTER 8

1. See Junod, *Warrior Without Weapons.*

2. Moreillon, *CICR et détenus politiques.*

3. The most well-informed, comprehensive, and critical account of the ICRC's contemporary problems is Freymond "Le Comité international de la Croix-Rouge dans le système international."

4. See Chapter 7 above. The breakdown of the ICRC system is also an implicit theme of Hentsch, *Face Au Blocus.*

5. See Freymond, "CICR dans le système international."

6. Ibid., and see Chapter 4 above with regard to the Zerka affair and shifting ICRC diplomatic positions. Also, it appears to be the case that during the war in Indochina various circles in the Comité were conducting different démarches.

7. See Davis, "International Relief in the Nigerian Civil War." He chides the ICRC for not making public its figures and suggests that the ICRC was less efficient than the churches in getting

relief into Biafra. During that war certain Western governments were unhappy over ICRC fiscal controls.

8. For example, at the 1975 session of the Geneva Diplomatic Conference and in preceding meetings the ICRC argued that it had never and would never offer itself without prior agreement as a formal substitute for a Protecting Power; rather, it would wait for agreement from a belligerent in order to supervise the law. However, in both 1956 and 1972 the ICRC had, without prior agreement, offered itself to conflicting parties as a substitute for a Protecting Power. See further Forsythe, "Who Guards the Guardians," and Moreillon, *ICRC et détenus politiques*.

9. This analysis is based on "Statuts et Reglement Interieur" (May 1974) of the ICRC. The author is responsible for translations from the French.

10. I am indebted to the late Pierre Boissier, official ICRC historian, for calling this point to my attention.

11. I am indebted to Donald D. Tansley, Red Cross study director, for formulating the issue in this way. See his *Final Report,* pp. 112–14.

12. The episode is recounted in Folke Bernadotte, *Instead of Arms* (London: Hodder and Stoughton, 1949), p. 36. Bernadotte at one time favored the internationalization of the Assembly, then changed his mind. See pp. 129–31, 163–66.

13. I am indebted to P. Vibert, ICRC head librarian, for calling this quote to my attention.

14. This breakdown of professions must be regarded as tentative. Some individuals fit into more than one category, and the professions of some early members are not known now for sure.

15. See Moreillon, *ICRC et détenus politiques.*

16. Young, *The Intermediaries,* p. 109.

17. Pictet, *Le Droit humanitaire,* p. 148: "Une chose est certaine: le droit humanitaire sera reçu et triomphera dans la mesure où l'on aura su se placer sur le plan de l'universal et dans la mesure où il sera conforme à l'interet réciproque et bien compris des diverses nations, car ce qui est utile à la majorité finit toujours par triompher."

18. Jacques Freymond has suggested that Swiss members of the ICRC have not been able recently to "denationalize" themselves and be fully impartial. This criticism is found in the *Journal de Genève,* 27 September 1972, p. 1. On the following day, that paper printed his criticism that ICRC delegates were frequently not well trained.

19. In addition to Tansley, *Final Report,* see *Red Cross at National Level—a Profile,* pp. 35–37, 62–63; and Magat, *As Others See Us,* pp. 17–22, 32–35. It can be recalled (as discussed in Chapter 4) that the ICRC has been accused of not being diligent enough in issuing Red Cross travel documents toward the close of World War II.

20. See Jacques Freymond, "Does the Red Cross Still Have a Future: The End of an Era," *Gazette de Lausanne,* 6 March 1974, p. 3. On secrecy in ICRC operating style, see also Tansley, *Final Report,* pp. 114–15. When this report was issued, the president of the ICRC was quoted as saying Tansley's study was a "pitiless inquisition" that had "gone too far" in saying the ICRC had an obsession with secrecy. President Eric Martin suggested discretion was necessary to the work of the ICRC, and that "discretion can be irritating" to others (*New York Times,* 19 October 1975, p. 21). On the subject of ignorance about the ICRC and what it does, see the works cited in note 19, above.

CHAPTER 9

1. U.S. Congress, House, Committee on Foreign Affairs, *Human Rights in Chile,* 93rd Cong., 2nd sess., 7 Dec. 1973; 7 and 23 May; and 11, 12, & 18 June, 1974, pp. 99–100.

2. Ibid., pp. 110–21.

3. Gidon Gottlieb, "International Assistance to Civil Populations in Civil Wars," *Israeli Yearbook on Human Rights, 1971* (Tel-Aviv: Israel Press, 1971), p. 354. Gottlieb also presents a conceptualization of humanitarian actors.

4. A favorably inclined survey of ICRC activity is found in Bissell, "ICRC and Protection of Human Rights."

5. See further Robert Heilbroner, *An Inquiry into the Human Prospect* (New York: Norton, 1974)

6. Charles Reich, *The Greening of America* New York: Random House, 1970, pp. 17–18.

7. Donald Schon, *Beyond the Stable State: Public and Private Learning in a Changing Society* (London: Temple Smith, 1971), p. 109.

8. See Freymond, "Confronting Total War," p. 679.

9. Bond, *The Rules of Riot,* p. 49.

10. Freymond, "Does the Red Cross Still Have a Future."

11. See *The Washington Post,* 22 June, 23 June, 23 July, 1975. This series of articles is the *Post's* analysis of ICRC prison reports from the war in South Vietnam, released by the United States government after that war under court order. It seems clear that: (1) the ICRC did help to achieve an improvement in detention conditions over time; and (2) it took a long time to achieve it, there being much suffering during the process.

12. The Yemeni conflict and use of gas is covered in Chapter 4; the ICRC's unusually candid and critical publication on the Middle East situation post-1967 is covered in Chapter 7.

13. In Chapter 1 I compared the role of UN peacekeeping and its utility in world affairs as an intermediate solution to violent situations.

14. *New York Times,* 28 September 1975, p. 2. Cf. ICRC, *The ICRC in Action* no. 226b (29 October 1975): 1.

15. Foudad Ajami, "Middle East Ghosts," *Foreign Policy,* no. 14 (1975): 94.

16. See further Gurr, *Why Men Rebel.* He discusses the trends toward, and reasons for, increased politicization of life and increased political violence.

POSTSCRIPT

1. Ali A. Mazrui, "The Red Cross and Politics in Africa," no date, mimeo; address given to the Regional Institute of the League of Red Cross Societies, Dar-es-Salaam, 23 November 1970.

2. See further A. H. Robertson, *Human Rights in the World* (Manchester: Manchester University Press, 1972).

3. Taylor, *Nuremberg and Vietnam,* p. 40.

4. See further Forsythe, "Who Guards the Guardians." The ICRC had wanted to protect its independence and avoid conflict with states.

5. Max Petitpierre, "Introduction," no date, mimeo, p. 2; address to a Red Cross meeting held in Montreux, Switzerland, 5–7 April 1972.

6. The GAO is the General Accounting Organization, a part of the American government. It is an independent investigating and reporting agency, responsible to Congress, but with authority to investigate affairs of the Executive Branch.

It may be useful, heuristically, to compare the ICRC also with the ombudsman, found in several European governments. The ombudsman is responsible for resolving problems in an alegal way by promoting agreements between adversaries. The ICRC could be considered to be, at times, a humanitarian ombudsman.

7. Bond, *The Rules of Riot,* p. 133.

APPENDIX C

1. See Appendix D.

2. See especially Brenda F. Brown, "Extradition and the Natural Law," *New York Law Forum* 16, no. 3 (1970): 581. See also, among others, Lora L. Deere, "Political Offenses in the Law and Practice of Extradition," *American Journal of International Law* 27 (April 1933): 248; and Manuel R. Garcia-Mora, "The Nature of Political Offenses: A Knotty Problem of Extradition Law," *Virginia Law Review* 43 (November 1962): 1237. For a sociological study of the concept "political crime," see Stephen Schafer, "Criminology: The Concept of the Political Criminal," *The Journal of Criminal Law, Criminology and Police Science* 62, no. 3 (19): 380–82, especially. Finally, see I. A. Shearer, *Extradition in International Law* (Manchester: Manchester University Press, 1971).

3. Yet at times in French law, a violent attack on a *person* in the government has been considered common murder, not political crime, despite the expressed intent of some would-be assassins to murder for "purely political reasons"—viz., to alter the government.

4. See Otto Kirschheimer, *Political Justice* (Princeton: Princeton University Press, 1969). See also Jon Van Dyke, "Are There Political Prisoners in America?—An Inquiry into the Definition of a Political Crime," March, 1971, mimeo.

5. Kirschheimer, *Political Justice.*

6. Van Dyke, "Political Prisoners."

7. This assumes the state-in-possession has adhered to the Convention and that the individual has not violated the laws of the state of refuge. The 1967 protocol to the 1951 Convention does not change the substance of the Convention, only the time span during which the Convention applies.

8. A copy of the Protocol was obtained from the U.S. Mission to International Organizations, Geneva; it is used by permission. The ICRC, in a press release in June of 1973, said with regard to political prisoners, "It is now obvious that the provisions of the Paris Agreement concerning these prisoners are not being applied," *The ICRC in Action* no. 198b (13 June 1973): 9. This somewhat unusual statement by the ICRC, noting violations of an agreement that did not directly pertain to it, was a prelude to the ICRC's offer to resume its visits to political prisoners in Indo-china.

9. Tom Farer, "The Laws of War 25 Years After Nuremberg," *International Conciliation* no. 583 (May 1971): 32.

10. ICRC, *Draft Additional Protocols: Commentary,* pp. 136–44.

11. Bailey, *Prohibitions and Restraints,* p. 169.

12. At the time of writing, the exact legal status of the Nuremberg Principles is unclear, as they have never been approved by the UN General Assembly in precise form!

13. The same trend is likely in Latin America, despite the existence of the Inter-American Commission on Human Rights at present, and the probability of a human rights convention in the future.

14. Lebanon is a modern example.

15. See Ivo D. Duchacek, *Rights & Liberties in the World Today* (Santa Barbara: ABC-Clio, Inc., 1974), p. 176.

16. Richard Kleindienst, quoted in Alan Dershowitz, "The Role of Law during Times of Crisis," in Harry Clor, ed., *Civil Disorder and Violence* (Chicago: Rand McNally, 1972), p. 132.

Index

Library of Congress Cataloging in Publication Data

Forsythe, David P.   1941–
  Humanitarian politics.

  Includes bibliographical references and index.
  1.   Red Cross. International Committee, Geneva.
2.   War—Protection of civilians.   I.   Title.
JX5136.F67   341.7′6   77–4781
ISBN 0–8018–1983–0

This book was composed in Times Roman text by The Composing Room. It was printed by Universal Lithographers, Inc. and bound by Delmar Bindery.